Grounding knowledge/walking land

McDONALD INSTITUTE MONOGRAPHS

Grounding knowledge/ walking land

Archaeological research and ethno-historical identity in central Nepal

By Christopher Evans
with Judith Pettigrew, Yarjung Kromchaï Tamu & Mark Turin

with contributions by Dorothy Allard, Eleni Asouti, Paul Craddock, Dorian Fuller, David Gibson, Alan Macfarlane & Ezra Zubrow

Principal illustrations by
Crane Begg & Andrew Hall

Published by:

McDonald Institute for Archaeological Research
University of Cambridge
Downing Street
Cambridge, UK
CB2 3ER
(0)(1223) 339336
(0)(1223) 333538 (General Office)
(0)(1223) 333536 (FAX)
dak12@cam.ac.uk
www.mcdonald.cam.ac.uk

Distributed by Oxbow Books
United Kingdom: Oxbow Books, 10 Hythe Bridge Street, Oxford, OX1 2EW, UK.
Tel: (0)(1865) 241249; Fax: (0)(1865) 794449; www.oxbowbooks.com
USA: The David Brown Book Company, P.O. Box 511, Oakville, CT 06779, USA.
Tel: 860-945-9329; Fax: 860-945-9468

ISBN: 978-1-902937-50-2
ISSN: 1363-1349 (McDonald Institute)

© 2009 McDonald Institute for Archaeological Research

Edited for the Institute by James Barrett (*Series Editor*) and Dora A. Kemp (*Production Editor*).

Cover illustration: *Kohla site plan superimposed with rendering of Tamang shamans' landscape-recital 'traverse'*
(see Fig. 5.6; after Höfer 1999, fig. 4).

Printed and bound by Short Run Press, Bittern Rd, Sowton Industrial Estate, Exeter, EX2 7LW, UK.

CONTENTS

CONTRIBUTORS

DOROTHY ALLARD
Analytical Resources, LLC, 1331 Waterville
Mountain Road, Bakersfield, VT 05441, USA.

ELENI ASOUTI
School of Archaeology, Classics and Egyptology,
Hartley Building, Brownlow Street, University of
Liverpool, Liverpool, L69 3GS, UK.
(formerly Institute of Archaeology, UCL, London)

PAUL CRADDOCK
Department of Scientific Research, British Museum,
Great Russell Street, London, WC1B 3DG, UK.

CHRISTOPHER EVANS
Executive Director, Cambridge Archaeological Unit,
Department of Archaeology, University of Cambridge,
Downing Street, Cambridge, CB2 3DZ, UK.

DORIAN FULLER
Institute of Archaeology, University College London,
31–34 Gordon Square, London, WC1H 0PY, UK.

DAVID GIBSON
Cambridge Archaeological Unit, Department of
Archaeology, University of Cambridge, Downing
Street, Cambridge, CB2 3DZ, UK.

ALAN MACFARLANE
Department of Social Anthropology, University of
Cambridge, Free School Lane, Cambridge, CB2 3RF,
UK.

JUDITH PETTIGREW
Faculty of Education and Health Sciences,
University of Limerick, Limerick, Ireland.

YARJUNG KROMCHAĪ TAMU
Tamu Pye Lhu Sangh (Central), Pokhara, Nepal.
(and Tamu Pye Lhu Sangh, UK)

MARK TURIN
Director, Digital Himalaya Project, Department of
Social Anthropology, University of Cambridge, Free
School Lane, Cambridge, CB2 3RF, UK.

EZRA ZUBROW
State University of New York at Buffalo,
Department of Anthropology, 380 MFAC-Ellicott
Complex, Buffalo, NY 14261-0005, USA.

Figures

Tables

Preface and Acknowledgements
The Assembly of Context

Foremost behind the fieldwork sit our local Nepali colleagues who hosted the project, particularly the Tamu Pye Lhu Sangh. It has been a great privilege to work with them. Many of that organization warrant naming, but here Major Hom Bahadur, Lieutenant Bhuwan Singh, Bhovar Palje Tamu and Lieutenant Indra Bahadur Tamu will have to suffice. Equally, the arrival of our expeditions must surely have proved daunting for our village hosts, particulary Tara Devi Gurung and family in Yangjakot and their remarkable hospitality is most gratefully acknowledged here.

David Gibson and Crane Begg were the core of the archaeological team in the first two seasons, with Josh Pollard joining us in 1995. The 2000 team consisted of Marcus Abbott and Alastair Oswald from the UK, being joined by Uddhav Acharya and B. Thapa of HMG, Nepal. Collectively, they gracefully endured a lot and, with Knut Helksog, proved good companions.

The project's 'archaeological stays' in Nepal have variously been enlivened, and our knowledge of the country and its people greatly furthered, by Gunnar Håland, Don Messerschmidt, Charles Ramble, Anne de Sales and Angela Simons. At 'home', we have been variously grateful for the support and insights of Mark Aldenderfer, Dorothy Allard, Tim Bayliss-Smith, John Bellezza, Richard Bradley, Dillip Chakrabarti, Hildegard Diemberger, Mark Edmonds, Ian Hodder, Caroline Humphrey, Michael Hutt, Mark Jobling, Alan Macfarlane, Tim Murray, Michael Oppitz, Corinne Pohl-Thiblet, Perdita Pohle, Tod Ragsadle, Mike Rowlands, Marie Louise Stig Sørensen, Peter Ucko, Torben Vestergaard, Piers Vitebsky, John Whelpton and the late Klaus Ferdinand.

Negotiating Nepal's intricate bureaucracies was greatly facilitated by the British Embassy in Kathmandu, and we are particularly grateful for the assistance of Sheila O'Connor and Andrew Mitchell. Equally, over the years, the various Directors General and Officers of the Department of Archaeology, HMG Nepal supported and smoothed the progress of the project in a spirit of open co-operation. Thereby, we are indebted to Shaphalya Amatya, Riddhi Pradhan, Kosh Acharya and Sukra Sagar Shrestha.

The project was funded throughout by the McDonald Institute for Archaeological Research at the University of Cambridge, and we have been grateful for its inspired support, and particularly that of Colin Renfrew and Chris Scarre. The project also received specific grants from the Frederick Williamson Memorial Fund and the Crowther-Beynon Fund of the University of Cambridge Museum of Archaeology and Anthropology, and in this capacity the encouragement of Robin Boast and Anita Herle must be acknowledged. Gratitude is also due to the Research Committee of the Society of Antiquaries of London for a grant towards the project's post-excavation research. In 1995 the British Academy funded the translation of the *pye*. Finally, we must acknowledge the intellectual support of the Cornell-Nepal Study Program of Cornell University, particularly Kathryn March, which led to the placement of Dawn Kaufmann who undertook a study of local Tamu-mai houses in 1999 (Kaufmann 2000) and whose sketches feature in this volume.

With political events in Nepal cutting short the project's fieldwork, the lack of 'hard' excavation data has provided greater scope to explore related themes. To wit, projects don't exist in isolation: knowledge and research frameworks interact with each other. In this case, Kohla's 'findings' and what has been made of them have, over time, resonated with other projects and colleagues, variously the Haddenham (Ian Hodder), Mergen (Caroline Humphrey) and Sinja Projects (Tim Harward), and which together constitute a singular Asian/Fenland genealogy. Evans would also like to thank Richard Darrah for his comments concerning the woodland management of Hobbemas's 'Middelharnis Avenue', which herein has been (re-)rendered by Vicki Herring.

Judith Pettigrew is grateful for the assistance of Kamal Prasad Adhikari. Eleni Asouti and Dorian Fuller wish to thank Sarah Walshaw for weighing and sieving the environmental samples and undertaking their initial sorting. The volume's graphics reflect the enormous skills of the Cambridge Archaeological Unit's Graphic Officers, variously Marcus Abbott, Crane Begg and Andrew Hall; the latter of whom drew the project's finds in Kathmandu, and was responsible for much of the final design of this book's figures. Unless otherwise indicated, the photographs within the volume are by Christopher Evans, and the text has benefited from the well-honed journalistic skills of his father, Ron Evans.

As to the nuances of the volume's authorship (i.e. what is implied by 'with'), its anthropological sections are, accordingly, specified. While Judith

Pettigrew's insights and deep knowledge of the local community have informed the text throughout, due to differences in disciplinary approach and 'scope', the responsibility for all but Chapter 2 is strictly Evans's alone. Evans is also grateful for Mark Turin's detailed comments concerning the introductory and final chapters, and for proof-reading and copy-editing the whole manuscript.

Finally, matters of nomenclature: the first is the reckoning of time, as Nepal has its own calendrical system. However, to facilitate international reference, all dates in this text should be read as '(B)CE', in other words relative to the 'Christian Era' (with the 'BP' of radiocarbon dating denoting 'before the present', that being 1950). The second point pertains to naming. Although the ethnic group under study is more widely known by their Nepali name, Gurung, here their name for themselves in their own language, Tamu or Tamu-mai will be employed. Otherwise, to all intents and purposes these terms can be considered to be interchangeable. Equally, there is little consensus-standard of local place-name spellings. They have been 'regularized' as far as reasonably possible, but due to problems of computer application, the use of diacritics is restricted to Chapter 2; however, in the subsequent chapter correspondence is indicated between *pye-* and site-titles.

Cambridge, Ely and Kathmandu

Now no chronicler nor historian can attempt to record all events; from the superfluity of happenings he must select what he regards as memorable. His selection is determined to a very small extent by his personal idiosyncracies, but on the whole by tradition and social interest. Indeed, save for personal memoirs and diaries, *the standard of the memorable is a social one*, dictated by interests shared by the whole community ... (Gordon Childe, *History*, 1947, 22; emphasis added).

Everyone is prone to forgetfulness, even under the most favourable conditions, and in a place like this, with so much actually disappearing from the physical world, you can imagine how many things are forgotten all the time. In the end, the problem is not so much that people forget, but that they do not always forget the same thing. What still exists as a memory for one person can be irretrievably lost for another, and this creates difficulties, insuperable barriers against understanding ... *It is a slow but ineluctable process of erasure.* Words tend to last a bit longer than things, but eventually they fade too, along with the pictures they once evoked. Entire categories of objects disappear — flower-pots, for example, or cigarette filters, or rubber bands — and for a time you will be able to recognise those words, even if you cannot recall what they mean. But then, little by little, the words become sounds, a random collection of glottals and fricatives, a storm of whirling phonemes, and finally the whole thing just collapses into gibberish (Paul Auster, *In the Country of Last Things*, 1987, 88–9; emphasis added).

Chapter 1

Introduction — Journeys and Knowledges

Christopher Evans

This is a book concerned with histories and journeys, and with land and identities. Framed in one way, it could be a story of high adventure, relating the discovery of Himalayan ruins and particularly the extraordinary site of Kohla at 3200 m above sea level (a.s.l.; Fig. 1.1). Reported to be the last place that the Tamu-mai/Gurung of central Nepal lived collectively together as a people (before dispersing to villages at lower elevations), it could equally have a quality of historical-inspired myth. History, of course, gives rise to mythologies. Think, for example, of Alexander's cutting of the Gordian Knot or Alfred's burning of the cakes: those moments when personal anecdote and grand narrative structures intercede with events. Yet, here, *context* is rather the prime concern, how the past is constructed in the present (and in 'the past' itself). Although it is crucial that the circumstances of the fieldwork are thoroughly documented, this volume must be far more than just an account of 'discovery'.

For upwards at least of two centuries, the Tamu-mai have practised terrace rice-agriculture in highland villages. Before that, they are largely attributed as having been transhumant pastoralists. Speaking a Tibeto-Burman language, they are the predominant group living in the Annapurna region of the Himalayas (see Fig. 1.7) and they number just over a half a million (there are also Tamu-mai communities in the east and south of the country, and in its urban centres). There is debate concerning their historical roots, with some having previously advocated a southern origin. However, they certainly see themselves (and all serious scholarship would now unequivocally have them) arriving from the north, from Tibet, China or even Mongolia. This accords with what have been held to be the physical (anthropological) traits of the Himalayan 'tribes', who have consistently been accredited as either being of a Tartar, Mongol or Tibetan/Chinese racial 'type' (e.g. Buchanan-Hamilton 1819, 9), and even Gurkha recruitment manuals have acknowledged this (e.g. Hodgson 1838; 1847; Northey 1928). Ultimately, the sense of dual

orientations is tied up with deep-seated stereotypic notions of the 'barbaric' wildness of hills and mountains (and their 'folk') as opposed to the 'civilization of the plains' and, equally, its corollary in the robust vigour of highland peoples in contrast to the effete decadence of lowland cultures.

The indigenous religion of the Tamu-mai is shamanism, with two main schools of practice, *Pachyu* and *Kyabri*. To this day, there are still as many as two to three shamans operating in each village, some even including urban Pokhara within their parish (though see Pettigrew 1995 and Tamblyn 2002 concerning religious pluralism). The role played by shamans is central to the maintenance of cultural identity and historical awareness. Undergoing many years of apprenticeship, during major rituals they regularly have to recite oral 'texts', some of which may take several hours to chant (the *pye*; see Chapter 2). Aside from detailing their cosmology and origins as a people, a *pye* narrates the migration southwards. It is an itinerary of successive villages, in which any geographic reference is relative and settlement information vague. If mapped, it describes a linear settlement genealogy and is, in effect, *a narrative trail* ('first we lived ... , then moved there ...'). Upon death, guided by a shaman, the soul retraces a length of this route north to the Tamu-mai 'Mountain of the Dead', *Oble*, from where it flies northward.

Although by appearance village-life remains traditional, it is not a 'pristine' or 'timeless' ethnography. The Tamu-mai are among the main Himalayan groups of Nepal from whom the Gurkhas have been recruited and widespread military service has had major ramifications for foreign travel, literacy and respect for book-learning, especially among retired officers (see e.g. Ragsdale 1990; Caplan 1995). They have, moreover, hosted a succession of social anthropologists and major monographs have been produced concerning them, including Pignède's *The Gurungs: a Himalayan Population of Nepal* (1966/1993), Messerschmidt's *The Gurungs of Nepal: Conflict and Change in a Village Society*

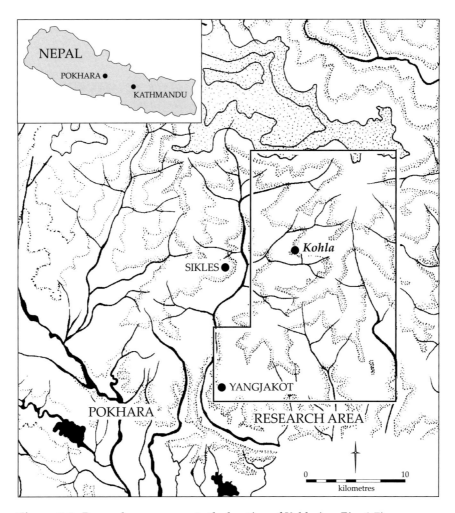

Figure 1.1. *Research area map: note the location of Kohla (see Fig. 1.7).*

(1976a) and Macfarlane's *Resources and Population: a Study of the Gurungs of Nepal* (1976; see also e.g. Messerschmidt 1976b,c; Humphrey 1978; Strickland 1982; Ragsdale 1989; Macfarlane & Gurung 1990; Pettigrew 1995; McHugh 2001). That the Tamu-mai themselves are a much studied people may have influenced the initiation of the Kohla project.

As further outlined in Chapter 2, the project came about in 1992. At that time, senior members of the *Tamu Pye Lhu Sangh* (TPLS), a major Pokhara-based Tamu-mai cultural organization, undertook a trek through the local highlands in an attempt to trace places mentioned in the *pye*. Accompanied by Judith Pettigrew (then a PhD student of Alan Macfarlane's at the University of Cambridge), upon reaching Kohla and inspecting its ruins, it was suggested that they should encourage archaeologists to investigate the site. (Remarkably, this exchange — the actual moment of the project's inception — was recorded on video.) Accordingly, during the course of excavating New Hall in Cambridge in 1993, Evans was approached and

asked if he would meet Judith and Yarjung (a senior Tamu-mai shaman) with a view to undertaking fieldwork in Nepal. Thereafter, things developed, but it needs to be stressed from the outset that the fieldwork was essentially commissioned.

Difficult paths

This volume has had to strike a difficult balance and operate at different scales of resolution. On the one hand, it deals with regionally specific data and sources, whose appreciation requires considerable background scene-setting. On the other hand, 'the local' invariably reflects upon more grand-scale themes, whose exploration must, to some extent, be inherently comparative. Given these issues (and the vexed character of Anglo-Nepalese relations), it is also held that a historical perspective has to be maintained throughout. It is not a matter of 'deep archaeology' and the ethnographic present alone, but of *communities realized in time*. Beyond these, two other themes run through and structure portions of this text. One relates to *walking land*. This focus upon journeys is appropriate, not only for the Tamu-mai's migration narrative, but also the trail-based archaeology which the project's treks involved. The other underlying thread is that of *different voices* and 'knowledges', as the text variously explores local/shamanic, anthropological and archaeological sources. While each will here be given its specific section, with the intention of accrediting all with comparable status, there are, of course, certain tensions. Formal methodologies ('science'), lay approaches and shamanic knowledge do not always easily dovetail, and issues of interpretative authority are not necessarily avoided by simply providing 'many voices'. This approach to the text is not adopted as any kind of knowingly ironic or post-structuralist strategy. Rather, it seems the only appropriate outcome from having the project's diverse co-Directors work together for more than a decade.

Although not always visible from the sites, the fieldwork occurred against the backdrop of the Annapurnas, among the highest and most celebrated mountains in the world. (Like the Matterhorn, but differing from Everest, this is largely a matter of having 'proper' unimpeded profiles that can be appreciated from inhabited, lower ground levels.) Their peaks provide a sense of framework both to the region's history and our researches. While the project involved working at altitude, this volume certainly does not celebrate mountaineering as such (see Macfarlane 2003 on the place of mountains in the Western imagination). *Expeditions* rather lie at its core, that is, *collective walking with a purpose*.

Ingold's celebration of walking as 'a form of circumambulatory knowing' (2004, 331) resonates in the circularity of much of our fieldwork, both as physical journeys and as a intellectual hermeneutic (i.e. 'circling towards knowledge'). What can variously be termed our walks, marches or treks, differed between their participants. While for the archaeological team they were, at times, indeed suggestive of expeditions of an earlier era, for at least some of our Tamu-mai colleagues they seemed to verge upon pilgrimage. Certainly, the 1992 TPLS trek outlined below had overtones of just that (the study area is also bracketed by major Hindu pilgrimage routes up to Muktinath in the northwest: see Chapter 5). It is almost as if by walking in the 'old ways', land and movement through it take on a moral value. Yet, for both parties, the journey was a matter of *grounding knowledge* or, in effect, 'clocking land' (i.e. putting time and history into it), and in this capacity the dynamics of ritual revelation and the (re)search procedures of more formal 'scholastic' investigation are not entirely unrelated.

Whatever nomenclature is applied, the itinerary of our journeys, amounting to many hundreds of kilometres, requires detailing. At the same time, the degree to which these travels frame this volume should also be elucidated, with Chapter 2 setting out the project's anthropology, and Chapters 3 and 4, respectively, its archaeological survey and excavation phases:

I. *1992*: TPLS trek (see Chapter 2);
II. *1994*: Survey of Kohla and other sites at Karapu and above (Chapter 3);
III. *March/April 1995*: Survey of sites in the immediate hinterland above the villages of Yangjakot and Warchok, with ethnoarchaeological study at the latter (Chapter 3);
IV. *September 1995*: Reconnoitering trek into Mustang and Manang (Chapter 4);
V. *April 2000*: Excavation at Kohla (Chapter 4);
VI. *December 2002*: Shamans' meeting in Pokhara (Chapter 5).

This only outlines the main fieldwork seasons; omitted are various visits to Kathmandu and Pokhara, both to negotiate the project and for the purposes of finds study. Arising from all this walking, three publications have appeared concerning the project's 'archaeology' (in the broadest sense of the term: Evans 1999; 2004; Evans *et al.* 2002) and two more anthropologically related papers have been produced (Pettigrew 1999; Pettigrew & Tamu 1999).

That the project arose at the request of the local community meant that these were seductive circumstances in which to conduct archaeology, conjuring up a sense of a calling or 'enlistment'. To whatever degree possible, however, the archaeological component tried throughout to maintain its academic independence and not be overtly sided. Indeed, it has always seemed that what the TPLS wanted the archaeologists to be were sympathetic *scientists* and that ultimately it was *facts* that mattered (as opposed to the deeper 'embeddedness' of anthropological practice). Yet, it certainly proved challenging to undertake fieldwork when archaeology so obviously counts. Returning to Pokhara after the project's treks, our findings and pronouncements were long mulled over. When we exhibited pottery found at Kohla and, upon learning that one had fingerprint impressions — the 'imprint of the ancestors' — some wept on touching it and the occasion was emotionally charged. These conditions cast fieldwork into a different context, leading us to weigh our words and interpretations more than would be the case in a European context. While at no point did we feel ourselves censored, there is no certainty that our Tamu-mai colleagues will wholeheartedly approve of this text with its ambiguities and 'alternatives'.

Figure 1.2. *The Pokhara Kohibo, above as under construction 1991. (Photograph: Y. Tamu.)*

Despite whatever contextual caveats may be rehearsed, the site of Kohla certainly sits at the heart of the project and this volume. This is only appropriate, not only for its quasi-mythical status within the Tamu-mai past, but also for the quality of its ruins and their impact. The site is quite simply extraordinary and this is only enhanced by its dramatic setting. No claim is here being made that we discovered it. Aside from the 1992 TPLS trek (and Yarjung's earlier visit: see Chapter

2), Pignède, writing in the late 1950s, noted that an informant had visited the site (1993, 197), and it was later inspected by other researchers, including Messerschmidt (1976b) and, in the early 1990s, by Temple (1993). Whereas the pastoralists, who for generations have camped among the ruins, obviously knew of the site's existence, the His Majesty's Government (HMG) of Nepal, Department of Archaeology colleagues who accompanied us in 2000 were the first official state representatives to see Kohla. They were astonished by the quality of the remains and, proclaiming that nothing was known like it within the country, felt certain that it warranted World Heritage Site status.

The conditions of fieldwork proved constantly stimulating and often trying. While members of the archaeological team had considerable experience of overseas expedition life, what distinguished the Kohla fieldwork was its extremes, both altitude and the primitive character of its living conditions, and the fact that getting to the research area itself required walking some distance. Usually involving up to a week's trekking, all equipment and supplies had to be portered in. There are no roads whatsoever in the area and our funds could not run to hiring a helicopter. Even if that had been a realistic option, it would probably not have been chosen. To do so would have entailed losing any experience of the land and our direct connection with the local populace (see Ingold's distinction between the broader experience of walking and 'groundless' travel: 2004, 221).

The conditions equally impacted upon the excavation and survey methods. Apart from our tents, there was no dig house or site office (no tables, chairs or showers, etc.) and there was never escape from the wet and cold. Without electricity, all surveying was done by theodolite, compass and tapes. This made Gibson and Begg's mapping of Kohla proper a truly daunting task, and only in our last season did the resources extend to a GPS (Geographical Positioning System; the area's satellite image was only acquired post-fieldwork). In short, things were basic and methodological sophistication should not, here, be presumed. The character of the landscape also influenced the field survey; step off a trail and there is thick forest. Add to this the progressive exhaustion of walking up through such highlands; St Paul's Cathedral could lie some tens of metres off the route and might well go unnoticed. While we did discover sites, this must invariably be an instance of *trail-based archaeology*. Biased to clearances and meadows, it was otherwise led by 'stories' and where things happened to have been seen before.

The fieldwork was cut short by Nepal's political circumstances in the first years of the twenty-first

Figure 1.3. *TPLS literature: museum advertising and membership flyers.*

century (Maoist insurgency; see e.g. de Sales 2000 and Pettigrew 2001; 2003; 2004; Shneiderman & Turin 2004) and, in 2002, we drew the project to a close with a meeting of shamans in Pokhara (see Chapter 5 and Evans 2004). This volume documents only one instance of the more general exploration of ethnic pluralism that occurred among Nepal's many minorities during the 1990s. Admittedly, the Tamu-mai case was unique in terms of commissioning archaeology; nevertheless, it only reflects the extreme of a wider phenomenon. Here, it is essential to recognize that this occurred beyond the level of ethnic localism. It should rather be seen in a context of changing trans-Himalayan identities, for which 'real' and perceived histories are increasingly playing a great part (Kraemer 1998; see also e.g. Fisher 2001 and Tamblyn 2002). While in these circumstances it is entirely appropriate to investigate the past of its diverse groups, it would be inexcusable to consciously provide historical grist to further ethnic rivalry.

This is potentially a matter of 'realpolitik' and, to understand this, Nepal's rich ethno-cultural mosaic must be appreciated. Extending over some 147,000 sq. km (approximately half the size of Italy), its population in 2007 of 27 million includes more than 65 ethnic minorities speaking over 90 languages. The Himalayas mark a great interface — between Hinduism and Buddhism (underpinned by shamanic traditions) on the one hand, and southern Aryan peoples (speaking Indo-European languages) with northern Mongoloid-type groups (and Tibeto-Burman tongues) on the other (see e.g. Turin 2006). In short, Nepal is an intensely multi-ethnic country.

The ultimate catalyst for much of what occurred in Nepal over the last 15 years (and even, distantly, the project itself) was the democracy movement of 1990, which led to constitutional change and the overthrow of the Panchayat system. Prior to that time, 'public' ethnic associations were forbidden on the grounds that they would erode national unity (though since the early 1950s there had been a few such underground groups). The changes of 1990 permitted much greater expression of sub-national identities and a flowering of diverse ethnic organizations and congresses, of

Figure 1.4. *TPLS seniors and shamans: top, inspecting the entrails of a sacrificed chicken prior to the 1994 trek's departure (right, TPLS's then-treasurer, Hom Bahadur and, left, its historian, Bhovar Palje Tamu); middle, shaman mannequins in the Kohibo Museum (cf. Fig. 2.4); below, the anthropological team (left-centre to right, Mark Turin, Yarjung Tamu and Judith Pettigrew) with the TPLS president, Idib Tamu.*

which TPLS was but one (see Fisher 2001, 3–5, 138–66 concerning the formation of a comparable Thakali league in Pokhara in 1983). The umbrella organization of these many associations is the *Janajati Mahasangh* ('Federation of Nationalities'), and the impetus towards greater ethnic representation and democracy is generally referred to as the Janajati Movement (see e.g. Skar 1995; Des Chene 1996).

Finally, in order to set the scene more fully, it warrants mention that during the latter half of the 1990s, Evans and Gibson also became involved in other research in Nepal, on the Sinja Valley Project in the west of country, recording the remains of the Khasa Malla kingdom (Fig. 1.7; Evans & Gibson 2003; see this chapter below and Chapter 5). Following a season of survey in 1998, this also saw its first and, as it transpired, last excavation season in 2000. Concerned with the recording of truly monumental 'dynastic' architecture and sculpture, the Sinja researches were, in many respects, antithetical to the Kohla Project and, for various reasons, serve as a counterpoint throughout this volume. Yet, what united the two was a conviction that fieldwork in these areas of Nepal could, through the production of appropriate guidebooks, encourage cultural trekking to benefit remote communities. While also furthering the discipline of archaeology in Nepal generally, it was held that the past could be enlisted to support the local present; in other words, practising an *engaged archaeology*.

Close retrieval — situating 'archaeology'

Despite whatever claims this volume has to mixed interdisciplinary participation and sources, the secrecy of certain knowledge-sets is also an underlying strand. As opposed to espousals of 'open' computer-age exchange (much of this book being put together trans-globally through electronic media), not all cultural knowledge is transparent and initiation is often a curtailing factor. In Chapter 2, we will see that Yarjung will only divulge some threads of his knowledge and not allow for the translation of all the *pye*'s entries (there are, apparently, also still 'hidden' Tamu-mai historical sources; see below). Equally, is anthropology's tradition of fictionalizing its study villages, which in this case involves Ragsdale's 'Lamnasa' and Messerschmidt's 'Ghasiu' (1990 and 1976a respectively: see Fig. 4.26). Practised in order to protect the confidentiality of informants, it also reflects the subject's concern with *abstract* social process; in contrast, archaeology is much more fixed in 'real' space and time (though we have had to mask the identity of our Yangjakot host family due to real political threat). This secrecy finds resonance in the activities of the few researchers/observers in the area prior to the later twentieth century.

Beyond the confines of the Kathmandu Valley, Nepal was closed to the outside world until 1950–51, with slavery, for example, only abolished in 1924. Much of the information gathered concerning its peoples and their history prior to its opening was collected by a succession of pundit-spies, 'adventurers' and political agents in the capital. Of the latter, Nepal's Himalayan peoples were first really discussed in any substantive manner by Buchanan-Hamilton and Hodgson. The former stayed for fourteen months in 1802–3, whereas Hodgson was Britain's Official Resident in Kathmandu between 1833 and 1843 (beforehand being Assistant in that post from 1825). Both were essentially East India Company 'fact-finders'. Very much a case of distant retrieval, by the constraints set upon the British Mission, they were unable to leave the Valley itself. They had to collect information almost entirely from secondary sources, including the commissioned travels of their local staff. Otherwise, Warren Hastings succinctly expressed the Company's desire for 'local knowledge' on commissioning Bogle's expedition to Tibet:

> … keep a Diary, inserting whatever passes before your observation which shall be characteristic of the People, their Manners, Customs, Buildings, Cookery, the Country, the Climate, or the Road, carrying with you a Pencil and Pocket-Book for the purpose of minuting short Notes of every Fact or Remark as it occurs, and putting them in Order at your Leisure while they are fresh in your Memory (in Teltscher 2006, 34).

In 1819, Buchanan-Hamilton published his survey, *An Account of the Kingdom of Nepal and of the Territories Annexed to this dominion by the House of Gorkha*. Providing much of this volume's historical data, it outlines the kingdom's history, its main ethnic groups and resources (for background see Allen 2002, 10–11 & 17–18 and also Sharma 1973 concerning Kirkpatrick's *An Account of the Kingdom of Nepal* of 1811). Although an extraordinary polymath and collector, Hodgson published relatively little and his extensive archives are only now being prepared for publication (see the various papers and Hodgson's bibliography in Waterhouse 2004). Hodgson's observations will be drawn upon later in the volume (see Chapter 4) and, at this juncture, only a brief note in the *Reports of the British Association for the Advancement of Science* for 1859 — the same year as Darwin's *The Origins of the Species* — need concern us. It announced a donation by Hodgson to the British Museum (Owen 1859). Propelled by the prevalent spirit of comparative ethnology of the day and the racist appraisal/ranking of nineteenth-century empire, he apparently gave some 90 Nepalese skulls representative of the Kingdom's various ethnic groupings (including Gurung/Tamu-mai examples; see also Arnold 2004).

Although acutely sensitive for the local people (and non-Western research generally), these activities need to be discussed in relationship to *orientalism* and the relationship between modes of Western 'scientific'

Figure 1.5. *Raw materials: wood, stone and clay. Top, behind-house storage in Yangjakot of poles, including bamboo (note corrugated steel sheet right and concrete repair of wall-seam left); below, Evans inspects stacked pots, Bhaktapur, April 1994. (Photograph: D. Gibson.)*

knowledge/discourse and those of local communities. On the one hand, there has been the apparatus of empire, turning people into racial/ethnic objects, with the Tamu-mai having seen the vexed benefits of Gurkha caricature, as a trustworthy, good-humoured 'martial tribe' (see below and e.g. Caplan 1995). Yet, on the other hand, and as is recently emphasized by Allen (2002), it was researchers of early orientalism that founded so much of the study of, and intellectual respect for, Asian traditions. Therefore, this is a difficult path to tread between a strict cultural relativism/localism and what have been 'grand' (imperial) Western knowledge categories. What is here seen as crucial is a sense of inter-cultural dialogue, akin to that of Said's *Culture and Imperialism* of 1994. This is not just a matter of the many things 'Asian' that adorn Britain's

A

B

C

D

E

F

Figure 1.6. *'Type' portrayal and material dialogues: A) Tamu-mai dancers at 'National Dialogue Conference on Indigenous and Tribal Peoples and Peace Building in Nepal', Kathmandu, January 2005 (note the males' plaid scarves; from NEFIN website); B) 'A Limbu and a Gurung', watercolour from Hodgson's Scrapbook (from Waterhouse 2004, pl. 23), note the downtrodden rendering of its subjects, especially 'The Gurung' (right); C) 'Gurung/ Tamu-mai ethnic-type' dolls in National Museum, Kathmandu; D) Bulbir Gurung of the Gurkha army, being one of a series of Indian portraits commissioned by Queen Victoria (which hung in Osborne House on the Isle of Wight, Royal Collection of Her Majesty the Queen; Mathur 2003, fig. 17) painted by the Austrian artist, Rudolf Swoboda, when he spent the summer of 1887 in the Punjab with Lockwood Kipling, Director of the Mayo School of Art in Lahore (see also the latter's son's, Rudyard, 1912 short story, 'In the Presence' concerning the extraordinary endurance of Subedar-Major Santbir Gurung of the 2/2nd Goorkhas); E) George Stubbs's Yak of 1791 (oil on canvas, Royal College of Surgeons, London; Myrone 2002, fig. 36); F) Tipu Sultan's tea-set (Clive Collection, Powis Castle; Jasanoff 2005, 191).*

museums, that influenced the decor of its houses and stocked its gardens (e.g. Evans 1990; Jasanoff 2005), but also the two-way contact of colonial experience (e.g. Gosden 2004). The dress of the Tamu-mai dancers shown in Figure 1.6 exemplifies this, with their plaid scarves being comparable to the Hong Kong silks often worn by women. This selection of 'the foreign' reflects the impact of Gurkha service, and even extends to families without enlisted members. However minor, this demonstrates the interpenetration of (material) cultures and is part of a spectrum of 'mixing' ranging from Swoboda's *Bulbir Gurung*, Stubb's *Yak* and Tipu Sultan's European tea-set to Nash's Brighton Pavilion of 1815–23 and Maharajah Duleep Singh's Elveden Hall, near Thetford of 1874–94 (see Fig. 1.6). In reference, therefore, to the dynamics of cultural exchange (however unbalanced at times) and while showing all due respect for the immediately 'local', it is here held that a comparative basis for discussing community/ ethnicity and history is possible and, indeed, essential. This seems the only reasonable response as, for most of the world today, we are all at times variously 'insiders'/'outsiders' or *participants and onlookers*.

In 1899 the Japanese monk, Ekai Kawaguchi (author of *Three Years In Tibet*; 1909), surreptitiously entered Tibet, coming up through Pokhara and Thak Khola into Mustang where he stayed for several months. His intention was apparently genuine: to further his studies of Buddhism in Tibet. While staying in India beforehand to learn Tibetan, he came under the tutelage of one Babu Sarat Chandra Das, the 'master' pundit who journeyed to Tibet (then also closed to foreigners) in disguise in 1879 and 1881, and who served as the model for Kipling's Babu in *Kim* (see Hopkirk 1996, 223–6 and Meyer & Brysac 2001, 212–20, and also Chapter 4 below concerning the activities of Hari Ram). In 1907 the Swedish explorer Sven Hedin entered Mustang and, in 1944, the Austrian climber Hans Kopp travelled through that region *en route* to Kathmandu, after escaping — together with Aufschnaiter and Harrer (the latter, the author of *Seven Years in Tibet*) — from an internment camp in what was then still British India.

With the opening of Nepal there were many expeditions into the area. In 1950 it saw both Tilman's and a major French mountaineering expedition (with cultural aspirations) of which Herzog was a part (1952). Thereafter followed the 1952 Swiss Geological Mission (with Toni Hagen) and, in 1953–4, large Japanese scientific expeditions. The latter also involved anthropologists and, prior to Pignède's 1958 stay among the Tamu-mai, in 1956 Snellgrove travelled widely through Nepal's inner Himalayan districts (1961), with Fürer-Haimendorf staying in

Lower Mustang in 1962 (1975; Vinding 1998 provides a full outline of subsequent anthropological research in the Thak Kohla area). In 1959, Mustang was again closed to foreigners and swathes of Manang became restricted during the 1960s and '70s, when CIA-supported Tibetan Khampa fighters entered the country escaping from the Chinese army (Messerschmidt *et al.* 2004, 49–50).

The expeditions of the renowned orientalist, Giuseppe Tucci (1902–84), twice took him to Pokhara, first in 1952 and, then, in 1954 (Tucci 1956; 1962; see Chakrabarti 2002; Chatterjee 2002). Primarily concerned with the spread of Buddhism and interested in Tibetology generally, he was in the area in order to strike into the west and northwest of the country, travelling in 1954 by yak caravan to Jumla *via* Tukche and Charka. However, among the more immediate findings of his 1952 expedition were the inhabited cave sites in the Thak Khola Valley (he had earlier seen comparable cave settlements in western Tibet; 1956, 10; 1977, 122, fig. 30; see also Aldenderfer 2005; Simons & Schön 1998). A scholar of great energy and intellect, a recent memoir by his photographer on a number of these treks, Fosco Maraini, provides insights into Tucci's character. For example, apparently even in the most remote corners of Tibet, he still insisted on being referred to in the prescribed manner of the Reale Academia d'Italia, 'Your Excellency' (Maraini 2000, 196).

Based on his researches in the 1950s, Tucci pronounced that knowledge of the Khasa Malla dynasty of western Nepal then amounted to little more than 'arid lists of names suspended in the void of chronological uncertainty' (1962). Despite the efforts of the Department of Archaeology of HMG, Nepal (established in 1953), this statement is still relevant for much of the country where the practice of archaeology is very much in its infancy (see Darnal 2002 concerning the history of its development, and Whelpton 2005, 15–16 and Pandey 1987 provide outlines of what is known of Nepal's prehistory). Most attention has been directed towards the Lumbini District of the southern Tarai (identifying Buddha's birthplace; e.g. Coningham & Schmidt 1998) and, also, the Kathmandu Valley itself. Consequently, the Kohla researches were something of a radical departure and, aside from Howard's surveys of forts (1995), there had been no fieldwork within this region of the country. However, the investigations of the Nepal-German High Mountain Research Project in the Kali Gandaki Valley, Lower Mustang (on the northern side of the Annapurnas), did provide some degree of context. Between 1992 and 1997 they surveyed and excavated a series of settlement and cave sites. Occurring very much in a 'grand project' tradition,

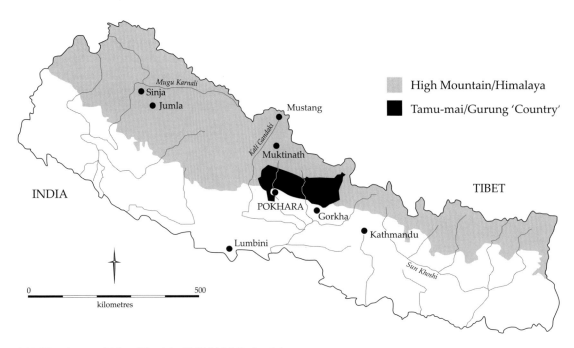

Figure 1.7. *Nepal map. (After Pignède 1993 [1966], fig. 1.)*

this interdisciplinary initiative included geographic land-use analysis, the recording of manuscripts and rock art, and also temple and village architecture studies (and, in relationship to which, our efforts always seemed entirely dwarfed). Referred to in detail below, interim reports of their work appeared in *Ancient Nepal* (nos. 130–34, 136, 137 & 153; 1992–94 & 2003), with their final publication in *Beiträge zur Allgemeinen und Vergleichenden Archäologie* (nos. 14, 17 & 18; 1994, 1997 & 1998; see also Simons 1997; Alt *et al.* 2003).

The Nepal-German Project found occupation dating back to the first millennium BC, and, elsewhere in the country, both Neolithic and Palaeolithic remains have been discovered (see Darnal 2002). From the outset, it must be stressed that, while never intentionally ignoring any facet of data, the Kohla Project was never so ambitious. There was never any question of trying to establish the general antiquity of occupation in the Annapurna region. Even aside from the ethno-historical emphasis of its specific research framework, our limited resources could never have stretched to such ends.

There is a telling schism within Nepali cultural studies, including its archaeology. On the one hand, reflecting the prevalence of Kathmandu's learned echelons, the primary axis of 'high culture' has been with India. Indeed, the Nepali archaeological state service appears to have been modelled on the Indian example. Yet, within a specifically Himalayan context, in recent years there has been an equally influential northward focus. First introduced by anthropologists,

with the closing of Tibet and growing interests in Tibet-Buddhism (and also Bon-po practices), in recent decades northern Nepal — particularly Mustang and Dolpo — has seen much research, almost as though the north of the country was a surrogate Tibet. Though Himalayan Nepal still clearly maintains its allure, over the latter half of the 1990s this began to change as outside research became possible within Tibet, where particularly noteworthy have been both Bellezza's and Aldenderfer's archaeological researches (e.g. Bellezza 2002; 2004; Aldenderfer 2003a,b; forthcoming; see also Aldenderfer & Yinong 2004).

Despite this background, to all intents and purposes, in terms of its archaeological component, the Kohla project was essentially a case of working blind. Without an established antiquarian tradition in the region (or the country as a whole), how does one evaluate the cultural associations of one site-type as opposed to another and gauge their age? Over the last two decades in Anglo-American archaeology, with the development of various schools of theoretical approach (under the generic umbrella of post-processualism) there has been a distinctly anti-scientific ethos and a questioning of concepts of truth — with all rather being seen as modes of 'interpretation'. This is a luxury that can only be afforded when basic chronological and typological frameworks have been so long-established that a base-line understanding can be assumed, becoming so deeply embedded that they somehow stop being 'scientific'. Undertaking archaeology in such circumstances as in Nepal can only make one long for more hard science and analytical rigour.

The Kohla project's community-based background has implications for the situation of archaeology (and anthropology) within nation-building paradigms, and the development of the discipline generally within Nepal. Recognizing the underlying need to contribute to a basic framework for the country's archaeology, the intention has never been an 'archaeology against the state'. There were, nevertheless, always potential tensions between local and national interests. Throughout, we attempted to undertake overseas archaeology in a 'non-Wheelerian' manner (i.e. 'imperialist'; see e.g. Chakrabarti 1988; Paddayya 1995). Yet, it was equally held that the work must not be an exercise in cultural relativism that could foster an historical ethnic chauvinism and, therefore, it needed to balance both 'sensitivity'/engagement and detachment.

Within the specific context of the project's researches, the definition of archaeology is, by necessity, broad. The excavation and site surveys can only be considered traditional, whereas, arising from the fieldwork, are aspects of ethno-archaeological study — for example, the recording of contemporary pastoralist shelters and village houses — behind which lies the idea that these somehow directly reflect upon 'the ancient'. Yet, beyond this are also aspects of singularly contemporary material culture study (albeit with indirect past relevance) that reflect upon phenomena in the 'modern world'. In this capacity, it can be considered as part of the 'archaeology of us' (Buchli & Lucas 2001); that is, as a facet of contemporary diversity, as opposed to casting the ethnographic 'other' as just some manner of primitivist cipher. This would include both developments in a new Tamu-mai public architecture and the entire context of the fieldwork itself. It is a matter of re-defining practice and pushing the subject beyond its normative limits. In other words, opening it up to embrace a wide range of material culture study in general, that being held as a crucial meeting-ground of archaeology and anthropology in the world today (see e.g. Gosden 1999 concerning the history of their interrelationship).

Evaluating stories — axes of history

As is the case throughout much of Asia — and for that matter as was prevalent in Europe prior to the early–mid twentieth century — in Nepal, there has been a strong tradition of (re-)studying written sources (and iconography). The situation is in some ways comparable to what Evans encountered when working in Inner Mongolia, where there is a very active historical research community, but an underdeveloped appreciation of original fieldwork, with the result that there, for example, *The Secret History of the Mongols* has been endlessly pored over and analysed. In Nepal, it is largely a matter of king lists. Variously documenting genealogical succession and taxation, these have come to intermesh with local ethnic and clan histories (i.e. essentially oral sources). In the end, it is a matter of trying to *evaluate* stories, in which one group's reading of the past may well conflict with another's. In a Himalayan context, this largely relates to the issue of historical origins, and the relationship to Hinduization and the imposition/adoption of caste. Ultimately, this comes down to the 'archaeology' or historical politics of domination and sub-set alliances. Yet, increasingly within the country, this is now considered a matter of 'true' and 'wrong' histories, with the past being publicly adjudicated (and even featuring in court-case disputes; see Glover 2004 and Chapter 5). The historical interfacing of Nepal's Himalayan groups with southern Aryan Hindu hierarchies has come to be seen as a betrayal of the former's collective northern origins. The risk is that, by focusing on a pristine sense of *source*, the less-than-ideal dynamism of subsequent histories becomes deflated or even denied (see e.g. Rowlands 1988 concerning myths of historical origins).

The problem with so judging history is its own judgment. In the long term, all the proponents have variously been colonized and colonizers. By whatever means, the Tamu-mai did *arrive* in the region and the land was surely then not entirely 'empty', just as the original impetus for the region's later Hindu(ized) overlords was their own displacement due to Muslim incursions into northwestern India. The Himalayas have been like a still hub, around and through which, over time, the great religious cultures of the world have flowed. Therefore, in order to frame the project's researches, it is appropriate that the relevant 'axes of history' are outlined:

The north - The conquest of Zhang zhung in the mid seventh century officially marks the introduction of Buddhism into Tibet (Aldenderfer & Yinong 2004, 42). It was not, however, until *c.* AD 1000 that the religious basis of the kingdom was thoroughly transformed. Pre-Buddhist cultural forms persisted throughout the time of the Yarlung Kings during the early seventh to mid ninth centuries, a period of military might and territorial expansion (e.g. invading India in the seventh century). Thereafter followed collapse, the fracturing of the kingdom and the end of its extra-regional ambitions. In 1207, the Tibetans submitted to Mongolian rulers, who were themselves defeated by the Manchus in 1720, when Tibet fell under their suzerainty (see Snellgrove & Richardson 1968 for general background).

Nearer at hand, Tibetan culture and Lamaist Buddhism impacted upon Mustang from, at least, the later tenth century and the 'Tibetan' Kingdom of Lo appears to have been established in *c.* AD 1380. By the fifteenth century, Lo had become a significant

Buddhist religious centre and, threatened by the Jumla Kingdom (see below), it was then that the fortified capital of Lo Manthang was built. After a 20-year war, in 1760 Mustang (Manthang) fell to Jumla, itself shortly to succumb to Gorkha. Though paying tribute to the latter's kings, Manthang was not invaded by its armies and still today retains an independent status as a distinct kingdom within Nepal (see Peissel 1992, 228–31; Vinding 1998).

The west (and south) - With its centre of power focused within the far west of the country, the trans-Himalayan Khasa Malla Kingdom lasted from *c.* AD 1100 to the late fourteenth century. The 'Khas' are thought to have immigrated into the area from the northwest (e.g. *Kash*mir or *Kash*gar), where they intermixed with both indigenes and Hindu Rajputs; the latter coming into the region fleeing from Muslim invaders in Rajasthan in the centuries after AD 1000. The kingdom included most of Nepal west of Gorkha (though they also attacked and held the Kathmandu Valley on a number of occasions from 1287–1334), and included Garwhal and Kumoan provinces in Uttar Anchal, India, and also Guge and Purang in southwestern Tibet. Supported by a network of royal roads and with its palace at Sinja, the dynasty fostered its own monumental architecture and sculpture (Fig. 1.7; see Chapter 5 below). Its kings were known to be Buddhists, though their religion later incorporated Hindu components. They employed Sanskrit, Tibetan and early Nepali texts, and encouraged the settlement of Brahmans to further scholarship. This highly de-centralized feudatory state was in decline by the mid fourteenth century, when it lost its Tibetan provinces, and by 1400, it was subsumed by the Jumla Kingdom. Thereafter, the political fragmentation of the west of the country continued until the seventeenth/eighteenth centuries, it being controlled by two loose federations — the 22 kingdoms of *Baisi Rajya* in the Karnali basin (of which Jumla was paramount) and the 24 kingdoms of the *Chaubisi Rajya* in the Gandaki region. At least in part founded by Rajputs fleeing Muslim expansion into India, these petty Hinduized states included the fifteenth-/sixteenth-century chiefs/princelings of Lamjung and Kaski, which are of particular relevance for the project's researches (see Buchanan-Hamilton 1819; Hutt 1994, 24–6; Bishop 1990, 105–23; Pandey 1997 and Whelpton 2005, 10, 23–5 for further general background).

The east - The establishment and subsequent periodization of the kingdom(s) of the Kathmandu Valley from at least the fourth century AD need not unduly concern us (see e.g. Hutt 1994, 14–23; Whelpton 2005, 35–49). However, emerging out of the political fragmentation of the 24 kingdoms of the *Chaubisi Rajya*, the rise of the Gorkha Kingdom (founded 1559) is of obvious relevance. From 1685, the leaders of this small principality commenced conquest and expansion. Capturing the Kathmandu Valley in 1768–9, the Gorkha thereafter subsumed both the western Khasa/Jumla Kingdoms and the east of the country. As a result, by the late eighteenth century, the new Kingdom of Nepal extended from the Kangra Valley to Sikkim. The Gorkhas were, though, defeated by the Chinese when they invaded Tibet in 1792 and again later, in 1814–16, by the armies of the British East India Company (see Hernon 2003, 468–94). In the ensuing treaty, the kingdom lost lands to the east and west, reducing Nepal to its current borders. (It was due, however, to their fighting prowess that the agreement was then made to employ 'Gurkha' regiments within the British Army.) In 1856 the Gorkhas invaded Tibet for a second time, only withdrawing in return for long-term indemnities (see e.g. Stiller 1973 for general background).

Within the sweep of history, these axes have all pushed towards the 'centre'. From this background, three main dating horizons are of particular relevance for the study area:

1. the influence of Tibetan Buddhism and culture in Mustang from the tenth century;
2. the establishment of Hindu(ized) principalities during the fifteenth/sixteenth centuries;
3. the conquest of the region and unification of Nepal by the forces of Gorkha during the later eighteenth century.

Village communities — framing ethnography

Villages frame our fieldwork. What we studied at Kohla was clearly a village (with associated hamlets) and, whether for shamans or the expedition's porters, when encountering Kohla's ruins, all were confident of its attribution as such. Equally, our host community, Yangjakot, is a settlement of comparable density — *a village*. Operating behind this is what is implied by the idea of the face-to-face *village community*. Until recently, villages have after all been the prime unit of anthropological study, held to reflect the 'totality' and fully express the social, economic and ritual life of 'traditional' cultures. As exemplified by Pignède's study (1993 [1966]), but also underlying Macfarlane and Messerschimdt's work among the Tamu-mai/ Gurung (respectively 1976 and 1976a), this viewpoint tends to overlook much 'going out' from settlements (see though Des Chene 1992; 1996; Macfarlane 1989; Pettigrew 1995; 2000). This has included both their transhumant pastoral component and overseas Gurkha service. More recently also involving urban migration and foreign labour, at any one time, therefore, much of a village is away. Nor are these entirely closed communities. While admittedly only usually a minor component, Tamu-mai villages will often include both Brahman households, artisan castes and members of other Himalayan/Janajati ethnic groups (e.g. see Macfarlane 1976, fig. A3.3–5 concerning the village of Thak and also the Digital Himalaya website for its subsequent development).

The epistemological construction of 'the village' has been persuasive and it has been seen as variously epitomizing communities and 'folk types' (e.g. Maine 1871; Gomme 1890; Dewey 1972). Yet, from an archaeological perspective, 'villages' can be viewed within a more fluid spectrum of settlement types, ranging, on the one hand, from camps to hamlets and, on the other, to towns and cities. Kohla has attributes that fly in the face of such easy 'village-as-type' identification, particularly the fact that it hosted 'kings'. Accordingly, questions of social hierarchy must here be explored. Especially relevant in this case are the Ghale Raja (in Tamu, *Klye Mru*) — the kingly lineage coming down from the north — as they reflect upon the idea of 'outside' or 'stranger kings' (see Helms 1988).

While verging on caricature in the face of the complex social matrix of villages and contemporary politics, here a deeper resonance is also apparent. As understood, villages have their poorer — usually in Nepal the Blacksmith and Tailor castes — as well as wealthier households. What has clearly occurred in the case of the recent Maoist movement is a particular understanding of the village economy/community; one opposed to the urbanism of Pokhara and Kathmandu. Whereas, within an archaeological perspective, villages have emergent hierarchical potential, as some may become towns and even cities (as, indeed, Pokhara has become over the last 40 years), the contemporary Maoist vision is singularly based in the present-day village community and motivated by a 'constructed' egalitarianism.

Villages are, nevertheless, an appropriate nexus through which to consider daily social life. Here, an example is relevant. Early in 2004, Evans and Pettigrew met to discuss this volume's structure, Judy having just come back from other fieldwork in Nepal, which included a visit to our host village, Yangjakot. Over the course of the last year, one of the local men who had worked for us on site had established a shop at a riverside ford (his wife being abroad as a migrant worker), which was swept away in floods; he perished with all his children; another acquaintance had died in a landslide. What of equivalence had occurred in Cambridge over the same period? — an acquaintance committing suicide, the wife of a colleague having a stroke, a friend breaking his knee and three births among co-workers. The difference lies in the extent that the impact of 'nature' tells of closer relations to land in Nepal. This equally reflects the degree to which the village is a hub of social (and emotional) life and, with it, the relative importance of face-to-face relations. Consequently, working in such 'situated' circumstances as in this project, one cannot but reflect on archaeological interpretation, making things seem far more real and less distantly academic.

To a large extent, perspectives on the past are a matter of scaling, with the grand scope of kingdoms — their comings and goings (and their taxes and armies) — *seeming* to contrast with the lingering immediacy of 'the local' or 'ethnographic'. It is telling that there is little written mention of any of Nepal's Himalayan communities prior to the eighteenth century. As essentially 'peoples without (written) history' (Wolf 1982), knowledge of their pasts must largely rely upon oral sources (and 'myth'). Accordingly, as identities are variously being forged and reinforced in the region, at least in the case of the Tamu-mai, the appeal of archaeology lies in its provision of time depth when history *per se* is otherwise weak or shallow. In effect,

it allows us to re-address the historical present. Given this, and in the awareness that identity is inherently relational (e.g. Boon 1982), what is known of the ethno-histories of the Tamu-mai's immediate neighbouring groups should be outlined:

The Magar - Inhabiting the hill-zone of central Nepal, the Magar are among its largest groups traditionally speaking a Tibeto-Burman language, with the degree of their Hinduization essentially dependent upon their south/north situation (see Hitchcock 1966; Lecomte-Tilouine 1993; 2002; Tucci 1977, 4–5 notes that prior to their Hinduization they lived in high fortified settlements; see also Oestigarrd 2000, fig. 6.43). Among those communities which Hitchcock investigated in the south-central part of their territory (Banyan Hill), there seemed to be no distinct sense of origin. Although sometime admitting 'When we came here' (from an unspecified source), others responded 'We have lived here always' (Hitchcock 1966, 4). Yet, in contrast to most of the origin stories for the northern (Kham) Magar, which tell of their local ancestry, one apparently relates the arrival of a clan from 'Mongolia' (Oppitz 1983, 200; 1999, 198). That the Magar language varies greatly has also led to speculation of their multiple origins: 'The term "Magar" was perhaps once simply a prestigious title that was adopted by numerous otherwise unconnected groups' (Whelpton 2005, 14; see Oppitz 1999 concerning their cosmology and traditional house architecture, and also e.g. de Sales 2000 on the role of the Kham Magar in the Maoist conflict).

The Thakali - While seeing considerable migration southward into the central hill-zone over the last two centuries, the homeland of the Thakali has traditionally been the Kali Gandaki Valley, south of Jomson (see Figs. 1.7 & 4.35). They were renowned as traders along this great corridor route between western Tibet, central Nepal and northern India. Like the Magar (and to a lesser degree the Tamu-mai), the basis of their religion is a matter of various combinations of Hinduism, Buddhism and shamanism. What is remarkable is that they make no claim of being a single ethnic group (Fisher 2001). Rather, their four clans arrived in the area (then already inhabited) from different regions. *Apropos,* there is apparently a saying among them, 'although we could not meet at our birthplace, let us meet at *our gathering place*' (Fisher 2001, 50; emphasis added). Their historical narratives outline the journey of the ancestor of each clan. These have been written down (the *rhab*) and are read in public during the great Lha Phewa festival, that occurs every twelve years. The story of the Bhattachen clan, for example, outlines their ancestor's travels in Tibet, whereas the Gauchan clan migrated to Sinja to join with the Khasa Malla, only afterwards leaving to travel eastward.

A popular oral tradition references the latter, as it describes how the Hansa Raja, putatively the son of the Raja of Sinja/Jumla, came to the region and married the daughter of the Raja of Thini. This is cited by some Thakali to assert their descent from higher caste Thakuri (Fisher 2001, 50–51, 147–8, 230; see 204–5 concerning the claim of having discovered the crown and sceptre of the Hansa Raja in a store room of the Thakali council, when — ironically, evoking Quixote's shaving bowl-helmet — the sad array of swords and a helmet that were eventually displayed proved disappointing). Many would dispute the entire basis of this claim, and the Hansa Raja is also associated with the founding of the Gorkha dynasty. However, as discussed below, this tale does reflect upon the relationship between the adoption of Hinduism and high(er) caste claims by affiliation to 'outside' authority (see Fisher 2001 and Vinding 1998 concerning general background, and Morillon & Thouveny 1981 for their traditional house architecture).

The Manangpa - Living in the Manang Valley on the north side of the Annapurnas (see Chapter 4 below; Fig. 4.35), these communities are equally renowned for their long-distance trade privileges, having first received royal tax exemptions to trade in salt during the eighteenth century (see van Spengen 1987 and Pohle 1988; 1993 concerning their socio-economic settlement patterns and house-forms). Their language, *Nyeshangte*, is close to Tamu, but also includes Tibetan elements. Apparently, in Tibetan the residents of Upper Manang are called *Nyeshangpa*, the 'people of Shang', which is thought to refer to an area of Tibet. While some think that their origins lie in the Manaslu or Jumla regions of Nepal, others cite a northern source (Tibet, Mongolia or China). There are written records of the area being inhabited from the twelfth century, when they first paid tribute to the King of Se-rib (and, thereafter, the Kings of southern Tibet and later Lo in Upper Mustang: Jackson 1976; 1998). However, it is generally admitted that there were Tamu-mai inhabitants in the valley prior to their arrival and that it was a Ghale King who captured the area from them. (While it is held by some that the Manangpa arrived as followers of Bon fleeing from Tibet in the thirteenth century, it is also said that it was Milarepa who converted its inhabitants to Buddhism in the eleventh century; the dates of the area's conversion are obviously not firmly established.)

Although also including some distinct Tamu-mai villages, the inhabitants of Upper Manang are predominately Tibetan Buddhist, with *Oble* or 'The Great Wall of Pisang' marking the divide with the shamanistic/Hindu communities below it. A Ghale King is said to have banished shamanism from Upper Manang. There is also a story of how a Buddhist Lama, enraged with animal sacrifice, eventually drove its practitioners from the area down along the lower Marshyangdi River into Lower Manang and Lamjung. Upon their departure, he apparently defecated in its waters, thereby symbolically marking their division (Messerschmidt *et al.* 2004, 15; see also for general background Mumford 1990 and van Spengen 1987, 138–40). However, widely attributed/claimed in their rule, it is known that one of the Ghale Kings joined with the Tamu-mai and, indeed, one of their clans is named as such, with 'Ghale' or 'Galle Gurung' spoken as a distinct dialect (see below concerning the Ghale, particularly Chapter 2). To this extent, there is real debate whether the Manangpa constitute a 'real ethnicity', as opposed to a geographic grouping with only a religious separation from the Tamu-mai.

The Tamang - 'Tamang' in Tibetan is understood to either mean 'horse traders' (e.g. Bista 1967, 48) or 'horse army'. Of the latter, it is thought by some that their ancestors had been part of a Tibetan cavalry that arrived in Nepal in the seventh century AD, and certainly their origins are considered to be northern (Ragsdale 1990, 8; Höfer 1999). With a population of 1.28 million, in the main, they occupy the northern and eastern hills of the Kathmandu Valley (Fig. 1.7). They are essentially Lamaist Buddhists and, using Tibetan as their ritual language, at times the pejorative label of 'Bhotiya' has been applied to them. Although locally well aware of themselves in relationship to immediate 'others', they would seem to have only a limited sense of any 'nationwide' identity. Rather, it has been argued that what primarily distinguishes them from the Tamu-mai/Thakali was their status within Nepal's caste hierarchy and designation as conscripted labourers (they were also forbidden service in the British Gurkhas, on the grounds that Nepal's rulers wanted to restrict geographic knowledge of Kathmandu's environs; Ragsdale 1990, note 19). In other words, the state's ascription of them as a group, itself encouraged their *en masse* identity (see Macdonald 1989; Whelpton 2005, 58–9, 178–9; and also Fricke 1986; Holmberg 1989).

Oppitz has observed that, in contrast with the relative localism of most of the northern Magar origin stories (aside from the one outlining a 'Mongolian' source), claims of distant origins are typical of Himalayan communities (1983, 199). In a further example, Caplan outlines another among the Limbus of east Nepal and in which a river's current provides a mechanism of 'divine' chance-relocation:

> In the beginning a large group of Mongolians came to the source of the Arun river. They were anxious to find a place to live, so they made a bundle of clothes and threw it in the river, and determined to follow it until it came to rest, for that would be the place which god had chosen for them. After many days they found the bundle on the river bank in the hilly region south of Tibet. They named the land *hidangna* 'the land chosen by god' (Caplan 1990, 137 after Chemjong 1958).

Generally, the extreme environment of the Himalayas has not been seen as a place in which 'peoples' have arisen, but have rather *arrived*. It is in relationship to this background, that the establishment, in 2002, of 'The Nepal Federation of Indigenous Nationalities' (NEFIN) must be appreciated. Having 48 member-organizations drawn from across the country, aside from acknowledging that every Indigenous Nationality is 'sovereign' and their rights to self-determination, its 'vision statement' demands the recognition of 'the inherent strength of Indigenous Nationalities in the unity of diverse groups with their distinct language, ethnicity, religion, culture and territory' (see Fig. 1.6). This ascription of indigeneity seems potentially problematic. With only a few exceptions, almost all of Nepal's groups/peoples are understood to have originally been 'outsiders', and to directly relate this status with territory flies in the face of its multi-ethnic landscapes.

History naturally gives rise to *admixture* and is, moreover, something that can be negotiated or at least re-emphasized. Skar's analysis of the development of lowland Tharu origin myths since 1990 serves as an example (1995). Previously claiming ancient descent from India (i.e. 'caste-climbing'), today their stories are being recast to portray the Tharu as the most original 'indigenous' people of Nepal. They thus trace their ancestry back to Buddha himself, who, of course, was born in the Tarai plains of Nepal, the ancestral homeland of the Tharu. This reappraisal of their historical identity would, therefore, seem clearly to reflect the impact of the Janajati Movement and Nepal's recent 'de-Hinduization' (see also Ganesh Gurung 1988 on ethnic/caste mobility).

Group identity is not itself necessarily fixed, but also a matter of 'becoming' (e.g. Sørensen 2002; Jones 1997). It is generally held that its nexus rests, to a greater or lesser degree, upon a common language, religion, kinship patterns and shared history, whether the latter be 'real' or imagined (see Anderson 1991 on

14

imagined communities). In further demonstration of the complex interaction of these many parts, the Man-angpa/Nyeshangpa offer a salient case. As attested to in the website-posted statements of, for example, the Manang Youth Movement, there is real debate as to whether they are a distinct ethnicity (they have recently removed themselves from official lists of 'indigenous' peoples). Are they essentially Gurung/Tamu who converted *en masse* in their history to Tibetan Buddhism, and is religious difference sufficient to define a 'people'? Certainly, history offers instances of comparable divisions on just such grounds. Apparently, during the 1756 French/British war in America, the Mohawks of Upper New York State split with those who had converted to Catholicism, moving north into French Canada and renaming themselves the Caughnawagas (O'Toole 2005, 70). Similarly, what of Sikhism, that was only established in the fifteenth century? — becoming 'something' new, to what degree do peoples cease to be what they were?

Alternatively, living in a pocketed enclave, how much has geography actually prescribed Manangpa identity? If so, what then when families and/or individuals migrate to towns or overseas and lose their immediate 'landed-ness'? Issues of scale are also relevant in this context. The 'ethnicities' outlined above are numbered in hundreds of thousands, with their 'home territories' extending over thousands of square kilometres. What then, for example, of the Dura, a 'tribe' of only some 3000 members, who are distributed around only a single hill in Lamjung District? Falling within the area of Tamu-mai lands, given such discrepancies of size, can these represent groupings of the same order/'type'? As in the case of the Thakali, must these larger 'ethnicities' invariably reflect a degree of group-amalgamation and confederacy? This is also potentially pertinent for past/present perspectives. As discussed by Zubrow in Chapter 4, a millennium ago the Tamu-mai may have had a population of only around 1000, whereas today they number over half a million. By this difference of magnitude, can they really be considered the same people? Surely such growth must have been accompanied by significant social transformations, and this equally raises the question of whether ethnicity (and its manifestations) actually had the significance in the past that it does today.

The (pre-) history of the Tamu 'tribe'

Before proceeding, the last phrase of this section's sub-title requires scrutiny. In the context of the Indian subcontinent (and Nepal), the use of the term 'tribe' is problematic. As discussed by Caplan (1990), drawing upon earlier studies by Bose (1941), Sinha (1965;

1973) and others, there has been an either/or dualism between 'tribes' and 'peasants'. Ultimately, the appellation of the former term derives from British colonial practices (e.g. Hodgson's 'martial tribes' of 1847; see also Gaenszle 2004), which focused upon their relatively egalitarian social relations in contrast to the caste-peasantry of Hindu communities. In Nepal, the result of this has been that 'tribe' (essentially in antithesis to 'caste') has been and is a broad catch-all category, encompassing hunting/gathering groups, long-distance trade specialists, pastoralists and mixed farming/herding communities. Nor is it just a matter of their diverse economic/technological basis, but also of social structure and political economy. Modes of kingship are not something usually associated with tribalism, but, to various degrees, this is what most of these groups have experienced since medieval times. As a result (and further blurring any boundary with 'peasantry'), most have only a limited basis of internal group authority and 'formal' social interaction beyond the level of their immediate villages; kingship having weakened, if not 'lopped-off', networks of clan/chiefdom hierarchy. This imposed tribe/peasant caricature overlooks, moreover, the interpenetration of these 'types' and that they have long co-existed in multi-ethnic settlements. This has led Caplan to suggest that the main distinction between the two might, in fact, reflect relationships to land; essentially as private property among non-tribal peasants as opposed, otherwise, to a symbolic facet of larger communal identity (1990, 139–40).

The detailing of Tamu-mai history is a central concern of this volume and need not be rehearsed at length at this time. What does, however, warrant attention are its key tenets/poles and the main published sources on this theme (see also Pettigrew 1995 and Des Chene 1996 concerning active history writing/researches among the Tamu-mai community themselves). Of the latter, the first to be considered are those portions of Chemjong's *History and Culture of the Kirat People* (1967) concerned with the Tamu-mai. This he largely drew together from references in the *Limbu Chronicles*, which, unlike comparable Tamu-mai documentation, was not destroyed (though Macfarlane 1997a, 193, alludes to the existence of other still secret documents). Awkwardly structured, sustained by conjecture and without adequate citation, Chemjong's text is not easy and his arguments are actually best appreciated as they are summarized by Ragsdale (1990, 5–7). He dates the arrival of the Tamu-mai in west-central Nepal to the seventh century AD and relates this to the expansion of Tibet by its first king, Songtsen Gampo. He has the Tamu-mai undertaking their migration eastward from out of northern Tibet, then south along the Mekong, Salween and Yangtze Rivers; next westward through Burma to follow the Tsangpo River to its conjunction with the Kali Gandaki; and then, finally, southward along the latter through the Himalayas. Chemjong would have the Tamu-mai as one of the 'seven tribes' of northern Tibet and arriving in Nepal as mercenary troops. Then said to be named the *Gyarung*, nine of their officers established a federation of village states in the Gandaki area, named the *Gya-Rong* or 'nine chiefs'. Songtsen Gampo's control and incorporation of the nomadic tribes of northern Tibet has been established by other scholars (e.g. Stein 1972) and, indeed, a seventh-century shift of 'tribes' into eastern Tibet could relate to the establishment of the small Gya-Rong states in the area of the Sino-Tibetan frontier (Ragsdale 1990, 6, note 12). Yet, while not denying the general affinities between the Tamu-mai and north/northeastern Tibet communities that, as a result of Chemjong's researches, Ragsdale has explored (1990, 7–8), the underlying problem with these arguments is that they turn on the root of the Nepali term 'Gurung' and not the original, 'Tamu-mai' (see also Turin 2006).

The only direct written source for Tamu-mai history is the *Gurung Vamsavali* (Narharinath & Gurung 1956; S.B. Gurung 1957). Originally dating to the seventeenth century, these are essentially dynastic chronologies and entirely reflect a Hindu/Brahmanical construction of their history. It chronicles the derivation of the name Gurung as reflecting the ability of one of their ancestors to mediate and, also a teacher, he was thus called 'Guru' or 'Gurung'. It codifies, moreover, a dual organization of Tamu-mai society into two hierarchical 'sub-tribes', the *Char Jat/Carjat* ('four clans') and *Sora Jat/Solahjat* ('sixteen clans'). Crucial is what has been held to be the more highly ranked caste status of the former, and that, in this version of history, their ancestors are held to include both a Chetri prince and a Brahman priest, who are said to have lost their Hindu caste status through ritual pollution (see Pignède 1993, 'Legend II', 160–62; Messerschmidt 1976a, 9–14).

The complexity of Tamu-mai social structure has been much studied (e.g. Pignède 1993, 157–85; Macfarlane 1976, 17–18; Messerschmidt 1976a, 4–16; Pettigrew 1995; 1999) and, as such, need here not be a major concern. However, Macfarlane (1997a) has recently questioned its 'standard' four-fold (plus *Solahjat*) structure. He cites that other, still 'hidden', Gurung *vamsavali* histories do not actually discuss the *Carjat* at all, but tell of three intermarrying groups (the *lama*, *lema* and *kona/kone*), with the fourth — the *kyle/ghale* — being distinct and itself sub-divided into three

intermarrying groups: 'In these early histories it is suggested that for a long time the "three-peoples" were separate, only joining up with the other groups and the *ghale* fairly recently' (Macfarlane (1997a, 194).

The entire issue of Hinduization and of (imposed) caste hierarchies has and continues to be variously painful, contentious and acutely sensitive for Tamu-mai, the crux being that, as portrayed in the Brahmanical histories, the *Carjat* can be construed as having a southern origin in northern India, with the remaining '*jat*' coming from the north. The historical account by Yarjung and Bhovar Palje Tamu included in the notes to the English edition of Pignède's *The Gurungs*, 'A Brief History of the Tamu Tribe' (1993; an abridged version also appeared in *Himal* of that year, 'The Long Road to Gandaki') is, in contrast, very much Tamu-mai-centred (*vs* 'Gurung'; see Chapter 5). This they had prepared prior to the advent of the Kohla project itself, and it was not informed by its findings. (Bhovar, a local lay historian, accompanied us during the 1994 fieldwork; Yarjung, in fact, had little input into this piece and it largely reflects the conjectures of his co-author.) Employing various versions of the *pye* as its main source, though also clearly informed by both ethnographic and historical data (and, too, calculating sequence on the basis of lineage-descent), it is explicit in its chronology. It starts with the 'beginnings of civilization', 8000–9000 years ago, and outlines how the 'first people' lived in *Chō* (Tso) *Nasa*, where they planted barley — the 'first grain'. This they locate in either western Mongolia or China (the Tu and Naxi/Nakhi people respectively of the Lanchow and Sichuan/Yunnan regions share the same name as two of the Tamu clans; see also Ramble 1997b concerning *Tso* origins). Thereafter, the migration southwards by various clans is related; one group arriving in the Lhoka region by 1000 BC, where they were known as *Tamu* and followed *Bon* (the pre-Buddhist religion of Tibet). Subsequently, some Tamu are said to have occupied the Bagmati region and become Tamang, and others may have settled in Mustang before 100 BC and certainly by the first century AD.

It was when living by the upper Marsyangdi River in Manang that the Tamu adopted a new chief or king, whose descendents then formed an additional clan (the *Klye* or Ghale). Tamu & Tamu date the crossing of the Himalayas to *c.* 500 AD and attribute it to hunting pursuits (1993). Apparently liking these highlands, grain was duly sown and, returning for a second visit, a good harvest was found:

> On the third visit peoples from three clans came and settled there in three groups, calling it Kohla Swomae Toh [*Kohla Sopreye*]. *It was the first historical village of the Tamus on the southern slopes of the Himalayas*

and it became the last united village too. Other Tamus migrated later from Manang and Mustang. Those remaining in Mustang became the Thakali when other Tibetan groups, and probably some Tamangs, arrived (in Pignède 1993, 484; emphasis added).

Thereafter, the basis of Kohla's social hierarchy and religious authority are explored. They note that an increase in population must have led to the dispersal out from Kohla and the establishment of new settlements in the area, and that 'It would appear that there were no other tribes in the Gandaki zone except for some Neolithic Kusundas' (Pignède 1993; see also Whelpton 2005, 11). Outlining that the Ghale Kings had seats in more than ten locations (including Kaski, Gorkha, Lamjung and Kohla), the paper goes on to describe the Tamu's contact with the Hindu Rajputs when they entered the Gandaki area in the sixteenth century (the Magar of the mid-western hills succumbing a century earlier):

> The Tamu were most resistant to the new faith, having a deep belief in the efficiency of their own priests and rituals … *The literate Hindu Aryans were experts in exploitation and dominating, introducing the idea of caste, making slaves, and pursing a policy of divide and rule* (Pignède 1993, 485; emphasis added).

The resistance and eventual defeat of the Ghale Kings is then discussed. This and other issues relating to this 'contact period' will be further explored below. However, the emphasis given to the construction of 'false' or 'pseudo' genealogies by the Hindus must be noted. By this means, the Tamu apparently were themselves said to have been Aryans and to have migrated into the region from the south:

> Through the use of the false genealogy, King Jagadi went on to capture the whole of Kaski. *The genealogy was stronger than hundreds of arrows or swords* (Pignède 1993, 487; emphasis added).

Clearly informed by reading and scholastic acquaintances (and free of the ambiguities that permeate more 'academic' texts), this historical sketch well-expresses the weight of the past upon contemporary ethnic identity. On the one hand, it privileges the primacy of the Tamu-mai; they are the carriers of the 'original religion', the Thakali and Tamang are accredited as being their off-shoots, and the southern Magar gave into Hinduization at an earlier date. At the same time, there is also the emotive quality of being robbed of 'true' identity through the imposition of caste, false genealogies and, with the latter, a different source of origin (south *vs* north). Yarjung and Bhovar's narrative, moreover, underlines if not the contradictions of history, then at least its changing fortunes, as it relates the Tamu-mai's decline from an 'expansive people' (the previous Kusundas in the Gandaki zone being dealt

with summarily) to the downtrodden. In short, theirs is a vexed history, which further highlights that there is never a simple or timeless 'ethnographic'.

Though drawn from only a limited sample, apart from near-common themes of distant northern origins, the ethno-histories of Nepal's Himalayan peoples outlined in the previous section reveal considerable variability. While for the Tamu-mai the emphasis is very much upon their 'distinct-group' northern origins (reinforced by single-axis migration), Thakali, and possibly Magar, identity seems to primarily relate to their amalgamated collectivity. The same may also be true of the Tamang, though it is argued that their broader identity may essentially stem from a relational, state-based designation of them as a distinct group (Whelpton 2005, 178–9). Even if only amounting to 'variations on a theme', each of these groups performs its ethnicity in a customary manner and they are acknowledged as having their own house-type, costume, rituals and language (albeit, in various instances overlapping). Against this, issues of language(-change) are paramount for the region's ethno-history, as they reveal deeper structures of mass-grouping. By the closeness of their vocabularies, it is widely held that the Tamu-mai, Thakali, Tamang and Manangpa shared the same proto-language (e.g. Vinding 1998, 67) and, based on the percentage of probable cognates, Glover tentatively concluded that this occurred prior to the mid fourth century AD (1970, 25; see also Pittman & Glover 1970 and Whelpton 2005, 12). Vinding has speculated that this unified 'tribe' may have referred to themselves as the *Tamu* (possibly meaning 'highlander'; Salter & Gurung 1996) and, citing Bista (1977), that they may have belonged to the Kirata people, who moved west into Nepal during the fourth–second millennium BC (Vinding 1998, 76; see also van Driem 2002 and Aldenderfer & Yinong 2004, 34–40).

Although the situation is by no means clear, on the basis of their ritual language, it has equally been thought that the Tamu-mai may have originally referred to themselves as *Se* (Strickland 1982, 1–2; 1987, 72). From this, and given that some Tamang clans also claim a Tibetan source, Ramble has proposed that the Thakali, Tamu-mai and Tamang may originally have been the *Se* People and arrived from Tibet (1997b). He notes, however, that it is presently unknown whether their migration occurred before or after their fragmentation into distinct groups. Nevertheless, as informed by what is now known of Mustang's archaeological sequence, this 'proto-grouping' — whatever its composition and immediate axis of migration — probably arrived in the north of the country during the first millennium BC.

17

The Kohibo — towards a new architecture

One of the project's original 'directives' was the recovery of uniquely Tamu-mai architectural forms. It was felt that there would have been shamanic training schools and grave settings at Kohla that could inspire present-day efforts. In the intervening years, while research funding was raised, the TPLS however went on to invent these structures (its membership including architects). Aside from experiments with funerary architecture, the most dramatic construction has been the great *Kohibo* meeting house in Pokhara (Figs. 1.2 & 1.8:A). Its cleanly abstract, concrete shell-like form seems almost to evoke the Sydney Opera House and it is one of the most striking modern buildings in Nepal. Yet it is actually laid-out according to principles of the Tamu-mai zodiac/cosmology (without 'knowing' international reference) and, like the illustrated grave example (Fig. 1.8:D), ultimately derives from the rice effigies that feature in many of their rituals (Fig. 1.8:C).

Two-and-a-half storeys high, the grander ground level of the *Kohibo* is essentially an empty meeting place, the upper storey being given to a museum/ethnographic display (for which, through a chain of personal inter-connection, they received funding from the Danish Overseas Development Agency, DANIDA: Figs. 1.3 & 1.4). Generally, it is a multi-purpose space that can house large meetings. Those we attended were generally formal events. Seniors (invariably male and usually having seen Gurkha service) and dignitaries (i.e. 'us' and other visitors) sit facing the audience, with the elder women (the source of much of the TPLS's infrastructure and crucial fund-raising) arranged around the back. It is a world variously of recital and lay expertise in which males front 'hidden', though very active,

women. Together, they are fighting a rearguard action to pass on a traditional culture amidst socio-economic circumstances now divorced from their village roots.

Very much a 'community of builders', you can only admire the TPLS's mobilization and energy. Having built the *Kohibo* (and then its associated crematorium), they then went on to fund-raise for another major building beside it, with the sponsorship largely coming from Tamu-mai groups in Japan and Brunei. Completed in 2002, it is intended to serve as a combination of lodge, shamanic school and an expanded museum (the latter reflecting the impact of the project's findings). Three storeys-high, this aspiring structure follows a more standard, modern Nepali 'grand mansion' style. However, on its roof is a full-size brick and concrete version of a typical Tamu-mai house (Fig. 1.8:E & F). Celebrating their vernacular (and 'roots'), architecturally, it is an awkward village-origins reference. The traditional house does not really survive such a radical translation into modern materials, and it is only when informed of its intention that one appreciates what was attempted.

This invention of a distinctly Tamu-mai architecture can only be considered something vibrantly creative. Subsequently, over the course of the later 1990s, the *Kohibo* was emulated by other Tamu-mai communities outside of Pokhara and, in 2002, we visited a recently built half-size version in a town some hours drive to the south (Fig. 1.8:B). Such is the way that an *invented* 'traditional' style can spread (see e.g. Ranger & Hobsbawm 1983 on the 'invention of tradition'). In some respects, this is reminiscent of yurt-inspired domes, that today crown the roofs of Inner Mongolian public buildings in China and, otherwise, the concrete 'solidification' of inherently temporary yurt architecture (see Evans & Humphrey 2002).

Walking, writing and seeing

Issues of aesthetics and the manner of the project's documentation underlie these researches. Spanning deep valley jungles and high Himalayan snow-capped passes, the fieldwork conditions were variously tough and exquisitely beautiful. Text can never adequately convey land, and to this end extensive use is made of graphics as a means of exploring different 'visualizations'. Ranging from free-hand sketches and satellite imagery to photographic mosaics, the intention is to explore various ways of *seeing, mapping and experiencing landscape*. (The use of a mosaic-technique is not undertaken as any kind of knowing experimental 'fracturing', but rather due to the impossibility of otherwise conveying such broad horizons; see though Gombrich 1982 concerning 'why appearances cannot be mapped', particularly mountain panoramas; 209–10, figs. 176 & 177.)

Walking and writing intermesh when undertaking such landscape-based researches. The route is simultaneously traversed and chronicled, and for most of the western staff (and Yarjung; see Chapter 2), journal-keeping became a key part of the rhythm of the day. It is difficult to know how, or even whether, to

incorporate such raw observations. Take, for instance, the first season's archaeological notebook: an A4 hard-bound science experiment-type. From previous expedition experience, it was known that maintaining its entries on a daily basis would be demanding, so, therefore, Evans didn't think there would be time for a personal record. In the end, the land got the better of him. While the first two-thirds is a 'proper' expedition record, full of measured sketch observations (and survey feature/structure indices and photographic logs, etc.: Fig. 1.9), progressing from its last page forwards as it were (i.e. reversed) the latter portion became entirely personal and was written as a long letter to his, then young, daughter. Does this have a place in this report? Throughout, the degree to which subjective experience features is undeniably problematic. Here, it is acknowledged, but not particularly privileged; with 'our personal' only taking a background role.

Beyond the inclusion of narrative chronicles (*Travelling up* and *Goin' north*; see also that concerning the 1992 trek in Chapter 2), the framed insets within this volume fulfil two roles. On the one hand, they provide a counterpoint between the project's anthropological (Chapter 2) and archaeological (Chapters 3 & 4) components: material culture studies intermesh

Figure 1.8. *Towards a new architecture: A) The Pokhara Kohibo; B) out-of-town, half-size Kohibo; C) full-size wooden replica of rice effigy setting within the Kohibo Museum, Pokhara; D) recent grave 'sculpture' also based on rice effigies; E) Yangjakot Village, exemplifying the vernacular house-style that is celebrated atop the Pokhara Kohibo site lodge-building ('F').*

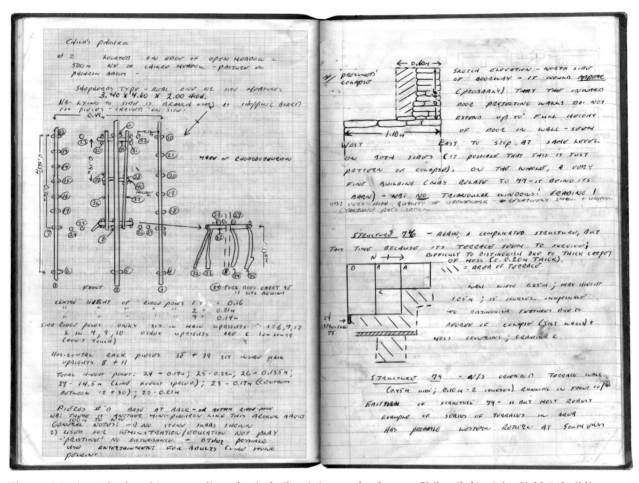

Figure 1.9. *A notebook archive: recording of twig-built miniature* phrohon *at Chikre (left); right, Kohla's buildings.*

with the more strictly anthropological studies and, equally, 'the ethnographic' penetrates the archaeological through transcribed interviews. On the other hand, these insets also provide a degree of fragmentation. These are conscious devices intended to address the complications of 'mixed' histories and offset the seeming unilineality of the Tamu-mai historical narrative itself (see Evans & Hodder 2006a,b in which comparable Kohla-related insets inform a British prehistoric sequence).

The researches reflect upon a number of general themes, among which is the character of oral records and materiality — where the past and identity are variously stored, embedded and/or embodied (and with it the nature of their maintenance and/or invention). In other words, *the conditions of remembering* (see e.g. Goody 1987; Coonerton 1989; Rowlands 1993; Mack 2003) and, in effect, the 'Kim's Game' of culture (i.e. the memory-game that features in Kipling's novel of that name). Issues relating to mass-group migration and the fact that communities move are equally relevant. Yet, once accepting a logic of migration, this need not

imply a single source or uniformity of mechanism. 'Neolithicization' has now become a recognized basis of mass movement (i.e. the spread of domesticates) as the evidence of plant genetics compels social migration, making it again an acceptable avenue of explanation (e.g. Bellwood & Renfrew 2002). However, within the context of Himalayan Nepal, religion has also been a basis of historical displacement. The widespread practice of shamanic animism throughout the region has, in part, been seen as relating to the *diaspora* from out of Tibet, with the adoption of Buddhism from the seventh century. This, combined with plant-based and linguistic evidence, raises the possibility of multiple waves of population shift.

With the Tamu-mai, we are reportedly dealing with a certain type of migration, one in which an entire 'people' move *en masse* so as to leave no obviously discernable 'parenting' homeland populace. Parallels for this kind of 'great trek' (or exodus) could be sought with the Celts' arrival into Italy during the fourth century BC, the fifth-century Huns, the Aztecs' long southward wanderings prior to their arrival in the Valley of Mexico in the thirteenth century, or even the eighteenth-/nineteenth-century 'drift' (and coalescence) of the Zulus. Yet, these were all 'events' occurring over one/two centuries (or less) and not sustained millennium-long journeys. The long migration of the Tamu-mai, nevertheless, resonates with the idea of the 'peopling of the world' and provides a high-level dynamic to counterbalance any sense of the enduring long-term stability of 'the ethnographic'.

Movement can itself become a facet of group identity, and communities can, in effect, transport their cultural landscapes with them. It is almost as though a blueprint of sanctified landmark-types and/or monuments must be re-enacted in the investment of land, and, in Chapter 5, the idea of serial cultural landscapes is explored. Such a perspective questions the simplistic determination of *a* landscape phenomenology (e.g. Tilley 1994). These perspectives are all the more relevant in the context of Nepal and Himalayan studies. The country's spectacular landscape draws various sport- and eco-tourists, who clearly believe that there they confront some manner of primal wilderness (i.e. 'nature'). Yet these are long-inhabited lands and 'crowded' cultural landscapes, whose diverse ethnicities have historically vied and intermeshed with each other. This makes it all the more essential that multiple landscape perspectives be explored.

Amidst these many complexities, and clearly relating to questions of migration, lies another crucial issue, that of 'archaeological cultures'. Ultimately arising from studies of type distributions and founded in the work of Kossinna and Childe, these are based on the presumption that there is a direct relationship between ethnicities and 'things'. In other words, a correspondence of distinct artefact types and discrete cultural groupings. Yet, one-to-one associations of 'people', material cultural and language have been shown to be, at best, inconsistent (e.g. Hodder 1982; Shennan 1989; Jones 1997, 15–26). In fact, writing in an orientalist context, it was Max Muller who first pronounced that there was no necessary co-relationship between these (see Stocking 1987, 59). Against this, and whatever the contemporary cause, it should not be assumed that we can naively read-off or assign peoples in the archaeological past directly from material culture.

Chapter 2

Anthropology and Shamanic Considerations

Judith Pettigrew, Yarjung Kromchaĩ Tamu & Mark Turin

Situating anthropology

In August 1992, I interviewed Major Hom Bahādur Tamu, treasurer of the *Tamu Pye Lhu Sangh* (Tamu Cultural and Religious Organization) at the ancestral village of Kohla:

'How does it feel to be in Kohla?' I asked,

'Great, it's our old village, the place of our ancestors'.

He followed this with, 'I think that we should get people up here with shovels to dig the place up and put the proof in the *kohībo*'.

I commented:

'If anyone is going to dig it up, there should be archaeologists involved as they will know how to dig without damaging the old buildings'.

Hom Bahādur nodded his head and replied: 'Yes, that would be a very good idea'.

The Kohla Project for Archaeology and Ethno-History which developed as a collaborative venture between University of Cambridge researchers and members of the *Tamu Pye Lhu Sangh* (TPLS), a Tamu (Gurung) religious and cultural organization, has its origins in this discussion which took place at the ancestral village of Kohla in August 1992.

The Kohla Project was concerned with archaeology and ethno-history as a 'community process'. Its multi-dimensional approach incorporated archaeological survey/excavation alongside the collection of oral histories and interviews with Tamu people regarding their views of the past. A 'project within a project', it was also concerned with how history is created in the present and the role that our work

played in this venture. A central feature of the Kohla Project was its commitment to the concept of multiple voices — separate but equal. The *Jana Andolan* (People's Movement) of 1990 in Nepal created new possibilities for organization, discussion and activism among the people who call themselves *janajāti* (ethnic minorities or minority nationalities) and *adivāsi* (indigenous peoples). Much of the immediate post-1990 discourse related to their position within the nation-state, their desire to negotiate new relationships to the state and to enjoy new rights within it. The demands were based on contemporary realities and the experiences of the past which, in the early and mid-1990s, were being carefully examined from the perspective of the long-term effects that they have had on *janajāti* groups.

Among the Tamu-mai, this re-examination took place on many levels and in talking to a wider national forum, the Tamu-mai also talked to themselves. The prime topics of discussion included the question of historical origin, the religion(s) of the Tamu-mai, the preservation of language, loss of culture and the effects of Hinduization. Of particular concern were the seventeenth- and nineteenth-century Hindu-authored genealogies (*bāsāvali*), which posited a mixed Indo-Aryan and Mongolian origin for the Tamu-mai and portrayed one group of clan lineages, the *Sõgi* (Nep. *cār-jāt*), as being 'superior' to another, the *Kugi* (Nep. *sohra-jāt*).

In the post-*Andolan* years, these discourses led to the foundation of a plethora of new ethnic organizations. One such organization is the TPLS which was founded in Pokhara in 1990. *Tamu Pye Lhu Sangh's* self-appointed mandate is to preserve and revitalize Tamu cultural traditions and in particular the shamanic traditions of the *pachyu* and *klehbrī* and the *'bön' lama*. The TPLS is concerned with shamanic interpretations of the past, the effects of Hinduization and status relationships between the clans. While a significant number of other Tamu organizations exist, including the national Tamu organization *Tamu Chõj*

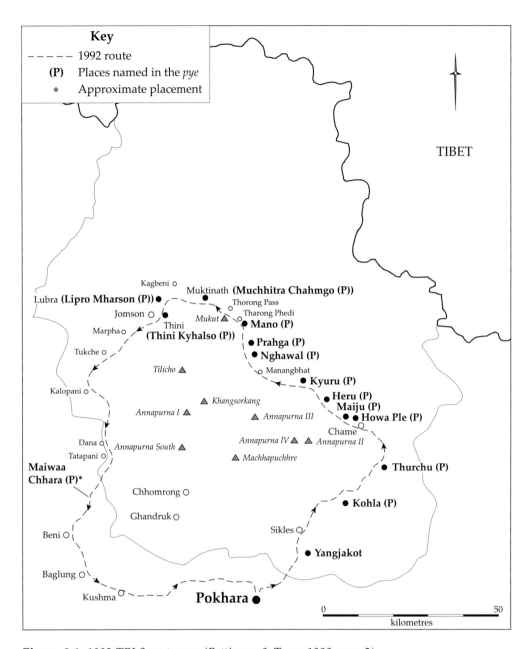

Figure 2.1. *1992 TPLS route map (Pettigrew & Tamu 1999, map 2).*

Dhī, the Kāski district organization *Tamu Dhī* and the Buddhist organizations *Bauddha Arghaun Sadan* and *Tamu Bauddha Sewā Samiti*, TPLS is the only organization directly concerned with the shamanic traditions and its position as such is uncontested. Its stance on the relationships between the clans, however, while widely supported at an overt level, is contested, often covertly, by those Tamu-mai who perceive that a hierarchical relationship does exist.

In the absence of documented sources, the present re-examination of Tamu history has proceeded along different lines of enquiry (see Des Chene 1996, 117). These include the search for evidence of Tamu

kingdoms, the re-evaluation of the place of the Tamu-mai in the Hindu kingdoms, the study of language and the study of religious history. The last of these is the approach taken by members of the TPLS.

Tamu shamans are considered by many Tamu-mai to be experts in indigenous knowledge and understandings of the past. What they know about Tamu history is based on knowledge contained within the 'oral texts' (*pye*), including texts such as the *Tõhdã* and *Lẽmakõ* (see below) which narrate the downward migration of the Tamu-mai, sections of which are retraced in reverse during the shamans ritual journey in the *pai laba* death ritual. As the shamanic version of history relates to a literal landscape, the search for a more authentic version of the past led TPLS members to travel into this landscape where they attempted to match text to geography. During a 1992 research trip, I accompanied TPLS members on their first expedition northward through the districts of Kāski, Lamjung, Manāng and Mustāng (Fig. 2.1). We 'discovered' that there are significant ruins at the historic village of Kohla. While shepherds and cowherders were fully aware of the village, they saw the ruins as a source of stonework for their temporary shelters, rather than as part of their heritage which should be preserved.

The purpose of the 1992 trip was to discover if the places listed in the *pye* exist in the physical landscape. The first part of the journey retraced the overlapping downward migration route of the Tamu-mai and the upward ritual journey route along which the shamans guide the souls of the dead in the *pai laba* death ritual (Fig. 2.3). While the ideal would have been to travel the entire length of both routes, in practice it was only possible to trace those sections of the journeys that lie within the districts of Kāski, Lamjung and Manāng.

The ritual journeys of shamans from different villages merge in the high pastures of Thurchu (some shamans do not have the *pye* which takes them to Thurchu and so they 'fly' from the village they are performing in). Prior to Thurchu, shamans from different villages have their own routes. On our journey, we followed the route of the shamans from the village of Yāngjakot. This route was chosen because several of the TPLS participants were originally from Yāngjakot. At the point on the trail where the soul journey ascended the large rock at Oble, we continued following the downward migration trail that overlaps with the landscapes referred to in several different *pye*.

Although the TPLS members already knew that most of the geographic places on the routes existed, they hoped that the trek would provide concrete (experiential but non-shamanic) confirmation and documentation of their existence. The journey was therefore not only of spiritual importance, but also of emotional, historical and political importance. It was simultaneously a pilgrimage to sacred places and a journey into the past. More importantly, it was a quest for origins — origins which are perceived to be 'somewhere in Mongolia' and intimately tied to the shamanic traditions. Oral texts narrate the northward soul journey, the downward migration route and a series of overlapping physical landscapes. Thus, it was not only the oral texts which were under scrutiny, but also the entire orientation of the shamanic world.

The TPLS trip members, none of whom, with the exception of the shaman and founder member, Yarjung Tamu, had visited more than a few places

on the proposed route, were very conscious of the implications of their venture (see below for an account of Yarjung's original visit). They knew that a successful trip would place them in a much better position to address questions about the past and the cultural embeddedness of the *pye-tā lhu-tā*. The term 'proof' was often used, and on several occasions I heard people saying that they were 'going to retrieve the proof'. 'Proof' referred to verification of the historical migration route as well as to the shamanic journeys. Not surprisingly, the trip received considerable attention among the wider Tamu community, particularly in the urban centre of Pokhara.

We left Pokhara on a sunny August morning in 1992. We were a group of sixteen — eight participants (seven TPLS members, two of whom were shamans, and myself), one guide, five porters and two cooks. Our first night was spent in the village of Yāngjakot, and the second at the site of the ancestral village of Khudu. On our third morning, we saw the historic village of Kohla for the first time: a small distant treeless area amidst the heavily forested south-facing slopes of the Lamjung Himal. Further along the trail at Chikrei, ruins were spotted and members of the group took rough notes and measured buildings.

On the fourth night, we camped in a dismal monsoon downpour above the treeline at Naudi Pak. Early in the morning, we walked the short distance to Kohla (Fig. 2.2). I knew of its importance as I had been told many times that it was the 'last joint village before the Tamu-mai split into smaller groups and moved down to the locations of the present villages'. I was not, however, expecting what we found — visible standing ruins of a very large village. With notebooks, measuring tape, cameras and a video recorder, the group moved through the ruins recording what we could see despite the high monsoon-fed overgrowth.

On the basis of what was visible to us, a process of ascription began taking place which was based on people's knowledge and their experience of contemporary architecture. The largest and most prominent house was thought to be the 'Klye (Ghale) chieftain's house'. The standing stone to its side, which stood in relationship to the house in a way that is still found today in house/stable complexes in extant Tamu villages, was the 'stable'. We couldn't locate the cemetery, but when the pachyu shaman Yarjung Tamu began to have pretrance sensations after touching some large stones, people said 'that's probably the cemetery or a place where rituals used to take place. The ancestors are nearby, that is why Thagu (eldest son) feels shaky'.

After leaving Kohla, we spent two nights in the shepherds' huts at Thurchu before crossing into Manāng district by cutting through the mountains. In Manāng, our route took on an added dimension. As well as being the trail of the shamanic soul journey, the ancestors' migration route

25

Figure 2.2. *A shaman's perspective: A) Yarjung and guide, Damarsingh, at Kohla during the 1992 TPLS trip (photograph: J. Pettigrew); B) Tamu-mai shamans gathered in Kathmandu, 2003 (there to record their chants and drumming for the CD,* Divine Ancestors, *made in collaboration with the School of Oriental and African Studies, London; note their prominent drums); C) a shaman's study (Yarjung's), Pokhara, 2005, including Kohla environs satellite image (1), a photograph of Yarjung in full regalia and 'performance' (2), his collection of flat-drums (with both Siberian and Irish examples) (3), a* Phai Lhu Chon *shrine to ancestors (4), a portrait of Yarjung's shaman father (5) and a bound series of Yarjung's transliteration of various* pye *'texts' (6; with detail right).*

and the salt trade route, the route had also become other peoples' trails — an important tourist route, the trail down which the 'Tibetan refugees spreading Buddhism' travelled, a route dotted with small Tibetan and Tamu villages. Tamu gods, shamans and ancestors thus share their landscape with foreign trekkers, Buddhist lamas, Tibetans and people from elsewhere who run the local administration.

At Oble, in the shadow of the large dome rock which deceased Tamu ascend to reach the afterworld, the group practised the singing and dancing of the pachyu Serga Pye. The Serga sends the deceased to the afterworld in the pai laba, the three-day death ritual. The section referring to the local landscape was to be sung at Maiju Deurāli, the site of an ancestral village, and the point on the route at which the human trail curves to the left while the trail of the dead goes to the right, up and over Oble.

As we continued our journey, we passed villages that are mentioned in the pye as ones in which Tamu ancestors had lived. The list corresponded to that given in the texts, and landscape corroborated the shamanic version of the past. In each case, the villages appeared in the order in which they are listed in the pye, many names were clearly the same although the pronunciation, and in some cases the actual name, was different. The ancestors, however, had left little trace of their habitation — the contemporary villages were all of Tibetan origin. The landscape was populated by gods that can be beckoned by contemporary Tamu shamans who live on the other side of the Himal. The valleys leading to Thorang La (Pass), famed and feared among trekkers, were inhabited by Tamu gods. Crossing the pass the following morning we looked down, in the early hours of the dawn, on a landscape which incorporated the famous Hindu pilgrimage site of Muktināth. In Tamu shamanic geography, this location is referred to as Muchhitrachamgoye.

A high point of the expedition was the side-trip to the village of Lubra (Lipro Mharsō in the pye), a place of past learning for the klehbrī shamans. The village was inhabited by Tibetan-speaking people who had no memory of the klehbrī and were bemused by the group's earnest enquiries. We were taken to see the Bön-po monastery. Excitedly, the group members examined the painted deities on the ceiling, which bore a great resemblance to those on the klehbrī urgyan ('crown'). As Yarjung filmed the images, he narrated the names of the gods to the camera. As we left the monastery, someone pointed to a miniature iron bird suspended just above eye-level and cried, 'look, it's just like the klehbrī bird'. Writer and historian Bhovar Tamu questioned the villagers, 'where did this come from?', 'what do you think it is?', but the locals had no idea. We were told of an old monastery that was on the other side of the ridge behind the village. There was talk of sending me and a couple of others up to film and photograph it, but there was no time. We left. There was a distinct but unspoken awareness that our excitement was not shared by the locals, a certain

disappointment that they did not realize how 'important and historic their village is to the Tamu-mai'. At a distance from the village, Ba Klehbrī chanted the section of the pye that refers to Lipro Mharsō. Lipro was 'reclaimed'.

We reached Jomsom. To the locals we were just another group of 'tourists' looking for accommodation, so we decided to press on. Time, money and what are always referred to as 'rations' were beginning to run short. Jomsom is not mentioned in the pye, but the nearby village of Thini is. There were only a few brief minutes in which to film and chant the section of the pye that refers to Thini (named Thini Kyhalsō in the pye). In Tukche we bought apples for friends and families and hired a porter to carry them down.

The next day we passed the large waterfall of Maiwha Chhara that is mentioned in Prōprō pye. Yarjung, who had never before physically visited it, recognized it immediately as a place that he had visited in trance. The pye tells that the mho (demons) that live in the waterfall used to be able to change into people. One day, a ritual was held in the village during which all the pots and pans were laid out. During the ritual, a ladle was stolen and from that day, the mho have been unable to transform themselves into humans. According to Yarjung, a 'king and queen still live in the waterfall'. We approached an old man weaving a bamboo basket. 'Do you ever hear the sound of bells and drums coming from the waterfall?' asked Yarjung. 'Yes we do', replied the old man.

We reached Baglung two days later. The new Chinese-built road to Pokhara was temporarily blocked due to a landslide creating a long delay. In the afternoon, we finally managed to get a truck which took us back to town. In slanting rain, huddled under sheets of plastic, we perched atop the Chinese truck. Through the rain, and between the hairpin bends of the new road, we passed the familiar villages of Birethanti, Nayapul and Lumle. As Dhampus came into view Yarjung said, 'My father had a bad fight with witches in that village about 30 years ago'. It was almost dusk when we finally reached Pokhara.

We met the following day — to celebrate, to apologize should we have offended each other in the difficult circumstances of the trip, to thank the porters, guide and cooks, and to watch the video. When we came together, we heard that we had received messages of congratulations from many people along with requests to watch the video.

The expedition recounted above is the second journey in the chronology of TPLS journeys into the land of the ancestors. It formed the basis for the construction of new historical narratives and, as 'our 1992 trek', it became part of the history that it was designed to discover. When those who participated in the journey talk about their historical research, they trace the beginning of the search for evidence to this trip which allowed them to see and experience first hand the relationship between the *pye*, the landscape and the shamanic journeys (as opposed to hearing about it from shamans, who usually have not visited the sites themselves). This evidence significantly shifted the discussion about history as it provided a firm foundation on which to counter versions of the Tamu past based on Hindu interpretations (for which the only evidence is the widely discredited seventeenth- and nineteenth-century genealogies). During and after the trip I spoke to TPLS members about the role that archaeology could play, and asked if they were interested in my making contact with archaeologists who could help with a research project on the history of the village of Kohla and other ancestral villages. They replied that they were, and on my return to Cambridge (to write up my PhD dissertation), my discussions with colleagues led to the suggestion that I contact Christopher Evans, Director of the Cambridge Archaeological Unit, which is part of the Department of Archaeology. In the summer of 1993, Yarjung Tamu (who was in the UK to work on a museum project at the Cambridge University Museum of Archaeology and Anthropology) and I met Evans. Out of this meeting and subsequent negotiations, the Kohla Project developed as a collaborative venture between University of Cambridge researchers and the TPLS (and subsequently the Government of Nepal's Department of Archaeology).

Archaeological research plotted new routes into the landscape of the ancestors. The land was re-mapped but in a different way, and the archaeological maps did not always coincide with existing interpretations. The maps provided by the archaeologists expanded indigenous understandings of the landscape and provided new material for interpretation. That the scripts were somewhat different, although a source of much discussion, was relatively unimportant. The interpretations co-existed in simultaneously overlapping and separate domains. Local people and archaeologists talked both to each other and past one another. What was important was the journey, for it was the journey that provided the context and the opportunity for interpretation and the construction of narratives. My initial role as a broker continued, and much of what I did as the anthropologist on the project was to act as an interpreter. My interpretation included the usual range of language and culture, but also included mediating between different modes of thinking, knowledge and interpretation as shamans, local people and foreign and Nepali archaeologists engaged in an ongoing dialogue about the Tamu past. Ethnographic research also included translation of the oral texts relating to Kohla (see below) and oral history interviews with people of different ages, genders and

generations in Kāski and Lamjung districts, as well as in Pokhara. These did not, however, provide significant material, as although all interviewees stressed that the Tamu-mai migrated downwards from a northern direction, and most had heard of Kohla, few could provide any additional historical information.

The encounter with archaeology created a degree of previously denied access to the ancestral world. The emotionality of journeying into the landscape of the ancestors (and conversely the landscape of the ritual journey) was further enhanced by actual physical contact with the ancestors' material culture. Unlike the original TPLS journey, the range of people who could at some level participate, who could 'touch and be touched', was now much wider. The first archaeological expedition's return to Pokhara attracted a wide audience to the *kohibo* who came to look at photographs of the trip, talk to the participants and touch the pottery of the ancestors.

Journeying of the type undertaken by TPLS members on their 1992 trek was an attempt to show that the places mentioned in the *pye* existed, and thus prove the historical authenticity of the shamanic version of history, which could be counterposed against what appeared as the historical inauthenticity of the Hinduized version. There was a moral dimension to the journey, suggesting the contemporary righting of past wrongs. Geography fostered a moral continuity with the past. Landscape and morality were linked in a manner that is reminiscent of that described by Basso (1984) for the western Apache. Among the Apache, moral narratives are constructed in landscape. One does not necessarily need to hear the stories but only to see or remember the landscape of the stories, 'the moral significance of geographical locations ... is established by historical tales with which the locations are associated' (Basso 1984, 44). What was different in the Tamu case was that the encoding of morality in landscape was based not on historical tales but on narratives constructed in the present, but which related to the landscape and memories of the past. It was also different in that it concerned historical morality rather than everyday conduct.

Landscape and morality were linked through the ancestors. The landscape had to be negotiated in a particular way: to be disrespectful to the land was potentially to be disrespectful to the ancestors. To simultaneously pay respect to ancestors and manage the pragmatics of everyday life required constant negotiation. The situation was similar to that described by Turner (1974, 182–3) for pilgrims. As the pilgrim moves away from home, s/he becomes increasingly sacralized as s/he meets shrines and sacred places and objects, and increasingly secularized as s/he must cope with the difficult practical demands of everyday life in a strange and temporary place. Those who journeyed confronted problems created by this juxtaposition of roles. Sometimes the subtle balance was lost. Following our brief 1992 visit to Kohla, it was suggested that we had become lost because we had not burnt herbs or said prayers to the ancestors. On another occasion, herbs were hastily burned because it was felt that we had constructed our toilet close to the dwelling place of an area god. The arbiters of morality in landscape were the shamans who decided when to appease or not appease the Afterworld. On our 1994 research journey to Kohla, the frequency of hailstones worried some members of the research team who often urged the shamans to burn herbs in order to keep the ancestors happy. The underlying fear was that we were making the ancestors unhappy, thereby causing them to send hail. The shamans, working on a different understanding of, and relationship to, the landscape, sometimes refused to burn herbs, explaining that it was the weather and not the ancestors. At a temporary resting place en route to Kohla it began to hail and Yarjung appealed to the place-god to stop the deluge. As he stood in the middle of the hailstorm burning herbs and chanting, the group watched, and his actions (and apparent success) were captured on film and video. Journeying, which required shamanic mediation between the landscape and the ancestors/ Afterworld, provided an additional domain of authority for shamanic practice.

While 'proof in the landscape' provided the basis for a reconstruction of history, I suggest that journeying was the *actual* construction of historical narrative — the writing (or walking) of history. Rather like committing a historical account to paper, journeying was the construction of a performative historical narrative located in landscape. As Tilley (1994, 28) writes, 'movement through space constructs "spatial stories", forms of narrative understanding'. As Tamu revivalists walked up and down the trails from the town to the high Himalaya, they constructed, both for themselves and others, a chronology which was simultaneously past and present, and past in the present. A narrative was constructed which included and interlinked the actors of the past with the actors of the present. In this way, a perspective was created which associated the contemporary actors with the telling of history, thereby establishing authority. As the shamanic and the historic interacted, the establishment of history-making authority was at once the enhancement of shamanic authority.

To understand the potential that journeying had in conveying an interpretation of history, it is necessary to consider the audience to which history-making was directed. While it was important to provide written accounts of the Tamu past for outsiders — to explain and share perceptions of the injustices of the past, to reinterpret, to assert an identity based on one's own cultural practices — it was more important to provide an account for one's own people. While published historical accounts might receive the attention of a small number of well-educated people, most Tamu-mai, whether urban dwellers or villagers, do not read them or have access to them. For some sections of society, understandings of the past continue to be based on the Hindu-authored genealogies. While in the early-mid 1990s, some people were engaged in the re-examination of the past, and others were aware of it and eager to learn more, there were (and continue to be) Tamu-mai who premise their understandings of social life on ideas of clan hierarchy and dismiss the perspectives of TPLS activists as 'the talk of people who have a chip on their shoulders'.

Of interest to most people are the local events of the village, the 'lived-in' experiences. Also of interest is the landscape — the forests above the villages where people go to cut firewood, the stones, rocks and rivers where the human and spirit worlds overlap. The ancestral landscape is one which the Tamu shepherds traverse, where people go to cut bamboo, gather herbs and walk through en route to Hindu pilgrimage spots. These places have well-known and emotive names, like Kohla, Chomrong, Thurju, Dudh Pokhari, places which a great many people from all clans aspire to visit, places which exist in consciousness, seen or unseen.

While the past as a written account, or even as a narrative account, normally does not receive much attention from people when detached from the landscape, the past 'located' in the landscape is a different matter. A high-profile visit by urban Tamu-mai with video cameras and maps, accompanied by foreign researchers and local porters who are 'going to the old villages to study Tamu history', gained enormous attention. So did the return trip a month later, and the subsequent showing of the video of the trip. This attention was reinforced by the hearthside recollections of the porters and support workers, hired from the villages, and the villagers' own stories of what the visitors did, where they went and what they said. Such stories were also reproduced in the town with people telling and re-telling what they had heard had happened and where it had happened. The stories were 'brought home' in a manner reminiscent of Kwon's (1993, 67–74) account of stories recollected in the evenings by Orochon reindeer herder-hunters from Siberia. As in the narratives of Kwon's herder-hunters, the stories of what happened in the landscape can only be shared if one 'has a certain shared map. The location, where an observation or a recollection is made, was not referred to by east or west' (1993, 67), but by the location of events or in relation to a particular geographical feature. The stories and places constructed thus reproduced each other (Tilley 1994, 33). As with the Orochon, Tamu stories create and alter social relations, and differentials exist between the old and the young. The teller of tales, however, could enjoy temporary elevation to a status 'above' that of his/her normal one.

Narratives were constructed and located in the ancestral landscape that they were intended to address — narratives that included the events of the journey, interspersed with images of the actual activities making history. In this way, an account of how the cook used to send *Thagu* ('eldest son', a support worker hired from a village) through the forest at Chikrei carrying mugs of tea and biscuits for the researchers and their helpers, who were measuring the old houses, drawing the *kuni* (rice grinder) we found near the trail and looking for the *chogō* (cemetery), was simultaneously a recollection of a rather amusing daily life event <u>and</u> the conveying of historical information. At Chikrei there were old houses, material culture which was continuous with the present, and the burial place of ancestors. The potential for reinterpretation was extensive. History became meaningful, relevant, close by. Links were created to the present — trails along which both past and present could be experienced. Events that were contemporary were interrelated with powerful visual images of the past. The ancestor's *kuni* could be looked at, touched, and held. It became a relic. The old buildings could be inspected and wondered about, and everyone could enter the discussion about why the *chogō* (cemetery) was not found.

Prior to departure and en route to the ancestral landscape, people told us of places and things to look out for. The possibility existed for everyone to be a historian, for stories about places, people, gods, spirits, ancestors to be remembered, brought out, constructed, interpreted and reinterpreted. The possibility, however, did not exist for everyone to be an expert; this remained the domain of the few, those who entered the landscape to research it, those who established the authority to investigate the past and make it speak in the present, those who had made the journey, those also, who had the knowledge to speak to the past, those who knew the *pye*, those who had the migration genealogies, in other words, the shamans. The research team could not have operated without a shaman as a central figure. For those who were interested, and many clearly were, shamanic practice narrated and located the past and by doing so, located itself.

As identity is bound up with place (Tilley 1994, 15), journeying contributes to the construction of identity.

Journeying associated those making the journey with what is considered to be quintessentially Tamu — the world of Tamu ancestors. Those who made the journey were simultaneously seen, and saw themselves, to be associated with the essence of a cultural past. Despite their residence in the town, by journeying they established their direct continuity with the culture of their ancestors. This went some way towards counteracting the widespread opinion that the purest most authentic form of Tamu cultural life is lived by those who remain in the villages. The people who went on these journeys, all members of the urban diaspora (except for the porters), showed themselves to be town-dwellers who 'could walk'. Thus, the stereotype of town people who 'cannot walk' was debunked. Not only could they walk, but they could walk further than many villagers who have never been in the *hye* (uplands). Journeying into the ancestral landscape and closely associating with the ancestors, not only established a direct continuity with the ancestral Afterworld but also a moral continuity that could be matched against the perceived 'immorality' of the town. It created a shared Tamu *hyula* (country/locale/homeland) — a *hyula* which included town-dwellers, villagers and ancestors. In other words, a common sense of landscape in which town and country, past and present could merge. Journeying was thus transformative in the sense that a pilgrimage is transformative (Turner 1974, 204–6); those who made the journey at some level transformed how they were perceived and how they perceived themselves.

Journeys into the landscape of history were simultaneously journeys into the geographical and metaphorical 'landscape' of the shamanic. Shamanic landscape overlaps with the landscape of history, reaching northwards to the Afterworld and origins, and southwards through history to the landscape of the present. Like the past, shamanic practice exists in other spaces and other times. To interact with the history of the landscape is to interact with the 'landscape' of the shamanic. The historical significance of landscape is enhanced through ritual, which 'invests historicity in sites that do not themselves embody events of the past' (Rappaport 1990, 153). The performance of ritual activities, as illustrated in the account of the journey described earlier, imbued (or reimbued) geographical location with both shamanic and historical significance. For the audience watching the video of the journey, the chanting of the *pye* at Maiju, Lubra and Thini not only invested these locations (which for many would have previously only been names) with historicity, but associated the conferring of historicity with shamanic action. The shamanic legitimized both history and landscape. In this relationship, the shamanic was the senior player. Shamanic action in landscape has been continuous (it had never ceased). History (in its non-Hindu interpretation) was discontinuous. History in landscape was relocated and re-created by those who had never left the landscape — the shamans. As interest was refocused on the past, it was simultaneously refocused on the shamanic. At a time when shamanic practice was seen as being on the decline and under pressure from other religious and secular ideologies (Buddhism as well as cosmopolitan secular ideas), this kind of history-making made a contribution to its revaluation. It also helped to remind the urban dwelling Tamu-mai, in particular, that this was their indigenous religion and that the shamans were the custodians of Tamu history. Since their beginnings in 1990, TPLS members have been very successful in re-centring the shamanic traditions and ensuring that they still have currency in the new national and international Tamu diaspora. The Kohla Project aimed to expand understandings of the Tamu past, and as such it brought out histories that had long been submerged. It also accorded a degree of attention and authority to the work of TPLS members, supporting their role as shamanist-activists.

Reflecting on the past and remembering the path
Yarjung Kromchaĩ Tamu, Mark Turin & Judith Pettigrew

This section is devoted to the perspective of the Kohla project's principal *pachyu* shaman and co-director, Yarjung Kromchaĩ Tamu. The truly interdisciplinary nature of the fieldwork endeavour and the research which ensued, combining anthropological, archaeological and shamanic forms of knowledge, was new not only for the academics involved, but also for the shaman. Moreover, while the lead anthropologist and archaeologist both have an extensive scholarly vocabulary at their disposal for articulating reflexive thoughts about knowledge production in their native English, this was not the case for the lead shaman. This collaborative fieldwork experience was truly experimental for Yarjung Tamu and challenging in ways that he could not have predicted.

How best then to represent the experiences and impressions of the Nepali- and Tamu-speaking lead shaman to an international audience in an academic publication? It was clear to the editors of this volume that in Nepal, narrative sequence and presentational style are intimately tied up with the cultural expectations of both the audience and the speaker. A canonical translation of the lead shaman's narrative, whether from a structured interview, a relaxed chat or from his own field notes contained in a diary, would likely not reflect his nuanced perspective of the experience.

Instead, it was decided to conscript the help of a linguistic anthropologist who has been working in the Himalayas since the early 1990s, had visited the project area and is fluent in Nepali. The other issue is that of trust, since Yarjung Kromchaĩ Tamu is concerned about the incorrect appropriation of his knowledge and all too aware of the importance of representing his ideas in an idiom which has currency and meaning to an international scholarly audience. The longevity of the relationships between Tamu, Turin and Pettigrew, including many successful prior collaborations in the realm of language teaching, publications and computer support, have done much to build and reaffirm this trust.

This chapter is divided into discrete subsections, each of which address a specific issue or concern of the shaman. Throughout the chapter, the voice is that of the lead shaman, Yarjung Tamu, and the text is therefore written from his perspective and in the first person. The contents of this chapter were elicited by Mark Turin over a period of sixteen months between October 2002 and March 2004, in occasional, if intensive, periods of questioning, recording and transliteration of Yarjung's written Nepali and Tamu. Four languages were used in the conversations between the linguistic anthropologist and the shaman, in decreasing frequency: Nepali, the vernacular Tamu language (called *Tamu Kyui* and hereafter referred to as *TK*), the ritual language known only by shamans from the ethnic group (known as *Cõ Kyui* and hereafter referred to as *CK*), and finally English. Important names, places and terms were written down both on paper and entered digitally into an Apple Macintosh computer in a Devanāgarī font which was later checked for spelling errors by the shaman. The chosen method of transliteration reflects well-attested and long-standing Indological guidelines and has been chosen by the linguistic anthropologist in the interest of compliance with international norms. It should be noted that this method of transliteration is at odds with Yarjung's own method which reflects a perceived phonetic reality of spoken Tamu but fails to take into account the phonology of cognate Tibeto-Burman languages. In particular, we had differences about how and where to indicate aspiration or breathiness on consonants, but have resolved to follow linguistic best practices rather than a local and indigenous method of transliteration. The material gathered by the linguistic anthropologist was supplemented with additional data collected over eighteen years of ongoing collaborative research between Tamu and social anthropologist Judith Pettigrew. This data did much to provide context as well as flesh out the shamanic narratives presented by Tamu.

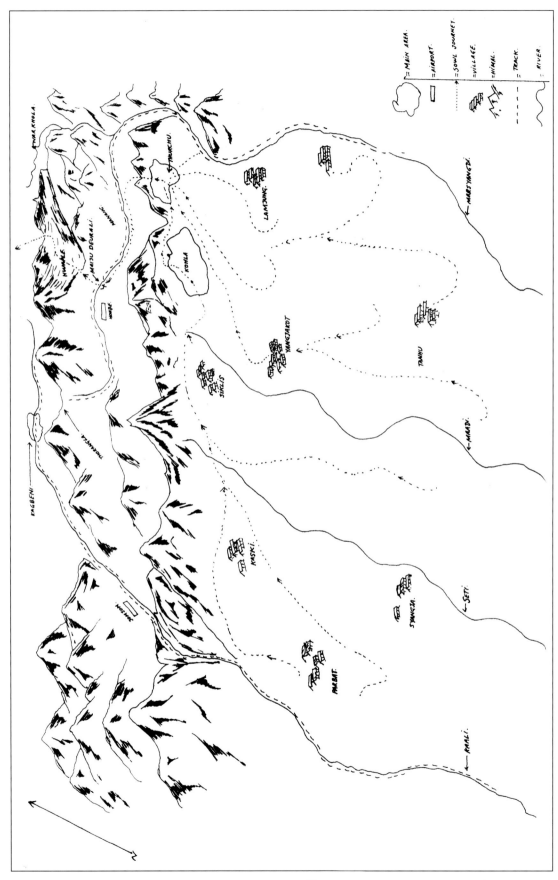

Figure 2.3. *Yarjung's mapping of the 'soul journey' north (note Hwaple/Oble top centre; see Fig. 4.34).*

The composition of the first team to visit Kohla

Kohla is a very important place for the Tamu-mai. Our *pye* and the oral history of the shamans tell us that many important things happened at Kohla. When I retired from the British army, I visited the Kohla area for the first time. In some sense, this felt like going 'home', even though it was a home I had never seen. I travelled with another ex-Gurkha soldier, also from my ethnic group, by the name of Bālā Singh. While not a shaman, Bālā Singh knew a fair amount about the places we would pass since he had worked as a cowherd. We took another guide with us, a 60-year old man called Buddhimān. Buddhimān was also not a shaman, but rather a shepherd. He didn't know the texts of the *pye*, nor did he know of the importance of our journey, but he had heard of or visited all of the places and locations mentioned in my shamanic texts. All three of us hailed from the Kromchaĩ clan, and we were related which gave us a sense of security and trust with one another. We also took with us a porter called Khorā. Of our group of four, then, Bālā Singh knew the layout and names of the lowlands areas through which we would pass (on account of his tending cows), while Buddhimān was better versed in the features of the higher pastures (since he tended sheep).

My father, Parsingh Kromchaĩ Tamu, had always believed that the places shamans mentioned in their chants and rituals were to be found on earth, and not in the sky as some others believed, and that the locations of the ancient migration route lay to the north. I had always wanted to visit these places and see them with my eyes, but had never had the time and money. Only now that I was retired did I have the money and time to make my dream a reality.

We set off on our journey on Sunday, July 22, 1990, departing from my home village of Yāngjakot. When we reached the high pastures, Buddhimān explained the landscape to us and told us the names of all the places along our route which I compared with the place names in the *pye*. Each time the *pye* described a village we could see evidence of a past settlement. We also found other places that are mentioned in the *pye*, like rivers (*syō*) and resting places (*nhe*). It took us a week to get to Thurchu, by which time all our rations and money were finished. Thurchu is at about 15,000 feet and is an important base for Tamu shepherds (Figs. 2.1 & 2.3). Thurchu is where the various ritual journeys of Tamu shamans meet up and also the location through which all the souls of the dead (*plah*) from different Tamu villages pass on their final journey to Targila (the Tamu Afterworld). We wanted to cross Ekrai Mountain into Manāng as Ekrai is the place where near-dead Tamu souls prowl in the hours and

moments before death, but Buddhimān said that we didn't have the equipment for climbing through the snow. At this point, we decided to turn back. Because of the hardship we sent our porter and Buddhimān back to Yāngjakot, while Bālā Singh and I returned by ourselves. On the way back, we got lost taking a shortcut in Lamjung, and the going was difficult. In total, the whole trip took us fifteen days. We had followed exactly the route of the chants. After this trip, I realized the strength of our traditions and knew that it was important to do more research. However, our journey had been self-funded and sadly, we had no more resources to undertake further studies.

The importance of the **pye**

The *pye* are the sacred oral texts of the Tamu *pachyu* and *klehbrī* shamans. They also explain the history of the Tamu-mai. At the beginning of a ritual before we start the *pye*, we chant and describe what we are going to do in the ritual. After that we start the *pye*. Some *pye* are effective by themselves, you just need to chant them to bring about change. *Pye* vary in length, some take 30 minutes to chant and others, like the *serga* in the three-day death ritual, take about ten hours to complete. Some *pye* describe actions or events, others call evil spirits or gods and ancestors. During a major ritual when a *pachyu* needs the extra protection of the *pachyu* god *Pakrei Klhyesōdi Prehsōdi* in his body, he chants a 'calling' *pye* so that he can enter trance. At the end of a ritual, we chant about the success of the ritual and for the protection of the participants.

Altogether there are perhaps three or four hundred different *pye*, so this is a very rich oral tradition, perhaps one of the richest in the Himalayan region. Shamans from different villages know different *pye* or slightly different versions of the same *pye*. I know over a hundred. The *pye* are chanted in a ritual language named *Cō Kyui*. *Cō* is the Tamu place of origin. Although we now speak *Tamu Kyui*, *Cō Kyui* is our original language. In some ways, it resembles a secret language, as nowadays few people understand or speak it. Many shamans don't know it and they just chant the texts from memory without understanding the content.

There are different types of *pye*. Some explain the origins of shamanic objects, animals, plants and other sacred things such as yeast (*prhama*) and millet wine (*pah*). Others tell the stories of gods, ancestors, famous people and famous shamans. There are also *pye* that tell of shamanic journeys and about shrines and ancestors. Others are about evil spirits, witches, stars, luck, illness, death rituals and funerals.

The *pye* also describe the Tamu past and list all the places we travelled through on our migration from

Mongolia. Some anthropologists refer to our *pye* as myths, but I do not think that this word is accurate as the *pye* contain historical facts.

The route that we walked and the importance of place names

I want to take the time to carefully explain the route that we took. It is important to me that readers should know all the names of the places that we passed and what these names mean. I also want to make it clear whether the names are modern spoken Tamu language (TK) or the ritual language which is only known to shamans like myself (CK).

We set out from my home village. In Nepali, the name of the village is Yāngjakot (Figs. 2.1 & 2.3), but we know it as Yōjku in my ritual language (CK). Villagers refer to the village as Yōju which is an abbreviation of Yōjku. The toponym derives Yōjku from the words *Yoja*, which is a clan name of an ethnic group, and *ku*, meaning 'nine'. It is thus the village where the nine Yoja brothers founded a village. The Nepali name Yāngjakot is derived from the indigenous term, and the suffix *kot* is clearly a term of Hindu provenance, likely from *kot* meaning 'guardroom, prison, station' and referring to the location that buffaloes are slain during the yearly ritual of Dasain. This Nepali term became common usage only after the rule of the Bhaise Chaubise Rājā (twenty-four kings).

Leaving Yōjku, we travelled on to Thāurō, a word from my vernacular (TK) meaning 'a species of inedible bead derived from a fruit'. It is believed that such beads were found in this place. From there, we journeyed on to Līduce, a place name which means 'veranda of a house' in my ritual language (CK), on account of the terraced landscape which is reminiscent of such a veranda. Thereafter, the path continues on to Cāsū, derived from the TK words *cā* 'bridge' and *sū* 'mouth', meaning 'mouth of the bridge' or more commonly 'gate'. Thence we trekked up to Cyuhjyu Ple, which means 'wet, damp and flat place' in my ritual language (CK), and derives from *cyuhjyu* 'wet, marshy' and *ple* 'flat'. As anyone knows who has visited this location, the name is fitting and requires no further explanation.

From Cyuhjyu Ple, we walked on to Kuniholdō, a place whose name derives from the spoken Tamu words *kuni* 'foot pestle' and *holdō* 'mortar'. The hole in the ground is still present for all to see where grains were beaten so many years before. Thereafter we travelled on to a place with a most interesting name: Mār Chōlō Chyāh. All of these three words derive from spoken Tamu (TK), with the following meanings: *mār* 'gold', *chōlō* 'putting shot' and *chyāh* 'to throw, take aim'. It is said that in this place, a

man who visited once found a gold shot-put on the ground. Delighted with his find, he hid the gold orb in his backpack which he then hung on a tree for safe-keeping while he went to collect wood. On returning to the tree, with a full bundle of kindling, the pack had disappeared and no matter how hard he tried, he never found it back. This is how this place came by its name.

Leaving Mār Chōlō Chyāh, we walked on to a place known as Sōgyāpūh Koyā. It is not commonly known that this place name is a mixture of ritual language and everyday vernacular: *sōgyāpūh* means 'junction' or 'crossroads' in CK, while *koyā* is a vernacular Tamu place name. This is an important junction as several paths meet here with routes leading to different villages. People walking through can bring diseases or evil spirits with them and sometimes witches pass by, so we bunch together a minimum of three and a maximum of nine thorny plants such as *palā* or *chutro*, and the eldest man — or a shaman if one is present — sweeps each person from head to toe as they leave the cross-roads. This prevents bad spirits and illness following the travellers and causing trouble on the journey. At any rate, the road splits at Sōgyāpūh Koyā, which in part explains the toponym. Soon after, we reached Krasa Nēh, another location whose name is a mixture of two languages. *Krasa* is the term for the purification ritual which a daughter conducts for her parents in the ritual language (CK), while *nēh* is a 'resting place along the path' in vernacular Tamu (TK).

Close to this area is a stone memorial to a hunting dog. In the past, hunting was a very important activity and hunting dogs were much loved. One day a hunting dog died, and his owner was so upset that he decided to bury him on the trail instead of bringing him back to the village. This way he could see his memorial and remember him when he walked along the path to and from hunting.

After a total of six hours walking, we ended our first day of trek in Sa Pu Cyo, a place name with the following etymological components: *sa* 'clay' (CK), *pu* 'pottery' (CK) and *cyo* 'hanging' (TK). It is said that in our history, the Tamu people populated this place and produced various forms of hanging clay pottery from the local supplies of clay. The toponym derives from this activity.

The second day started with a brisk walk to Kōhkyā, a place name which is made up of two vernacular elements *kōh* 'upper' and *kyā* 'path', (both TK), and whose name is indicative of which path we took. After leaving Kōhkyā, we ascended to Dōth Kharka, in which *Dōth* is a proper name in vernacular Tamu and *kharka* means 'land around a village, pasture' in Nepali. The name relates to the arable land in this location. From Dõth Kharka we continued on to Krapu Pro and thereafter onwards to Krapu itself, a total of four hours walk from Sa Pu Cyo. *Krapu* is a proper name in spoken Tamu (TK), while *pro* means 'steep ridge' in the same language. The path closely follows a ridge and then evens out at Krapu. Krapu is the highest peak in the area and at Krapu Deurāli, which is a kind of 'gateway' between the village and the wilderness, we prayed to the local gods and placed flowers on the stone offering place to ask them to help make our journey a success. On our return, we gave thanks for a safe journey and another flower offering. Deurālis are always positioned in the middle of the path and when going out, people pass on the left side and when returning, they pass on the right side.

The next location we reached is called Kudami Coh Lhidī, a toponym based on words from both ritual and vernacular Tamu. *Kudami coh* means 'sternum or tip of a ridge' in vernacular Tamu while a *lhidī* is a bamboo tent rather like a yurt in my ritual language (CK). This name refers to two sides of the path: one side resembles a ridge while the other has the characteristics of a temporary shelter. As this place is shaped like a breastbone, we say that a heart is housed inside, and we believe that if you go to the top of the peak and make an offering and pray, your *sai* or 'heart-mind' (TK) will become very strong.

Thereafter we came to Sīyõ Kharka, known for its plentiful stocks of firewood. In the vernacular Tamu language, *sī* means 'firewood' and *yo* indicates availability, while *kharka* means 'land around a village, pasture' in Nepali. From Sīyõ Kharka we moved on to Kowār Kharka, and then Phulu Kharka. *Kowār*, in the vernacular language, is a type of round bowl and the toponym Kowār Kharka describes the round pasture land in this area. In the ritual language (CK), *phulu* has the meaning 'pleasant' or 'good', and Phulu Kharka is indeed an excellent patch of land for farming.

We left the three kharkas behind us and continued on to Khũidõ Toh which is invariably cold, as its name would suggest: in the ritual language known to shamans, *khũidõ* means 'cold, freezing' while *toh* means 'village'. We spent the night in Khũidõ Toh, only moving on to Klye Pal Ti Nẽh the next morning. This is a very important location and a very interesting place name. In the ritual language (CK) as well as in the vernacular (TK), *klye* refers to the Ghale ruler, while *pahl* means 'foot, leg' in vernacular Tamu (TK), *ti* means 'to kill' and *nẽh* is a 'resting place'. In Tamu history, this location is known to be the place where the Klye Mru (Ghale Rājā) was chased by villagers, chopped in the leg and felled. There is an interesting variation in the name, which also reflects a different ending to the story of the Klye. The Lamjung Tamu

refer to the place as Klye Pal Ti Nẽh 'the resting place where the Klye was chopped in the leg and killed', while the Yāngjakot people use the toponym Klye Pal Tu Nẽh 'the resting place where the Klye was chopped in the leg and wounded'.

Leaving Klye Pal Ti Nẽh, we moved on to Chyomsyo Yosī, a toponym derived from the ritual (CK) word *chyomsyo* 'nun' and the vernacular (TK) word *yosī* meaning 'long nail', on account of the land being so long, angular and thin in this place. Above Chyomsyo Yosī lie Cõmrõ Toh and Cõmrõ Nẽh. Cõmrõ is derived from Tamu ritual language *cõ* 'distant or high place' and *ro* 'to see', while *toh* means 'village' and *nẽh* is a 'resting place' in the vernacular. These places are so called on account of the long vistas.

After leaving Cõmrõ Toh and Cõmrõ Nẽh, we continued on to Ngyoi Plā Ngyoh. This complicated place name is made up of three elements of vernacular Tamu: *ngyoi* 'traditional woman's dress', *plā* 'to wash by beating' and *ngyoh* 'lake, pond'. It is told that this location was used our foremothers in the Kromchaī clan to wash their soiled clothes after giving birth. On account of the blood pollution, Kromchaī clan members may still not drink the water. As a Kromchaī clan member, visiting this location was very powerful for me. Slightly above Ngyoi Plā Ngyoh lies Cikrē Toh, *Cikrē* being a proper name and *toh* meaning 'village'. This place was originally inhabited solely by members of the Kromchaī clan, which explains why their womenfolk would wash their clothes in the lake below.

Moving on from Cikrē Toh, we came to Põmrõ Hāju Toh and Põmrõ Hāju Nẽh. *Põmrõ Hāju* is simply the proper name of this settlement which lies essentially opposite Kohla, although separated by a river. This village was once a Tamu settlement of mixed clans. After Põmrõ Hāju, we came to Taprõ Toh and Taprõ Kharka. *Taprõ* means 'crow' in the ritual language (CK), so the place names could be translated as 'Crow Village' and 'Crow Pasture' respectively. From there we moved on to Mihjāī Toh, a village by the name of *Mihjāī*, and thereafter Ladã Lidã Ngyoh, a pond or lake called *Ladã Lidã*. This then lead to Ngyoh Kõh, a pond or lake shaped like a *kõh*, a 'backbone, spine' in the vernacular Tamu language. At the next stop, Sa Pu Nẽh, there is a fork in the path, one of which leads to Kohla. The place name Sa Pu Nẽh derives from the ritual terms *sa* 'earth', *pu* 'pottery' and the vernacular *nẽh* meaning 'resting place'. It is said that people used to make clay and earthenware pottery there. Soon thereafter we reached Kohla Sõmpre Toh, the destination of our journey. *Kohla* is the place name, *sõmpre* is made up of the elements *sõ* 'three' and *pre* 'part', while *toh* means 'village'. The combined meaning is thus 'the village of Kohla in three parts'.

Leaving Kohla, we travelled to Kokar Kharka in which *Kokar* is a place name in our ritual language (CK) and *kharka* is the Nepali word for 'pasture'. Thereafter we walked on to Naudi Pakh, a term derived from Tamu ritual language *naudi* 'steep, uphill' and from Nepali *pākho* 'side, hillside, land', and from there on to the steep pasture land at Naudi Nĕh. From Naudi we made our way on to Sāurō Kharka, *Sāurō* being a proper name in the ritual Tamu language (CK) and *kharka* meaning 'pasture' in Nepali. Soon after Sāurō we came to Nghedku Nĕh, a toponym derived from the term *nghedku* in our ritual language meaning 'plentiful milk, fertile' on account of the excellent pasture in the area.

We arrived in Sāurō Syō on Tuesday, July 24, 1990. This place derives its name from its first settler, a Tamu by the name of *Sāurō*. *Syō* means 'river' in the ritual language (CK), and true enough there is a stream which runs through the land. The following place we came to is named Kane Kō, two words in our ritual language which refer to the outstretched body of a large animal lifting or arching its back. The hill is so named because it has the form of such an animal. From there we travelled on to Talle Coh, derived from *talle* 'sharp, long, fine, pointed' in the ritual Tamu language and *coh* meaning 'ending, summit' in the vernacular (TK). This place name accurately reflects the topography in this place, and it is plain for all to see why our ancestors named the place Talle Coh.

From there, we walked on to Kudrē which means 'winding hill' in our ritual language, and then onto Khĕbi which carries the meaning of 'den or resting place for wild animals, a territory occupied by wild animals who roam'. From Khĕbi we moved onwards to Khĕ U, so named because it refers to a nest or resting place for wild birds in our secret ritual language (CK). From the wild territories, the path levelled out in Khudi Kharka, in which *khudi* means 'flat river bank along the source of a river' and *kharka* is a borrowed word from Nepali meaning 'pasture land'. We then turned uphill once again to reach Sargē, a toponym meaning 'a steep uphill or winding path to a summit' which perfectly described the path we took. After Sargē we came to Puhrju Nĕh which derives its name from *puhrju* meaning 'holy, pure, sacred' in our ritual language and *nĕh* meaning 'resting place' in Tamu vernacular. Leaving Puhrju we came to Pagrē, the name of a very powerful ancestor spirit after which the hill has been named. Leaving Pagrē we came to Thurchu, a rather even pasture whose name fittingly means 'flat place' in our ritual language. The last part of our journey led us from Thurchu to Homa Nghaīru Ngyoh which is now a place of pilgrimage for Hindus and known in Nepali as Dudh Pokhari. In our ritual language, *homa* is a holy word or mantra, *nghaīru* means 'white, milky water' while *ngyoh* is a 'pond' in the Tamu vernacular. This 'holy pond of milky water' is so named on account of the consistency of the lake and is a very spiritual place.

My own thoughts on reaching Kohla

I was naturally very proud and excited to locate all these places and to see them with my own eyes. Our *pye* describe the landscapes of different areas, but I didn't know exactly where these places were. Before my father Pachyu Parsing passed away, he and I had many discussions about the landscape mentioned in the *pye*. While I visited these places spiritually, I had never seen them physically and so I wondered if these places really existed and also in the order that we chant them. Because of my doubts, my father suggested that I travel into the mountains to try to find them. Each evening after we set up camp we sat around the fire discussing the match between the *pye* and the landscape. It was very interesting for us: while Buddhimān knew the landscape, he didn't know the *pye,* and while I knew the *pye*, I didn't know the landscape. Putting them together was really exciting and I was very impressed. I had studied the *pye* for 25 years, since I was a young boy, and had often argued with my father as I had strong doubts about whether these places actually existed. Now I could finally say that I had seen them for myself.

It was particularly important and meaningful for me to visit the villages from which my own clan ancestors had migrated, and it gave me an excited chill inside to think that I may have been the first person from my clan to touch the places that we shamans chant about in our rituals. Finding Kohla also gave me more respect and appreciation for my father and what he taught me, and his unwavering belief that these ancestral villages existed on our plane and not in the heavens. Aside from the existence of Kohla, it was amazing to find all these ruined villages, to walk through what I think English people might call the 'sacred geography' of the past, and to see the layout of the whole region. It is natural that the finding of Kohla should be given some priority given all the incidents narrated in our history which deal with the place and the historical importance and prominence of the then Klye chieftain, but we also uncovered many other villages which we should investigate. The *pye* which I chant mentions 80 habitations in Kohla at that time, and the village ruins that we found were quite substantial with some surrounding land, indicating a large settlement. Since visiting Kohla, many people have asked me whether I felt as if I was on a pilgrimage as I walked up the hill that first time in search of the ancestral settlements. The answer is that I was not on a pilgrimage or on a spiritual journey in any sense. I do enough of this in my chanting, so I know what journeys into the ancestral realm are like. No, the trek to Kohla was something very physical and actual. On spiritual journeys a shaman reaches his destination by chanting, on physical journeys you get somewhere by walking and sweating. For me, this whole first expedition was because I was simply interested to discover whether the places which I sung about in my ritual texts actually existed. Having left the army, with the time and resources to do so, I was able to prove to myself that they did.

Going up the mountain and going back in time

In certain ways, going up the mountain was equivalent to going back in time. This was primarily on account of the practicalities of the travel and the hardship of the journey. While quite used to living without comforts, it was an adventure to sleep in caves and have to search for firewood to cook our meals. All of us in the group marvelled at how our ancestors could have survived, and even flourished, in such a place. Every time that we came to a new settlement, the first thing that we thought of was where the graves of our ancestors might lie. I would often stop and meditate on the locations of such graves and also try to find some connections to the bodies of individual forefathers. Working out the pattern of the settlements was not always easy since shepherds had more or less destroyed what was left of the settlements for useable resources such as firewood, stone or larger rocks. On trek, I and others in the party would attempt to get in touch with ancestors in our dreams. Many ancestors spoke to members of the group in our dreams, pointing us in the directions of their graves, but we never actually found the specific locations of graves.

Both Bālā Singh and I often went into trance during the journey, even though Bālā Singh was not a shaman, he was accepted by the main god *Pakraī* who entered his body and made him go into trance. In such cases, we felt that the best thing to do would be to make a fire and burn some incense. Our guide, Buddhimān, had thoughtfully brought some fuel with him in case I should go into trance in a remote location where wood was hard to find or when it was too wet or windy to make a fire. By the time that we reached Homa Nghaïru Ngyoh, Bālā Singh and I were in trance. Buddhimān was used to seeing trance and knew what to do, but Khorā wasn't and was quite afraid. Buddhimān, then 60 years old, insisted on bathing in the freezing lake three times to purify and cleanse himself.

My relationship to archaeological knowledge

Over the years, the Tamu people have met and worked with many anthropologists, but not with archaeologists. On returning to Pokhara after visiting Kohla, we started having meetings with other Tamu who were also interested in our history, religion and culture. In Kārtik 2047 (October–November 1990), we founded an official organization to study Tamu cultural traditions and our indigenous shamanic religion, the *pye-tā Lhu-tā*. Almost all of the founding members are ex-Gurkha soldiers and officers. Our organization is called *Tamu Pye Lhu Sangh* (TPLS). All Tamu-mai are welcome to become involved in TPLS and help us study and preserve our cultural traditions, language and indigenous religion which are now endangered. The study of shamanic history is also very important as it tells us that there are no 'higher' and 'lower' clans among the Tamu-mai. Nowadays, many people, especially the young, thankfully no longer accept these old ideas that have caused such problems in our society.

Some months after we founded TPLS, we met Judy Pettigrew, a social anthropologist, who was a student of Professor Alan Macfarlane at the University of Cambridge. At that time, Judy was doing research for her PhD on Tamu cultural traditions.

In August 1992, TPLS organized a trip through the districts of Kāski, Lamjung, Manāng and Mustāng to discover if the places listed in the *pye* existed in the geographical landscape. The first part of the journey retraced the downward migration route of the Tamu-mai with the overlapping upward ritual journey route along which shamans guide the souls of the dead in the *pai laba* death ritual. We wanted to travel the entire length of both routes, but for practical and financial reasons it was only possible to trace those sections of the journeys that lie within the districts of Kāski, Lamjung and Manāng. The ritual journeys of shamans from different villages merge in the high pastures of Thurchu.

Prior to Thurchu, shamans from different villages have their own routes. As on our previous journey, we followed the route of the shamans from the village of Yāngjakot. At a point on the trail known as Māijyu Deurāli, where the soul journey goes up and over the large rock at Oble, we continued following the downward migration trail which overlaps with the landscape referred to in several different *pye*.

Of all the journeys I have been on, this was the greatest as we found many ancestral settlements and each time a place was mentioned in the *pye* it was there in the land. We were a large group so many people had a chance to see the correspondence between the landscape and the *pye*, and this delighted me. At Kohla I video-taped a conversation between Judy and TPLS treasurer Major Hom Bahādur Tamu during which

Hom Bahādur said that he thought we should get people to come to Kohla to dig it up and put the proof in the *kohĩbo*, our Tamu cultural and social centre in Pokhara. Judy suggested that if anyone was going to dig things up then there should be archaeologists involved, as they are the experts in doing this kind of work. When I heard her talking about developing a research project and getting archaeologists to work with us it felt like a dream, as previously I had no idea how we could involve archaeologists as I had never heard of such people before. Amazingly, this was a dream which came true!

This was actually my first visit to the settlement of Kohla as on our previous trip we hadn't quite reached it. I was naturally very excited to finally see such a famous place. At all the important places on our journey, the *klehbrĩ* shaman and I chanted our respective *pye* referring to the specific location we were in. At Kohla I couldn't chant as I was hyper-sensitive and could hardly even touch the stones without shaking and getting other pre-trance sensations.

I really didn't know anything about archaeology, what it was, how it worked or what kinds of information archaeologists collect, before I met Chris Evans. I had a sneaking suspicion that archaeology had something to do with baking breads in large ovens. Perhaps they bake their 'data' in large ovens! In my opinion, and this is only my perspective, archaeologists are looking for proof and evidence while anthropologists are more on the look out for stories, tales and history. I see archaeology as studying facts, and anthropology as studying ideas and memories. Scientifically, then, it strikes me that archaeologists are more rigorous in their methods. Since they don't ask living people any questions, they are not so often deluded by their local 'guides'. Anthropologists, on the other hand, are far more contingent on their guides and can only represent what people tell them. Archaeology is therefore more likely to be truthful. But there is another side to this also: while anthropologists have to be smarter and more critical to be able to differentiate between truth and lies, archaeologists can just rely on their machines to sort out the wheat from the chaff for them, as they just have to collect the facts. While archaeology is more scientific, I think that you have to be smarter to be a really good anthropologist.

This is how archaeologists follow leads, find data and form their ideas: they work methodically, step by step, formulating ideas, opinions and thoughts, and they test them out at every point along the way. This is not how shamans work. Shamans, like me, just know things. We believe things since they are written in our texts, and more often than not, we are proven right. Archaeologists are particularly helpful and useful in uncovering and understanding small things such as pottery shards and pieces of necklaces. When we find them, we simply have no idea what they are, but archaeologists can read such kinds of data far more accurately than shamans can. In fact, archaeologists and anthropologists are pretty similar, like related cousins really. The only difference is that anthropologists can write what and when they want, but archaeologists have to find things first before they can write about them.

Archaeologists are not always satisfied with my historical accounts and the stories in my ritual texts. They find them interesting, but as they are proper scientists, they can't just trust my oral history about how many houses there are in Kohla, for example. Well, I told them that there would be 80 habitations in Kohla, but they found more than one hundred. So my aim was right, but they ended up excavating more details than my texts had told me. There are other examples of the difference in approach between my kind of knowledge and that of archaeologists. One particularly interesting example was when they found some rocks in a cluster and then some human bones nearby. When I asked the archaeologists what they had found, they thought that it might be a cemetery. I disagreed since I know that we Tamu people do not bury people within the boundary of a village, but rather outside of a settlement in a northerly direction, as this is the direction of heaven. Then they thought that it might be a burial site for children, but still I disagreed since I know that we just don't do that. I wanted to find the *chogõ* 'cemetery' so that we could locate the bones of our ancestors and offer them proper respect and make sure to not disturb them during our work. We searched every part of the village and the surrounding area but we were not able to find the *chogõ*. This puzzled me, but Chris felt that we were unlikely to find our ancestors bones, as there is so much acidity in the ground at Kohla and also lots of erosion. During the excavation season in 2000, the ancestors told me in a dream where they were buried and I found the cemetery hill, but large trees had grown on top of it and it was quite inaccessible. I took Chris to the location and he agreed that I might be right, but as they did not have time to excavate, I was not able to get actual proof. I was very disappointed not to get a physical reminder of the ancestors.

On Kohla expeditions, with one anthropologist and a team of archaeologists, my role was actually pretty minor. After all, I already had found my interest and calling, then anthropology found me, and together we found archaeology. I was the shaman — the holder of oral history — and I gave information whenever it was needed. Obviously, many of the things I know are secret and I don't give such information away. I make careful decisions about what information to make public, but too many shamans have taken their knowledge to their grave and then it is completely lost. To save our traditions and to help people learn more about our true history, nowadays it is important to share our knowledge. During Kohla Project trips, I was also a kind of co-ordinator or manager, making links between people, keeping everyone happy, explaining to villagers what we were doing and why. In the army we would call this job a quartermaster. This is not a very glorious role, but it is an important one, since I helped to make things happen.

On our archaeological trip, the first thing that I did when we arrived at a location was to burn *pru-mai* 'herbs' to the local *sildo naldo* 'god of the area' and to the *khe-ma* 'ancestors' to let them know that we respected them and also to ask their permission to do our research in their area. The first time we visited Kohla was during the monsoon and because the grass was so high, it was difficult to see clearly. When we re-visited, I immediately saw *um-ta-te*, the very large stone from which the village caller would send out his messages. *Um-ta-te* is mentioned in the *pye*. Nearby there was a small rock cave where we found the body of a dead cow. Chris thought that this was a shrine as he felt that the space was laid out in a formal manner as one would expect in a ritual place. He thought that maybe the cow had been sacrificed. I don't believe that it is a shrine. The dead animal must have been old and not able to keep up with the others, so the cowherders probably left it in the cave with grass and water and that's where it died. On the 1992 visit, at one of the other places that Chris called a 'shrine', I started having pre-trance shakes. I believe that this place must have been the house of a *pachyu* shaman. I agree with Chris that the place on the other side of the village is indeed a shrine.

En route to Kohla during the 1992 TPLS trip and the Kohla project survey in 1994, we hit a very bad hail storm, and on both occasions I conducted a ritual to control the weather. It hailed because we made too much noise and disturbed the ancestors and the locality gods. They are sensitive and you shouldn't speak loudly in the uplands. In 1992, the gods were angry because a TPLS colleague and I had an argument about Tamu history, and in 1994 our large team of porters were noisy and made the place dirty. After that I spoke to the porters and told them to be quieter and to be especially careful about where they went to the toilet. I also spoke to the ancestors and the locality gods and asked them to excuse us if we had done something wrong and I explained to the ancestors that we were coming to learn more about their lives and

the places in which they lived, and in this manner I asked for their protection and assistance.

During our trips to Kohla, I spent a lot of time alone in the forest. When I was on my own, I ran with the locality gods and with other jungle spirits. They beckoned me with their secret calls and I followed them. I ran all over the jungle with them but I never got lost as they always brought me back safely to where I started. When I run with spirits I get a special kind of energy and I feel very good. This energy helps me afterwards when I am doing healing rituals. Above Kohla is a long flat piece of ground where our ancestors used to race horses. Several times, I ran with the spirits in this area. I found a tree that had been split by lightning. I gathered wood from this tree as it is especially good for making tools such as the weaving implements that women use. If you keep a piece of wood from a tree like this in your home, your house will be protected against lightning. I also took some of the bark of the tree as it can be used as a medicinal herb and also for making amulets.

During our survey trip to Kohla, my father told me in a dream that before we started excavating, we must sacrifice a goat and present it to the ancestors and the locality gods. He told me that if we did this, then we could excavate the village without problems. So when we returned in 2000 to excavate, we brought a goat with us and sacrificed it on the first morning of work before we started digging. There was also a visiting shaman present on that day and we both chanted after the sacrifice and before the work began. Because of this, I believe that our work was successful and we didn't experience any problems.

In terms of what the archaeologists actually did, I am happy with their findings. They worked hard even though the conditions were difficult, and did their dating on two objects. I do think, however, that we should not stop here but continue to dig deeper since this is where older artefacts are likely to be preserved. After all, they only excavated in one place, in the centre of the village, and very little is still known about the outlying villages. The charcoal which they found was tested and found to be around 1000 to 1200 years old. I believe the settlements in the area to be much older, perhaps between 1600 to 1900 years old. I have my own scientific reasons for believing this, which I explained to the archaeologists when they asked me for my opinion on the dates. My father told me that the texts of the Tamu people predate our civilization and our establishment as a stable and unique ethnic group. These sacred texts existed before letters and writing were invented, when the Tamu people were still living like wild men in the jungle. There are trees in Kohla which are most likely more than 1000 years old. I believe that these trees would only have been planted, or sprung up, after humans settled there. The humans settled there before the trees, so the site is surely older than the dating shows.

I would like to return to Kohla from time to time, as it is a very important place both spiritually and historically. We need to do further archaeological research but given the present political situation and the activities of the Maoists, this is impossible. In the future, I do hope that the Kohla Project will resume. We need to talk to Tamu people about what should be done with Kohla. It could become a site for pilgrimage, or even a healing centre as it is an area where many and varied verbs are grown. The future of Kohla is for all Tamu people to decide and it will be important to have consultations with as many of our community as possible.

The nature of recording: a glimpse into a shaman's diary
In my field log book or diary, I wrote down an exhaustive account of each and every day: what time I got up, when I left the tent, how long we walked, what problems we encountered and whether I conducted protection rituals for the group in cases of high risk or danger. While I was writing this down, others were recording the situation with a video camera. I noted down the things that happened, such as the big hail storm which threatened to slow us down. For us to continue, the hail storm had to stop, so I conducted another ritual for this.

I wrote down all of these events and wrote about how they affected me and the efficacy of the expedition. There was another added danger: since we might be walking on decomposed bodies and perhaps even digging near the bones of the ancestors, they could have reason to be angry with us. I had to pacify the spirits and explain what we were doing and why, and part of this meant burning herbs in the evenings and praying. I simply had to inform the ancestors that we were coming and that we meant them no harm and no disrespect, and whenever I conducted a ritual of this sort, I noted it down in my book. Other times, during discussions between the archaeologists and the village elders, I took notes on how they presented their views. Often I would make an effort to meet with the village elders and headmen of the places we came through in order to explain what we were doing and to reassure them that the foreigners were not tourists but researchers, and were conducting important work. Sometimes these discussions took the form of lectures or little speeches, and I would often make some notes in my book beforehand to make sure that the event went smoothly and to ensure that I didn't forget to mention any important points.

Another topic on which I took notes on was the health of the group. If people got ill, which they did, I would write down what they were feeling, what they were eating and also try and keep an eye on their physical and mental state. I was very concerned about the food, both in terms of making sure that our group members were eating enough and also checking that what we were eating was healthy and clean. My occupation with the health of the group concerned all members: from the foreign archaeologists to the porters whom we had hired. All of this writing about the daily routine of our group meant that my note books read more like a trip log than a research diary. I didn't usually write down much about the research itself, although if there were particularly interesting finds or events I would jot those down. My part of the scientific documentation project was using the video camera to capture the moments on film. The archaeologists were less interested in the video than I expected them to be, but then I suppose they have their own way of recording facts. For me, the video camera was a way of setting in stone the reality of what we saw, and showing others the footage means that no-one can ever say that it was different. I take video footage and photographs in the way that I like, and use the images as visual proof in a way similar to the way that archaeologists use the finds that they dig up from the ground. When people later ask the archaeologists what they did, Chris and his team can show them the bits of broken things which they found and this counts as their proof. When my villagers and community ask me what I did on this project and what we found, I want to be able to show them the video proof. Taking a camera, tape and batteries along was not the archaeologist's idea, it was Judy's and my idea and this should be seen as a contribution that I made towards the scientific documentation of what we did. The first video camera belonged to Judy and the second one belonged to my brother while the still camera was my own. Archaeological photography is very different to how I take photos. Archaeologists measure things and use photography only as a tool for their science, while I use photography and video both as a way to document a scientific proof and also for my own personal reasons, to record where we went and how. Dates and places are very important to me.

On anthropological responsibility to the community
Many PhD degrees have been granted to foreign scholars, many of them anthropologists, who have worked with the Tamu communities of Nepal. While these people then call themselves Doctor, we Tamu cannot say that we benefit in practical ways from their knowledge and few, if any, of the scholars have

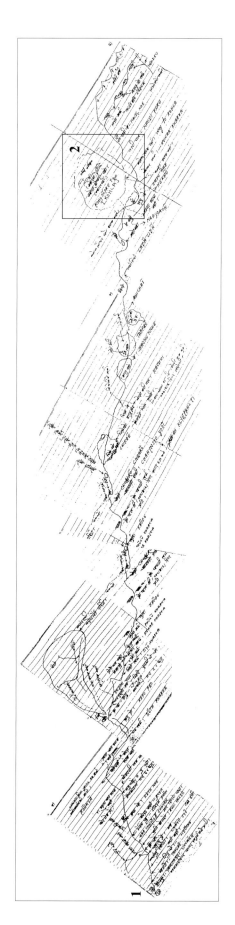

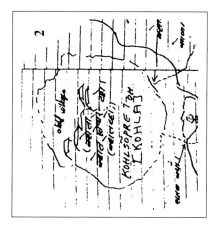

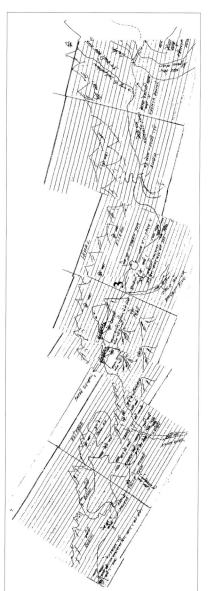

Figure 2.4. *Yarjung's depiction of the migration route of the Tamu-mai (part I, southern length): 1) Yangjakot; 2) Kohla (with enlarged inset lower right); 3) Thurchu.*

41

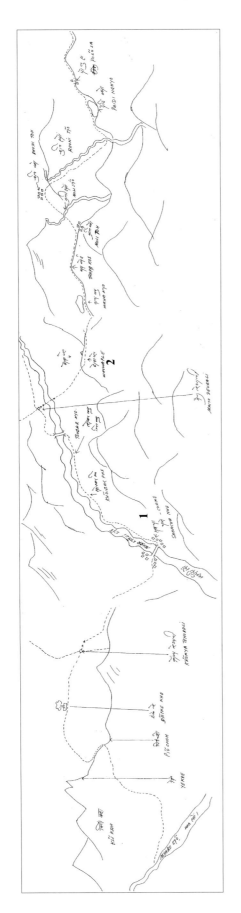
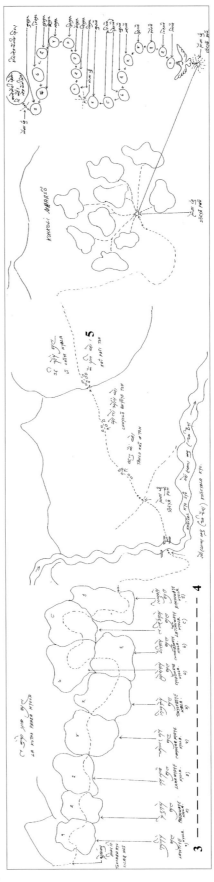

Figure 2.5. *Yarjung's depiction of the migration route of the Tamu-mai (part II; northern length with origin of world lower right-end): 1) Chame; 2) Whowaple/ Oble; 3–4) Lines 85–101 of the pye referring to 'countries' or 'homelands'; 5) Kai Patiye, Line 39 ('Kai Pati Toh').*

worked really collaboratively. Judy Pettigrew is the first anthropologist to have listened to what the community wanted and worked in an equal way with local people to help them get what they wanted: in this case, we wanted the archaeologists. You see, we Tamu had no idea where to find these archaeologists but Judy did, and she brought them to us. This is a point which must not be forgotten.

Some of my scientific findings
The full name of the village we reached is Kohla Sõ Pre, and this has an interesting and important local meaning in my language. *Sõ* means 'three' while *pre* means 'part, division', thus the full meaning of Kohla Sõ Pre is 'Kohla of the three parts'. The archaeologists gave these parts the names KI, KII and KIII. But what is the meaning of these parts? To this day, there are little streams which separate the three parts of the village, and this may give us some indication as to what once happened there. In fact, the text of the Tamu *pye* tells me the meaning:

Ha Ha Kohla Sõpre Tohmiyā Suji Cūmaiba?
Ha Ha Yoja Kohl Lemmai Nohmae Khemaiji Kohla Cūmaibā!

Question: *Who founded the village of Kohla?*
Answer: *The founders of Kohla are the ancestors of the three clans known as Yoja, Kohl and Lemmai!*

The story that I know goes like this: the three ancestors did not each settle one section of the village, as many people think, but rather settled and lived together at the beginning. They happened upon the location of Kohla one day when hunting, and they chased a deer into the clearing which is the present site of Kohla. As they entered, they witnessed the fantastic location and decided to settle there after killing the deer. The hunters had carried some grain with them in their quivers, which they immediately planted at Kohla. They reasoned that if it sprouted and did well, then the location was habitable and fertile. Next year, when they returned to see how their crops had grown, they found a herd of animals eating the succulent crops. Realizing that the land was fertile, they decided to live there and promptly set off to call their families and villagers who were living higher up the mountain at Rabrõ Toh above Kohla. Kohla is known as 'the three villages' on account of the many people who came to settle there after our ancestors first moved there. The settlement soon became so large that it had to be divided into three sub-divisions. Many people think that Kohla is the first place that our ancestors all lived together, but the reality is really the opposite. Kohla is actually the last village at which all our ancestors were

gathered together in one place and is the final village on our historical migration route. Our ancestors had been living together for a very long time before they all moved to the fertile lands of Kohla. This is why I believe that Kohla may be much 'younger' from an archaeological perspective than other ruins of villages higher up the mountain from which our ancestors migrated.

To be quite clear, the first settlement in the whole area for the ancestors of all the Tamu people was Cõ or Ũicõ Hyul. When our ancestors were here, they were not known as Tamu or Gurung but rather as *mihnāku*, a term which has no meaning to my knowledge. (According to Turin, the first element of this interesting ethnonym, *mih*, may be a reflex of the well-attested Tibeto-Burman lexical item *mi* 'man, person, human'. Moreover, it is worth noting that a settlement north of Kangding, in dkar mdzes/Ganzi prefecture in Tibet, is known as 'Mynak', written Tibetan *mi nyag*. The area is known to be inhabited by nomads and agriculturalists, and is home to many Buddhist monasteries of the Sakya school which is also the sect overwhelmingly represented in Mustāng gompas. Originally the home of speakers of the now extinct Tangut language, who were known as Minyag by the surrounding Tibetans, there are still some speakers in Mynak who speak a little-known Tibeto-Burman Qiangic language notable for its phonemic tone.) Only after our ancestors came down the hill and settled in Sa Pu Ti Kyhālsā did they come to be known as *Tamu*, through interbreeding with other people. There is a detailed explanation for this, all of which is mentioned in the *pye*, but some of it is secret. Only after our ancestors settled in Kohla, did they come to be known as *Gurung*. This name was given to the Tamu people by the local Hindus, who wanted some way to distinguish between their own Hindu *guru* 'learned one, teacher, religious practitioner' and Tamu shamans, which they called *Gurung*.

The tale of the two sisters
One day, many years ago, two Tamu sisters were lying asleep together. At midnight, the elder sister called Kali Gyhāmu stood up and walked off in her sleep, got lost and turned into the Kāli River. In Nepali, this river is known as the Kāli Gandaki, while we Tamu still refer to it as Kali Syõ because Kali Gyhāmu walked quietly and the river also moves silently. Anyway, in the early morning, the younger sister called Mharsyõ Gyhāmu arose, noticed that her sister had gone, and crying copiously, set off to find her. As she ran, she made lots of noise and screamed loudly, and she turned into what the Nepali speakers call the Marsyangdi river, which in Tamu is known as Mharsyõ Syõ. This explains why the Kāli Gandaki is such a silent river, while the Marsy-

43

angdi is so noisy. All of this is also explained in the *pye*. The parents of these two sleeping sisters are the direct ancestors of the Thakāli people, since they lived in this valley. In the Tamu ritual language (CK), *tha* means 'to reach, find', and *Kali* was the name of the daughter they were looking for.

The story and origin of the Klye (Ghale)

The man popularly referred to as the Ghale Rājā 'the Ghale king' or 'king of the Ghales' was actually the bastard son of Guru Rinpoche and a nun. Guru Rinpoche was ashamed of having impregnated a nun, so he asked her to say nothing of this event to anyone else. The nun emerged pregnant from a long period of meditation, and when questioned about her state, she explained that a mouse had made two holes in the walls of the mountain cave in which she was meditating and that sunlight from one side and moonlight from the other shone on her stomach at the same time, causing her to become pregnant. To this day, the Klye's ancestors are know to the Tamu people as 'sunbeams' and 'moonbeams'.

At the time of Kohla's prominence, there were many other branches of Tamu peoples living in villages and settlements of a smaller size. The man known as the Ghale Rājā was not really a king—he was just the village leader in one of the places that Tamu people settled — and he quickly demanded their loyalty. In the Tamu ritual language (CK), the Ghale Rājā was first known as Kyālbu Ruju, then he became known as Kyālbu Krōh and finally as Klye Mrũ. The meanings are as follows: *kyālbu* is a clan name, *ruju* literally means 'horn', but also has the metaphorical meaning of 'someone who fights with others and shows his strength', *krōh* means 'leader, headman of a village', while *mrũ* indicates someone who is a visionary and has foresight or who is a born leader.

Long before Kohla was settled, Klye Mrũ wanted to become king and leader of the area. The Tamus didn't like him nor did they accept him as their undisputed leader, so they left the five villages of Lisõ Yhul in Manāng to settle in the primarily Ghale village of Maiju where they intermarried with the Ghale people. One day, there was a massive landslide in Maiju, after which the Tamu people were completely dispersed and settled in different places. The Klye Mrũ nevertheless demanded allegiance, and while most Tamu clans gave in and agreed, two or three clans resisted and were forced to leave the area to settle elsewhere. After Kohla was settled, the Klye Mrũ became angry since people were settling in and around Kohla and establishing new settlements without accepting his sovereignty of the region and also without clearing their movements with him first. The Klye Mrũ insisted that all the villagers pay tax to him in exchange for his permission to settle

in the area. In Kohla, serious disagreements emerged between Tamu ancestors about whether or not to ally with the Klye Mrũ. The Tamu eventually got rid of the Klye Mrũ and in Klye Pal Ti Nềh, below Kohla, they chopped off his leg as described above.

The Klye Mrũ was the first king under whose control our ancestors came, and it was by no means a positive experience. Our Tamu people had leaders and headmen, but not kings, and the clans and social divisions in Tamu society predate the arrival of the Klye Mrũ. The fractions and tensions in our society date to the period of the rule of the Klye, and artificial divisions were created in Tamu society at this time causing tensions and disagreements which exist to the present day. We have the Klye Mrũ to thank for the tensions and divisions in Tamu society today. As a historical footnote, I should add that the Tamu people only came under the control of the kings of Kāski and Lamjung after the destruction of Kohla.

Lẽmakõ Rõh Pye

JUDITH PETTIGREW, YARJUNG KROMCHAĨ TAMU & MARK TURIN

Lẽmakõ Rõh Pye is chanted by the *pachyu* shamans in the *serga* ritual on the third day of the *pai laba* death ritual and is part of the process of sending the dead to the Afterworld. It is a 'question' and 'answer' *pye* as the shamans form two groups with one group chanting the questions and the other the replies. *Lẽmakõ* is one of the longest *pye* and differs from other texts in terms of topic and content. Most *pye* relate the story of specific local events and people. *Lẽmakõ*, on the other hand, is an epic as it speaks of human and animal origins, the names of the places the Tamu-mai migrated through, deals with conquest, affiliation and resistance as well as recounting a series of events in Kohla and its environs.

Lẽmakõ Rõh Pye is 509 lines long and can be subdivided into a series of different sections. Lines 1 to 15 are preparatory. They explain the significance of the *pye*, why it should be performed and what will happen if it isn't. Whatever their topic, *pye* begin with the creation and origins of the main actors and the subsequent section recounts the creation of humans, a people called the *minakuju*, animals and birds.

In the following sequence, the *minakuju* look out over their locality and then they move (Figs. 2.4 & 2.5). There are no explanations as to what prompted them to relocate, although we are told that they moved in a southwards direction and that members of the group scattered out in different directions. At Kaipatiye, they changed their name and become *mhinakugi*, which according to Yarjung is because they split off from a larger group. Lines 42 to 79 recount the meeting with a man named Nochani followed by a series of discussions regarding his origins, his ancestors, what food he ate, his physique and what work he did. He asked to stay with the *mhinakugi*, was given permission and married and had children. His children were named Lam, Lem and Kon and they were the ancestors of the present-day Sōgi clans. At this point in Sa-Pu-Ti Kyhalsaye, the group became Tamu.

Line 80 marks the beginning of another series of migrations which took the Tamu-mai through a series of named but undescribed localities (see Fig. 2.5 above). By line 110 they had reached Muchhitracham-goye (Muktinath). In Upper Manāng (Lho Mantāng) they encountered a Tibetan king named Khamba Rājā. This meeting is not included in Yarjung's version of *Lēmakō Rōh Pye* below, however, some *pachyus* have stories about this ruler. The Tamu-mai moved into present-day Manāng where they met the Klye (Ghale) chieftains who ruled the area. The biggest Tamu village in the area was Maiju where they lived for a long time as it is surrounded by good hunting forests. Following a landslide at Maiju (which is the place where the paths of humans and those of the dead separate), the pattern of reconnaissance and migration continued and they moved down towards Kohla. The Klye followed them, and on top of Ekrai Mountain (which is above the town of Chāme in Manāng) demanded that they subjugate themselves to him. Some clans agreed and remained behind but others did not and moved away.

Line 144 describes how some clansmen came across Kohla when they were hunting. Line 150 describes the founding of the village and the arrival of the Klye ruler. Lines 155 to 171 provide descriptions of the number of houses in the various villages in the wider area. In line 186, the Klye announces the introduction of taxes. The remainder of the *pye* (lines 187 to 492) deal with the story of Lēmakō, the chieftain's assistant, who was appointed tax collector. The story chronicles the difficulties he faced when trying to collect taxes from his mother's brother, his curse, his death, the incorrectly perfomed death rituals which led to his inability to reach the Afterworld, his subsequent redemption and the redoing of his death rituals which freed him from liminal purgatory and enabled him to reach the Afterworld (for a summary of this story see Pettigrew & Tamu 1999).

Lēmakō Rōh Pye, chanted on the third day of the three-day core ritual of Tamu life, the *pai laba*, serves as a reminder that the rituals of death cannot be performed without certain essential objects, the co-operation of kin and the performance of appropriately trained ritual specialists. The consequences for deviating from these prescriptions are severe as

the deceased does not reach 'heaven' or become an ancestor. Rather, such deceased are trapped 'betwixt and between' the world of the dead and the living and between the human and animal form. *Lēmakō Pye* recounts the story of the beginning of taxation, how the social relations of hierarchy changed and how people resisted that change. Despite the emphasis on the importance of reciprocal kinship relationships, this *pye* also draws attention to individual agency as people sometimes go against what is believed to be the correct way to behave towards kin. *Lēmakō* was the last event that was made into a *pye*.

Interviews conducted in 2001 with 90 shamans confirmed the centrality and consistency of this text as they all have it in their repertoire. While some referred to the *pye* as *Chyumi Huidu Pye*, in all cases the story remains the same, although the perspective from which it is told may be different. In the version presented below, the story recounts the experiences of Lēmakō. When the *pye* is titled *Chyumi Huidu*, the emphasis is on the story of Lēmakō's mother's brother named Chyumi Huidu.

1   *sula sumaye pye sele? pedā klhyemaiba*
    Which *pye* to chant? *Pedā Klhyemaiba*[1]

2   *sula sumaye lhu sele? lhudā klhyemaiba*
    Which *lhu* to chant? *Lhudā Klhyemaiba*[2]

3   *tamu hyalsa hyulsaye pye sele pedā klhyemaiba*
    Let's chant the *pye* about the Tamu countries

4   *tamu hyalsa hyulsaye lhu sele lhudā klhyemaiba*
    Let's chant the *lhuda* about the Tamu countries

5   *lēmakō rōhmaye pye sele pedā klhyemaiba*
    Chant the *pye* of Lēmakō Rōh

6   *lēmakō rōhmaye lhu sele lhudā klhyemaiba*
    Chant the *lhuda* of Lēmakō Rōh

7   *tamu hyalsa hyulsaye pye aasesyā khaiju tamoba?*
    If we do not chant the *pye* about the Tamu countries, what will happen?

8   *lēmakō rōhmaye lhu aasesyā khaiju tamoba?*
    If we do not chant the *lhu* of Lēmakō Rōh, what will happen?

9   *targi la nibai mhargi tihrō chohlo aakhābago*
    We cannot reach Targi La Nibai Mhargi Tihrō[3]

---

[1] This *pye* is owned by *Pedā Klhyemaiba* (a guru, teacher, master). *Pedā* refers to the chants.

[2] *Lhudā* refers to the shamanic techniques, rules, guidelines, ways of behaving, being, concepts, etc.

[3] Two of the many names for 'heaven' in *Cō Kyui*.

45

10 *tamu hyalsa hyulsaye pye sesyā khaiju tamoba?*
If we chant the *pye* about the Tamu countries, what will happen?

11 *thori nghaisōye nasarō chohlo khābago?*
Can we reach Thori Nghaisō?

12 *tamu hyalsa hyulsaye pye sedo pedā klhyemaiba*
Chant the *pye* of the Tamu countries

13 *tamu hyalsa hyulsaye lhu sedo lhudā klhyemaiba*
Chant the *lhu* of the Tamu countries

14 *lēmakō rōhmaye pye sedo pedā klhyemaiba*
Chant the *pye* of Lēmakō Rōh

15 *lēmakō rōhmaye lhu sedo lhudā klhyemaiba*
Chant the *lhu* of Lēmakō Rōh

16 *tela mhide sōmade kemmnāmī khanarō kemaiba?*
Where were human beings created?

17 *mara krōngai nasarō mhi kekhamai*
Humans were created in Krōngai[4]

18 *singai nasarō mhi kekhamai*
Created in Singai[5]

19 *tohngai nasarō mhi kekhamai*
Created in Tohngai[6]

20 *sangai nasarō mhi kekhamai*
Created in Sangai[7]

21 *sangai nasrō khanarō kemaiba?*
Where in Sangai?

22 *ta uī chōye hyularō mhi kekhamai*
Humans were created in Uī Chōye country[8]

23 *uī chōye ye hyularō toh kedimai*
Villages were created in Uī Chōye country

24 *uī chōye ye hyularō syō kedimai*
Groups of villages were created in Uī Chōye country

25 *kyhāye kyhūye chahmaiji syō plīdimai*
Rivers filled up with fish

26 *pāhnam phonama chah maīji kōh plīdimai*
Jungles filled up with animals

27 *mhiye kōhjaye chahmaiji hyula plīdimai*
The country was filled with humans

28 *chyah kōhjye chahmaī ji syōdō nādō plīdimai*
Trees and bushes filled with birds

29 *ta chōye hyalsa hyulasaye tōhrōmi khaijyu tamaiba?*
What happened in Chōye country?

30 *chōye hyalsa hyulsaye tōhrōmi mhinakuju tadimai*
Mhinakuju were created in Chōye country

31 *mhinakuju rōhmaye chāmaiji hyula plīdimai*
The country was inhabited by the *Mhinakuju*

32 *chōye hyalsa hyulsaye tōhwaji ple nghyo khamai*
They looked out from their village in Chōye country[9]

33 *chōye hyalsa hyulsaye syōwaji ple nghyo yumai*
They looked out from their location in Chōye country

34 *ta uī chō whamaye hyularō khaijyu tamaiba?*
What happened in Uī Chō country?

35 *syaje, nhuje, lōje, chyōhwaje mhinakuju pūh yāmai*
East, west, south, north, the *Mhinakuju* spread out in all directions

36 *mhinakujuye khemaimi khaiju nghegaiba?*
What about the ancestors of the *Mhinakuju*?

37 *mara lōchhyobai tīhsa waji ple nghyo yumai*
They looked towards the south

38 *mara kaī patiye hyulara ple nghyo yumai*
They moved down to Kaī Patiye country

39 *kōhri syōride thoy umai mhinakugimai*
The *Mhinakugi* crossed rivers and travelled through different landscapes[10]

40 *sa-pu-ti kyhalsaye tohrōmi ple nghyo yumai*
They saw and moved down to Sa-Pu-Ti Kyhalsaye

41 *sa-pu-ti kyhalsaye tohrōmi suni tohmaiba?*
Who did they meet at Sa-Pu-Ti Kyhalsaye?

42 *nochani rōhmaye kheni charō tohmaiba*
They met Nochani Rōh

43 *kyōmi sula sumaye puh bhiji ngyoisu lamaiba*
They asked him who his family was

44 *kyōmi sula sumaye puh bhiji pōsu lamaiba*
They talked to him about his family

---

4 The first stage of creation. All animate things move through this and the following stages.
5 The second stage of creation.
6 The third stage of creation.
7 *Sangai* is earth. When beings and things are created, then they create other beings and things on earth.
8 *Hyula* is a *Cō Kyui* word which is now also used in *Tamu Kyui* to mean 'country' or 'homeland', but in this context it means 'locality' or 'territory'.

---

9 *Ple nghyo khamai* refers to 'reconnaissance' and looking for another place to move to.
10 At Kaī Patiye, nine ancestors separated from the larger group, the *Mhinakuju*, and became the *Mhinakugi*.

45 *kyōmi khanai pachhaī khalo, nochani rōhgo?*
'Where have you come from, Nochani Rōhgo?'

46 *kyōmi khanai mha chhaiñ khalo, nochani rōhgo?*
'Where have you wandered from, Nochani Rōhgo?'

47 *marō lōchhyobai tīhsa waje ple nghyo khalo*
'I have come from the south'[11]

48 *kyōye khe mai mi khaiju nghegaiba*
They walked about the ancestors

49 *kyōye khemāmi sugo bhimaība?*
'Who were your ancestors?'

50 *thebse thebai khemi mayām di goba*
'My most senior ancestor was Mayām Di'

51 *chahye prhirbaye khemi masyām di goba*
'Next was Masynām Di'

52 *chaye prhirbaye khemi paim nhāgyā goba*
'Next was Paim Nhāgyā'

53 *chaye prhirbaye khemi paim tihrgyō goba*
'Next was Paim Tihrgyōgo'

54 *chaye prhirbai khemi nhanāba khorlo goba*
'Next was Nhanāba Khorlogo'

55 *nhanāba khorloye chahmi nochani rōh goba*
'Nhanāba Khorloye's son is Nochani's Rōh'

56 *nochani rōhmi ngasyo mhinakugimai*
'Mhinakugimai, I am Nochani'

57 *kyōye chabai kāi jumi khaiju nghegai ba?*
'What food do you eat?'

58 *kuhlu whamaye syami ngaye kāigo ba*
'I can eat a whole goat or sheep in one go'

59 *kuiñdi kuboye nhojumi ngaye khugo ba*
'I can drink a large pot of wine'

60 *nhaju whamaye rijumi tino prīmō ba*
'One of my ears reaches to the ground and I sleep on it'

61 *nhaju whamaye rijumi neon prīmō ba*
'One of my ears covers me when I sleep'

62 *kyōye kedā kejumi khaiju nghegai ba?*
'What kinds of things can you do?'

63 *kaiñdu waji khabai pahleñ koilo khāmo ba*
'I can stop the monsoon streams which come from above'

64 *kyoro waji khabai nhāmru ya koilo khāmoba*
'If a hurricane comes from below, I can stop it'

65 *kyōye toh nibai syōrōde chhyonō pinoba*
'Let me stay in your village'

66 *tille, nghille, sōlle plhille, nhalle, nghachhyābu timai ba*
He stayed for one, two, three, four, five years

67 *tuhlle, ngille, prehlle, kulle, kuchhyābu timai ba*
He stayed for six, seven, eight, nine years

68 *ngeñbu teñhbu de kramo bhimai nochanirōhmi*
Nochani said 'I would like to marry'

69 *ngeñbu teñhbu de krano priñmai nochanirōhji*
Nochani got married

70 *ngeñbu krabai lisōra khaiju tamaiba?*
What happened after the marriage?

71 *puhja puhmaide khāno priñmai nochani rhō la*
Nochani had children

72 *chahsō wamade khāno priñmai nochanirhō la*
Nochani had three sons

73 *lam, lem, kōnade khāno priñmai ba*
Lam, Lem and Kōn were born

74 *klhyapai phipaide tano priñmai sa-pu-ti kyhalsō ra*
There was a *pai* at Sa-Pu-Ti Kyhalsaye

75 *tagrā hogrāde tano prīmai sa-pu-ti kyhalsō ra*
There was an argument at Sa-Pu-Ti Kyhalsaye

76 *kugi rōhmaye khemaini ngiya kōbago*
'Can we join the *Kugi* ancestors?'

77 *tamu whamade aata bisi tāju chhomaiba*
They had a meeting to decide 'yes' or 'no'

78 *tamu wamade tamu bisi tāju solaje*
They discussed this at a meeting

79 *sa-pu-ti kyhalsaye hyulaji tamu pō chhyāmai*
From Sa-Pu-Ti Kyhalsaye they became Tamu

80 *sa-pu-ti kyhalsaye hyulaji ple nghyo yumai*
They looked down from Sa-Pu-Ti Kyhalsaye

81 *syaje, nhuje, lōje chyōhje tamu pōhyam ai*
East, west, south and north the Tamu-mai spread out

82 *chhyōlō bhyōba ye nheni tahlu kaiñ ye hyularō chohyu je*
They arrived in Chhyōlō Bhyōba country

83 *khōsyala syōrō ple nghyoyu mai*
They saw the river of Khōsyala and moved down

---

[11] *Nochani* arrived from a place that was south of where the *Mhinakugi* were settled at that time.

84 *kohñri syõride tho yumai tamu rohñmai mi*
    Tamu people crossed many rivers and hills

85 *riñmyũwaye hyularõ ple nghyoyu mai*
    They saw Rimyũwaye country and moved down

86 *kohñri syõride tho yumai tamu rohñmai mi*
    Tamu people crossed many rivers and hills

87 *la tihiũwaye hyularõ ple nghyoyu mai*
    They saw La Tihiũwaye country and moved down

88 *kohñri syõride tho yumai tamu rohñmai mi*
    Tamu people crossed many rivers and hills

89 *chhairiñ waye hyularõ ple nghyoyu mai*
    They saw and moved down to Chhairiñ country

90 *kohñri syõride tho yumai tamu rohñmai mi*
    Tamu people crossed many rivers and hills

91 *sydõ waye hyularõ ple nghyoyu mai*
    They saw and moved down to Sydõ Waye country

92 *kohñri syõride tho yumai tamu rohñmai mi*
    Tamu people crossed many rivers and hills

93 *timyu kreye hyularõ ple nghyoyu mai*
    They saw Timyu Kreye country and moved down

94 *kohñri syõride tho yumai tamu rohñmai mi*
    Tamu people crossed many rivers and hills

95 *chyõhgara myaye hyularõ ple nghyoyu mai*
    They saw Chyõhgara Myaye country and moved down

96 *kohñri syõride tho yumai tamu rohñmai mi*
    Tamu people crossed many rivers and hills

97 *lam myabai hyularõ ple nghyoyu mai*
    They saw Lam Myabai country and moved down

98 *kohñri syõride tho yumai tamu rohñmai mi*
    Tamu people crossed many rivers and hills

99 *phreduñ waye hyularõ ple nghyoyu mai*
    They saw Phreduñ Waye country and moved down

100 *kohñri syõride tho yumai tamu rohñmai mi*
    Tamu people crossed many rivers and hills

101 *layutiye hyularõ ple nghyoyu mai*
    They saw Layutiye country and moved down

102 *kohñri syõride tho yumai tamu rohñmai mi*
    Tamu people crossed many rivers and hills

103 *sisarangi ni thõsara kyurõ ple nghyoyu mai*
    They saw Sisarangi Ni Thõsara river and moved down

104 *polusa polunghyorõ ple nghyoyu mai*
    Saw Polusa Polunghyorõ lake and moved down

105 *kohñri syõride tho yumai tamu rohñmai mi*
    Tamu people crossed many rivers and hills

106 *rhuni toh rhunisyõra ple nghyoyu mai*
    They saw Rhuni village and Rhuni river and moved down

107 *kohñri syõride tho yumai tamu rohñmai mi*
    Tamu people crossed many rivers and hills

108 *muli tõhnibai mulisyõra ple nghyoyu mai*
    They saw Muli village and Muli river and moved down

109 *kohñri syõride tho yumai tamu rohñmai mi*
    Tamu people crossed many rivers and hills

110 *muchhitra chahmgõye tohrõ ple nghyoyu mai*
    They saw and moved down to Muchhitra Chahmgõye[12]

111 *kohñri syõride tho yumai tamu rohñmai mi*
    Tamu people crossed many rivers and hills

112 *thĩni kyhalsõye hyulami ple mrõkha mai*
    They saw Thĩni Kyhalsõ

113 *thĩni kyhalsõye hyulami ple nghyoyu mai*
    They saw Thĩni Kyhalsõ and moved down

114 *thoye hyalsa hyulsa waji ple mrõkha mai*
    They saw the area of Thoye[13]

115 *thoye hyalsa hyulsa waji ple nghyoyu mai*
    They saw Thoye and moved down

116 *syõye hyalsa hyulsa waji ple mrõkha mai*
    They saw a river area

117 *muchhitra chahmgõ waji ple nghyoyu mai*
    They saw Muchhitra Chahmgõ and moved down

118 *manõ hyalsa hyulsa ple mrõkha mai*
    They saw the area of Manõ[14]

119 *manõ hyulaye tohrõmi khaiju tamaiba?*
    What happened in the area of Manõ?

120 *uiñ sõye hyulara paihju mruñ tamaiba*
    Uiñ Sõye country[15] had a Tibetan king

121 *lisõye hyulara klyeju mruñ tamai*
    The low country had a Klye king

122 *tagrã hogrã de tano priñmai manõ hyulara*
    In Manõ there was an argument

---

12 Present-day Muktināth.
13 Present-day Thāk Kholā.
14 Present-day Manāng.
15 Present-day Lho Mantāng.

48

123 *mhina kumaiye khemaimi charō chohyu mai*
The *Mhinakugi* ancestors arrived

124 *mhina kumai chohbai lisōra khaiju tamai ba?*
What happened after the *Mhinakugi* ancestors arrived?

125 *klyejuwhamaye rujuri mruñ tadimai ba*
The Klye became king

126 *prahaaga, nghawala, kyuruye tohmai ya charō tadimai*
There he founded the villages of Prahāga, Nghawala and Kyuru

127 *tagrā hogrāde tano prīmai manō hyulara*
In Manō there was an argument

128 *manō hyalsa hyulsaye tohwaji ple nghyokha mai*
He looked out from Manō

129 *maiju whamaye hyularō ple mrōyu mai*
He saw and moved down to Maiju country

130 *toh nibaisyōa chyōnō prīmaiba*
He made a village

131 *maiju whamaye hyularō khaiju tamaiba?*
What happened in Maiju country?

132 *tyudā tyuijuji myarno priñmai maiju hyulami +++*
A landslide covered Maiju country +++[16]

133 *lhaju phrebai hyula tano prñimai maiju hyula mi*
At Maiju the routes separated

134 *maiju whamaye hyulaji ple nghyokha mai*
Looking out from Maiju and moving down

135 *tara yekre ye lharōmi khaiju tamaiba?*
What happened on top of Ekrai?

136 *klyeju mruñmi charō chohdi mai*
The Klye king was there

137 *yuñma tāteñye chohrōmi pahlju theñmai ba*
He planted his feet wide apart on two stones on the path

138 *ngaju koiñbaye mhi maimi khōji kyulyado*
'Those who accept me, pass between my legs'

139 *krōmchhaiñ, mhauchhaiñ, kyapchhaiñ, lhegaiñ, yobchhai, kubchhaīn ye khemaimi mha aā kyulago +++*
Krōmchhaiñ, Mhauchhaiñ, Kyapchhaiñ, Lhegaiñ, Yobchhai and *Kubchhaīn*[17] ancestors did not pass between his legs +++

140 *hyurplā plenade toyamai mhinakuju mai*
The *Mhinakuju* returned

141 *thurchu wamaye toh waji ple nghyokha mai*
Looking out from Thurchu and moving down

142 *rabrō whamaye toh waji ple mrōkha mai*
Looking out from Rabrō

143 *rabrō whamaye tohwaji ple nghyokha mai*
Looking out from Rabrō and moving down

144 *kohla sōpreye tohmaiñ ya ple mrōkha mai*
Looking out to see Kohla Sōpreye

145 *kohla sōpreye tohmi ya suji chuñmaiñ ba?*
Who founded Kohla Sōpreye?

146 *pammai, kohlmai, lemaiye khe maiji kohla chuñmaiñ ba*
The *Pammai, Kohlmai* and *Lemai* founded Kohla[18]

147 *phaiblō barōde nheyuma charō chohyumai*
They discovered it while hunting

148 *mrōmrō toride mrōnō priñmaiba?*
What did they see?

149 *cheplā hyabaye hyulade mrōnō priñmaiba*
They saw a flat place

150 *tohde syodenga de syonopriñmai kohla tohrōmi*
They made a village

151 *klyeju whamaye mruñju mi charō chohyu mai*
The Klye king arrived

152 *tela kohla sōpreye tohrōmi khaiju tamai ba?*
What happened in Kohla?

153 *klyeju whamaye rujui mruñ tadi mai*
The Klye became king

154 *lēmkō hamaye rohñmi dware tadi mai*
He made Lēmko his assistant

155 *kohla sōpreye tohrōmi kuñju mi khaiju tamaiba?*
How many houses were at Kohla?

156 *kohla sōpreye tohrōmi prechyu kuñ chyomai*
At Kohla Sōpreye there were 80 houses

157 *kohla hyalsa hyulsaye tohrōmi khaiju tamaiba?*
What happened in Kohla?

158 *kohla hyalsa hyulsaye tohrōmi tōhju chyuñmaiba*
In the area of Kohla villages were founded

159 *ma krapu kohgarai tohromi khaiju kuñ mumai?*
How many houses were at Krapu?

[16] This line is followed by some secret lines which are only known to initiated shamans and have therefore not been translated.
[17] These are clan names. This line is followed by untranslated secret lines.
[18] This refers to the three clans who founded Kohla.

160 *ma krapu kohgarai tohromi nghyusyu kuñ chyomai*
In the area of Krapu there were 20 houses

161 *khuñidõ whamaye tohromi khaiju kuñ mumai?*
How many houses were at Khuñidõ?

162 *khuñidõ whamaye tohromi chyu kuñ chyomai*
In the area of Khuñidõ there were 19 houses

162 *chõmrõ whamaye tohromi khaiju kuñ mumai?*
How many houses were at Chõmrõ?

163 *chõmrõ whamaye tohromi pre kuñ chyomai*
In the area of Chõmrõ there were eight houses

164 *chikreñ whamaye tohromi khaiju kuñ mumai?*
How many houses were there at Chikreñ?

165 *chikreñ whamaye tohromi nghyusyu kuñ chyomai*
In the area of Chikreñ there were 20 houses

166 *pamrõ, hachu, mhichuye tohromi khaiju kuñ mumai?*
How many houses were at Pamrõ, Hachu and Mhichu?

167 *pamrõ, hachu, mhichuye tohromi sõchyu kuñ chyomai*
In the area of Pamrõ, Hachu and Mhichu there were 30 houses

168 *naudi rabrõye tohromi khaiju kuñmumai?*
How many houses were there at Naudi Rabrõ?

169 *naudi rabrõye tohromi ngago kuñ chyomai*
In the area of Naudi Rabrõ there were five houses

170 *lelkhu whamaye tohromi khaiju kuñ mumai?*
How many houses were there at Lelkhu?

171 *lelkhu whamaye tohromi chyu kuñ chyomai*
In the area of Lelkhu there were 10 houses

172 *tasa whamaye khowarõmi khaiju nghegaiba?*
What was at Tasa Khowa?

173 *tasa whamaye khowarõmi ta chyõmaiba*
Horses were kept at Tasa Khowa

174 *ta thullheye tohromi khaiju nghegaiba?*
What was at Thullhey?

175 *ta thulheye tohromi rabrõ, kyubrõde chyono priñmaiba*
Goats and sheep were kept there

176 *taprõ mhijyaye tohrõmi khaiju tamaiba?*
What happened at Taprõ Mhijya?

177 *chyumi huñdu ye khemi charõ chohdimai*
Chyumi Huñdu's ancestors arrived

178 *sula sumaide bisi ngyuisu lamaiba*
'Who are you?', asked the villagers

179 *sula sumaide bisi põsu lamaiba*
Villagers talked about who they were

180 *ngami lẽmakõ rohñmaye aasyõ kumaiba*[19]
'I am Lẽmakõ's mother's brother'

181 *chharga puhrga de sõnõ primai aasyõ kumaiji +++*
Mother's brother introduced himself +++

182 *nhasõ whamaye padõra khaiju tamaiba?*
What happened after that?

183 *kyalbo whamaye rujuimi chharga sõmaiba*
Kyalbo made an announcement

184 *kyalbo whamaye rujuimi puhrga sõmaiba*
The Kyalbo chieftain gave information

185 *chu kohla sõpreye hyulami ngaye hyulago*
'The Kohla Sõpreye area and country is mine'

186 *sermã whamade sailado hyulai mhimaiba*
'Villages have to pay tax'

187 *sermã sõmade saila pago lẽmakõ roh-mai*
'Lẽmakõ will collect the taxes'

188 *sermã sõmade saila pago dware rohñ mai*
'My assistant will collect the taxes'

189 *hyarplã plenade toyamai lẽmkõ rohmai ba*
Lẽmkõ went

190 *hyurplã plenade toyamai dware rohñmai ba*
The assistant went

191 *ma krapu kohñgarai tohrõmi lẽmkõ chohnimai*
Lẽmkõ reached Krapu village

192 *tagrã hogrãde tano primai lẽmkõ rohmi*
There was an argument with Lẽmkõ

193 *sermã sõmade sailal khãmai lẽmkõ rohji*
They paid tax to Lẽmkõ

194 *hyarplã plenade tokhaje lẽmkõ rohmi*
Lẽmkõ returned

195 *chohma khanarõ chohkhaje lẽmkõ rohmi*
Where did Lẽmkõ go?

196 *kya pomrõ hachuye tohrõmi lẽmkõ chohnimai*
Lẽmkõ reached Pomrõ Hachu village

197 *sermã sõmade sailalado tohngai mhimai ba*
He asked the villagers for tax

---

[19] *Āsyõ* means 'wife giver' and refers to those who have given a daughter in marriage to Lẽmkõ's lineage.

198 *sermā sōmade sailalado aangi chyōmai ba*
He asked Āngi Chyōma [mother's brother] for tax

199 *aasaila whamade aasaila lēmkō rohmai ba*
'No, no, won't give it to you, Lēmkō'

200 *tāju chhono priñmai tohngai mhimaini*
Villagers discussed this

201 *sermā sōmade aapiñmai aangi chyōmaimi*
Āngi Chyōma didn't give tax

202 *hyarplā plenade toyaje lēmkō rohmaimi*
Lēmkō returned

203 *kohla sōpreye tohrōmi lēma chohnimai*
Lēma reached Kohla Sōpreye

204 *sermā sōmade sailalano primai kohla sōrami*
He asked for taxes in Kohla Sōra

205 *tagrā hogrāde theno priñmai kyalbo ruji*
He argued with Kyalbo

206 *kyalbo rujuye ngarōmi lēma chohnimai*
Lēma returned to Kyalbo

207 *chharga puhrgade seno priñmai kyalbo rujuni*
He told Kyalbo what had happened

208 *kyōjabai tohrōmi khaiju nghegaiba?*
What happened in the other villages?'

209 *pomrō hachuye tohrōmi khaiju nghegaiba?*
'What happened in Pomrō Hachuye?'

210 *tagrā hogrāde theno priñji kyōjabai tohrōmi*
'There was an argument in the other villages'

211 *kyōye aasyō kumaye sermāmi khaiju nghegaiba?*
'What about mother's brother's tax?'

212 *aasaila wamade aasaila aasyō kumaila*
'I didn't bring it, I didn't bring [tax] from mother's brother'

213 *tagrā hogrāde theno priñji pomrō hachura*
'There was an argument in Pomrō Hachu'

214 *sermā whamade saila pago aasyō kumaila*
'You should bring tax from mother's brother'

215 *sermā whamade aasailasyā khaiju nghegaiba?*
'If I don't bring tax, what will happen?'

216 *kyōye kahuride pehñ wamo lēma roh go*
'I will sack you, Lēma, from your position'

217 *khaila khailade tanoprīmai lēma rohmi*
Lēma wondered what to do

218 *hyarplā plenade toyamai lēma rohmi*
Lēma went

219 *ma chhyodo wamaye syōrōmi lēma chohnimai*
Lēma reached the river of Chhyodo

220 *aangi wamaye chyōmaini lēma chohnimai*
Lēma reached Āngi Chyōma

221 *tagrā hogrāde tano priñmai chhyodo syōrami*
There was an argument in Chhyodo Syōrami

223 *hyarplā pleññade toyamai lēma rohmi*
Lēma left

224 *ta pomrō hachuye toh rōmi lēma chohni mai*
Lēma reached Pomrō Hachu

225 *tagrā hogrāde tano priñmai aasyō kumai ni*
He had an argument with mother's brother

226 *tagrā hogrāde tano priñmai toh nibai syōni*
He had an argument with the villagers

227 *kyāju thobaiye tāju chhomai lēma rohñmi*
'Lēma, this will be the end of our relationship'

228 *mhikareñ chokimai khuno priñmai lēma rohñji*
Lēma called the village leaders

229 *pahaye kuiñdi de krānō priñmai aasyō kumaila*
They charged mother's brother one pot of millet wine

230 *mghebai mejude pehnō prīmai aangi chyōmaila*
They charged Āngi Chyōma one milk cow

231 *tibai kregi ni hyobai kahyade pehno priñmai aasyō kumaila*
They charged mother's brother one *kregi* [turban]

232 *syōrbai chhyodo whamade phuno priñmai aangi chyōmaila*
They destroyed Āngi Chyōma's water mill by the river

233 *chihdō whama de thonō priñmai aasyō kumaila*
They punished mother's brother

234 *ngheju whamade thonō priñmai aangi chyōmaila*
They punished Āngi Chyōma

235 *mudō tihrbaye tagrā tano priñmai lēma rohmaini*
The argument with Lēma could be heard in the sky

236 *sadō tihrbaye hogrā tanō priñmai sasyō kumaini*
The argument with mother's brother could be heard in the river

237 *tagrā hogrāde tabai lisōra khaiju tamaiba?*
What happened after the argument?

238 *hyarplā pleñna de toyamai lēma ōrohō mi*
Lēma returned

240 *sabu tihrbai krolu jhonō priñmai aangi chyõmaimi*
Āngi Chyõmaimi cried very loudly

241 *mbu tihrbai krolu jhonō priñmai sasyō kumaimi*
Mother's brother cried very loudly

242 *pahrje sõmade põnō priñmai aangi chyõmaiji*
Āngi Chyõmaiji put a big curse on him

243 *pahrje sõmade põnōpriñmai aasyō kumaiji*
Mother's brother put a big curse on him

244 *kyõmi kohla sõpreye tohrōmi mha aa chohdo ba*
'You will not reach Kohla Sõpre'

245 *kyalbo whamaye rujuni mha aa tohdoba*
'You will not meet Kyalbo'

246 *neye chhainibai rhñye chhaini kyō tohdoba*
'You will get a horrible disease'

247 *nhãgabai nã aa nhõbaye padõra kyō mhadose*
'You will get lost before sunrise'

248 *ngesabai nã aa riñ bai padõra kyō sidose*
'You will die before sunset'

249 *kohla sõpreye mhimaini mha aa tohdoba*
'You will not meet the people from Kohla Sõpre'

250 *chhyodo syõrbai mōmaini kyō tohnese*
'You will meet the ghost of the water mill'

251 *pahrje sõmaje põnō priñmai aasyō kumaiji*
The curse given by mother's brother

252 *pahrje sõmade põnō priñmai aangi chyõmaiji*
The curse given by Āngi Chyõmai

253 *pahrje sõmade põbai lisõra khaiju tamaiba?*
What happened after the curse?

254 *neye chhai nibai rhiñye chhaini lēma tohnimai*
Lēma met with a horrible disease

255 *mōnibai hāniga lēma tohnimai*
Lēma met a ghost

256 *tuñje ryuino ga tayamai lēma rohñmi*
Lēma began to vomit

257 *muñje syalano tayamai lēma rohñmi*
Lēma began to get diarrhoea

258 *tahñyā koiba mhaiñsa phyobade tano priñmai ba*
The sun could not help him, the night could not help him

259 *thaami syomide nghyonō priñmai lēma rohñ mi*
Lēma's eyes became glazed

260 *Mharsō khlyo khlyo de noyamai lēma rohñ mi*
Lēma died

261 *Mharsō khlyo khlyo de noyamai lēma rohñ mi*
Lēma died

262 *kohla sõpreye tohrōmi mha a chohmaiba*
He could not reach Kohla Sõpre

263 *nhãsō raye padōra khaiju tamaiba?*
What happened after that?

264 *mhingaī mhichhyōde tanō priñmai kyalbo rujumi*
Kyalbo was very upset

265 *klhye paipde lēmo bhimai kyalbo ruji*
The Kyalbo chieftain performed a *pai* for Lēmo

266 *pachyu ni pahiñbo mhai chyõmai*
He didn't call a proper *pachyu* or *pahībo*[20]

267 *syaje mhaimāmi syaje aāyōmai*
He looked to the east, but couldn't find one

268 *nhuje mhaimāmi nhuje aāyōmai*
He looked to the west, but couldn't find one

269 *chyōhje mhaimāmi chyōhje aāyōmai*
He looked to the north, but couldn't find one

270 *pachyu mhaimāmi pachyu aāyōmai*
He looked for a *pachyu,* but couldn't find one

271 *pahiñbo mhaimāmi pahiñbo aāyōmai*
He looked for a *pahībo,* but couldn't find one

272 *khaiju whamaye pye tasi chu tamai?*
Why did this happen?

273 *aasyō wamade aapa bisi chu tmai*
Mother's brother didn't come

274 *syōla syõkōide aayōna chu tamai*
He didn't receive a gift of cloth from mother's brother, so it happened

275 *aoli kaiñde aayōna chu tamai*
He didn't receive a gift of rice from mother's brother, so it happened

276 *sundo chyu de aayōna chu tamai*
He didn't receive a gift of millet from mother's brother, so it happened

277 *nhasō wamade padõra khaiju tamaiba?*
What happened after that?

278 *ma lōji khabai syōla pachyuye chahriya charō chohh khamai*
From the south, a strange *pachyu* arrived

[20] This is the CK word for *klehbrī.*

52

279 *tāju wamade chhono priñmai kohla tohrami*
They gossiped in Kohla

280 *tagrā hogrāde tano priñmai kohla tohrami*
There was much discussion in Kohla

281 *pohñgi kaigide tano priñmai kohla tohra mi*
There was an argument in Kohla

282 *negai chhaigai de tano priñmai kyalbo rujuni*
Some people shouted at the Kyalbo

283 *syōla pachyuye chahjimi pai chyōmaiba*
The strange *pachyu* did the *pai*

284 *nha aa syobai mi aa syobai paijumi charō ladimai*
A *pai* that had not been seen or heard before

285 *thēhchu kyakyāde achōna pai chyōdimai*
The *pai* was done without the offer of a *thēhchu kyakyāde*[21]

286 *kohkyu thukyude aapina pai chyōdimai*
The *pai* was done without the offer of a *kohkyu thukyu*[22]

287 *playō kaiñ chanō charō ladimai*
The *pla* was made to eat rice[23]

288 *playō tāseno charō ladimai*
The *pla* was made to talk

289 *playō kyu thunō charō ladimai*
The *pla* was made to drink water[24]

290 *tiro whamaye pai lamai syōla pachyuji*
This strange *pachyu* did a one-day *pai*[25]

291 *pye aa rhiñbai pai lamai syōla pachyuji*
This strange *pachyu* did a *pai* without *pye*[26]

292 *lhu aa rhiñbai pai lamai syōla pachyuji*
This strange *pachyu* did a *pai* without *lhu*[27]

293 *nha sōraye padōra khaiju tamaiba?*
What happened after that?

294 *hyarplā plenade toyamai syōla pachyumai*
Syōla the *pachyu* left

295 *targila nibai mhargi tharō lēmko mha aa chomaiba*
Lēmko could not reach Targila and Mhargilharō[28]

296 *khebreñ la nibai mhabreñ lani mha aa chomaiba*
He couldn't meet the male and female ancestors

297 *thori nghaiñsōye hyularō mha a chohmaiba*
He couldn't reach Thori Nghaiñsōye

298 *khaiju whamaye hyularō lēmko chohnimai?*
What kind of place did Lēmko reach?

299 *ta heni nhobai chhajarō lēmko hcohnimai*
Lēmko reached a place between the mountains and the high pastures

300 *mhiji aachyobai chyhjyude leñmā chyōdimai*
He lived with creatures that people have never seen

301 *khaiju whamade chyōdimai leñma rōhmi*
What kind of a body did Lēma have?

302 *suñmi chyhsuñde payh dimai lēma rōhmi*
Lēma's mouth looked like a bird

303 *pahle siñye pahlju payhdimai lēma rōhmi*
Lēma's legs looked like wooden legs

304 *kohmi mraye kohjude payhdimai lēma rōhmi*
Lēma's body was like a door

305 *chabai kaijude ayōna meye kli chadimaiñ*
He couldn't get food, so he ate cow dung

306 *thuñbai kyude ayōna mye kuñ thuñdi mai*
He couldn't get water, so he drank cow urine

307 *peñju wamade peñjuli charō nghedi mai*
The sound of the voice was 'peju, peju'[29]

308 *kōhidulu mara khabai padōra pyedā klhyemaiba*
At the beginning of the monsoon, Pyedā Klhemai

309 *pyhadulu tusyuñ ye padōra, lhudā klhyemaiba*
At the beginning of the summer, Lhudā Klhemai

310 *chyhōmchhyobai tihsa waje pyedā klhyemaiba*
From the north, Pyedā Klhemai

311 *muchhitra chahmgōye hyulaji lhudā klhyemaiba*
From Muchhitra Chahmgōye, Lhudā Klhemai

312 *pachyu ngi nibai paihbo kumai ya charō chohyumai*
Seven *pachyu* and nine *paihbo* arrived

---

21 The *thēhchu* is a goat that is sacrificed by *pachyu* at the beginning of a *pai*. The *kyakyāde* is the goat that is sacrificed by the *klehbrī* during the first night of a *pai*.

22 A *kohkyu* is a sacrificial sheep which represents the deceased and the *thukyu* is the 'friend' sheep who acts as a companion on the journey to the Afterworld.

23 The *pla* is an effigy of the deceased.

24 These goings-on were considered to be bizarre. In a usual *pai*, activities such as eating and drinking are undertaken by representatives of the dead person such as a sheep.

25 The *pai laba* is a three-day ritual.

26 It is not possible to conduct an activity in a shamanic ritual without describing it first.

27 This refers to the shamanic objects without which it is impossible to perform.

---

28 Part of 'heaven'.

29 A strange, high-pitched noise.

313 *peñju wamade peñj li nghenō themaiba*
They heard the sound 'peju, peju'

314 *na kō wamade mi kō charō lamaiba*
They listened carefully with their ears, looked carefully with their eyes

315 *mrō mrō toride charō mrōmaiba?*
What did they see?

316 *suñmi chyhasuñ de mrōnō primai pa-chyu ngimai ji*
The seven *pachyu* saw that its mouth looked like the beak of a bird

317 *pahle sñye pahle mrōnō primai paihbo kumai ji*
The nine *paihbo* saw that its legs looked like wooden legs

318 *mraye kohdōya charō mrōmaiba*
They saw a body that looked like a door

319 *kyōmi sula sugode bisi ngyoisu lamaiba?*
They asked 'who are you?'

320 *kyōmi sula sugode bisi pōsuñ lamaiba?*
They said 'who are you?'

321 *ngami ma kohla sōpreye hyularbai lemā rōhgo ba*
'I am Lēma Rōh from Kohla Sōpreye' [he replied]

322 *kyōmi khaiju taside chu taloba?*
'How did this happen to you?' [they asked]

323 *ngami aasyō kumai ye pahrje ji mharsō khlyoyalo*
'I died from the curse of Āsyō Kumai'

324 *aangi chyōma ye pahrjeji mriñsō noyalo*
'I died from the curse of Āngi Chyōma'

325 *aasyōmai syōla syōkōide aayōna chu tasimo*
'I didn't get the special cloth from mother's brother, so this happened'

326 *kyāju wamade aatōna la kyā aayōmai*
'The route wasn't clear so I didn't find the way to La Kyā'

327 *thehëchu aayōna nghikyā aayōmai*
'I didn't sacrifice the goat, so I couldn't find Nghikyā'

328 *kohju, thujude aayōna thu aayōmai*
'I didn't sacrifice the sheep, so I didn't get a friend'

329 *syōla syōkōide aayōna tuhi nibai whai aayōmai*
'I didn't get Syōla Syōkōide, so I don't get warmth and shade'

330 *ngaye kohdā sōmaiya mha aa yōgoba*
'I didn't get a sheep to represent the body'

331 *targi la nibai mhargi tihrō chohlo mha aa yōgoba*
'I couldn't reach Targila and Mhargi'

332 *thori nghaisōye hyularō chohlo mha aa yōgoba*
'I couldn't reach Thoringhaisōye'[30]

333 *pabai pachyude pago bhimami*
'A real *pachyu* should have done it'

334 *aapabai syōla pachyude pano priñmaiba*
'The unreal *pachyu* did it'

335 *pabai paihbode pago bhimami*
'A real *paihbo* has to do it'

336 *aapabai syōla pachyude pano priñmaiba*
'An unreal Syōla *pachyu* did it'

337 *kyāju, tihju,nheju, mha aa yōgoba*
'Couldn't find the correct route and the resting-places along it'

338 *pye aa rhiñ bai pye laje syōla pachyuji*
'Syōla *pachyu* did it without a *pye*'

339 *lhu aa rhiñbai lhu laje syōla pachyuji*
'Syōla *pachyu* did it without a *lhu*'

340 *lhoyo wamade musyāna pachyu ngimaiba*
'Be kind', seven *pachyus*

341 *lhoyo wamade musyāna paihbo kumaiba*
'Be kind', nine *paihbos*

342 *marō kohla sōpreye tohrami chharga sōbino*
'In Kohla Sōpreye village, chant the story'

343 *marō kohla sōpreye tohrami puhrga sōbino*
'In Kohla Sōpreye village, explain the problem'

344 *phyoguru nhig gade lanō primaiba*
The creature bowed to them seven times

345 *hyrplā pleñnade toyamai pa-chyu ngimai mi*
The seven *pachyu* went

346 *hyurplā pleñnade toyamai paihbo kumai mi*
The nine *paihbo* went

347 *ma kohla sōpreye tohrami pa-chyu ngimai chohni mai*
The seven *pachyu* reached Kohla Sōpreye village

348 *ma kohla sōpreye tohrami paihbo kumai chohnimai*
The nine *paihbo* reached Kohla Sōpreye village

349 *sōgyāpuhñye kohisōra pa-chyu ngimai chohnimai*
The seven *pachyu* reached the village crossroads

---

30 Part of 'heaven'.

350 *sōgyāpuhñye kohisōra paihbo kumai chohnimai*
The nine *paihbo* reached the village crossroads

351 *tōkhu syōkhu tano priñmai sōgyā puhñrami*
The villagers gathered at the crossroads

352 *paimo wamade aapaimo toh ngain mhimaiba?*
'Did anyone die in this village?'

353 *mhaimo wamade aa mhaimo syōngai mhimaiba?*
'Was anyone from this village lost?'

354 *tōimo wamade aatōimo toh ngain mhimaiba?*
'Did anyone from this village leave?'

355 *ngyoisu pōsu de lano priñ mai toh ngain mhimaini*
They asked the villagers

356 *aapa wamade aapaimo pachyu ngimai ba*
'Nobody died, seven *pachyu*'

357 *aamha wamade aamhaimo paihñbo kumai ba*
'Nobody died, nine *paihbo*'

358 *aatō wamade aatōimo pachyu ngimai ba*
'No one died, seven *pachyu*'

359 *tōimo, mhamo, paimo de bhino priñmai pachyu ngimaiji*
'Someone must have died, must have died', said the seven *pachyu*

360 *leñmā rohñ ride pano priñlo pachyu ngimaiba*
'One Lēma died, seven *pachyu*'

361 *leñmā rohñ ride mhamo priñlo paihñbo kumaiba*
'One Lēma died, nine *paihbo*'

362 *lēmā rohñ ride tōno priñlo pachyu ngimaiba*
'One Lēma died, seven *pachyu*'

363 *klhyapai phipaide lanō priñje kyalbo ruji*
'Kyalbo did the Klhyapai Phipaide'[31]

364 *targi la nibai mhargithirō chohlo khājegō*
'He reached Targi La and Mhargithirō'

365 *thedo wamade thedose tohngaiñ mhimaiba*
'Listen, listen villagers'

366 *thedo wamade thedose syōngaiñ mhimaiba*
'Listen, listen friends'

367 *targi la nibai mhargithirō lēmā mha aachohgoba*
'Lēma did not reach Targi La and Mhargithirō'

368 *thori nghaisōye hyularō mha aachohgoba*
'He did not reach Thori Nghaisōye'

369 *kheni wamaye māniyā mha aachohgoba*
'He did not meet the male and female ancestors'

370 *ta heni nhobaye chhajārō leñmā chohnimu*
'Lēma is not between the mountains and the high pastures'

371 *suñmi chyhasuñde pyhadimo leñmā rhoñla mi*
'Lēma's mouth looks like a bird's beak'

372 *kohmi mraye kohjude pyhadimo leñmā rhoñla mi*
'Lēma's body is like a door'

373 *pahle siñye pahlede pyhadimo leñmā rhoñlami*
'Lēma's legs look like wooden legs'

374 *chabai kaiñjude aayōna myakli chadimu*
'He has no food, so he eats cow dung'

375 *thuñbai kyude aayōna myakuñ thuñdimu*
'He has no water, so so drinks cow urine'

376 *peñ ju whamade peñjuli charō nghedimai*
'He cries "peju, peju"'

377 *lasu sebaye padōra kyalbo choh khaje*
During this story Kyalbo arrived

378 *shharga sōmade selo khāje pa-chyu ngimaiji*
The seven *pachyu* finished telling their story

379 *puhrgade sōmade selo khāje pahibo kumaiji*
The nine *pahibo* finished telling their story

380 *chharga puhrgade seba ye lisōra khaiju tamaiba?*
What happened after the story?

381 *tagreñ wamade kreno priñmai kyalbo rujumi*
Kyalbo got on a horse

382 *hyarplā plenade toyamai kyalbo rujumi*
Kyalbo went

383 *yhurplā plenade toyamai kyalbo rujumi*
Kyalbo went towards that place

384 *chohmami khanārō chohnimai kyalbo rujumi*
Where did Kyalbo go?

385 *ta heni nhobai chhajarō kyalbo chohnimai*
Kyalbo went to the place between the mountains and the high pastures

386 *peñju wamade peñjuli nghenō thimaiba*
He heard the 'peju, peju' sound

387 *kyōmi ngaye leñmā rhñgode bisyāga*
'If you are my Lēma' [he said]

---

[31] CK word for *pai*.

388   *phyoguru lajide kohibora syokho se*
'Bow to me and come to my lap'

389   *chharga wamade sōji khadu hyapyōmai*
He said this and threw down the shawl

390   *kuthu wamade kuthuli phyoguru lamaiba*
He bowed nine times

391   *khadu wamade puhrōmi lēmā syokhamai*
Lēma came to the shawl

392   *hyarplā plenade toyumai kyalbo rujumi*
Kyalbo returned

393   *hyurplā plenade toyumai kyalbo rujumi*
Kyalbo returned

394   *ma kohla sōpreye tohrōmi kyalbo chohyumai*
Kyalbo returned to Kohla Sōpreye village

395   *khaima khaijude lababisi tāju chhomaiba*
He organized a meeting to decide what to do

396   *klhyapai phipaide labo tāju chhol khāmai*
We will have to do the *pai* again

397   *pachyu nibai pahibō maini ngyoisu lamaiba*
He asked the *pachyu* and *pahibo*

398   *Pachyu nibai pahibōmaini pōsu lamaiba*
He requested the *pachyu* and *pahibo*

399   *syōla syōkōide aayōsyā sipai mha aa tagoba*
'Without a cloth from mother's brothers, we cannot conduct the death ritual'

400   *kohdā sōmade aayōsyā rhipai mha aa tagoba*
'Without a sheep to represent the body, we cannot conduct the death ritual'

401   *thechu, kyakyāde aayōsyā sipai mhaa ta*
'Without a sacrificial goat, we cannot conduct the death ritual'

402   *kohkyu thukyude aayōsyā syopai mhaa ta*
'Without a companion sheep, we cannot conduct the death ritual'

403   *aasyō kumaye hāsyulu sodo kyalbo ruju*
'You have to invite mother's brother, Kyalbo chieftain'

404   *tohkhu syōkhude ladose kyalbo ruju*
'You have to invite the villagers, Kyalbo chieftain'

405   *mhōkhu synokhude ladose kyalbo ruju*
'You have to invite the relatives, Kyalbo chieftain'

406   *riñni chahmimai khudose kyalbo ruju*
'You have to invite the female relatives, Kyalbo chieftain'

407   *tahkhu ngeñ khude ladose kyalbo ruju*
Kyalbo gathered his relatives

408   *chharga puhrgade sōlo khāje pachyungimaiji*
The *pachyu* gave the messages

409   *chharga puhrgade sōlo khāje pahibokumaiji*
The *pahibo* gave the messages

410   *hyarplā plennade toyamai kyalbo rujumi*
Kyalbo went

411   *hyurplā plennade toyamai kyalbo rujumi*
Kyalbo went

412   *kya pnomrō hachuye tohrōmi kyalbo chohnimai*
Kyalbo reached Pomrō Hachuye

413   *yodō whamade aakurna chihdō kurnimai*
He started to bow

414   *ra ru whanade aakurna kyu ru dō kurnimai*
He bowed like the horns of a sheep

415   *kehñti pahtide noyamai kyalbo rujumi*
Kyalbo took bread and wine

416   *mar te mai tede noyamai kyalbo rujumi*
Kyalbo took gold and silver

417   *kregi kohilide noyamai kyalbo rujumi*
Kyalbo took a turban

418   *phyola phokurude lano priñmai kyalbo rujumi*
Kyalbo bowed again

419   *syōla syōkōide nonose aasyō kumaiba*
Give the cloth, mother's brother

420   *syōla syōkōide nonose aangi chyōmaiba*
Give the cloth, Āngi Chyōmaiba

421   *syōla syōkōide mha aa pimai aasyō kumaiji*
Mother's brother did not give the cloth

422   *syōla syōkōide mha aa pimai aangi chyōmaiji*
Āngi Chyōmaiji did not give the cloth

423   *hyarplā plenade toyamai kyalbo rujumi*
Kyalbo left

424   *hyurplā plenade toyamai ukyalbo rujmi*
What happened next?

425   *kya kohla sōpreye tohrō kyalbo chohnije*
Kyalbo reached Kohla Sōpreye Tohrō

426   *nhasō whamaye padnora khaiju tamai ba?*
What happened next?

427 *phaanle warabai rohñride thahnō priñmai ba*
He chose a cunning person

428 *pobaji tōhaa korbai padōra kyalbo ruji*
Before dawn, Kyalbo chieftain

429 *chyahbra chyuhbaruji hyul aa korbai padōra kyalbo ruji*
Before the birds wake, Kyalbo chieftain

430 *obaji nā aa nhōbai padōra kyalbo ruji*
Before the cock crows, Kyalbo chieftain

431 *mhainō baye padōra kyalbo ruji*
At midnight, Kyalbo chieftain

432 *warbai rhōriya kulnō primaiba*
He sent the cunning person

433 *hyarplā plenade toyamai warbai rhō mi*
The cunning person went

434 *kya pōmrō hachuye tohrōmi chohno priñmaiba*
He reached the village of Pōmrō Hachuye

435 *asyō kumaiye tohrō chohno priñmaiba*
He reached mother's brother's village

436 *klhyaye mharbasōra chohnimai Asyō kumaila*
He reached mother's brother's house

437 *phiye mriñsōra chohnimai angi chyōmaila*
He reached Āngi Chyōmaila's house

438 *kiñ kiñ toride kino priñmai warbai rhoñji?*
What did the cunning person take?

439 *rheñdo myurbai naaride kinō priñmaiba*
He took a little bit of left-over millet from the hole in the centre of the quern

440 *rheñdo phyolude kinō priñmaiba*
He took a small piece of cleaning cloth from the quern

441 *kundō dhuñrbai suiñngrā de kino priñmaiba*
He took a little bit of left-over rice from the foot grinder

442 *hyurplā plenade toyumai warbai rhñmi*
The cunning person left

443 *kohla sōpreye tohrōmi warbai chohkhaje*
The cunning person reached the village of Kohla Sōpreye

444 *kohla sōpreye tohrōmi khaiju tanaiba?*
What happened in Kohla Sōpreye?

445 *klhyapai phipaide tanō priñmai leñmā rhōla mi*
The *pai* began[32]

446 *sipai rhopaide tano priñmai leñmā rhōlam*i
The *pai* began[33]

447 *kohidi kohipade chhono primai leñmā rhōlami*
It was arranged for Lēma

448 *kohidi kohiside dhōnō primai leñmā rhōlami*
It was arranged for Lēma

449 *rhalmō rhiñye mhajimi kyā lōmaiba*
The soul of a goat was sent as a friend

450 *rhalmō rhīye mhajimi teh chumai ba*
The goat started the ritual[34]

451 *lhuye whamaye kohñjaji koh chyuiñmaiba*
The sheep represented him

452 *lhuye whamaye kohñjaji thu chyuiñmaiba*
The sheep became his friend and porter[35]

453 *rheñdō myurbai naariji sundō chyu lamaiba*
Millet from the centre hole of the quern was given as special grain

454 *rheñdō wamaye phyoluji syōla syōkōi lamaiba*
A piece of cloth collected from quern was used as mother's brother's cloth

455 *kuni dhuñrbai suiñngrāji oli kaiñ lamaiba*
Rice from the foot grinder was cooked and made into rice offering

456 *tabai wamaye rhijega rhitemai*
Doing the correct ritual

457 *rhalmō wamaye rhiji mai chyōmai*
Completed with the goat

458 *chyhane kone rhiñji ne kōmai*
Completed with the birds

459 *klhyapai phipai lano khāmai leñmā rhōlami*
Lēma's *pai* was finished

460 *targi la nibai mhargi tihrō leñmā chohnimai*
Lēma reached Targi La Nibai Mhargi Tih

461 *aaji khenibai aajimāni leñmā chyhlni mai*
Lēma joined Āji Khe and Āji Mā[36]

---

32 The type of *pai* which is conducted immediately after death and in a house with an ancestral shrine.

33 The type of *pai* which is conducted some time after death and for a house that does not have an ancestral shrine. This *pai* is less elaborate and less expensive.

34 This refers to the sacrificial goat without which a *pai* cannot begin.

35 This refers to the 'friend' sheep and is different from the one which represents Lēma. The role of this sheep is to act as a friend and porter to carry his things on the way to 'heaven', and to assist and make things easier for him.

36 The male and female ancestors from the place of creation.

462 *khebreñla nnibai mhabreñla ni leñmā chyhlni mai*
Lẽma joined Khebrenla and Mhabreñla[37]

463 *lakuti nibai nghikutini leñmā chyhlni mai*
Lẽma joined the nine moon and the nine sun ancestors

464 *thori nghaisōye hyularō leñmā chyhlni mai*
Lẽma reached the area of Thori Nghaisōye

465 *iñji tehwa chaiñgiye singarō leñmā chyhlni mai*
Lẽma reached Iñji Tehwa Chaiñgiye Singa[38]

[The next three lines are secret. They explains that unless this text is chanted, it is impossible to reach heaven]

466 *chaye wamaye pyerō +++*

467 *chaye wamaye lhurō +++*

468 *pūhda jhōnn +++*

469 *nhāsō wamaye padōra khaiju tamiaba?*
What happened next?

470 *tagrā hogrā de tano primai kohla hyularō*
A fight began in Kohla Hyula

471 *pōhgi kaigide tanō primai kohlai hyhular*
An argument began in Kohla Hyula

472 *negai chhaide tanō primai kohlai hyular*
That fight got worse in Kohla Hyula

473 *pōmrō hachuye tohwaji pōhgi chhaimaiba*
The argument reached Pōmrō Hachu

474 *chigreñ whamaye tohwaji pōhgi chhaimaiba*
The argument reached Chigreñ

475 *chōmrō khuñidoye tohwaji pōhgi chhaimaiba*
The argument reached Chōmrō

476 *krapu kohñgarai tohwaji pōhgi chhaimaiba*
The argument reached Krapu

477 *ta naudi nghidkuye tohwaji pōhgi chhaimai ba*
The argument reached above Naudi Nghidku

478 *rabarō lelkhuye tohwaji pōhgi chhaimai ba*
The argument reached above Rabarō Lelkhu

479 *chharga sōmade chhomaiba hyulai mhimaiji*
People all over the Hyula knew of the argument

480 *pōhda kaidade tano primai ba*
The argument continued

481 *khaiju whamade tsiga negai tamaiba?*
Why did this fight happen?

482 *khaiju whamade tsiga chhaigai tamaiba?*
Why did this argument happen?

483 *kyalbo whamaye rujumi mha aa khoibago*
Kyalbo did not understand

484 *kyalbo whamaye rujuji kōichhyā aalabago*
Kyalbo did not care

485 *sermā sōmade syoji chamaiba kyalbo ruji*
Kyalbo took the taxes and ate them

486 *khwaye whamaye nhōrōmi theñlo mhaibago*
He wanted to put everyone under his feet
[i.e. dominate them]

487 *chabai saimaiye ruju tahñmaiba*
The headman selected the best food

488 *thuñbai whamye kyu ruju tahñmaiba*
The chieftain selected the best water

489 *nhasō whamaye padōra kyalbo rujumi*
Next day, Kyalbo chieftain

490 *tiryai tano primai kyalbo rujumi*
Kyalbo was alone

491 *miryai tano primai hyulai mhimaimi*
Separate from the people of the area

492 *mhainhobaye padōra kyalbo rujumi*
At midnight, Kyalbo chieftain

493 *Parawa mharawa kiside plena de pleñ yamai kyalbo rujumi*
He took his family and left

494 *tiro, nghiro, sōro, pliro, ngaro roli kyalboye parawa mhachyō mai*
First, second, third, fourth and fifth of Kyalbo's family[39]

495 *syaphre tōhlode khānō prīmai tohngai mhimai mi*
Villagers looked to the east, west, south and north

496 *nhuphre tōhlode khānō prīmai tohngai mhimai mi*
Villagers looked to the east, west, south and north

497 *lōdohre tōhlode khānōprīmai tohngai mhimai mi*
Villagers looked to the south

498 *chyōhphre tōhlode khānōprīmai tohngai mhimai mi*
Villagers looked to the north

499 *chhyopliye nhōsōwaje klyemai nhechyōmai*
They looked in all four directions for the Klye family

---

37 Other male and female ancestors from the place of creation.
38 A part of 'heaven'.

39 This means they disappeared and were not seen for this number of days.

500   *ma khuiñdō whamaye tohrōmi klyeri syamaiba*
       They caught the Klye in Khudo

501   *klye whamaye pahlride chonō primai ba*
       [The Klye] had broken his leg

502   *klyeju whamaye puhmaimi syara chohnimai*
       The Klye's family went east

503   *klyenilamriye chahmai mi syara chunimai*
       His sons went east

504   *kaasi whamaye chahmi rimi lōji chu nimai*
       The youngest daughter went south

505   *nhasō rhaye padōra khaiju tamaiba?*
       What happened next?

506   *syaje nhuje lōchhybai tiñhsarō tamurhō pūhya mi*
       East, west and south, the Tamu people spread out

507   *Lēmkō rhōmaye pye seje pyedā klhyemai ba*
       Chant the Lēmkō *pye*

508   *Lemakō rhōmaye lhu seje lhudā klhyemaiba*
       Chant the Lēmkō *lhu*

509   *Bundsa khedu +++*

Looking back — looking forward
JUDITH PETTIGREW

The Kohla Project began with my conversation with Hom Bahādur Tamu that opened this chapter. How then do those who 'commissioned' the project evaluate it thirteen years later? In December 2005, I put this question to Yarjung, who replied:

> The Kohla Project was important, but because it was cut short we didn't really achieve very much. We identified our ancestor's villages and we found some material culture which originated from the north which helped provide proof of our northern origins. We dated some objects, but I do not think these were a good sample, and I think that the actual age of Kohla remains unknown. I am very excited that the numbers of houses at different villages listed in the *pye* make sense when calculations are done based on our contemporary population. This is fantastic and provides additional evidence for the historical accuracy of our oral texts. In the future, some of our young educated people will hopefully carry this work on. Nowadays no one is really interested in this research, people don't talk about it and they don't think about it. Maybe once our books are published they will become interested. I hope so. There are many Tamu-mai living in different parts of the world and I feel that we should be able to support such work ourselves. There is no reason why the Tamu-mai cannot raise funds for this research.

They can, and I believe that to preserve our cultural heritage, they must.

Despite Yarjung's relatively modest evaluation of the impact of the project, I think that there are achievements that he has overlooked. The Kohla Project is an example of a successful multi-disciplinary collaboration between community activists, foreign and Nepali archaeologists, a social anthropologist and a linguistic anthropologist. Multi-agency and professional-activist collaborations along these lines are relatively rare and have not previously taken place in Nepal. The Kohla Project opened up new ways of working for local communities, archaeologists and anthropologists, and plotted a potential route for how ethnic communities might collaborate with government archaeologists in the study of their past.

The project has undoubtably made a unique contribution to the study of Tamu ethno-history as the detailed archaeological findings of this book clearly attest. It was at times difficult to define a clear role for ethnographic research and this was made more complex by the findings of oral history interviews which provided little or no significant data. Furthermore, there were tensions both in the fieldwork and in the production of the text, as the project was overwhelmingly archaeologically orientated, which at times diminished the more implicit achievements of ethnographic enquiry. Despite the high profile of the archaeology, however, anthropology was intrinsic to the development and success of the work as it was dependent on the networks, linkages, cultural understandings, insights and brokerage skills that developed out of in-depth and long-term ethnography.

Political insecurity as a result of the Maoist insurgency prevented planned research on the *pye* in different districts. The meeting of shamans in December 2002, however, provided an alternative which enabled the essential comparative work on *Lēmkō Pye* to be undertaken. Further work on the *pye*, and its associated cultural knowledge, remains an essential element of research on the Tamu past, and a documentary project on the *pye* is due to begin in 2009. As additional work is undertaken, the full extent of the resource becomes clearer and the depth of the contribution it can make to understanding the history of the Tamu-mai better appreciated. The work undertaken to date has an important role to play in reminding Tamu-mai, regardless of their clan affiliations, that their coalesence as an ethnic group is rooted in antiquity. As the *pye* illustrates, clan tensions and arguments are not new. However, the ongoing over-attention to the Hindu-authored genealogies and their impact has distracted attention from the longevity and depth of these alliances formed in antiquity. Tamu-mai of *all* clans share a long history of collaboration, migration and co-existence. They have been together for a very long time, and there is much to celebrate in their shared past.

The involvement of linguistic anthropologist, Mark Turin, in the latter stages of the project highlighted the need for ethnolinguistic analysis, and this remains an important avenue for future exploration. The major publications arising out of the Kohla Project, this manuscript, and a planned anthropology-led book, should not be seen as the conclusion of the work but rather a catalyst for additional research. Furthermore, if Yarjung is correct, then publications such as these will continue to engage the Tamu community, thus increasing the possibility that further studies will be undertaken.

Chapter 3

A Trailside Archaeology — Survey Results

Christopher Evans
with contributions by Dorothy Allard & David Gibson

This chapter is concerned with the project's survey results. Before presenting these formal records, it is worth sketching something of the landscape and the route up to Kohla (the next chapter concludes with a comparable section, outlining our trek through Manang and Mustang, *Goin' north*). Trying to find an appropriate language to express land and its walking is always a challenge. It is not possible to capture the slog, rhythm and humour of the trail, nor the wrenching beauty of the country. Certainly there are words not to use ('poetics' or 'majestic', etc.) and neither a travelogue nor academic vocabulary seems right.

This section does not so much aspire to be a narrative or diary account, as a general chronicle (from the perspective of the archaeologists). It is intended to provide some sense of both the trail and camp-life, and convey something more than just 'the conditions of fieldwork'.

Travelling up

First, frantic days tearing around Pokhara in taxis, buying supplies and outfitting the local men (blankets, shoes, shirts and sweaters), who eventually come down from their vil-

B

C

Figure 3.1. *Travel rites: A) A shaman sits behind a chop figure during a Kohibo departure ceremony; B & C) a shaman's performance in Yangjakot, 1995.*

Figure 3.2. *Preparations: Yarjung oversees organizing of gear in Pokhara (top), packing the bus and distributing the loads for the trek ahead (below; top and middle photographs by A. Oswald).*

is usually a final group meal with the TPLS, with a chicken being slaughtered, whose entrails are first consulted (one season announcing 'the way will be difficult and the funds will run short ...') and then, following the ritual, it was duly consumed.

Then, at last, the leaving. We pack into (and on top of) a hired bus for a shaky hour's drive through the town's sprawling suburbs, and then up the river valley. From here on, it's on foot, four to five days up to Kohla. We're a party of some 25, including 15 men from the villages for portering — all food (including vast quantities of rice), fuel and supplies must be carried up. Upon stopping, loads are distributed; roughly 40–60 kilos each, with a man assigned to carry the survey equipment (a borrowed theodolite and knocked-up drawing boards: Fig. 3.2). The first day will get us to Yangjakot. It is along a major trail that serves a series of villages and, for part of the way, is common with the route to Siklis, and there are usually people on it.

The way goes over what we'll come to count as only high hills, and then down through the floodplain of the River Madi. After passing through fields, we cross the river on a spindly suspension bridge, having lunch under the shade of a great tree further up the far bank. (In 2000, some of our group were stopped near this spot, and questioned by a pair of earnest young men, 'Who are we and what are we doing in the country?'. Our naive explanation obviously sufficed, as we only later learned that they were local members of the [Maoist] Communist Party of Nepal.) Thereafter, the way is up. Basically, it's a long stairway along the ridges up through Hindu-community villages and terraced fields below, till, after four hours or so, Yangjakot is reached. Here, we'll stay for two to three days. It's a large village of some 400 houses, strung along the top of a ridge (there are no other villages above this level: Fig. 3.3). Coming up to it from the southwest, you enter its public space — first a corrugated steel-shed school, then a muddy watering hole, a temple up on a hill and a volleyball court. (There are also a couple of small shops, but they don't sell much and, apart from agricultural produce, people get what they need from Pokhara.) Perhaps a quarter of the houses lie on a separate knoll to the south, the bulk of the village lying on the north side. They're linked by a main throughway trail, a wide stone path running the village's length. The houses are densely arranged about it, terraced above and below. Though its very much a hard, stone-paved space, it has an almost nest-like quality (Fig. 3.45).

Coming in, we're a procession — kids, of course, gawk and trail behind, and people are pleasantly curious. After about ten minutes passing through, with a turn downslope, we've arrived at our host's house. (She's an extraordinarily vibrant and forceful individual, running the whole scene of the household-cum-farm. She was remarkably generous in her hospitality, and displayed great perseverance in the face of what must have been the stress of our eccentric record-

lages and assemble in the Kohibo. There formalities occur: various meetings, usually a reception (many speeches and garlanding) and then, before departure, a long ritual with shamans chanting, off in a corner in front of a ritual rice figure (bits of which must be consumed by those going up: Fig. 3.1). To those of us unfamiliar with local ritual practice, the extraordinary thing is that, apart from the final 15–30 minutes of some six hours, the ceremony goes on little noticed amid the chaos of departure — the sacred falling to second place behind the jostle of the profane. There

Figure 3.3. *Yangjakot village from the south.*

ing of her home, and the long questioning of her and her neighbours on matters of village life.) The house is big and well-appointed, and the men and gear crowd into the front yard. There are introductions (and later renewals, presents and pleasantries), with neighbours around to linger and stare. Many of our men come from the village and they will sleep in their homes. The cooks set up their kitchen in the yard for eating. Generally, there's a lot of simultaneous lingering and pandemonium; most socializing occurs on the porch, only the invited going into the house. Tired after the day's walking, bed is early.

The next day, there are things to organize. By late morning, needing respite from all the public hubbub, the archaeological team go off to view and later record a 'site' on the south side of the village. Later, it's time for the Mother's Dances — its a big event, with an awning erected in the yard, into which friends and neighbours are packed. It's vibrant and lively, and is accompanied by a fair amount of drinking of local beer and spirits. (It is usually in the 'exposed' atmosphere of the village that one or more members of the team get ill, having a few unpleasant days thereafter.) People linger long into the night, the archaeological team escaping early; it's still early days, and the need for some privacy still counts.

In 1995, we surveyed sites in the high ground, immediately above Yangjakot and the neighbouring village of Warchok. This required extended stays in both villages and trekking steeply upward for one to two hours each day. In an effort to ensure local support and explain what the project involved, we had a video-deck carried up to Yangjakot. Having to porter-in a hired generator and large television for viewing, this made for an absurd sight on the trail. We duly convened a meeting of the village's seniors, showing them both the plans and tapes of our work at Kohla from the

year before (Fig. 3.4). Well received, that evening we hosted a grand event in the village's central court. It was dusty and hot as hundreds crowded in to watch a public video screening (all hard-pressed given the size of the screen). They sat respectfully through the project's tape, thereafter growing a little restless through another that Yarjung had made of his father's life (also a renowned shaman). Then came the 'entertainment', as we also had brought other films. Yarjung's choice, Mr Bean, went down poorly, its humour being lost in translation (and misunderstood body language). The night ended with Jurassic Park, then recently released. The villagers' reactions indicated that, while much of its plot went unappreciated, they clearly warmed to the dinosaurs.

The following night, there was a 'Rodhi event' — the Rodhi being a type of chaperoned club for Tamu-mai young people. Usually involving dance parties, in this case an inter-village highland run had been arranged. Having reached the village, it was party time in the fields. With drums and the proverbial dancing, the festivities were punctuated by an old man (two sheets to the wind) firing off an ancient flintlock musket into the starry night skies (Fig. 3.4:B). (When surveying Nadar Pa on the rise above Warchok, late one day we were disturbed by a hunting party coming down from the uplands. It had been organized by a Gurkha officer, home on leave, though such pursuits are illegal within ACAP's territory. Involving some 10–15 men, bristling with guns, the group had the air of a safari. Having them come across us while working isolated in the woods, left us feeling vulnerable and exposed, and this encounter later served as a cautionary warning once the Maoists started operating in the area.)

On leaving Yangjakot, the men arrive early; there are new provisions to be redistributed, goodbyes and then

Figure 3.4. *Project meeting with village elders at Yangjakot (A); B) Rhodi event; C) Tinker's Band on leaving Yangjakot in '94.*

off once more. Above the village, the trail only rises slowly and, much of the day, it remains uncomfortably hot over this length. There are still a lot of people on the route, variously off to visit other villages and collecting wood or spring plants in the higher ground. An early lunch is taken after some hours by the spring point of Yangjakot's water. Just below, there's said to be the remains of a village. However, apart from a mortar husking stone and a few suggestive stone alignments, there is nothing too convincing. After-wards, it's off, first through forest (passing a man's shrine to his hunting dog) and then a steep climb. Camp is made at

a pastoral campsite, where there's water nearby. It's grassy and pleasant and a wise decision to stop, as we 'outsiders' are still getting used to the walking. As will become rou-tine, the men sleep and cook en masse in one of the large buffalo-type shelters. We've brought a big, gaudily-striped plastic cover to go over its standing timber frame, which can then serve as a group marquee (Fig. 3.10). It's cosy and fun inside, but generally, due to the needs of privacy (and in reaction to the noise and smoke within the 'circus big top'), the overseas team tend to sleep in their own tents. A small, upright stone has been erected near the spring point, *that has a few ritual offerings set about it. Similar settings will be encountered* en route. *When we ask our local colleagues about its significance, all are pretty dismissive, as such stones are relatively commonplace.*

The next morning, up again through dense forest, it's long and hot up to a high cliff, just below Karapu. The going's a bit dangerous, as the path up is narrow and steep. But, getting above the ridge, things change as there are stretches of open grassland and it's cooler. From here, it's only an hour's walk along the ridge to the ruins at Karapu and its dharmasala *lodge (this being a long open-room building, where local people, working or passing through an area, can take shelter, cook and sleep). There, we stop early to view and record the remains, and this proves an important turning point. The place is beautiful, with terrific views down over the cliffs and across the lowlands below to the south. The crest of the rise is commanded by a square, stone-walled enclosure, that seems to be some manner of fort. Around it are various walls, mounds and cairns. Yarjung is convinced that this is a large village site. Certainly, there are many stone settings (including more mortar stones) and probably a few ancient houses, but there are also a number of still-utilized pastoral shelters and many other settings, that could be of similar, albeit older, origin. (On the way down — having experienced real 'ancient' ruins — we have to re-appraise the site plan, downplaying its 'village' elements and upgrading its pastoral components.)*

Once gaining the cliff up to Karapu, the nights are much colder and there is often frost. (Leeches can be bad in the woods, and one advantage, as things cool, is that their numbers lessen.) At times, the deep rumble of avalanches from the Annapurna IV glacier can be heard. The mornings are superb, and the peaks of the Annapurnas are clearly in view. From here onwards, far fewer travellers are encountered. Taking the ridge-back trail north (much of the time along deeply cut erosion channels in the woods, but also at points along the steep scarp edge), the forest is thicker. Swathes of ash dot the steep slopes below, where woodland has recently been burnt-off and, at a distance, are blooms of smoke from slash-and-burn field-preparation. Down in the sides of the erosion channels, on the ridge itself, burning lines can be traced in their profile over distances. At some time, it should be investigated whether this is the result of sporadic forest fires or earlier arable burn-off.

An easy walk gets us to Khuindo, set in a small, alpine meadow valley. The ruins are different and the structures along its southern, wooded edge are robust and well-made. There is none of the ambiguity of their 'ancient' attribution, as there was at Karapu. From here, the trail goes up through meadow, then forest, and then a long, steep climb up to the ridge-top at Tapron. Above the tree cover, there is a rest lodge, where we stop for midday food. Awaiting its preparation, we go up to the ridge proper. At c. 3500 m a.s.l., it's the highest point on this route, and from here you can look

Figure 3.5. *Trailways: A) the rest platform with memorial to where the Ghale Raja lost his leg; B) lost in the jungle below Kohla; C) at the Tapron lodge.*

deep into the valley of the Gouch Khola. There, on the other side, breaking the cover, Kohla can at last be spotted (Fig. 3.6). It's a terrific moment, and appropriate location-fixing photos are taken. Yet it's not really this that strikes you, but the impossibility of the perspective beyond. From here, Kohla lies just below sight-level on forest ridges, but, incredibly higher, the peaks of the Annapurnas and the Lamjung Himal loom above. You're now that much closer that they fill three-quarters of the vertical. They're icy, and white-cold radiates from them. Savouring the moment — knowing that neither words nor snapped images will do it justice

Figure 3.6. *Approaching Kohla: the view from Tapron (arrows indicate Kohla's location on slope opposite).*

Figure 3.7. *Kohla's ruins (Structure 3) with the peaks of the Annapurnas behind.*

— *then its back to the lodge, for lunch. After that, the trail doesn't go over the ridge, but veers off to the east, around the back of the high ground. It's a good path, wide and well-trodden. Gaining the ridge shoulder, after a short while, we're called down off the trail, as some 50 m below there's another route, and here it's marked by ruined buildings on either side, as if guarding the way (Chromo). Following their inspection, a short walk — no more, it's pleasant and horizontal — gets you to Chikre. Situated on the east side of a very high alpine meadow plain (with a similar 'guard' or posting station-like building in its middle, beside the trail), the ruins are arranged along the cliff-side, and their setting is staggering.*

The trail then goes along the ridge, through meadows dotted with pastoralist camps. Eventually, it begins to go down through Rhododendron forest (vivid red, some of the porters partake of their flowers, more in show than conviction that they provide energy). The way comes out to Tapron, a broad grassy vale. There's a range of mounded pastoralist shelters arranged along the eastern side, the ground before them being wet and spongy. It's dotted with livestock carcasses and the air is torn with the swooping cries of crows. We'll camp at the rest lodge up on the west side. It's a pretty god-forsaken spot as here, right before the Annapurnas, it's as cold and windswept as hell and things freeze come dark.

From here, we have to go down to the river to get up to Kohla. First, through open park-like ground with tall evergreens, while at the riverside itself (with great scree-strewn boulders) there's dense bamboo jungle (Fig. 3.5:B). Each time, crossing the valley bottom, the trail is lost for some time. Worry then moves through the group: 'Will we gain Kohla that night?', and, on the 2000 trip, we had to camp on the grassy terraces lower downstream on the far side. Then, the problem is finding the upward route, as the slope is steep and the grass wet, making the way treacherous for men with loads. Finally, however poor, a path is found and the escarpment line is gained. There is a good route going along it, which at points opens onto broad meadows, with the remains of pastoralist camps. We take this trail along the ridge, the steeper slopes all carry high grass cover, with the forest confined to erosion valleys. Things are wilder up

A

B

Figure 3.8. *The 1994 fieldteam at Kohla (A) and a visiting TPLS delegation (posed beside the 'King's tethering stone'; B).*

here and there's more evidence of animal life. Mountain pheasants are heard and a musk deer sighted; elsewhere, pawprints of both wildcat and bears are seen by the men.

After steady going for two hours or so, we hit another forested valley and the trail weaves up. After about 20 minutes it flattens into clearings and then you see the first really high standing ruins — Kohla. It's impossible to adequately convey the impact of the site. It's situated in a small valley and, ringed by bare-stone escarpments behind, it has the feeling of a natural amphitheatre, and to the south the view is open and broad. Although dotted with trees (growing up on the site's walls with a girth of upwards of

5 m) and also a few recent phrohon settings, the central portion of the site is open and it's dominated by the building ruins. Its distinct western and eastern 'quarters' stand amid woodland, and the stonework is draped in thick moss. All the same, generally standing 1–2 m high and at points up to 4 m, the ruins are striking. Their quality and setting lend the site an air of drama and it does seem to be a special place (Fig. 3.7). Contributing to this is an extraordinary natural 'monument': a great plate-like boulder, poised on huge stone uprights, mid-way up on the back scarp (Fig. 3.38:A). On arrival, it offers a 'commanding presence' and this seems confirmed when, approaching it, we notice that a box-stone shrine has been built into the recess beneath the great capstone. (This sense of a ritual presence seems to be furthered when, in the first year, the corpse of a cow lay at its mouth, though there was no evidence whatsoever of any sacrifice.) The interpretation of this megalith-like setting — becoming known as the 'flying saucer' — was the source of some consternation and later re-appraisal, which is more fully outlined below and in Chapter 4.

The first time up, we spent 18 days at the site, in 2000 only ten. You get into a strange rhythm up at Kohla. Despite all the bounty of this staggering nature, apart from work, there's not much to do and certainly it's not the kind of landscape to encourage free-time exploration by the party's members. As an experiment, during the first season we arranged a group 'away-day' to view the sites mentioned by Messerschimdt in the high ground above. First, up through Rhododendron forest to pine lands and 'The Horsetrack' (with one building only set near an oddly cleared linear valley, it's pleasant if not terribly convincing), then a few hours climb up to 'The Cave of Nuns' (Fig. 3.9). The way is dangerous, with deep, weakly crusted snow and there's fear that someone will break a leg, as we regularly fall through (there's no serious medical aid easily at hand up here). Finally, soaked to the skin and all pretty exhausted, we reach the cave: a great boulder overhang with a bit of drystone wall in front. (While clearly not a 'nunnery', like comparable examples in Mustang and Manang, this could have been a hermitage cell, albeit in a rather extreme location.) Despite the pleasure of also seeing yak herders' shelters at this altitude, when we eventually get back late in the day, all forswear ever having another day off.

Even at midday, however autumnally pleasant, it never seems warm at Kohla. During the morning, at least in late Spring, the clouds start coming up from the valleys below. At night this can result in fantastic lightning storms and by late morning or early afternoon there's often hail. Its comes down violently, the size of marbles, and lies thick on the ground, appearing like snow. We get wet, things get wet: its time to eat, work-up notes and nap, then work again late in afternoon and into the evening.

The living conditions remain much as they were on the trail. Like some sort of 'bubbled' suburbia, we alienated 'outsiders' stay in our individual tents. The men outfit one of the large pastoralist shelters with all the coverings that are available, and a kitchen and eating stall are established at one end (Fig. 3.10). Over time, in an effort to combat the cold nights, it's padded throughout with juniper boughs. In the first season, upon slaughtering an accompanying goat, its meat was hung up in the rafters to smoke. Together this, and the evergreen interior, gave the shelter an oddly festive, if primitive, atmosphere, approximating what you imagine life in a Huron longhouse might have been.

Having to carry in all food (and what few delicacies can be managed), the limited diet soon begins to tell. The men eat daal bhaat twice a day; occasionally enlivened by whatever livestock are brought on the hoof, it's basically lentil-dal and rice, literally eaten in washbowl-full quantities. The Western staff usually only partake of this once a day, otherwise having a starchy alternative. When combined with the strain of constant work at altitude (bend down too much, drawing or digging, and you're left dizzy), the low nutritional level of the diet leaves one feeling lethargic and debilitated. Various events and gags are organized to promote espirit de corps, but exhaustion soon mounts up.

Eating en masse in the shelter, there is first the formality of the evening's local millet alcohol intake — thereafter, group-eating, songs and joking around, and then we retire — often preceded by further spirits imbibed by the archaeological team (at least as long as supplies hold out). At night, the tents and everything within, freeze, and any encouragement to numbed sleep is welcome …

The daily routine of work on the site was broken by 'official' visits, variously delegations of shamans and/or TPLS members. (Many of their participants were gentlemen nearly twice our age, casting our rigours of the trail into perspective; though they, too, clearly felt it: Fig. 3.8: B.) These tended to last for two to three days, with half a day usually given to site tours. The most fraught of these visits occurred in the first year, when a team of shamans stayed for an extended period. We duly demonstrated what we were doing and our survey techniques, and then went on to discuss matters of interpretation. Reaching the 'flying saucer', intense debate broke out. What we were saying (through interpreters) was clearly felt to be wrong and certainly it had no basis in contemporary village-based analogy (their guiding framework of reference). Evoking severe reaction, relations were markedly cool over the next two days and there was a sense of interpretative showdown. Finally, early one morning, the most senior shaman of the group was observed going up to the great boulder to undertake a ritual. Thereafter, everything changed and the air of tension deflated. (Though, in hindsight, whether all of what we then purported to be correct is probably questionable; see Chapter 4.)

Coming back from Kohla, the route is much the same, though the pace is somewhat quicker on account of being

Figure 3.9. *Goin' up: en route to the 'Racetrack' (main picture) with its valley/course inset above right; upper left, Damarsingh just below the 'Cave of Nuns' (note the outline of the ruins of a Yak herders' shelter immediately to his left).*

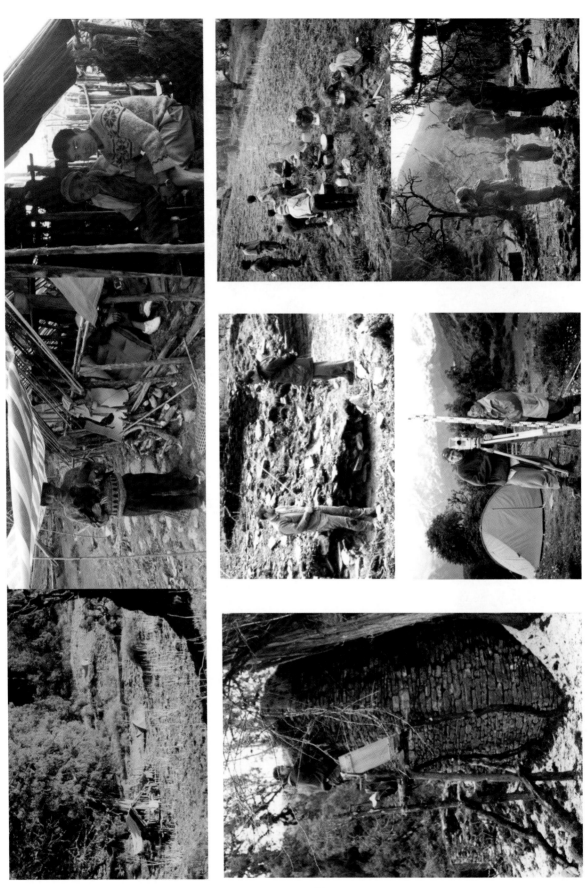

Figure 3.10. *Camplife: at Kohla 1994 and 2000.*

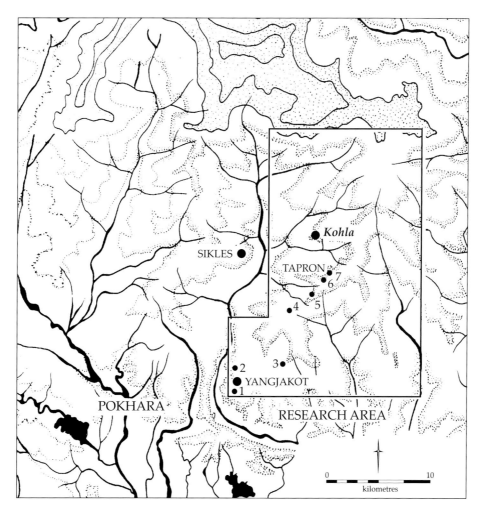

Figure 3.11. *Site location: 1) Yangjakot 'Palace'; 2) Kui Choh; 3) Nadr Pa; 4) Karapu; 5) Khuindo; 6) Chromo; 7) Chikre Toh.*

that much more downhill. The first time down, it was decided to at least roughly survey all the sites seen coming up. Chikre proved difficult. It was late in the season and the monsoon conditions were trying. By 9–10 am, the misty cloud cover was so thick that you couldn't read the theodolite over more than a 10 m distance. On top of this, some of the porters were suffering from the altitude. The result was that, aside from two of us and the same number of 'help', the rest of our party had to be sent down to Khuindo. While spending the next days recording the site in the few hours available, staying at the one-room rest house at Tapron, we got to know the location all too well.

The first time down we were paraded through Yangjakot with one of its Damai Tailors bands. With exotic drums and horns, it all seemed appropriately otherworldly and we newcomers were enthralled (Fig. 3.4:C). During the 2000 season, we decided to pull out the stops to convince our government colleagues of the degree of grassroots support the project carried. Arranging for all the village's bands and Mothers' and Ghato Dance groups to participate, on our

departure the procession took a good half-hour to weave its way through the village.

Finally, getting down and catching the bus again into Pokhara, the men and equipment go off to the Kohibo. We jump off to first hit the bank (to pay them off), then it's to one of the riverside bars and cold beer and snooker — the jukebox perpetually playing, like before, To the End of the World. *Things come to a close at the Kohibo, with pleasant formalities and speeches and garlanding.*

The survey sites

The cultural reckoning, mapping and appraisal of landscape are themes that are dealt with later in this chapter. However, before proceeding a sense of a scientific base-line must be established. Involving its own specialist language, faced with the variety and lushness of the land, such 'hard' description was beyond our abilities. Here, we were particularly fortunate that Dorothy Allard (then a student in the Department of

Geography at Cambridge) had undertaken her PhD researches within the area, in part within Kohla's immediate environs, and she was able to provide the following commentary.

Study area environs
DOROTHY ALLARD

Although the project's observations extended over a broader area, the main study area consisted of a 17 km-long transect-corridor running northeast from the village of Yangjakot, a few kilometres east of the Madi River, to Kohla. This transect extended from 1500 to 3550 m a.s.l. in elevation, thus passing from a warm temperate to a cool temperate vegetation zone. Because the geographic extent of my studies of vegetation and forest dynamics in the sub-alpine fir forest zone south of Lamjung Himal (Allard 2000) fortuitously happened to include the Kohla study area, its present-day vegetation can be detailed.

The phytogeographic regions of Nepal have been described by a number of authors (Karan 1960; Stainton 1972; Shrestha 1989; 1993; Sill & Kirkby 1991). Stainton recognized the area south of Annapurna and Himal Chuli, which contains our study area, as a unique subset of the phytogeographic region which he called the Central Midlands. Stainton described the Central Midlands as a meeting place of forest types occurring in the Western Midlands and the Eastern Midlands, with Western Midlands forest types being dominant on south-facing slopes, and Eastern Midlands forests occurring on north-facing slopes.

Stainton described the vegetation of the area south of Annapurna and Lamjung Himal as differing from that of the rest of the Central Midlands, because it is strongly influenced by a higher-than-usual annual precipitation. This is due to a lack of hills to the south, which would otherwise impede movement of monsoonal rains. These conditions are too wet for some types of forest that would otherwise occur at this latitude in the Central Midlands. Stainton observed that forests of pine (*Pinus roxburghii, P. wallichiana*) are completely lacking from this area, as is hemlock (*Tsuga dumosa*) and juniper (*Juniperus recurva* = *J. wallichiana*); some oak forests are also missing (*Quercus incana, Q. lanuginosa, Q. semecarpifolia*), and fir forests (*Abies spectabilis*) are not as abundant as they are in the rest of the Central Midlands. At the same time, some vegetation types become relatively more common. Forests dominated by *Rhododendron* species, or with rhododendrons in the understorey, are particularly prominent at elevations above 2500 m a.s.l. Although in agreement with most of Stainton's assertions, during my research a strong presence of *Abies spectabilis*, usually in combination with rhododendrons, was

found. I also found some stands co-dominated by *Abies* and *Juniperus recurva*. These vegetation types will be described in more detail below.

Annual precipitation in the study area increases with altitude, and falls as snow for part of the year in the vicinity of Kohla. Although there are no weather stations nearby, average annual precipitation as predicted from isobars is estimated to be between 4000 and 4500 mm (Sill & Kirkby 1991). The greatest amount of precipitation falls during the monsoon months of June to September.

The bedrock in the study area is comprised of gneiss, schist, and phyllite, metamorphosed from sedimentary rocks of the Tethys sea floor (Sill & Kirkby 1991). Landslides are a common feature of this young mountain chain, sometimes caused by earthquakes, and sometimes by downwasting after heavy rains. During the monsoon months, active landslides can often be heard, that sound somewhat like distant thunder.

Soils of the area are poorly studied. In the broad sense those of sub-alpine forests may be classified as inceptisols, with some profile development and with a sandy to loamy texture (Sill & Kirkby 1991). Soils of lower elevations are considered to be alfisols and have clay accumulation in the 'B'-horizon, although tilling and erosion have often altered soil conditions.

The lower, subtropical reaches of the study area are terraced and cultivated to a large extent. Forests below about 1800 m a.s.l., when present, are dominated by a combination of *Schima wallichii* and *Castanopsis indica* and are highly impacted by lopping for firewood, grazing, and erosion. Above these forests is a zone with a mixed broadleaf canopy and a subcanopy and shrub layer dominated by species in the Lauraceae. This is also highly impacted by human habitation and cultivation.

Proceeding upwards, the first forest to have relatively little human impact is dominated by *Quercus lamellosa*, occurring between 2000 and 2600 m a.s.l. in elevation. The oak trees are large and buttressed; the forest interior is dark and covered with dense vegetation, including many epiphytes and mosses. Above this is another type of mixed broadleaf forest in which maples (*Acer campbellii, A. pectinatum*) and *Rhododendron arboreum* are abundant, but occur along with a number of other deciduous and evergreen broadleaf species (*Ilex, Prunus, Sorbus*).

Present-day forests of the higher elevations in the vicinity of Kohla (2900–3500 m a.s.l.) are dominated either by rhododendrons (*Rhododendron* spp.) or by Himalayan silver fir (*Abies spectabilis*) with an understorey of rhododendrons. Again, these forests are very wet, and clouds and mist are almost constantly present during the growing season. *Abies* towers above the rhododendrons to a height of over 40 m, and in some parts of the study area trees more than 2 m in diameter have been recorded. The firs are at least 15 m taller than any trees in the understorey.

Although Nepal is rich in rhododendron species, only three species of 'tree rhododendron' occur in the study area: *Rhododendron arboreum*, *R. barbatum*, and *R. campanulatum*. By far the most abundant species of this zone is *R. barbatum*. The three species form an overlapping altitudinal gradient. *R. arboreum* is present throughout the subalpine forest zone, but reaches its greatest development at lower and middle elevations; *R. barbatum* is dominant in the middle of the range. *Rhododendron campanulatum* is present only in the higher elevations, occurring as an understory tree in *Abies spectabilis* forests above 3300 m a.s.l. or alone as 'scrubs' above the limit of *Abies*, starting at about 3500 m a.s.l. in elevation. The three rhododendrons also form a gradient of size, with *R. arboreum* achieving the greatest height and diameter, *R. campanulatum* both short and of small diameter, and *R. barbatum* of intermediate size.

Scattered broad-leaved deciduous trees may occur in fir/rhododendron forests of this area. These include two maples, *Acer pectinatum* and *Acer campbellii*, a birch, *Betula utilis*, and *Sorbus foliolosa*. They achieve a height somewhere in between that of *Abies spectabilis* and the rhododendrons. *Viburnum nervosum*, a shrub, is almost always present in fir or fir/rhododendron forests of the area.

The ground layer in these forests may be lush, with vegetation up to a metre in height. Ferns are often important. Bamboo (*Thamnocalamus spathiflorus*) is abundant in some areas, and is thought to increase as a result of fire. It may achieve a height of two metres or more. Epiphytes are common on fir trunks and branches and on deciduous trees. Rhododendrons support some epiphytes, but their flaky bark prohibits extensive epiphyte development; mosses often cover the ground and the trunks of firs and deciduous trees.

At the highest elevations (above 3400 m a.s.l.) and in drier situations on south- to west-facing slopes, *Juniperus recurva* becomes a canopy codominant. At these elevations, *Abies spectabilis* no longer achieves its great height, as accomplished farther down, and is matched in height by juniper. As always, rhododendrons are abundant in the understorey.

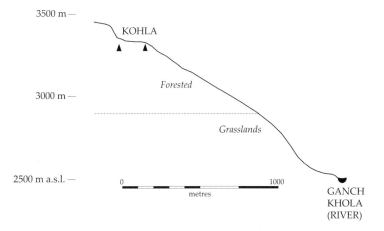

Figure 3.12. *Schematic elevation profile of the Ganch Khola/Kohla valley (top); below, expedition camp at Karapu (1994) with erosion-elevated tree-bowl right.*

Within the matrix of fir, fir/rhododendron, and fir-juniper forests, are open areas. Open lands are limited to landslides, sub-alpine grasslands, cliffs, and herb-dominated forest openings of anthropogenic origin. Of greatest interest, from a vegetation standpoint, are the semi-natural grasslands and the forest openings. These are dealt with in detail in Allard (2000), but brief mention will be made here. The sub-alpine grasslands near Kohla are not a common feature of the landscape in the region south of Lamjung Himal, and it is interesting that they are in greatest abundance near Kohla. They are probably caused and maintained by a combination of frost and drought (Miehe 1982). They occur on steep, convex surfaces of south-facing slopes, where winter insolation prevents much snow accumulation (Fig. 3.12). As a result, the ground is unprotected and freezing and thawing of the soil

A

B

Figure 3.13. *Chuni-Holden: A) the characteristic village-type artefact (see Fig. 3.50:2); B) girls operate a husking mortar in Yangjakot village.*

occurs repeatedly. Both the freeze–thaw action and the resulting droughty soil prevent the growth of trees. The grasses that replace the trees are fire-tolerant and perhaps even fire-adapted, and so fire — whether of natural or anthropogenic origin — may play an additional role in maintaining these areas in non-forested condition. The grasslands near Kohla are dominated by a type of bunch grass, *Danthonia cumminsii.* If the tough, fibrous leaves of this grass are removed by fire, tender new shoots sprout from the tussocks and are favoured by livestock.

Anthropogenically induced and maintained forest openings are part of the present-day landscape, and surely were also present during the time of Kohla's inhabitancy. They are used for the grazing of livestock brought up from lower-elevation villages during the summer months. Today's forest openings are dominated by weedy herbaceous and graminoid species, including species that do

well with nitrogen enrichment. Their flora does not overlap to a great degree with either the sub-alpine grassland flora, or with the ground layer vegetation within the forests.

Landscape dynamics

A degree of circularity, or at least reappraisal, informed our fieldwork recording. Essentially taking the same trail up and back to Kohla during our main research trips (and also through Manang; see Chapter 4), allowed us to re-visit a number of the sites first recorded in 1994 again in 2000 (Fig. 3.11). As will be apparent, ultimately by its scale and the length of our stay there (i.e. extended familiarity), Kohla came to dominate the recording of all these sites and provided a sense of base-line reference. This is a key point underpinning our travels and researches generally. 'Travelling up', of course, generated immediate ideas and first associations, but these invariably lacked context. It was only coming back down on their return legs that our observations were informed by a sense of relative perspective.

The fieldwork conditions clearly affected the outcome of our surveys. It was very much a case of a trail-based 'linear' archaeology along established routes and, due to exhaustion and dense cover, one rarely ventured too far off the path. If unknown by our colleagues, any site lying 30 m or more off to one side or the other could have easily escaped detection. Among the environmental factors affecting the archaeology is extreme erosion and down-cutting, which the landscape obviously sees during monsoon downpours and spring melt-off. At many points, the trail follows steep outwash gullies and, almost corridor-like, these are up to 1–2 m deep. Trees growing within them can stand perched to this height, above the eroded ground-level, the soil beneath being protected by their root-boles (Fig. 3.12). Similarly, the base of stone-lined trails approaching villages from above can be eroded by such flood action, to leave their flanking walls standing 0.5 m or more proud above their (unpaved) bases. Although the opportunity did not arise to detail these phenomena, this extreme down-cutting, and otherwise the influence of protective capping, would impact upon archaeological survival. Potentially this could create a height-based inversion relative to age. In other words, 'things' capped earlier appear to stand higher. One expects, for example, that the many mounds which dot the meadow at Khuindo reflect these processes (Fig. 3.26). The extreme impact of these natural forces obviously explains why so much public-yard space in villages today is paved, as indeed was also the main square at Kohla itself. In fact, the apparent cleanliness of that surface within the settlement might well be the result of water scouring; refuse and finds being washed down the steep valley slope below the site and now many kilometres away.

For our Tamu colleagues, chuni-holden stones were among the main type-artefacts demonstrating settlement, and, indeed, these were present on all the main sites (often in some numbers). They are essentially boulders with a single, large cupmark depression in their centres (*c.* 35 cm in diameter and 20 cm deep) and attest to the operation of crop husking mortars, as are still seen in villages today (Fig. 3.13; see Gajurel & Vaidya 1994, 310–14). These are big pieces of 'machinery' with complex timber superstructures, and are unlikely to have ever been used in mobile pastoralist circumstances. While, therefore, a logical attribution of settlement (*per se*, as opposed to pastoralist activity), this does not remove an element of ambiguity. The most obvious case was the 'village settlement' that our colleagues claimed lay just below Yangjakot's water-point, a half day's march above the village proper, Yarjung's *Kuniholdo* (see Chapter 2; 28°16.523'/84°07.097'/1910 m a.s.l.). Despite investigating this stretch of the trail four times in the course of the project's travels (upward and return legs), yes a chuni-holden was there, but otherwise never any convincing evidence of a village site as such.

There was a complicated relationship between our more formal survey recording of sites in 1994 and what our local colleagues had distinguished in the course of their trek two years before. Yarjung kept his own notebooks throughout, including sketch-mapping. These he essentially maintained as private documents. Nevertheless, it was clear that — combining evidence from the *pye* and what had been seen on the 1992 trip — he had tallies for the number of houses at the village sites (see Chapters 2 & 5). These invariably proved to be much higher than ours, in some cases substantially so. Karapu, for example, provides a relevant instance and, in discussion with him, it was obvious that he enumerated its pastoralist shelters among the attributed houses. This is not at all surprising and reflects upon the construction of context and analytical procedures. As outlined above, it took time and extended exposure to a range of sites for us to get 'our eye in', and even then some attributions must remain ambiguous. Relevant in this context is the work at Khuindo, where the archaeological team made its main site 'discovery'. We stopped at this meadow at the instigation of our colleagues, but it eventually emerged only long after the fact (and then hesitantly) that our local colleagues thought the pastoralist shelters which dotted its open ground were, in fact, the settlement and that they had not seen the building ruins along the meadow's forested edge.

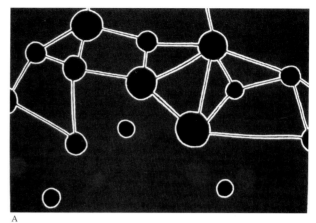

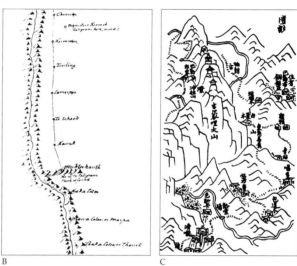

Figure 3.14. *Seeing land: A) Australian sand painting (Michael Aspinall); B) section of Crawford's 1802/03 map of the Kali Gandaki River trade route (note Muktinath, lower centre); C) Son Yun's 1792 campaign map showing the route of the Tibetan army through the Himalayas north of Kathmandu (Boulnois 1989, 91).*

Reading and scaling land

Writing in the mid nineteenth century, Hodgson described the Himalayas as a 'mighty maze without a plan', which indeed it then was. Even today, in such an extreme landscape, mapping and the experience of land seem to have little direct co-relationship. Yes, you can appreciate on paper the build-up of contours, getting a feel for the highs and lows ahead. Yet this tells little of the ruggedness of any route and just how steep it will prove. This is more than just a matter of a generically 'embodied' experience of land as opposed to its abstract 'reading', with the real closed surround of dense forest cover and steep ravines (from some of which there will be no ready way out) only occasionally broken by great sweeping vistas.

There is a correspondence between the earliest trade route maps of the wider area (e.g. Fig. 3.14:B, Crawford's map of 1802–3: see Graafen & Seeber 1992–93) and Yarjung's (Figs. 2.4 & 2.5). They are basically lines linking named places and convey little of the land itself. Today, the Himalayas are often portrayed in Tibetan Buddhist world-view landscapes; their jagged peaks run across the foreground, with Lhasa commanding the centre beyond. Yet, otherwise, apart from pictures within highly stylized pilgrimage guides, there seems to have been little 'indigenous' means of visualizing the land (though see a shaman's drawing of the 'palace of the gods' in Mumford 1990, fig. 7 and Losty 2004 concerning Hodgson's employment of local artists to record monuments and his fig. 5.15). There is, for example, no equivalent of the Chinese scroll-painting tradition, wherein mountain ranges unwind as long panoramas (though see Fig. 3.14:C and Boulnois 1989 for Chinese maps of Nepal and a scroll painting relating to the 1788–92 Tibet-Gorkha War). Based on learning/perception studies among 'traditional' rural communities within Nepal (including the Gurung/Tamu-mai), Dart & Pradhan (1967) similarly remarked upon their powers of landscape abstraction:

> The propensity of the Nepalese for making maps (whether verbal or graphic) which are *sequential* rather than spatial constructs is not limited to school children. In a land of foot trails, where literacy is too low to justify the use of signs, this propensity has been a source of consternation to more than a few travellers of Western upbringing! We, too, in reply to our inquiries as we travelled, were given instructions or 'maps' which, like *a string of beads*, list in correct sequence the places we should pass though without giving any clue as to distances, trail intersections, changes of directions, and so on (1967, 653; emphasis added; see also Boulnois 1989, 90 concerning time-distance calculation in Nepal and McHugh 1989 concerning concepts of Tamu-mai personhood).

Much of the population of Nepal is still only functionally sub-literate. In terms of any cognitive and/or phenomenological 'reading' of the world (or the past), this is clearly a major perceptual barrier — can the literate ever understand the 'un-lettered' world-view? Attesting to poverty and the inadequacies of the state education system, when travelling through Nepal images of trees or ploughs will be seen painted upon walls in villages and towns. These are the symbols of the country's political parties and thus are, in fact, word-replacing *signs*. By way of contrast within an Asian context and reflecting upon the 'high' literacy of the Tibetan-Buddhist religious hierarchies, in response to the Younghusband expeditionary force of 1903, Tibet's lamas apparently arranged stones on mountain sides along the way, spelling-out appropriate 'go home' slogans addressed to the forces (Allen 2002; see Macdonald 1973 for a Lamaist perspective on Everest expeditions); though, without translation, few of them, of course, would have appreciated their messages. While working in Inner Mongolia in 2000 on the Mergen Project (see Evans & Humphrey 2003), Evans observed that the Chinese state had transcribed comparable, environmentally encouraging mottos to its populace on the flanks of the highlands — not so much a matter of landscape as palimpsest, as, quite literally, *writing on land*.

The question of illiteracy also reflects upon modes of graphical rendering and model representation. When asking our locally hired men to explain the operation of something, such as the chuni-holden mortars, despite being offered pen and paper for the purposes of sketching, they would instead quickly mock-up in bamboo, quarter-scale models of what was intended. Equally, while recording one of the highland sites (Chikre, see below) we came upon miniatures of pastoralist shelters. Up to 70 cm long and *c.* 25 cm high, these had been carefully made of *Rhododendron* twigs (Fig. 1.9, left-side). They were not sufficiently robust to have withstood any kind of sustained 'play' and, when questioning the local pastoralists about their use, it was confirmed that they were for the *instruction* of children in the eventual construction of such full-size structures (see Evans forthcoming). It was disconcerting stumbling upon these, set as they were on the edge of a pastoralist camp-site meadow that was dotted with the standing full-size frames of their 'originals'. Monsoon mists lay thick over the ground and you could not see more than a few metres, and the resultant lack of perspective meant that you could not immediately distinguish the models from the 'real thing'.

The one traditional mode of landscape 'depiction' throughout the region are *Torma* dough renderings. These are of *sacred landscapes*, and involve lump-like mountains and area gods (e.g. see Diemberger 1997, 313–16, illus. 6.3 & 6.4; Mumford 1990, fig. 2). Like the small dough-animal effigies that are 'ritually killed' in place of these creatures' real sacrifice, such 'landscape trays' do not seem so much a matter of representation as *substitution* and relate to an ethos of reincarnation (see Hegewald forthcoming for 'solid' cosmological modelling amongst the Jains, and Höfer 1999, 226 on how the ritual altars of shamans are effectively a miniaturized model of the universe).

The first formal mapping of the Annapurnas and the Himalayas as a whole occurred during the Great Trigonometrical Survey project of 1817–43 (the GTS). This was only achieved through distant triangulation from the northern Indian border. Because its surveyors were unable to enter the Kingdom of Nepal, their peaks were literally fixed from the 'outposts of empire' and were shot in from twenty yard-high stone towers, built to elevate the project's enormous theodolite (see Keay 2000; Macfarlane 2003, 188–90). Apart from the subsequent detailing of the region's topography through the operation of native pundit agents (particularly Hari Ram: see Montgomerie 1875; Gurung 1983), Nepal was only glimpsed from a distant 'imperial gaze' (see generally e.g. Stone 1988; Evans 1990; Duncan 1990).

Coarse trekking-quality contour maps of the study area are now widely available (the army having restricted use of those of higher resolution). In an effort to offset this, it was only in the latter part of 2000 that a satellite image of the area was obtained (Fig. 3.15). This had to be commissioned and was then troublesome to achieve due to near-constant cloud cover. (The final picture is a mosaic, as it is a merged split-view image taken under only 'best possible' conditions.) Although at first it is difficult to get one's bearings due to the degree of altitude difference and extent of forest cover (i.e. what is 'up' and 'down'?), it nevertheless well expresses the overwhelming quality of its topography. While it is still hard to appreciate its ridgeway routes, once having distinguished the rivers, the valleys can be read and the general east–west lay of the land grasped.

Mountaineering has its own lexicon of landscape expression (see e.g. Macfarlane 2003). Knowing that such imbued phrases as the 'spine' or 'bare bones of the planet' are singularly inappropriate (the Himalayas being geologically young), from this image and being in the land you can understand why it is so difficult to render and conceptualize. Without exact mapping techniques, it is impossible to bind it up in anything other than a strictly relative system of local reference (e.g. *the* valley by *a* mountain crossed by *that* route).

Musing over the digital satellite image, one is struck by the contrast this poses with the world's more seemingly uniform landscapes, such as tundra, steppe, desert or the outback. Though in reference to the latter, superficial parallels could be drawn with the linear route of Yarjung's map and Aboriginal 'song-lines', in actuality, nothing would seem further from the truth. The painting shown in Figure 3.14:A presents a case in point (it hangs in Evans's dining room and, as such, has 'informed' this book). Its white line-linked black circles depict the view down through constellations; raised in subtle sand-relief behind are the streams and pools of underground water sources. The land is simultaneously shown from above and below — from

both outer space and the subterranean. Having the quality of an X-ray, *there is no middle ground* and the surface of the earth is only the flat red of the canvas (see Ingold 2000 and Bender 1999 concerning 'map perception' generally, and specifically the latter for the network of Mughal tunnels *imagined* to exist beneath Lahore and linking their capital to Delhi and other provincial centres). This is not the superabundant, or at least overly extreme, landscape of the Himalayas, where *surface is so all-pervading*. As in Tibetan Buddhism, Tamu-mai cosmology has its own many levels of heaven and the underworld, but aside from *Oble* these are not localized systems closely situated within the immediate landscape (though see Ehrhard 1997 and Diemberger 1997 concerning the Tibetan Buddhist tradition of 'hidden lands'). Ultimately, the Australian tradition may relate to a need to map, or better 'fix', widely distributed resources. Although the Himalayas has its nodal points (e.g. critical passes), water for instance is generally available and the restriction of resources is, otherwise, essentially vertical.

Across the upper third of the satellite image there is more open ground and swathes of rock, that being the higher ground just below the peaks of the Annapurnas and Lamjung Himal proper. Local communities have never practised any form of 'sport' mountaineering. They go high for pasture and resources, and regularly negotiate passes at altitude, but there has been no tradition of scaling peaks for the sake of it. Generally, mountain tops are where gods live and only outsiders would presume to append personal names to them (though obviously they are all also locally named). Named in 1856 to commemorate the GTS's superintendent of 1823–43, Everest is a classic example of this; Tibetans refer to it as *Chomolungma* — the 'Mother Goddess of the World' — its Nepali equivalent being *Sagarmatha* ('Forehead of the Ocean' or 'Goddess of the Sky'). Closer at hand, *Machhapuchhare*, which commands Pokhara Valley, provides a similar instance. Mountaineerer Jimmy Roberts came within 50 m of its summit in 1957, only to have his Sherpas rebel against going any higher, due to its sacred character, and since then it has been closed to expeditions. (With its name translated as 'The Fish Tail', there is only speculation as to the basis of its religious association; see also Herzog's 1952 account of scaling Annapurna I, *Annapurna*.)

Village environs and fort sites
Yangjakot (c. 1500 m a.s.l.; Fig. 3.11:1)
Located on a low hill-top immediately south of the village, the so-called 'Hindu palace' site (this appellation deriving from TPLS information), sketched in the first season, was formally surveyed in 1995. Appropriately

Figure 3.15. *Satellite image with location of Kohla indicated.*

enough, this raised more questions than answers and it remains our most ambiguous 'site'. The main ovoid wall-enclosure appears to be a 0.85 m+ high terrace (base not visible; 12.5 × 18.5 m total area: Fig. 3.16). Inspection of a collapsed length revealed that the 'soil' behind the main wall did not seem dumped as such, but rather simply revetted. Whilst it is possible that this is the (high) platform of an ovoid building (7 × 13.5 m), it is more likely the remains of an 'old' hill-crown fieldsystem (former terraces can be traced across the hill), and an outer wall circuit runs 1–2 m beyond that which defines the flat crown of the mound/hill.

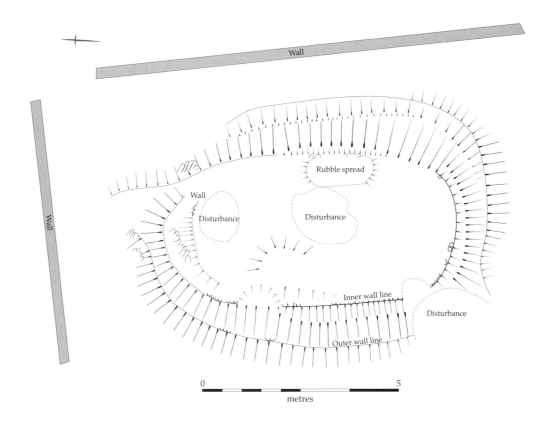

Figure 3.16. *Yangjakot 'Palace' Site: survey plan (top); below, its mound from the south. (Photograph: D. Gibson.)*

In both seasons, quantities of pottery were recovered from an area of pitting to the west, and where burnt clay horizons were visible in the sides of the cuts. The option was fully considered (and for a time adopted) that this material was just derived from manuring, with the burning being the by-product of stubble firing. Yet, given the amount of pottery recovered (otherwise not informally found in the other present-day villages we visited), and that fragments of burnt clay/daub were also present, there does seem to be a site of some description at this locale. It has to represent more than field-related activity; but

Figure 3.17. *Yangjakot village from the south with the location of Kui Choh (1) and Karapu (2) indicated above.*

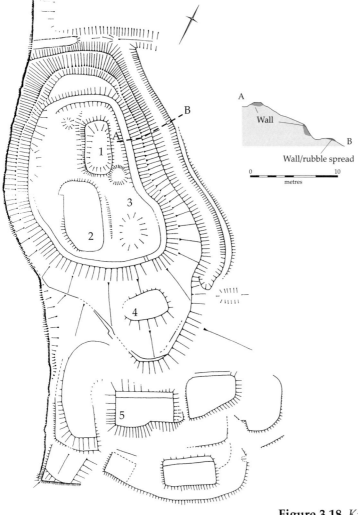

Wall

Wall/rubble spread

0   10
metres

Figure 3.18. *Kui Choh: survey plan.*

0   40
metres

whether it was a 'palace', village or only a backfilled quarry is impossible to say.

On each of our subsequent visits to the village we informally inspected this site. By 2000, it had been impinged upon by a newly constructed ACAP office and campsite. During that trip, it was drawn to our attention that Yangjakot implies a fort; we duly inspected the central hill-top within the main core of the village (by its temple) and were able to recognize low walls across its crown, perhaps relating to its fortification.

Kui Choh (Fig. 3.11:2)
Situated along a high ridge some 500 m north of Yangjakot (*c.* 200–250 m higher), the ruins extend for 85 m east–west (Figs. 3.17 & 3.18). The site is confined by cliffs on the southern side and traces of terracing continue down the densely wooded, more gradual north slope, and beyond the 60 m width that could be reasonably surveyed). As is the case for many other peaks in the region, the ridge is said to be the home of a god (in this case one for single women). Its locus, however, seems to lie west of the ruins, within an area of flat table-stones (one with cupmark impressions).

Encircled by terraces on its eastern and northern sides, the core of the site is a walled, bivallate enclosure (Fig.

3.18). Of ovoid/'kidney bean-shape' plan (16.5–21.5 × 30 m), the inner enclosure is defined by a 1.2 m-wide drystone wall, that survives up to four courses high (0.30 m) in relationship to the interior ground surface and ten courses high (1.2 m) on its exterior face (Fig. 3.19). Two definite (and one 'possible') ovoid-plan house structures lie within its interior. These are low/denuded and their walls generally only stand 3–5 courses high (0.15–0.40 m), though at one point up to nine courses (0.70 m) were visible:

Structure 1 - 4.1–4.75 × 9 m.

Structure 2 - 6.6 × 12 m; some manner of extension, possibly a stairway, is apparent on its northwestern side.

Figure 3.19. *Kui Choh: the outer enclosure wall, south side.*

Structure 3 - *c*. 3.5(+) × 9 m disturbed by a large charcoal burning pit, the existence of this building must be considered 'possible' only.

Along the northwestern end, between the main circuits, is a minor terrace (1.5–2.5 m wide), whose sides drop *c*. 1 m and which bears traces of walling. Otherwise, the northwestern exterior is marked by a 'cross-ditch'. Some 4 m wide and *c*. 1.5 m deep in its centre (deepening on either side of the ridge), this runs straight across the width of the ridge. Clearly a feature in its own right (i.e. cutting off movement along the ridgeway), a separate ditch extends from it to form the northern outer circuit of the enclosure. The latter is 2–2.5 m deep on its enclosure/ridge-top side and 3.5–4 m wide. It has traces of drystone revetment along its interior face up to ten courses high (0.9 m); the ditch is up to 0.6 m deep in relation to its exterior side.

Along the western wide of the enclosure, the edge slopes steeply down from the side of the inner enclosure to the ridge-side cliff. Along the northern and northwestern sides, there is a 2–3.5 m-wide berm behind the exterior circuit. The exterior ditch continues for a length of 22 m along the enclosure's northeastern quarter, terminating at this point; at its southern end, a 'hollow-way'/path runs eastward.

Although not ditch-enclosed, along its southern and southwestern sides the outer circuit is marked by a terraced wall up to 15–17 courses high (*c*. 1.5 m). At its southeastern end it deviates from the standard between-circuit berm interval and there it expands to enclose a wedge-shape swathe (14 m long; 6–18 m wide). This accommodates another low ovoid house structure that extends over 4.5 × 7.7 m (No. 4).

Divided by paths/hollow-ways, a series of terraced platforms arranged in an 'outworks' fashion were distinguished along the southern side of the ridge. Delineated by walls two to five courses high (0.1–0.6 m; 0.7–1 m wide), this includes at least one other sub-rectangular house structure (No. 5; 3.6 × 9.3 m).

The ruins at Kui Choh would essentially seem to be that of a small *fort* (with associated settlement). Although more impressive and of a different plan configuration than that at Karapu (see below), both would seem to share comparable strategic locations — on the crests of high ridges at the junction of trails.

Nadr Pa (Fig. 3.11:3)
Ruins extend for some 365 m along the spine of the ridge high above Warchok (Fig. 3.20). At the southern end lies what is locally referred to as a 'palace', a very impressive two-cell building (7 × 11.6 m, Structure 1; Figs. 3.21 & 3.22). At its corners, this stands 1.2–1.8 m high and, along its southern front, 2.1 m high (39 courses), the middle portions of its walls having, for the most part, collapsed. It is constructed of a fine-grained limestone schist and includes very long slabs, 0.5–0.8 m in length (one up to 1.05 m); the quality of the drystone construction must be a product of the local stone as comparable walls were also observed within the village of Warchok. A circular hermit's cell (2.90 m dia.: Fig. 3.21:C), standing 1.45 m high, has been inserted into a corner of the building's interior, as has also what seems to have been a rest or meditation platform (Fig. 3.21:D). Our informant (in 1995) reported that the hermit had abandoned his retreat some 17–18 years ago.

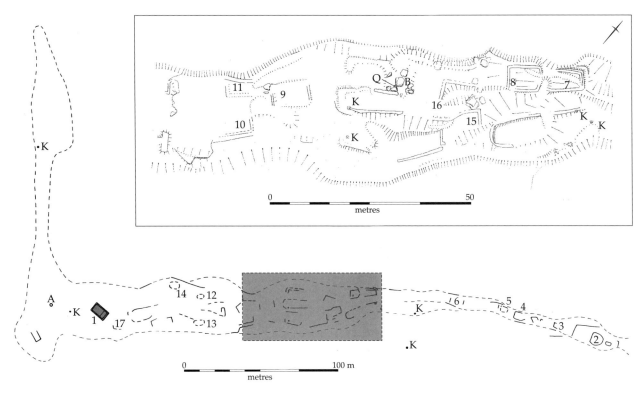

Figure 3.20. *Nadr Pa: survey plan with detail of central village inset ('K' indicates position of chuni-holden; 'Q' = quern; 'A' = cairn; 'B' = cupmark boulder; note highlighted location of 'palace'/Structure 1).*

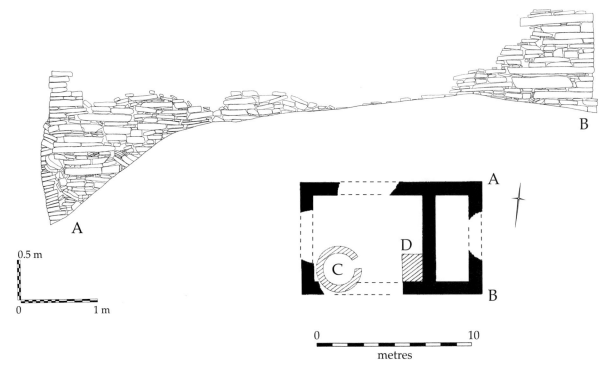

Figure 3.21. *Nadr Pa: plan of Structure 1 'palace' with elevation of its eastern face (A–B); C) hermit's cell; D) porters' rest platform.*

Figure 3.22. *Nadr Pa: A–C) The Palace, note the quality of its masonry (B) with 'A' showing the great serpentine tree and 'C' the shrine at its foot; D) Hermit's cell, note triangular recess.*

By its size (81.2 sq.m), this building would correspond with the larger (though not the largest) of Kohla's buildings, and certainly its construction techniques/quality would compare with the architecture of the more upland sites. Yet all our colleagues were adamant that this was a 'palace'. This might be a matter of context as — lying at a remove — this is much more substantial and carefully constructed than the building ruins within the adjacent village site. Yarjung reported his father having said that when he visited the site in his youth (c. 50–60 years ago), arrow firing-holes were to be seen in the palace's walls, which then stood much higher. Perhaps, a more likely explanation is that these were for first-storey floor joists, such as were found in Structure 6 at Kohla. Obviously, having undergone considerable damage during the twentieth century, the building's once greater height may well have contributed to its attribution as a palace.

It is difficult to know whether this building was entirely isolated or was part of a larger complex. Aside from a conical stone cairn built on the edge of the promontory in front of it (Fig. 3.20:A), some short lengths of wall were also just visible in the area. Thickly overgrown, it was felt inappropriate to clear these due to the fact that the palace is also a place of active ritual. A stepped shrine has been constructed of fallen stone beneath a great serpentine tree, rooted within the wall along the building's southern side (Fig. 3.22:C). The spot is considered very sacred, and the Village Ward President, who accompanied us, immediately performed ritual at the shrine upon our arrival. He told the story that its attribution relates to when a man was travelling with a heavy load. Upon stopping to rest at this point, an enormous snake emerged. He was duly terrified, but apparently the snake — at the god's insistence — went off peacefully and hence this was recognized as the place of a god. The President also reiterated that when a man out hunting deer in the vicinity a few years ago shot a snake, all three of his children mysteriously died within 15 days.

The main village site proved to be denuded, suffering from extreme damage through erosion, and has evidently been disturbed by pastoralists (old walled shelters dot the ridge). Nevertheless, there is extensive evidence of village-settlement terracing and, down its eastern slope, agricultural terracing. Apart from eight *chuni* and two rotary querns (Fig. 3.50:1), much pottery was recovered from both the palace end and the village site, leaving no doubt that this was a major settlement (Figs. 3.20 & 3.23:A). (As was the case at Kui Choh, a *chuni* was found lying on the grass, beside a trail approaching the site. Clearly removed from the ruins, they appear to be used as 'site' markers.) Large *Rhododendron* trees grow on the walls of the ruins. The

trees are estimated to be perhaps 200–400 years old, and a local informant from Warchok suggested a date of 300 years ago for the village's abandonment.

The houses generally seem to be defined by ovoid/sub-rectangular platforms, retained by low stones walls up to 0.50 m (five courses) high, and appear similar to those at Kui Choh. Of those recorded, only two — Structures 7 and 8 — can be said to be 'definite', and of the rest there must be some degree of ambiguity concerning their attribution (Fig. 3.20). Having even a greater level of doubt as to their status, three further house sites were also noted (15–17). What makes the identification of buildings so difficult on this site is the degree of water-cut erosion scarring, the quantity of terrace walls along the ridge, and the subsequent activity of pastoralists. Ten *phrohon* settings were recognized (not listed below); some of these may mask houses, just as some of the houses may actually have been pastoralist shelters:

Structure 2 - Ovoid/rounded 'square' platform (8 × 8 m); 0.40 m/four courses high.

Structure 3 - Ovoid/sub-rectangular platform (2.5 × 3 m); 0.20 m/two courses high.

Structure 4 - Ovoid/sub-rectangular platform (4.5 × 7.5 m); 0.40 m/four courses high.

Structure 5 - Possible (only) ovoid/sub-rectangular platform (3 × 5 m); 0.2–0.3 m high.

Structure 6 - Possible (only) sub-rectangular platform (3 × 8.5 m); 0.1 m high.

Structure 7 - Definite sub-rectangular platform (4.5–5.4 × 8.5 m); 0.3 m high.

Structure 8 - Definite ovoid/sub-rectangular platform (6.4 × 8.5 m); 0.3–0.5 m/four courses high.

Structure 9 - Possible (only) sub-rectangular platform (6 × 9.6 m).

Structure 10 - Possible (only) sub-rectangular platform (4+ × 9.5 m); 0.5 m/four to five courses high.

Structure 11 - Possible (only) sub-rectangular platform (3.5 × 6.5 m+).

Structure 12 - Ovoid platform (c. 3 × 5 m); 0.5 m/five courses high.

Structure 13 - Possible (only) ovoid platform (c. 3.5 × 7 m).

Structure 14 - Ovoid platform (4.5 × 7 m); 0.5 m/five courses high.

It warrants mention that within the middle of the settlement site is a very large boulder with cupmark impressions (Figs. 3.20 & 3.23:B).

The site is important for a number of reasons. It was the only example recorded in which the settlement is laid-out along the crest of a ridge, in the

A

B

Figure 3.23. *Nadr Pa: A) Chuni-holden set into end of main village-site wall; B) the central cupmarked boulder.*

manner of contemporary Tamu-mai villages (e.g. Warchok and Yangjakot). The situation of the village and distanced 'palace' is also intriguing — were they contemporary or successive? Equally, given that a god is said to inhabit the palace ruin, the site provides insights into the interrelationship between religious ascription and past remains. Our Tamu-mai colleagues and local informant were convinced that the god had lived there, and that it was known, before the site's occupation. Yet, the identification of the place of a *snake* god, at the base of the extraordinarily serpentine tree growing into the ruins, is unlikely to be coincidental. It suggests that the site's religious association may only have been 'identified' following abandonment (see Pignède 1993, 316 for a similar 'chicken/egg' tree-to-shrine relationship in the village of Mohoriya).

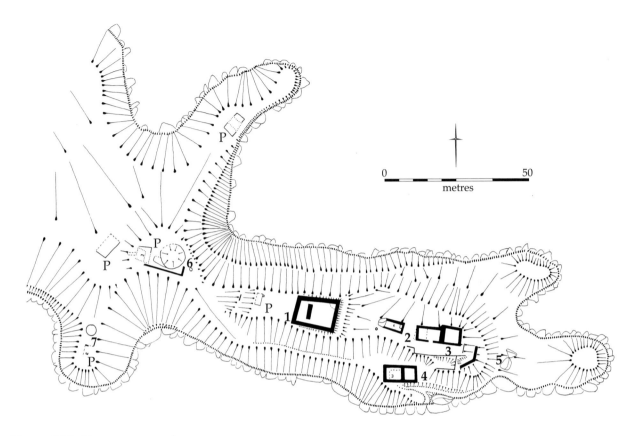

Figure 3.24. *Karapu: survey plan.*

The state of the Nadr Pa ruins also testifies to the extent of disturbance caused by pastoralist activity. This has relevance for some of the first season's sites, such as Karapu, where Tamu-mai oral 'texts' state substantial villages existed, but of which few traces remain. Yet, as discussed below, the relatively poor quality of the house remains could also reflect changes in building tradition. Again, as was the case at Karapu (see below), our Tamu-mai colleagues were not able to recognize the old *phrohon* from the house ruins. In fact, our Warchok informant had never heard of pastoralists camping on the ridge. This further supports the impression that a pastoralist sub-sector of Tamu-mai society seems largely ignored or even unrecognized; whilst 'age' and 'identification' are attributed to village ruins, this seems not the case with pastoral camps.

Karapu (28°18.526'/84°08.927'; 3240 m a.s.l.;
Fig. 3.11:4; Ch. 2, Krapu, Lines 159 & 160)
This dramatic promontory is dominated by what seems to be a fortified, or at least very substantial, building (Structure 1, Fig. 3.24:1; see also Figs. 3.17 & 5.4:D). Of quasi-trapezoidal plan (9.5–11× 15 m; 153.7 sq.m), it fills the width of the ridge and blocks passage along it. The drystone walls of its main perimeter are 1.2–1.3 m wide and stand to a maximum height of 0.8

m/seven courses high (Fig. 3.25:A & B). A north–south oriented wall (0.6 m high; 1.2–1.4 m wide) divides off the eastern third of its interior; a semi-circular heap of stones in the northeastern corner may either relate to the base of a structural feature (tower?) or, more probably, a denuded cairn.

Further evidence of this structure's defensive character was provided by portions of walling traced along the break of slope on the ridge's southern side at this point and, too, in the earthworks of its eastern approach. Of the latter, although much stone rubble masks its contours — suggesting collapse from either a 'high' building and/or a defensive perimeter — the dramatic ground slope has here been tiered or stepped and is suggestive of fortification.

The traces of pastoralist shelters lie scattered across the escarpment. Much more ambiguous is the attribution of three stone-built structures that lie on the eastern end of the promontory, beyond the defensive enclosure (Fig. 3.24).

Structure 2 - This rectangular structure (3.5 × 7 m), with walls 0.6–0.7 m high, was constructed to incorporate and utilize a large boulder (1.9 m high) as its western wall.

Structure 3 - A two-celled rectangular structure (5/6 × 16 m) with walls 0.3–0.8 m wide and up to 0.3 m high. The eastern cell, whose

A

B

C

Figure 3.25. *Karapu: A) the rise of the main tower fort from the west; B) detail of its masonry (with small box-shrine lower left); C) south aspect of cairn/shrine (no. 7).*

northern wall projects 1 m beyond that of the eastern, has a box-type stone hearth within it. Both cells have stone platforms in their eastern halves, and doorways through their southern walls.

Structure 4 - A two-celled (internally sub-divided) rectangular structure (4.75 × 1 m) with walls 0.3–0.4 m wide; both cells have stone-paved platforms in their western portions and there is a stone-set hearth in the western 'room'.

It is difficult to know whether these should be attributed as robust *phrohon* or poorly made buildings (or

buildings later re-utilized by pastoralists). On the one hand, they are without the gabled end-walls characteristic of stone-built shelters in the uplands. Yet, on the other hand, their coursing is generally poor, and the presence of internal stone paving, a paucity of rubble and stone slab-set hearths is common in the pastoralist's constructions. Of these structures, number 4 seems the most likely candidate to have been a building *per se*, with Structure 3 the least plausible. A series of stone walls enclose and frame these structures, with '5' being the most substantial.

Two other major features of note are also present on the ridge. Sitting centrally on a spur that juts south from below the main promontory is a large prayer mound/cairn (3.5 m dia.: Figs. 3.24:7 & 3.25:C). Still evidently seeing active ritual, this has a slab-built niche in its southern side and quasi-anthropomorphic stone settings ('footed pillars'). The other, '6', is a much larger cairn that sits at the apex of the escarpment's spurs, its situation being pivotal to the configuration of the site complex as a whole. It is of barrow-like proportions, *c.* 10 m in diameter and stands 1.3 m high. Consisting of a 'jumble' of soil and stones, one side is retained by a kerb-stone wall; the northwestern side being severely eroded. A low wall, 0.5 m wide and 0.3–0.4 m high (1–3 courses) frames its southern and southeastern sides. While possibly being no more than a 'formally' set (i.e. wall-framed) mound, this could alternatively be collapse from a large stone-built structure, perhaps even a tower relating to the main ridge-top building/fort.

Upland sites

Mention need be made that of the upland sites' naming, none coincide with recognized place-names and, rather, they solely derive from Yarjung's *pye*-based ascription. This being said, 'Tapron'/Taprang' — *Tapro Mhijya* of the *pye* (Ch. 2, Line 176) — is formally named and officially mapped as such and Kohla's ruins have been so-identified by other Tamu-mai sources (see below; Messerschmidt 1976b, 171–2 and Temple 1993).

Khuindo (28°19.772'/84°09.953'; 3064 m a.s.l.; Fig. 3.11:5; Ch. 2, Khuido Toh/Khunido, Line 161 & 162)
Aside from a sub-square structure at the foot of a central southern mound/hill (Structure 6), the settlement essentially consists of an alignment of three buildings along the western, forested edge of an open meadow (Figs. 3.26 & 3.27:A & C). All of these are well-built and are generally comparable to buildings at Kohla. The northernmost structure (3) is distinguished by the fact that it lies upon a 2–3 m-high mound:

Interview: Pachyu shamans from Warchok and Bachok (Nada Pa, April 1995)

In terms of its archaeological relevance, this interview reflects upon issues of 'translation' and getting the 'survey eye-in'. It was conducted shortly after our arrival at the site and attests to how difficult it was to distinguish its houses and even define its many pastoralist shelters.

JP = Judith Pettigrew
WP = Warchok Pachyu
YT = Yarjung Tamu
BP = Bachok Pachyu

JP: How did this place get its name?

WP: A pachyu came from Kohla. He carried a very heavy load on his back known as a *dausa*. The *dausa* was very heavy, but his head shaman said to him 'Do not rest anywhere until you reach your destination'. As it was so heavy he couldn't carry it and as he felt very tired he took a rest. He wondered what was in his load which made it so heavy. He opened the basket and inside was a python which came out and moved away. There was a tiny pond and people played with a golden ball there. That's as much as I know, my cousin-brother here might know more.

BP: It was called Nhada, as that means rest-place but nowadays it is called Nada [tells the same story]. In Nepali, it is called Lamtri because a snake is called *lamkira*.

YT: How did the Tamu-mai come from Kohla? Tell us what you know.

WP: In Kohla, there were too many people and so they had to spread out as the land wasn't enough.

BP: The crops did not grow well in Kohla. That's why they came down.

WP: Tanting, Siklis, Sidi. If you plant one grain of rice you, only get one grain, it doesn't become a family. If you go down further and plant one grain of rice, you get a couple of fistfuls. In Warchok village they plant maize, when it grows they give it more soil. At that time in Baraldhanda [a village at a lower altitude] they haven't even begun to plough or plant. Later on, Warchok's maize is not ready to be eaten but in Baraldhanda the maize is already eaten!

YT: This village was founded by Namju Kromchhains [Kromchhain clan from the village of Namju]. How old do you think that it is?

BP: More than 300 years.

YT: Thank you. We know this is a Tamu village, others say there was a king who lived in a palace here. Did the Tamus come before the king or did the king come before the Tamus?

WP: The Tamus must have been here first. The Tamus were stupid, that's why they were conquered by the king.

BP: Without people there isn't a king. I think this was at the time of the 24 kings. We don't know the exact year.

YT: Were the 24 kings Tamu or Bahun [Brahmin]?

WP: Must have been Bahun!

BP: There were the kings and their sons. We don't know which king was king on this hill.

WP: Must have been a king who came from lower down so they must have been Bahun.

YT: [to BP] Your opinion, Tamu or Bahun?

BP: [hesitates] There were 24 kings, maybe one might have been Tamu.

YT: The archaeologists think there wasn't a village here. They think there were only shepherd's huts. They found one shepherds' hut below Nada Pa and one above. What do you think?

WP: There were only two shepherds' huts in this area, one below and one above. I have not seen any other shepherds' huts here in 55 years. Maybe my cousin-brother knows.

YT: So, for 55 years there haven't been any shepherds huts here?

WP and BP: No.

WP: If a village was here, the water would be near here and there would be a path, but we haven't found a path to the water point in this area.

YT: The archaeologists said that maybe people took stones from the ruins and built houses in the village. [This is a misunderstanding, as it was never thought that the ancient settlement had been robbed of its masonry to build the current village that lies upwards of a kilometre away, but rather for the site's pastoral shelters/the 'shepherds' huts'.]

WP/BP: That's not true!

JP: Previously there was a village here but now we can't see any houses, so where have they gone?

BP: They left the houses and later on the houses were broken and the stones were moved.

WP: Nowadays some people make a tiny house without stone walls with bark and leaves. Maybe they made houses here with tiny stone walls and after that they used bark and leaves. Later, after they left, the leaves and bark would become rotten and we can't see them. That's my idea!

JP: OK.

YT: Was this a good place for a village?

WP: Yes for us it was a very good as we always stay in a high place!

JP: Why?

WP: If you went below you got malaria and that's why we stayed in the high hills.

BP: If you stay in the hills there is good air.

YT: Some Tamus planted apple trees and cut the trees here. Did they not know that this was a Tamu-mai village and the palace of a king?

WP: Everybody knows that there was king's palace and Tamu-mai village here. Everybody does rituals here but I don't know why they did that.

BP: They made it by mistake but now someone has stopped them.

YT: If people plant apples [uses English word 'apple'] the ruins will be destroyed. Will Tamu people be worried or not?

WP: If they plant apples it might be good as they make a profit, but they destroyed our ancestor's village. They shouldn't destroy our ancestor's village. They shouldn't plant here. They can plant on other hills but we must preserve the historical places rather than the apples.

BP: That's right.

YT: Today on Friday 24th, Chait 2051 you came to our ancestors' village to do an interview, thank you!

Despite the formal ending the interview continues.

YT: The archaeologists asked about pottery. In the past we didn't have contact with people from below who made pottery which means that the Tamu-mai must have made pottery. When did they stop making pots?

WP: I don't know if the Tamus made pottery.

YT: When did we start using pottery?

BP: [hesitates] I heard that we made pottery before, but when we met the pottery makers from below we stopped making pots.

YT: How many hundreds of years ago did we stop making pottery?

BP: [hesitates, stops, thinks] Maybe we stopped 100 years ago.

YT: How old are the villages of Warchok and Bhachok?

WP: More than 200 years.

YT: When you make a house, how many hundreds of years will it last?

WP: If I make a house in my lifetime it will be destroyed in my life and I'll make another house, so I don't know how long it will last! Before my house was a round house and I destroyed it and built a new one! [laughs] If we make house and the roof is of stone and grass, when it starts leaking the wood will become rotten and the house will be destroyed. If we look after a house it will last 70 to 80 years.

YT: Why was rice not planted here?

WP: Around here they planted wheat and barley. There was a rice grinder here, but I think that they brought the rice from below. How can you plant rice here? For rice you need terraces and water. How can you get water in this place? There is only a place for drinking water here, how can you plant rice?

JP: What grows here?

WP: Millet, maize, wheat, buckwheat, potatoes.

YT: Beans, vegetables.

WP: There is no water for rice.

Structure 1 - A two-celled rectangular building (6.6 × 15.7 m) standing to a maximum height of 0.75 m/nine courses. The southern unit (4.9 × 6.85 m internally) has a 1 m-wide doorway opening in the southern end of its eastern wall. There is another door (0.95 m wide) situated centrally in the northern end wall of the other cell (4.9 × 6.15 internally). The latter appears to access a porch terrace (3.9 × 6.6 m) on the northern end of the building, whose walls continue to partially flank its eastern and western sides. It is, though, just possible that, rather than a porch, this was a ruined room within the building itself (i.e. upper northern wall totally denuded). A paved terrace also projects for 5.2 m from the southern end of the building.

Structure 2 - A single rectangular cell (6.4 × 8 m) with a 1 m-wide doorway in its eastern side; maximum height, 0.5 m/6–7 courses.

Structure 3 - This is a substantial two-celled rectangular structure (6.5–7 × 14.3 m), its plan being slightly trapezoidal. The southern unit (7 × 7.7 m) appears to be primary, with the northern 'square' being an addition. Heavily overgrown, its walls survive only 0.4 m/five courses high; at the foot of a large tree growing upon its fabric midway along the western side is a small stone slab-built box shrine (recently 'active', with bamboo milk-stick offerings inside). What makes this building seem singularly impressive is that it sits atop a c. 2 m-high knoll/mound (16 × 21.5 m), whose lower sides are reveted by two tiers of terrace walling.

In front of Structure 3, a great natural boulder has been partially paved over to level its top, and four rough-laid steps have been built on its flank (Structure 4). Just south of this point, alongside a reduced trail leading westwards, is a stone-built rest platform (Structure 5; 0.3 m/3–4 courses high). Otherwise, the meadow is dotted with old pastoralist shelter settings and a series of mounds. One of the latter is approximately 16 m in diameter and stands 2 m high, and also has a disused shelter site upon it. (Extant/active circular pastoralist camps are still in use at this locale.) However, there are also smaller mounds (4.5–9 m dia.; 1.5 m high) that seem more 'cairn-' or 'platform-like'. Other features recorded include a standing stone set amid the reduced-trail approach from the south (Figs. 3.27:A & 4.27:C). Similarly, at the base of an immense natural boulder perched along the eastern valley-side scarp, is a stone box shrine and, on its top, a stone slab has been set upright (Figs. 3.27:B & D, 4.27:D).

With its eastern line of buildings and the central standing stone, the formality of Khoido is striking. The

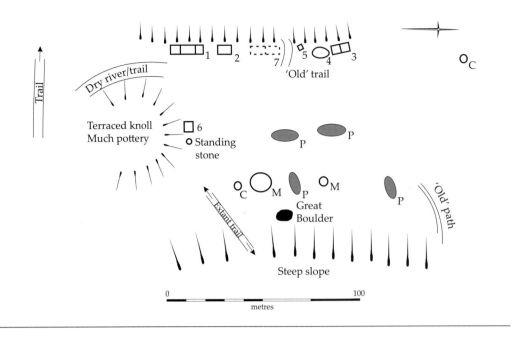

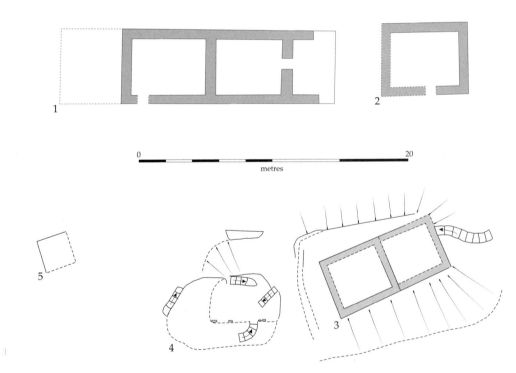

Figure 3.26. *Khuindo: sketch survey plan (top: C = cairn; M = mound; P =* phrohon*); below, detail plans of Structures 1–5.*

removed terraced knoll-top setting of Structure 3 speaks of status differentiation or a distinct function. While reminiscent of Kohla, the sense of planning at Khoido seems perhaps all the greater due to the small number of buildings and their size/scale. The site seems somehow pristine (the line of buildings lacks the organic quality of those at Chikre described below) and its character could even suggest some manner of administrative complex rather than village settlement. This being said, much pottery was recovered from the northern half of the southern hillside. This, and its platform-suggestive terraced contours, could suggest that other buildings may have once dotted its flanks and, therefore, that this might have been a separate hamlet.

Figure 3.27. *Khuindo: A) looking north along meadow with standing stone centre (see Fig. 4.27:C); B) Structure 1 (note tree-growth on walls); C) the great boulder with 'D', the box-shrine at its foot.*

Chromo (28°20.293'/84°11.011'; c. 3320 m a.s.l.;
Fig. 3.11:6; Ch. 2, Chromo, Lines 162 & 163)
Lying *c.* 0.5 km southwest of Chikre (see below), two structures straddle either side of an old trail (*c.* 50 m south of the extant track: Fig. 3.28). Of particular note are the 'window' openings in the southeastern building, as these seem to directly match those in the immediately trail-side building at Chikre.

Structure 1 - A single-celled unit (4 × 7.2 m) which stands 1.7 m/30 courses high. The building's long axis is aligned with and flanks the trail; two lintel-capped, now ground-level 'window' openings are present in the north wall, with another centrally situated in the eastern.

Structure 2 - Although much disturbed by pastoralist *phrohon* constructions, this rectangular unit (4 × 5.4 m) still stands 0.9 m/ten courses high. A 1 × 2.4 m rest platform (0.2 m/two courses high) conjoins its southern, trail-facing wall. A worked stone 'paddle' was found in the rubble associated with this building.

Behind Structure 2 a line of natural boulders (i.e. unworked) border the trail-side; additional stones appear to have been inserted to enhance this barrier.

Also at this general location (*c.* 120 m to the northeast) and appearing 'ancient', is a substantial stone wall — *c.* 7 m long, 1.5 m wide and 0.4 m+/five courses high — that dams a *c.* 40 m-diameter pond.

Chikre Toh (28°20.363'/84°11.318'; c. 3450 m a.s.l.;
Fig. 3.11:7; Ch. 2; Cikre Toh/Chikren, Lines 164 & 165)
Perched on a cliff-edge, five/six buildings lie along the spine of a ridge overlooking a meadow pasture; another lies isolated, some 70 m to the west beside the main trail (Fig. 3.29). While the avenue-like alignment of the buildings is, in some ways, reminiscent of the site at Khoido, the cliff-top situation of the Chikre ruins is extraordinary. There is only a *c.* 0.5 m berm between the two northwesternmost buildings and the cliff, and a step in the wrong direction would result in a fall of more than 100 m (Fig. 3.30:A & B).

Three structures are located at the extreme end of the western promontory ridge, the land dropping steeply on three sides:

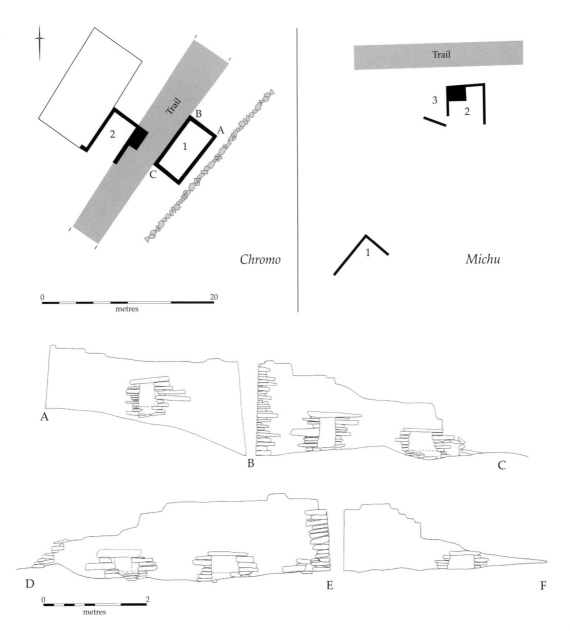

Figure 3.28. *Chromo and Michu: survey plans (above); below, 'toll station' elevations (top Chromo Structure 1; below, Chikre Structure 10: see Figs. 3.29 & 3.30:C).*

Structure 1 - A single-celled rectangular unit (4.5 × 5 m); 1.2 m/18 courses high.

Structure 2 - Very difficult to distinguish, this rectangular unit (3.4 × 4.7 m) conjoins Structure 3 and may be part of the same building.

Structure 3 - A rectangular unit (4.8 × 11.8 m) with possible evidence of an internal wall; maximum height, 1.2 m/17 courses.

To the southeast, further buildings are arranged along the northern cliff-side:

Structures 4 and 5 - Although separated by a *c.* 2.1 m-wide 'corridor', aligned and sharing the same width — and unified by a continuous *c.* 1 m-wide platform terrace along their northern side — these two buildings seem interrelated. The larger rectangle (5.9 ×

10.7 m), Structure 4, stands 0.65 m/nine courses high; its southeastern wall appears to project across the width of the front terrace. The other unit (5) (5.9 × 6.7 m) stands 0.5 m/eight courses high.

Structure 6 - Located south in front of Structure 5, a 0.5 m-high wall runs south for 2 m from the southeastern corner of this rectangular cell (2.5 × 4 m).

Structure 7 - An internally divided, two-celled rectangular unit (6.7 × 9 m) standing only 0.3 m/four courses high. The northern wall continues west beyond the building for 1 m, at which point it returns northwards (for 3 m).

Southeast beyond this a rather unusual arrangement of walls was distinguished. A northwest- to southeast-oriented wall (Structure 9), 0.3 m/four courses high,

Figure 3.29. *Chikre Toh: survey plan.*

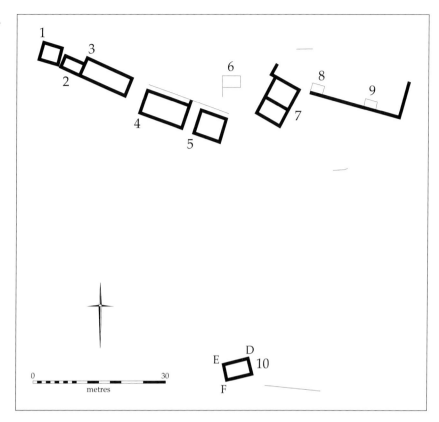

extends for 20.8 m along the crest of the ridge; at its western end it returns northwards, towards the cliff-side, for *c.* 8 m. The western end of this wall roughly corresponds to the line of the northern projecting wall of Structure 7 and together they seem to define an enclosure. Two 'solid' rectangular masonry blocks (both Structure 8; 1.6–1.7 × *c.* 2.7 m), 0.1–0.15 m/2–3 courses high, conjoin the northern side of the main Structure 9 wall. Otherwise, a series of more minor terrace walls was noted around the site, including one length along the cliff-edge.

One further building was recorded, Structure 10. This lies isolated *c.* 35 m south of the other ridge-top structures and is located beside the main trail, which crosses the lower meadow. This single-celled structure (4.2 × 6.5 m) sits on a *c.* 0.5–1 m-high mound. Clearly well made, its walls stand up to 1.5 m/15 courses high; three lintel-capped openings/'windows' are visible in the building's lower fabric (i.e. at ground level: Figs. 3.28 & 3.30:C).

It is difficult to imagine why any community would choose to live in such circumstances. It can only be presumed that defence or control must be the key, and the substantial drystone wall that enclosed the eastern end of the ridge may have had a defensive function. The location of Structure 10, with its various openings, is very similar to the Chromo buildings and equally suggests the regulation of trails.

Hachu and Michu (Ch .2, Hachu & Mhichu, Lines 166 & 167)

These two 'sites' are both located in the vicinity of Tapron. Involving detours off of the main routes used up to Kohla, these locales were only examined briefly in 1994 and neither was re-visited on the return-leg that year, or again in 2000. Accordingly, neither was surveyed using a GPS, and it is difficult to evaluate their status and both would benefit from more sustained scrutiny. (Note that no chuni-holden stones were present at either site.)

Hachu is located at a junction of trails along a small valley up from Tapron. Only one structure is present. It is a 'definite' building and there are no pastoralist shelters in the area. Two north–south walls survive (0.6 m thick and up to 1.8 m high) and define an area of 4 × 6.3 m. A square hole is apparent in the fabric of one, and a block of solid masonry bordering the other is probably a porter's rest place. Therefore, although accredited as being a 'village site' by our local colleagues, in all likelihood this represents no more than a 'toll station' and could be compared to the structures at Chromo.

Located some kilometres away on the edge of a meadow beside a trail, Michu is even more ambiguous. Two, possibly three, buildings are definitely present; though as many pastoralist shelters are sited there, some structures may have been completely

A

B

C

Figure 3.30. *Chikre Toh: A & B) showing cliff-edge location of site, with arrows indicating wall position; C) outlying trailside structure from north (10).*

robbed away or have otherwise gone unnoticed (Fig. 3.28).

Structure 1 - Only defined by two surviving walls, this rectangular setting (4.3 × 7.7 m) stands to a maximum height of 0.8 m.

Structure 2/3 - In the main (i.e. Structure 2), this seems to consist of a sub-rectangular setting (*c.* 5.2 × 5.6 m+) that stands to a maximum height of *c.* 1 m; a solid block of masonry (2 × 2.1 m) in its northern side is probably a rest platform. A 3.4 m-long wall extends at an angle from the western wall of Structure 2. While this may denote another building *per se* (Structure 3), alternatively it may only mark an adjoining porch or ancillary extension of the main building.

Structure 1 at Michu lies some 20 m south of Structures 2/3, whose northern side (and with it the rest platform) borders the trail. Again, this would seem to have been a 'toll station-type' setting, though other buildings may lie in the vicinity.

Kohla (28°22.757'/84°11.111'; 3350 m a.s.l.)
Consisting of 55 buildings, the ruins extend over 6.5 ha. Yet, true to the site's name, *Kohla Sopre/Sopreye* — 'Kohla, the Three Villages' (see Chapter 2 above) — they are separated into three distinct 'quarters' (Figs. 3.31 & 3.32). The central is by far the most dense and village-like, and there is evidence of formalized public space. By comparison, the eastern and western sectors can only be considered of 'hamlet-like' scale. The central and western portions are separated by a stream, whose channel flows down through a deep erosion gully; the eastern portion lies on a slight scarp overlooking the central settlement. Despite these topographic factors, the locale is relatively flat, with only a 25 m difference in height between its various parts. The ground falls away sharply to the south, with the southernmost alignment of buildings in the central sub-site being perched along its edge. As outlined in the narrative section introducing this chapter, the settlement is set in almost a natural amphitheatre — a 'bowl of space' (Fig. 4.2). It is framed by high, wooded ridges to the east and west; the back, northern aspect is ringed by a scarp edge, *c.* 5–10 m high, above which the ground shelves for some 100 m. Behind this, a very steep, almost cliff-edge face rises for some 100 m (estimated), up which a steep path winds to the high ground above.

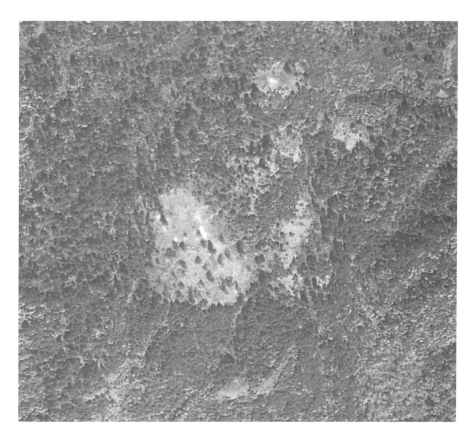

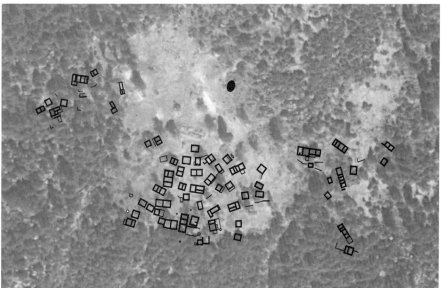

Figure 3.31. *Kohla: satellite image of site's clearing with plan of ruins superimposed below (see Fig. 3.15 for location).*

The settlement's sub-divisions are obvious and have been noticed by its earlier visitors, though on those occasions not all its sectors were necessarily distinguished. (While dotted by mature trees, the main site is essentially open meadow; the western and eastern portions are heavily wooded and their ruins are not immediately visible from the central core.) Visiting the site in 1992, at the suggestion of Alan Macfarlane, Mark Temple and his party (their guide, Damarsingh of Tangting, also accompanied

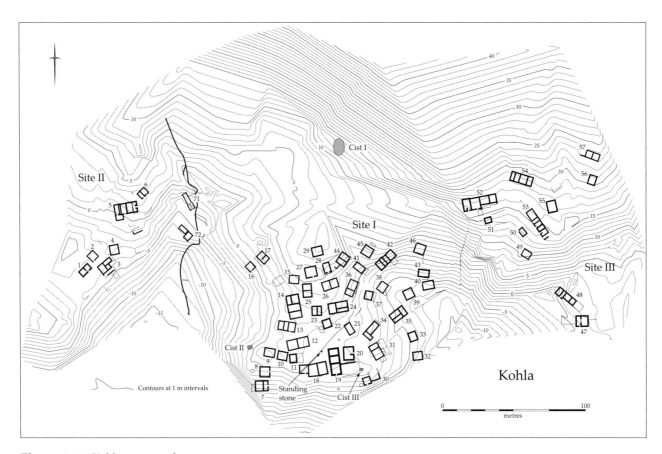

Figure 3.32. *Kohla: survey plan.*

us) made a sketch plan of the central and western portions of the settlement, though they apparently did not see its eastern sector (Temple 1993). In addition, they also rendered quite an accurate 'plan of [a] large house to the west of the settlement' (our Structure 5; see below). Messerschmidt had visited the site 20 years before and also rapidly surveyed it. Though he has not published a plan, his 1976 paper in *Human Ecology* included a lengthy footnote outlining the attribution of the settlement's major components, and also discussed other sites in the vicinity, including The Horsetrack and the Cave of Nuns (*chamsyo ngar*; 1976b, note 10). At Kohla itself he clearly identified its three sectors, attributing the so-called Ghale Raja palace (*Klemai darbar*) in the west and also a stream-side millhouse. Yet he also records visiting what he termed 'Khhol North, a site on a hill several hundred meters north of Khhol Central ... comprised of several structures and is called the "ruins of the underworld demons" (*mo lhu*)'. Though intensively searched for, we were unable to locate this spot, and can only presume that it relates to mis-identified *phrohon*, as there are a number of campsites in that general area. Perhaps the most contentious aspect of Messerschmidt's description was Khhol/Kohla East, which he states is remembered

as 'Lhegi Village' (Lhegi being a Tamu-mai clan) and notes that it was said to house the village blacksmiths, thereby raising the spectre of caste-based distinctions. Arguing that the main track from Kohla runs directly to a high ridge above Ghanpokhara, Messerschmidt privileges the connection which that large Tamu-mai village and its adjacent settlements have with the site. Apparently one of its leading families, the Lamichane 'Subba', maintains exclusive rights to Kohla's grazing and one of the clans of a nearby village is the *Khhol-mai* — the 'people of Khhol/Kohla' (1976b, 171–2).

As further discussed in the context of the central sub-site, it is difficult to estimate the scale of the damage caused by the long-term encampment of pastoralists on the site itself. It is quite likely that some early buildings, along the northern side of the main settlement, have been totally robbed of their stone in the course of their shelter construction.

In this section, the site's survey data are presented (the excavations being described in the chapter that follows). Essentially, organized by the site's sectors, this is a gazetteer of its structures and includes both buildings as such and ancillary constructions. (Note that, in relationship to the project's interim accounts (Evans *et al.* 2002; Evans 2004), the site's system of enumeration has here been more conveniently rationalized. Largely relevant for the western sub-site, this should be held as its 'official' version.) Standing between *c.* 0.2 and 4 m high, the individual survival of the site's buildings varies greatly. This, the extent of their 'cover' (i.e. moss and tree growth) and the quantity of rubble collapse upon them, influences the extent to which their plans and architectural details can be distinguished. Doorways, for example, could not be identified in all instances and there was considerable ambiguity over whether some 'cells' are sub-divided by internal walls. A formal spatial analysis of its components follows.

Kohla Central (I)
Extending over 1.3 ha, the central village seems to have twice the building density of its flanking hamlets (Fig. 3.32). Curtailed by the stream on its west side and low wet ground to the east (at the foot of the Site III slope), its buildings extend from the crown of a slight, *c.* 8 m-high knoll in the north down to the edge of the steep southern scarp-side. Packed into this space, there is much greater evidence of downslope terracing within it. There is equally evidence for the organization of formal public space. The putative King's House along the southern side opens onto a large square or plaza where a large standing stone is set beside it. Running north from this yard area, behind the westernmost line of buildings, there is a definite 'avenue' or hollow-way (see Fig. 4.1).

There is also some evidence of the zoning of its buildings. Although, for example, small single-celled units are located throughout the (sub-)settlement, there is a distinct concentration of such structures along its eastern margin. The implications of this kind of patterning, and the distribution and character of other 'types' will be more fully explored below.

Structure 7 - An internally divided rectangular unit (7.65 × 9.7 m; 74.2 sq.m) with 1 m-wide central doorway in eastern wall: eastern portion 2.6 × 6.2 m internally; western 4.9 × 6.2 m. A large, projecting terrace porch has been added to its western side; overall building height, 1.1 m/17 courses.

Structure 8 - A large single 'square' unit (7.6 × 7.75 m; 58.9 sq.m) with 1.2 m-wide doorway in the east wall and a 'formal' shelf (framed with top and bottom lintel slabs) within the interior face of the north wall (Fig. 3.33:A); 1.18 m/19 courses high.

Structure 9 - Single rectangular cell with no doorway or internal division apparent (6.4 × 8.15 m; 52.2 sq.m); 0.7 m/10 courses high.

Structure 10 - Basically as Structure 9 (i.e. 'matching'; 6.4 × 7.65 m; 49 sq.m); 1.3 m/17 courses high.

Structure 11 - This seems to be a two-celled structure (6.4 × 10 m; 64 sq.m), though the eastern half has been extensively disturbed through pastoralist shelter construction:

A

B

Figure 3.33. *Kohla: A) detail of Structure 8 stone shelf; B) Structure 1 doorway.*

A) original western 'square' (5.6 × 6.4 m);
B) eastern addition (4.40 x 6.4 m).
Maximum building height, 0.25 m/four courses.

97

Figure 3.34. *Kohla — The Structure 19 'King's House': A) as seen from the north; B) showing the quality of its masonry (southwestern elevation); C & D) the 'tethering stone' upright immediately beside it ('D' as exposed in 2000, Trench X).*

Structure 12 - A two-celled range (7.35 × 16 m; 117.6 sq.m):
    A) an original eastern 'square' (7.35 × 8.5 m);
    B) a secondary western 'square' (7.35 × 7.5 m).
Maximum building height, 1.3 m/18 courses.

Structure 13 - A two-celled rectangular structure (6.6–6.95 × 12.95 m; 88.6 sq.m):
    A) an original eastern rectangle (6.95 × 9 m), with an internal cross-wall and a *c.* 0.95 m-wide door in the western end of the southern wall;
    B) a rectangular unit (3.95 × 6.6 m) added to 'A'.
Note that the lower eastern wall face (of 'A') has a series of 'holes' through it; maximum height, 1.3 m/17 courses (Fig. 3.7).

Structure 14 - A large three-celled rectangle (9.3–9.7 × 16.7 m; 160.6 sq.m: Fig. 3.42) whose sequential construction was from north to south:
    A) an internally divided rectangle (7.05 × 9.7 m);
    B) a rectangular unit (5.05 × 9.7 m);
    C) a rectangular unit (4.65 × 9.3 m) whose eastern side is inset from the face of Cells A and B.
Maximum height, 1.88 m/29 courses.

Structure 15 - A single rectangular cell (6.3 × 7.65 m; 48.2 sq.m); maximum height, 1.34 m/19 courses (Fig. 3.35:B, see also Chapter 4 below).

Structure 16 - Single 'square' cell (5.3 × 5.8 m; 30.7 sq.m) with *c.* 1 m-wide doorway in southwestern end of southeastern wall; 1.4 m high/17 courses.

Structure 17 - Internally sub-divided rectangular cell (6.15 × 8.10; 49.8 sq.m) with a projecting porch on southwestern side; southeast portion, 3.4 × 4.8 m internally; northwest, 2.7 × 4.8–1.88 m high/26 courses.

Structure 18 - This phase-built/compounded building (6.4–9.25 × 20.8 m; 157.7 sq.m) seems to consist of two originally separate structures:
    A) a western 'square' (6.4 × 7 m) with a 1.08 m-wide doorway on its southern side;
    B) a large rectangular unit (7.2 × 9.25 m) with a possible doorway identified in its eastern wall.
The 5.4–6.5 m-wide gap between the two (they are not parallel) has been infilled with the construction of a trapezoidal-plan cell (5.2–7.45 × 8.9 m), whose construction definitely post-dated 'A' and, in all likelihood, Cell B. Its full definition is, however, difficult due to disturbance caused through the construction of a pastoralist shelter. Maximum building height, 1.57 m/22 courses.

Structure 19 - A two-celled range (7.8–8.05 × 19 m; 150.2 sq.m: Figs. 3.34:A/B & 5.1):
    A) an internally sub-divided, rectangular unit (8.05 × 11.2 m);

B) a square unit added to the southern side of 'A' (7.8 × 7.8 m) with a 1.2 m-wide doorway in its central southern wall (2.15 m + high), that is probably flanked with in-turned stub-walls. The building incorporates an enormous natural boulder within the fabric of its eastern wall; a 'hole' is apparent in its southeastern side, and a 0.12 × 0.3 m vertical slot was evident in the wall of Cell A (cf. Structure 5). Overall maximum height, 2.75 m/*c*. 40 courses. (Note that this structure may well have a direct interrelationship with Structure 20; this will be further discussed below.)

Structure 20 - A large 'square' unit (7.95 × 9.65 m; 76.7 sq.m); some manner of internal sub-division (?stub-wall) marks the southern side of the 1 m-wide door within the middle of its eastern wall. Maximum height, 0.4 m/six courses. (Note that this building has a 'corridor-like' relationship/divide with Structure 20 and the two may have been directly related.)

Structure 21 - A rectangular single-celled unit (5 × 8.35 m; 41.7 sq.m) with a possible 0.9 m-wide doorway on south side; 0.65 m/eight courses high.

Structure 22 - Though difficult to define, this seems to be a square single cell unit (6.6 × 6.6 m; 43.6 sq.m), with traces of porch terracing in the southern front; 0.44 m/four courses high.

Structure 23 - An internally sub-divided 'square' (6.95 × 7.45 m; 51.8 sq.m): east portion internally 2.3 × 5.5 m; west, 2.95 × 5.5 m; 0.42 m/six courses high.

Structure 24 - A two-celled rectangular building (7.75 × 14.55 m; 112.8 sq.m); the eastern rectangle (7.75 × 9.1 m), that appears to be primary, is longitudinally sub-divided; the western cell extends over 5.4 × 7.75 m (Fig. 3.42). Although no doorways are apparent, stairs, or more probably stepped porch terraces, are located along the eastern and southern sides; maximum building height, 0.56 m/six courses.

Structure 25 - A two-celled rectangular unit (6.9 × 9.8 m; 67.6 sq.m): north cell 4.95 × 3.9 m; southern, 4.95 × 3.95 m. There is evidence of a possible door in southern side; the structure is 1.32 m/24 courses high.

Structure 26 - A two-celled rectangular unit (6.7 × 11.9 m; 79.7 sq.m), though no evidence of phased construction is apparent:
    A) western 'square' (6.8 × 6.7 m);
    B) eastern 'square' (6.2 × 6.7 m; both measurements include central cross-wall).
Maximum height, 0.46 m/six courses (Fig. 3.42).

Structure 27 - A single-celled 'square' (7.35 × 8 m; 58.8 sq.m), with a 1.1 m-wide doorway in the southern side; maximum height, 1.5 m/18 courses (Fig. 3.42 and see Chapter 4 below).

Structure 28 - A rectangular single-celled unit (5.5 × 7.45 m; 41 sq.m), with evidence of a 0.48 m-wide terrace porch in front (west wall projects also; there is a separate porch/ledge conjoining the southwest corner); 0.65 m/12 courses high (Fig. 3.42).

Structure 29 - An extremely disturbed 'square' single cell (7 × 8.1 m; 56.7 sq.m), with evidence of a terrace porch projecting for 0.6 m on southern front; 0.14 m/two courses high.

Structure 30 - This seems to be a complicated structure which, unfortunately, has been extensively disturbed through the construction of a pastoralist shelter. The primary eastern unit is a rectangular cell (7.45 × 7.8[+] m), which has a small 'square' added slightly offset to its southwestern corner (5 × 5.3 m; 84.6 sq.m combined total); the latter has a 0.9 m-wide doorway in its southern wall. A terrace porch projects south beyond the eastern cell; a square masonry block (2 × 2 m) lies just beyond and parallel with the southwestern square. Maximum building height, 1.4 m/18 courses.

Structure 31 - A large, internally sub-divided rectangle (7.10 × 11.1 m; 78.8 sq.m) that has been complicated due to exterior additions. There seems to be a stair on its northwestern corner, and it has terrace porches on both the southern end of its northeastern wall and over the eastern half of the southeastern wall. Maximum building height, 1.6 m/22 courses.

Structure 32 - A single 'square'/rectangular cell (6.2 × 7.2 m; 44.6 sq.m), with a possible terrace porch on its east side; 0.4 m/six courses high.

Structure 33 - A single 'square' cell unit (6.05 × 6.85 m; 41.4 sq.m); 0.34 m/four courses high.

Structure 34 - A two-celled 'L'-shaped range (5.1–7.35 × 12.65 m; 72.3 sq.m):
    A) western rectangle (3.45 × 7.35 m);
    B) eastern rectangle added longitudinally at right-angles to 'A' (5.1 × 9.2 m).
Maximum building height, 1.46 m/23 courses.

Structure 35 - A two-celled rectangle (7.55 × 11.95 m; 90.2 sq.m):
    A) original, longitudinally divided, western unit (7.55 × 8.45 m);
    B) an eastern rectangle added across the width of 'A' (3.5 × 7.55 m), greatly disturbed by pastoralist construction.
Maximum height, 1.26 m/16 courses.

Structure 36 - A two-celled unit (6.3 × 11.40 m; 71.8 sq.m):
    A) an original northeastern 'square' (6.3 × 7.15 m);
    B) a southwestern rectangle (4.25 × 6.30 m).
A terraced porch runs along the southeastern side of Cell A, overlapping 'B' by 1.1 m.

Structure 37 - A single 'square' cell unit (5.8 × 6.4 m; 37.1 sq.m); 0.2 m/three courses high.

Structure 38 - A single 'square' cell unit (6.2 × 7.25 m; 44.9 sq.m); 0.54 m/five courses high.

Structure 39 - A single 'square' cell unit (7.1 × 7.2 m; 51.1 sq.m); 0.18 m/three courses high.

Structure 40 - A single rectangular cell unit (6.15 × 8.55 m; 52.6 sq.m); 1.16 m/17 courses high.

Structure 41 - A single rectangular cell (5.1 × 8 m; 40.8 sq.m), with evidence of a terrace porch along its southeastern end; maximum height, 0.8 m/ten courses.

Structure 42 - A two-celled rectangular range (6.55–7.2 m x 15.4 m; 105.4 sq.m: Fig. 3.42):
    A) original western 'square' (7.05 × 7.2 m), with internal cross-wall and possible evidence of a southern door;
    B) a later added eastern rectangle (6.55 × 8.35 m), whose north-western side is inset from 'A'. Internally divided by a cross-wall, it is possible that its two portions were themselves phase-built; an exterior yard-terrace conjoins its southeastern front.
Maximum height, 0.64 m/seven courses.

Structure 43 - A single rectangular cell unit (5.65 × 8.3 m; 46.9 sq.m); height, 0.40 m/four courses.

A

B

Figure 3.35. *Kohla: A) Structure 6; B) Structure 15.*

Structure 44 - An internally sub-divided 'square' unit (7.4 × 8.8 m; 65.1 sq.m.); southern side seems joined by an 'L'-shaped wall, probably porch-related. Maximum height, 0.46 m/six courses.

Structure 45 - A single 'square' unit (7.25 × 7.65 m; 55.5 sq.m.). There is evidence of a terrace porch on its southern side, and it has an unusual 'double' reinforcing of the northeastern wall (1.9 m wide); beyond the latter — by 2 m — there is a parallel rectangle of stone (possible resting place). Maximum building height, 1.1 m/15 courses.

Structure 46 - A single 'square' cell unit (7.6 × 7.8 m; 59.3 sq.m.); 0.7 m/nine courses high.

Kohla West (II)
Six buildings are located within the western sector that lies amid woodland along the rise above the stream that separates this portion from the Sub-site I core (Fig.

3.32). Its buildings appear to be grouped into two clusters. To the south, there are four that might relate to two pairs; in each a single cell unit being associated with a more complex house structure (Structure 1/2 and Structures 3/4). Lying somewhat removed, the northern group is another 'pairing' — Structures 5 and 6 — but in this case, both are quite extraordinary. Although relatively small, the latter is the highest building on the site, and was definitely two-storeyed. The former, Structure 5, attributed as being the palace of the Ghale Raja, is among the largest in the settlement and certainly has the most elaborate architectural details.

Structure 1 - A rectangular unit (5.25 × 9.15 m; 48 sq.m) with a 0.95 m-wide doorway in its eastern wall that has 0.50 m-long (beyond wall) in-turned flanking walls on both sides; these do not seem to go up to the full height of the wall-build. It has an internal sub-division (with a doorway gap 2.3 m wide) separating the northeastern (3.2 × 3.7 m) and southwestern portions (3.6 × 3.7 m). Very well made/finished (i.e. uniform build), the two southern wall corners appear to stand to full single-storey height (2.7 m/41 courses high). Note that the doorway itself appears to go up through the full height of the build (i.e. probably capped only by its roof); at the base of the doorway two large 'lintel' stones seem to bed upon foundation courses (three — 0.15 m high/deep), possibly indicating a raised interior (Fig. 3.33:B).

Structure 2 - Single-celled unit (6.5 × 6.3 m; 40.9 sq.m) with 1 m-wide door in southeast wall; southern wall projects by 0.5 m eastward beyond doorway; maximum height, 1 m/14 courses.

Structure 3 - Compounded 'square' (7.1 × 8.2 m) with a rectangular cell that projects for 3.2 m beyond its northwestern side (3.6 m wide; 69.7 sq.m in total: Fig. 3.42). It is difficult to distinguish its components owing to thick moss-cover throughout. It seems, nevertheless, to consist of three main rooms (internal dimensions):
    A) western rectangle (3.9 × 5.8 m);
    B) southeastern 'square' (2.4 × 2.8 m);
    C) northeastern rectangle (2.3 × 5.6 m).
Stub walls project northeast from the southern wall of Room/Cell B and southeast from the western wall of A; these probably relate to the porch terrace that continues around its southern front (including a terrace wall dividing its two levels). No doorways are apparent within the building itself, which survives to a maximum height of 1.05 m/15 courses.

Structure 4 - Single-celled unit (6.9 × 7.15 m; 49.3 sq.m), west wall continues for *c.* 1.2 m beyond the north wall (no doorway apparent); maximum height, 0.45 m/seven courses.

Structure 5 - Compounded 'L'-shaped range (16.6 × 7.85 m) with a rectangular room conjoining its southeast side (3.6 × 5.95 m; 130.3 sq.m in total). This building is rich in architectural details (shelves,

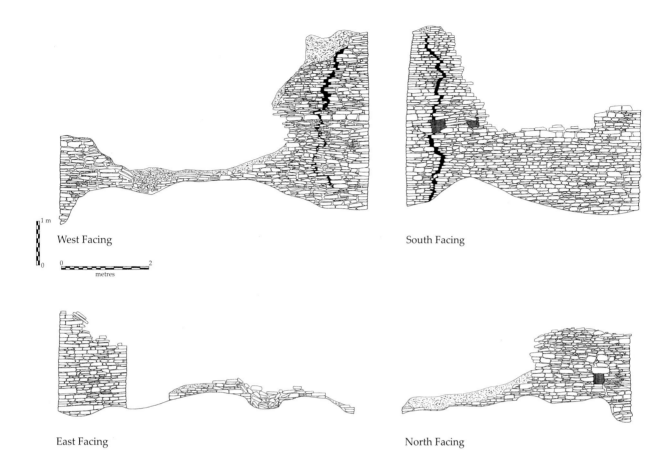

West Facing

South Facing

East Facing

North Facing

Figure 3.36. *Kohla: Structure 6 elevations.*

windows, etc.). The main range consists of three units (from northeast to southwest):

A) an internally sub-divided 'square' (7.85 × 8.3 m) with a 1.5 m-wide 'formal' doorway (flanked by in-turned side walls) set centrally in the eastern wall;

B) a rectangular unit (7.7 × 4.7 m — internal width dimension) with southern exterior door access (0.95 m wide);

C) a rectangular unit (5 × 7.8 m) with 1.05 m-wide doorway in southern wall; the rectangular room conjoining its southern side also has possible doorway access through its southern wall.

Maximum overall building height, 2.95 m/48 courses. Note that the architectural sequence and details of this building are more thoroughly discussed below.

Structure 6 - A 'squarish' rectangular unit (5.5 × 7.1 m; 39 sq.m), with an interior wall dividing it into two portions: northeast, 3.3 × 4.35 m; southwest, 1.95 × 4.35 m. There is a definite doorway within the eastern wall of the latter, 0.95 m wide (going down to ground level). There is also the possibility of a raised doorway to the northeastern portion in the eastern wall, but which cannot be identified with certainty. Well-made of large part-dressed stone, this is the highest surviving building on site (4 m/62 courses), with a storey-division marked by joist holes and a levelling stringer course (Figs. 3.35:A & 3.36).

Kohla East (III)

The nine buildings, and what are two very distinctly small units (possibly rest platforms; Structures 49

& 50), that make up this sub-site are located on the *c.* 5–10 m-high scarp-edge above the main settlement (Fig. 3.32). As a group ('hamlet'), they are relatively dispersed, with the two southernmost buildings (Structures 47 & 48) lying at somewhat of a remove on a lower terrace, some 5 m below the rest. Whilst as a whole this cluster includes a variety of building types, one — Structure 53 — is a uniquely long, narrow range, that is without parallel elsewhere on the site.

The buildings are set amid woodland (and for the most part are thickly covered in moss), except for three in the north (Structures 55–7) which are, instead, set on the side of a grassy plain that extends northwestward. At points, this swathe seems to be bordered by traces of low stone walling and it may have been an area of open fields; the flatish land across the top of the scarp on this side seems to be the only area where arable could have been readily possible. (The site's environs were explored for any evidence of terraced fields — including the steep slope's below the main settlement — with no evidence whatsoever being forthcoming; though see Macfarlane below.)

101

Structure 47 - This appears to be a large rectangle sub-divided by a north–south internal wall (8 × 9.15 m; 73.2 sq.m); the west cell seems to have a southern doorway *c.* 0.85 m wide; maximum height visible, 0.20 m/three courses. Note that there is much moss-covered rubble in association, and there may be a poorly preserved cell or an earlier building on the eastern side.

Structure 48 - A long three-celled rectangular range (5–6.15 × 21.7 m; 116.3 sq.m):
    A) an internally sub-divided rectangular unit (6.15 × 6.75 m) with a 0.9 m-wide doorway in the southwestern wall of the southeastern portion;
    B) an internally sub-divided southeastern extension to 'A' (5 × 8.9 m), offset from its southwestern front;
    C) possible-only, southeastern extension to 'B' (very disturbed/faint; 5 × 6.05 m).
Maximum building height, 0.35 m/two courses.

Structure 49 - A poorly preserved, single rectangular unit (5.45 × 6.7 m; 36.5 sq.m); maximum height, 0.20 m/two courses.

Structure 52 - This is a very large, east–west oriented range (6.35–9 × 24.95 m; 189.7 sq.m: Fig. 3.42). Of phased construction, it consists of three cells extending eastward:
    A) a rectangular unit (6.1 × 9 m); a 0.95 m-wide door in its southern wall has an in-turned wall flanking its western side;
    B) a 'square' unit (6.85 × 8.6 m) with a 0.95 m-wide door in its southern wall;
    C) an internally sub-divided rectangle (6.35 × 11.95 m).
The latter extends longitudinally from the eastern side of 'B', and a 0.9–2.3 m-wide terrace porch runs along its southern front; at either end, it is framed by stub-walls extending south from the eastern walls of Cells B and C. Maximum building height, 1.43 m/20 courses.

Structure 53 - A most unusually long range (5.8 × 20.7 m; 120 sq.m: Fig. 3.42). Although having five cross-wall sub-divisions, it seems essentially to be of one unified build. Its internal sub-divisions are set at distances/widths of (from northwest to southeast):
    A) 6.35 m (no doorway);
    B) 2.19 m, with a *c.* 1 m-wide doorway in the southwestern wall (west end);
    C) 2.65 m, with a *c.* 1.05 m-wide doorway in the southwestern wall (east end);
    D) 2.3 m (no doorway apparent);
    E) 3.2 m, there is a *c.* 1 m-wide doorway in the western end of the southwestern wall, with an in-turned stub-wall flanking in its southeastern side.
Note that 1.65 m beyond the end of 'E' is a low parallel wall. Apparently associated with the building, this may either relate to an 'open shed' or a porters' rest point; maximum building height, 2.05 m/27 courses.

Structure 54 - A two-celled rectangular range (7.1 × 16.4 m; 116.4 sq.m):
    A) a southeastern, cross-wall divided rectangle (7.1 × 9.95 m);
    B) a northwestern, cross-wall divided rectangle (6.45 × 7.1 m).
There are traces of a terrace porch before both of the units; maximum building height, 1.18 m/15 courses.

Structure 55 - A single cell with possible internal sub-division (7.1 × 8.6 m; 61.1 sq.m); its southern wall has been incorporated into a pastoralist shelter. Maximum height, 1.33 m/16 courses.

Structure 56 - A single rectangular unit (5.75 × 7.15 m; 41.1 sq.m); maximum building height, 0.55 m/eight courses.

Structure 57 - An internally sub-divided rectangular range (5.4 × 10.2 m; 55.1 sq.m). Much disturbed through pastoralist activity, the western extension of the southern wall may indicate another dismantled unit; maximum building height, 0.63 m/seven courses.

Other structures
Two relatively small, stonewall structures are located before Structures 52 and 53, near the edge of the scarp on the east side of Kohla III (Fig. 3.32). Of only 'shed-like' proportions, they seem much too small to be any manner of houses or even animal byres. Rather, they may either have been porters' rest points (Structure 50 has a bench along one side for this purpose) and/or 'toll stations', such as were found at Chromo and Chikre, and possibly also Michu and Hachu.

Structure 50 - A small rectangle (4.35 × 6 m; 26.1 sq.m), with a rest bench added to northwestern end; there is a vertical slot in the southwestern face (0.25 × 0.58 m) that appears to go through the wall. Maximum building height, 1.75 m/23 courses.

Structure 51 - A small rectangular cell (4.45 × 5.45 m; 24.2 sq.m); maximum height, 1.7 m/23 courses.

Two rectangular 'box' structures, oriented northwest–southeast lie in the valley base, parallel with/beside the stream separating sub-Sites II and III (Fig. 3.32). Said to be millhouses, given their plan-form and location this assignment would, indeed, seem valid (Harrison 1996, 34 illustrates the operation of such mills, and see also Gajurel & Vaidya 1994, 300–306). Note that 25 m downstream from these a large east–west oriented 'wall', 3.5 m long and 1.8 m wide (1.1 m/ten courses high), appears to have been cut by the stream. While possibly part of a more major structure, it is conceivable that this related to a small dam.

Structure 71 - This consists of a rectangular 'box' (2.4 × 7.3 m) with large walls flanking a 0.6 m-wide chute at its southern end (3.5 × 3.6 m). Standing 0.7 m high, this would seen to be a horizontal-type watermill.

Structure 72 - While no chute is evident, this is probably another mill and comparable to Structure 71. It seems to consist of two conjoining rectangular 'units' (3.6 × 6.75 m and 4.65 × 5.9 m) standing 0.75 m high.

Ritual features
As mentioned, when we first arrived at Kohla our attention was immediately drawn to a great 'saucer-like' capstone, balancing on enormous outcropping boulders (Cist I). While obviously of natural origin, centrally situated midway up the northern scarp behind and overlooking the main village, it struck the archaeological team as a commanding 'geological presence' (Fig. 3.38:A). That it was indeed held to have been 'special' was further indicated by the fact that a

large stone-slab shrine had been built within its interior (in the cavity opening onto the site itself). Further confirmation that this was a ritual 'architecture' seemed forthcoming by the fact that apparently similar (though smaller) 'cist-like' settings were identified on either side of the southern portion of the main village (Cists II & III).

Cist I (*The 'Saucer'*) - The great capstone is 3.4–5.9 m wide, some 7.5 m long and up to *c.* 1 m thick (Figs. 3.37 & 3.38:A & B). Its southern front overhangs by 2.5 m the two huge boulders on which it is balanced (it is also carried on a third at the back end). In the *c.* 1.4 m-wide gap between the two front boulders, has been set a stone-slab shrine. This consists of an upright (rough worked?; 0.9 m wide, 0.75 m high and 0.4 m thick), on which is balanced a large boulder (0.8 × 0.8 × 0.9 m), whose shape is vaguely evocative of a human head/face. At the base of the upright is a drystone altar, four courses high (0.5 m; 1.1 × 0.7 m), whose flat top is covered in one large slab. Above this, the cavity is void for *c.* 1 m (front opening 2.4 m high in total), with the soil below, retained by the shrine, sloping down from below the capstone along the length of the interior (i.e. soil appears higher further back within the inaccessible interior, eventually leaving only a slight gap with the capstone roof).

Cist II - Lying on the western margins of the main village (and evidently opening in that direction), this setting projects beyond the line of a north–south wall that retains a terrace adjoining Structure 9. It appears to consist of large stones packed around and set flat across a series of natural boulders (continuously over an area of *c.* 2.4 × 2.4 m: Figs. 3.37 & 3.38:C). At its western front, a capstone (0.8 × 1.65 m × 8–10 cm) lies balanced between two outcropping boulders to define a cavity *c.* 0.6 m high and 1 m wide (soil-filled, the depth of its interior is unknown). While this may just represent levelling to create a flat paving, the setting certainly suggests a 'box-cist'.

Cist III - Facing east, this is built into the side of a raised terrace that lies behind Structure 20 (south of) and seems to relate to the boulder-retained 'square' before Structure 30. It consists of a capstone (1.25 × 1.6 m × 10–15 cm), propped upon stacked drystone settings (0.2 m & 0.5 m high) to leave an interior cavity, *c.* 0.3 × 0.6 m (Figs. 3.37 & 3.38:D). Filled with soil, the depth of its interior is unknown; pottery, however, was recovered from it upon cleaning.

Just west of the Structure 19 'King's House', a large standing stone rises 1.65 m above the ground surface. By association (i.e. proximity), it is said to be where the King tethered his horse (this was tested during the 2000 excavations, see Chapter 4, Trench X below).

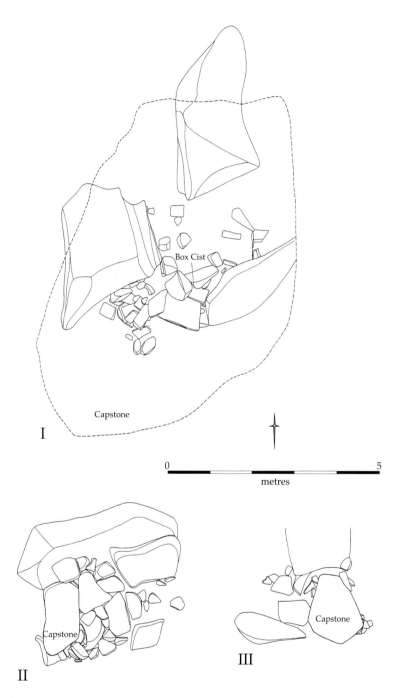

Figure 3.37. *Kohla: Cists I–III plans.*

Kohla — building studies and settlement space

In this section, the layout of Kohla will be analysed in terms of the 'grammar' of its buildings. This will variously draw upon formal architectural principles and spatial models, and be informed by the vernacular construction traditions of Himalayan villages. The sheer quantity of building-related data makes us rely upon a more strict analytical language (e.g. 'units',

A

C

B

D

Figure 3.38. *Kohla: cist settings: A & B) Cist I, 'The Saucer' from south (i.e. village site-facing view; A) detail of interior box-shrine with remains of cow at its foot (B); C) Cist II; D) Cist III, note paved surface before.*

'cells', 'types', etc.) than was employed by earlier visitors to the site. Moreover, with the investigations cut short by political events in Nepal, the emphasis given to this kind of formal spatial study is greater than would otherwise have been exercised had the excavations progressed further.

Excluding the Structures 50 and 51 'sheds' and the stream-side mills, Kohla's buildings range in size from 24.3–189.7 sq.m. Whereas with 40 buildings extending over an area of 1.3 ha (130 × 100 m), the central settlement is densely packed and its layout is suggestive of a village *per se* (Kohla I), the eastern and western portions are more 'hamlet-like'. Less constrained by their density, the layout of the main residential units within Kohla II and III seem to relate more to the prospects afforded to their long 'range-fronts' (Fig. 3.39). (Their arrangement is not linear, but offset from each other so as not to block the views of neighbours.) Respectively, with six and nine buildings, Kohla II and III each, at least superficially, seem more akin to the small settlement sites recorded at Chikre and Khuindo (though, at the latter, we do not know how many buildings have

been destroyed on its central knoll). At these two other sites the buildings are arranged linearly along the edge of slopes, each thereby having its own view. They lack — but then did not require — the 'deeper' and more 'fan-like' arrangement of Kohla II and III's buildings. Equally, at none of the other sites is there comparable evidence of formal public space, as at Kohla Central (e.g. paved squares and 'proper' avenues), and altogether it seems a different order of settlement.

Large complex buildings are distributed throughout all three of the village's sectors (100 sq.m+; 11 in total: Fig. 3.39). While the central sub-site would have the greatest overall number (six; Structures 12, 14, 18, 19, 24 & 42), as indicated in Table 3.1, Kohla East

Table 3.1. *Sub-site distribution/ratio of large buildings at Kohla.*

Settlement sub-sector	Total no. of buildings	No. of buildings >100 sq.m	Ratio >/<100 sq.m
I	40	5	1/7
II	6	1	1/5
III	9	4	1/2.5
Total		55	10	

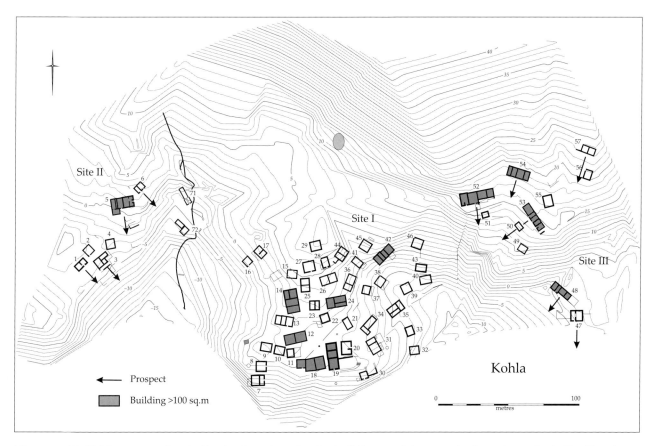

Figure 3.39. *Kohla: survey plan indicating location of major buildings and 'prospect' orientations of sub-Site II and III's structures.*

would have the greatest proportional density (four in total; Structures 48, 52–54), with Kohla West only having one building of that category (Structure 5).

The largest structure is 53 (189.7 sq.m) in Kohla East. Thereafter, by size, the next fall within the central settlement — Structures 14, 18 and 19 — which have floor areas of between *c.* 150 and 160 sq.m. The smallest of the latter is the central King's House (19; 150.2 sq.m), with the putative Ghale Raja's palace in Kohla West — Structure 5 — only extending over 130.3 sq.m. In other words, neither of these 'attributed' buildings is the largest on site. However, because of their 'special' status, it is worth considering them in greater detail.

The Kings' Houses/Palaces
Standing nearly 3 m high (48 courses), the putative Ghale Raja's palace (Structure 5) in Kohla West is certainly an impressive building. The quality and unique number of its architectural details — and the degree to which its development sequence can be 'read' — makes it suitable for more intensive study (Figs. 3.40 & 3.41):

Cell A
1) Main doorway (1.05 m wide) with in-turned flanking walls.
2) Probable door through cross-wall (*c.* 1 m wide), though certainty of its identification is impossible due to rubble collapse.
3) Inset wall recess in exterior wall face, with its base raised by *c.* 0.55 m above ground level. While possibly indicating a blocked doorway, the inset face is, in part, tied into the main wall and, therefore, may have had some other purposes (e.g. purely decorative or intending to hold an inset panel).
4) A vertical slot (0.1 m wide and 0.34 m high) that appears to go through the wall.
5) Collapsed triangular window (sides *c.* 0.3 m long) set in upper wall, 1.70 m above ground level.
6) 0.15 × 0.18 m 'hole' in the wall, set 0.63 m above ground level, that does not appear to go through the fabric.

Cell B
7) Definite doorway (0.95 m wide).
8) Possible location of collapsed doorway in cross-wall shared with Cell C.
9) Possible position of original north wall (see '11' below).
10) Triangular window, set 0.5 m above exterior ground level; exterior opening — base, 0.28 m; sides, 0.34 m; interior — base, 0.17 m; sides, 0.27 m.
11) Recess 0.4 m wide, 0.44 m high and 0.3 m deep; continues 'behind'/sealed by cross-wall shared with Cell C.
12) 0.18 × 0.24 m 'hole' above window (penetrates 0.3 m deep into fabric).
13) High recess 0.23 × 0.29 m; 0.3 m deep, with vertical slab set in back.

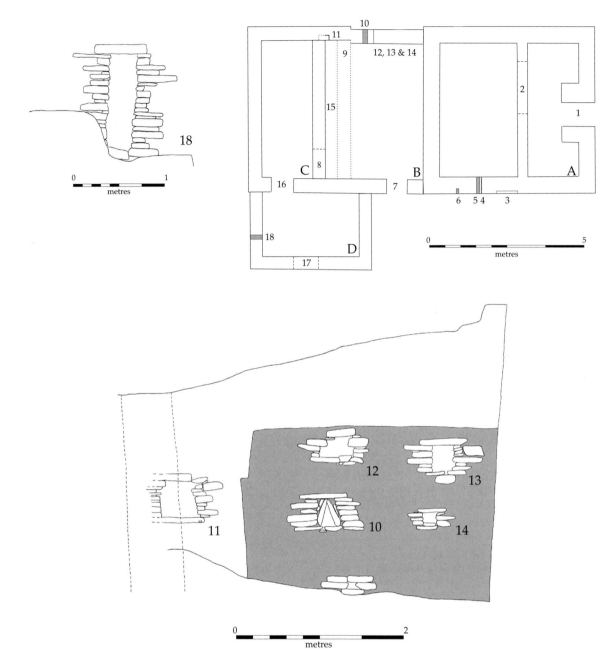

Figure 3.40. *Kohla: plan of Structure 5 with architectural details indicated (top), with elevation of interior face of Cell B north wall below (grey tone indicates original wall-build) and Cell D wall 'slot' left.*

14) Small hole below '13' (0.15 × 0.15 × 0.2 m).
15) Low-level 'hole' (0.28 × 0.24 m) that goes through the fabric of the cross-wall.

Cells C & D
16) Doorway access into Cell D (*c.* 1 m wide).
17) Possible (only) collapsed doorway location.
18) Vertical slot (0.26 m wide and 1.02 m high) with lintelled top; goes through wall just above exterior ground level.
19) Two scaffold holes (7 × 12 cm and 12 × 12 cm, both *c.* 0.25 m deep into wall) set on top of each other in outer face of Cell C wall. There are other potential candidates for same in immediate area; alternatively, these could have supported a timber superstructure (e.g. stairway).

Cell/Room B is clearly secondary to 'A'. This is not only apparent in the building division in the lower wall face between the two, but also that the northern wall of B was inset from that of the eastern unit. The primary status of the latter is indicated by the fact that the fabric of 'B' clearly went over the top of that of 'A', along the cross-wall that divided them. While possibly resulting in some demolition of the upper courses of the eastern room, it is reasonable to presume that the building west of this point was higher. This could attest to the existence of a second storey for the added

Figure 3.41. *Kohla - Structure 5: A) north elevation; B) doorway in eastern wall; C) interior of northern wall, Cell B; D) exterior elevation, Cell A.*

portions. The evidence is, unfortunately, ambiguous, as relatively little rubble fills the interior of Room B (though it may have been cleared by earlier visitors to the site; e.g. Temple's party), and there is no distinction of an upper storey by stringer courses or regular joist holes, as in Structure 6.

Among the most distinct features of this building as a whole is the inset portion of its northern wall over 2.5 m in Room B. From this it could, in fact, be inferred that it was a later addition, linking 'A' with 'C' in the west, with the latter standing independently and, at least in part, contemporary with the eastern (A). (By this logic, the position of the original eastern wall of Room C would have corresponded with the inset in 'B', this wall subsequently being dismantled and re-built further west. However, any corresponding 'build' divisions within the southern wall of Rooms B/C necessary to support this sequence were not apparent.) There seems no doubt though that the projecting wing/porch, 'D', was a secondary addition to Room C, and could not have originally been integral to it (though it is conceivable that C/D stood independently together, only later being linked to A *via* Room B).

What singularly distinguishes this building (apart from its general height) is the number of windows and recesses in the northern wall of its middle room (Room B). Apart from the vertical slot in the southwestern wing/porch (18), there is nothing that is particularly noteworthy within the building's western range alone (Rooms C/D). The same, however, is not true of Room A. Aside from the stub-wall-flanked doorway, centrally situated in its eastern side, are the recesses and window/slots in its southern wall. By this, it could be inferred that the function of Room B (a later addition) was originally fulfilled by 'A' (if, at first, standing alone, Rooms/range C/D were not in anyway 'special'). From this, it could be argued that, while as it first stood Room A was a 'common-size' building (62.4 sq.m), it was, nevertheless, *distinguished* from the outset.

How are we to envisage this building and is this to be considered a 'monumental' architecture? If so, it was not particularly sophisticated. There is no question of there being any direct internal doorway access between Rooms A and B. Like the other complex 'long' ranges on the site, the unification or inter-

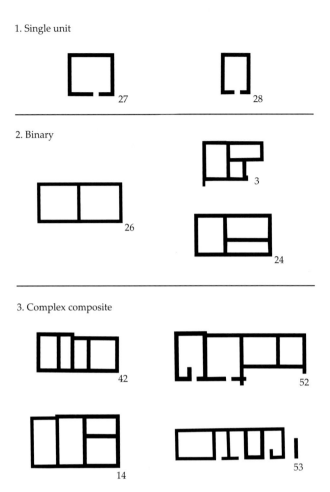

1. Single unit

27 28

2. Binary

26 3 24

3. Complex composite

42 52 14 53

Figure 3.42. *Kohla: building types.*

connection of rooms seems largely to have been facilitated by facade-exterior terrace porches. In this case, these internal divisions could either suggest multiple household/familial residence (i.e. by kin) and/or discrete functions under one roof. By this means, Room B could, for example, have functioned as some manner of shrine or in an 'official' capacity. What otherwise uniquely distinguishes this building is its formal 'L'-shaped plan. This is unique among Kohla's buildings. Whereas, in the case of other 'L'-arrangements, individual cells are simply offset or project beyond the facade of their ranges (e.g. Structures 34, 48 & 52), in this instance Room D has been added entirely against and at right-angles to the main facade, as if, in effect, to create a new wing.

While still nevertheless very impressive and well-made, the other so-called King's House, Structure 19, is altogether simpler (Figs. 3.34:B & 5.1). It has a clear, two-phased construction sequence; that the west wall of its southern square cell is inset by *c.* 0.2 m from that of the northern two-room rectangle leaves no doubt of its secondary status. Unusually,

the northern unit has an enormous upright boulder built into its southeastern corner, whose flattened face is flush with and incorporated into the wall. Otherwise, the building only has two architectural features of note: a small vertical slot in the western wall of the southern unit (0.12 × 0.3 m); and its massive stub-wall-flanked doorway in the middle of its southern side. With a width of 1.2 m, the latter rises through the full height of the wall's surviving fabric (2.15 m high) and is, thereby, comparable to the 'high' door in Structure 1.

In the case of the Structure 5 'palace', the reasons for its entitlement seem obvious within the context of the site as a whole. Its walls are generally high and it includes a unique series of niches and windows. Yet, other buildings on the site also have isolated examples of slots in their walls (e.g. Structure 50); an interior shelf recess is present in Structure 8 (Fig. 3.33:A), and Structure 13 has a series of low window-like openings in its eastern front (like the 'toll stations' elsewhere). What really marks this building is the array and density of its architectural features, particularly the occurrence of triangular windows, which are not present in any of the other ruins. (Pignède illustrates a tiered village shrine at Ghandrung, with a prominent triangular recess and which is associated with the worship of its royal/princely family; see Fig. 4.28)

Although lacking such elaboration and the detail of Structure 5, Structure 19 is nonetheless a large building and it is prominently situated fronting onto the main Kohla I 'plaza'. While the proximity of the nearby standing stone has probably also been influential in its assignation, perhaps the key factor has been its association with Structure 20 beside it (Fig. 3.34:A, C & D). When first shown this 'King's House', it was explained that this latter structure was also a part of it and it was only through the ensuing surveys that the corridor-like divide separating the two was distinguished. They may still, of course, have been related and, if not recognizing this divide, a combined Structure 19/20 would have seemed the largest single building complex on the site.

However imposing individual buildings may seem within Kohla, there seems to be no particular evidence of a 'monumental' architecture. The 'design' of its large buildings is not particularly sophisticated. They basically consist of a series of individual cells, either accessed internally (i.e. room-to-room), or from their frontage, and there is no evidence of interior corridors. The site's big buildings are essentially enlarged houses, and none seem constructed on a 'grand-scale' from the outset, but are rather the sequential expansion of typically domestic-type units.

Structural dynamics and building types

Through the analyses of the building's plans and their construction phases, it is clear that the site's largest buildings were all initially much simpler and smaller, being 44.8–90.2 sq.m in area (with the primary form of Structure 34 being distinctly smaller at 25.4 sq.m: Table 3.2). This demonstrates the uniformity of the basic building unit, and they were all essentially rectangular single-cells (with some internally sub-divided across their width; cf. Structure 34). Stripped down in this way to its primary form, a complicated multi-cell building such as Structure 14 becomes equivalent to such simpler structures as Number 7; a complex range like Structure 18 — upon removing the secondary central-linking cell — becomes reduced to two separate single-room buildings, variously equivalent to structures like Structures 16, 22, 33 & 37 and 8, 10 & 40. Similarly, simple origins can also be distinguished among the most complex 'long' range-type buildings in the flanking hamlets (e.g. Structures 5 & 52). What this effectively attests to is a loss of variability and distinction between buildings in the primary phases of the settlement. Interestingly enough, though, at just over 90 sq.m, Structure 19, the central settlement's 'King's House', actually becomes the largest primary form (i.e. as 'stripped down') of any expanded building on site by almost 20 sq.m, which may tell of its early 'distinction' and status.

The emphasis upon 'expanded' denotes that building's distinction from Structure 53 in Kohla East, which is certainly among the most 'special' buildings within the settlement. It consists of a long narrow range with five internal sub-divisions (between which there is no internal access): one is 'building-sized' (6.35 m), with the other four being a series of small rooms, 2.19–3.2 m across (Fig. 3.42). Its layout is unique at the site, and could suggest either storerooms or workshops. (Its proportion is only similar to the overall layout of Structure 1 at Khuindo, but that seems to respectively involve a porch and open terrace at its long ends: Fig. 3.26.) However, what perhaps more than any other factor marks out this building is that it seems to have been *a unified construction.* In other words, there is no obvious evidence of phased expansion; it extended over 120 sq.m from the outset.

Table 3.2. *'Stripped-down' buildings. In their primary form, these have a mean of 58.7 sq.m, as opposed to the 119.9 sq.m of their expanded versions (i.e. representing a c. 100% increase).*

Structure	Original form		Developed
	Size (m)	Area (sq.m)	Area (sq.m)
>100 sq.m buildings			
5	7.85 × 8.25	64.8	130.3
12	7.35 × 8.50	62.5	117.6
14	7.05 × 9.70	68.4	160.6
18A	6.40 × 7.00	44.8	157.7
B	7.20 × 9.25	66.6	157.7
19	8.05 × 11.20	90.2	150.2
24	7.75 × 9.10	70.5	112.8
42	7.05 × 7.20	50.8	105.4
48	6.15 × 6.75	41.5	116.3
52	6.10 × 9.00	54.9	189.7
53	5.80 × 20.70	120.0	120.0
54	7.10 × 9.95	70.6	116.4
<100 sq.m buildings			
13	6.95 × 9.00	62.5	88.6
34	3.45 × 7.35	25.4	72.3
35	7.35 × 8.40	63.4	90.2
36	6.30 × 7.15	45.0	71.8

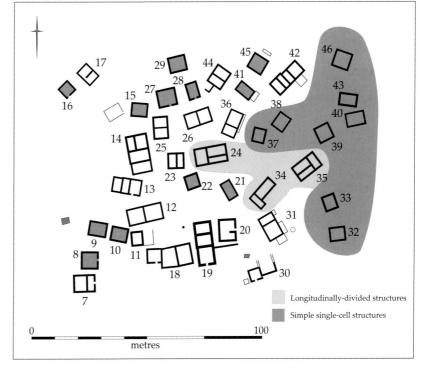

Figure 3.43. *Kohla: the central village core (sub-Site I) showing the distribution of building types.*

As shown in Figure 3.43, if the demonstrable additions to the central village's buildings are stripped away, the settlement's plan becomes much more open. This, of course, can only be a caricature of its early layout and not all of these buildings would necessarily have been contemporary. Equally, in other cases, the phased construction of some multiple-cell structures (e.g. 24 & 26) may not have been identified.

Otherwise, this leads us to the question: what are the generational conditions of large buildings? It may be a matter of some households having greater access to resources or just familial histories (i.e. more successful breeding). Modelling of the development sequence of the site's 'great' buildings does, nevertheless, provide insights into the basic construction of the settlement's buildings as a whole. Their primary, simple-cell units — in most instances, the equivalent of many 'full' or final-form buildings — would surely have been determined by expediency. With a limited available labour force, in the first instance the need to have a completed house of some form up and built before the onset of winter snows (however far falling short of its final intended scale), would have been paramount. Equally, building traditions and available materials (e.g. the span of timbers) may have also limited the basic scale of rooms and/or primary units. Moreover, the block-by-block expansion, and arguably the 'conceptualization' of buildings might have curtailed their possibilities, as regards the lack of corridors, etc. (Issues of construction detail, such as roof design will best be discussed in the light of the site's excavation in Chapter 4 below.)

In the light of these arguments, it is now worth returning to the main site plan to consider the dis-tribution of specific building types and their potential interrelationships. The most obvious such zoning is along the eastern margin of the central sub-site. There, over an area of 3030 sq.m, single-cell structures occur exclusively (Fig. 3.43). Situated alongside the main route into the site (a natural access-way), a number of possible functions suggest themselves for these small simple structures, ranging from traders'/porters' inns to shops. Yet, given the simplicity and frequency of these structures there (relative to the village as a whole), these seem implausible interpretations. Rather, either housing for the settlement's poor or byres for the main households' animals seem more likely explanations, with the latter the most convincing.

Based on their immediate proximity, cases of simple single-cell and complex building pairing can be recognized. This would include Structures 1/2, 3/4, 16/17, 56/57 and 53/55 (and possibly also 7/8). If representing a basic form of combined house and animal byre module, then their total floor area would range from 80.5–181.1 sq.m. There are also paired clusters of larger complex and small structures, but the latter's two-cell plans could indicate something more than just a byre/barn. This can be seen in the arrangement of Structures 47/48 and also 5/6, and it suggests a more complex ancillary building relationship. While perhaps involving no more than animal penning and agricultural storage, Structure 6 — the ancillary building in relationship to the putative Ghale Raja's place (Structure 5) — was two storeys high and could even have been an associated tower, and/or housed ancillary members of the household. Recognizing these kinds of dynamic building relations, raises many possibilities, particularly whether

---

Tamu-mai houses and villages

The Tamu-mai are justifiably proud of and clearly identify with their houses and villages. These show a strong sense of aesthetic; public space tends to be well-appointed with large-stone paved 'ways' and yard-squares that are generally kept clean. Their villages are situated on the upper slopes of highland ridges, between 1800 and 2600 m a.s.l. They effectively lie at a littoral and not below that height: that is for other communities. Looking west, for example from Yangjakot, it can readily be appreciated that the Tamu-mai villages on the western side of the Madi River Valley (Thak and Siklis) fall at the same approximate level, high above the valley floor and to reach them can involve hours of walking up steep stairways.

Perhaps as a legacy of the 'distant' husbands in Gurkha service, the maintenance of public space — open squares, porters' rest platforms and main trails and stairs — is ultimately organized by Mothers' Dance Groups. They 'forcefully' perform their routines for visitors and at village events, and the contributions they raise go toward the hiring of young men to maintain the village's stonework.

Usually laid-out along ridges (and along through-trails), villages tend to be terraced with houses facing south or east (Figs. 3.3, 3.17 & 3.45:A). Many have paved front yards (or otherwise adjoining), the houses themselves being set on raised platforms to provide a level base (Fig. 3.45:D). Generally built of mud-mortared, rough-hewn stone, the size of houses varies from c. 15–75 sq.m (based on the Warchok sample; see below). While such stone houses are usually one-and-a-half storeys high (there being an attic storey beneath their ridged, stone-slate roofs), this upper level is missing in smaller, wood and mud-built houses (that more often are thatched).

Again, perhaps in part attributable to husbands away in the military (and, earlier, involved in pastoral activities), the houses are heavy and closed, with a premium placed on security. Traditionally windows, restricted to the upper storey, are small with wooden screens. Where a more modern-style has been used, windows are larger and also occur in the ground storey, but often have steel-bar grills. (New houses in Pokhara have the capacity to be tightly locked, for fear of roving gangs of thieves, tales of whom abound.) Houses represent a massive investment of labour. Writing of the situation in the late 1950s,

Figure 3.44. *Warchok village and houses: A & B) general views (note that the Nadr Pa site lies on top of the promontory ridge visible in background of A); C & D) false front houses with new stone-built range replacing original verandas (note build-line visible in side of background left building in C).*

Figure 3.45. *Yangjakot houses: A) general view indicating settlement 'packing'; B–D) showing verandas and, in 'D', paved forecourt (note use of corrugated steel in the case of 'C').*

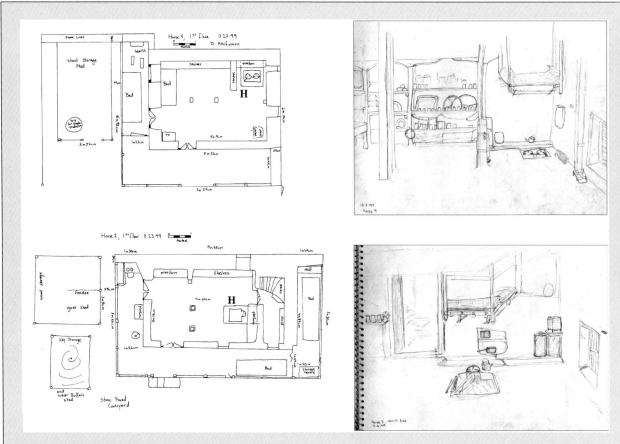

Figure 3.46. *Kaufmann's plan-renderings of Yangjakot houses (left), with the position of their hearths indicated ('H'; note television within 'House 4'); left, her pencil sketches of their respective interiors (note the extent of shelving in the top 'House 4' image and the wooden drying racks suspended above the hearths in both.*

Pignède calculated that, on average, they amount to 4000 rupees expenditure, at a time when a day's wage was worth 1.5 rupees (1993, 72). In other words, the equivalent of more than seven year's full-time investment.

Perhaps the most singular trait of Tamu-mai houses is their prominent verandas (Figs. 3.44 & 3.45; see e.g. Macfarlane 1997b). A half-enclosed space betwixt the interior and yard, this is somewhere to sit, converse and escape the sun. They generally extend right the way across the front length, and often also continue back around one or both of their short sides. Much of the houses and their ancillary space is given over to storage, with bulk food stuffs held in enormous baskets up in the attic story, and heavier pieces of equipment (e.g. husking mortars) in either of the verandas' side-aisles.

The exteriors of most houses are, at least in part, mud-plastered. Above the porch level, they are painted white and, below that, they are left in red 'earth'. The interior of the lower storey is also plastered. This includes the floor and built-in fixtures (e.g. hearths, base of upright timbers, etc.). This fragile surfacing gives rooms an organic, almost cave-like quality. Larger houses are often divided into two main rooms by a wooden partition; one for general purposes, the other being the kitchen, with the hearth built into its floor. Above the latter is a wooden drying frame and the ceiling above tends to be completely blackened through sooting (Fig. 3.46). Sleeping occurs in both

rooms, but never in the attic storey (see Pignède 1993, 70–72 concerning the crucial role of the fireplace and the importance of familial gathering and group sleeping arrangements).

Vernacular architecture is not, of course, something timeless and the villages are not pristine. Siklis now has electricity and water is being piped into some houses; at Warchok, corrugated plastic was seen being used for roofs (see also Fig. 3.45: C), and in Yangjakot, at least one porch is surfaced in concrete (see also the television indicated within interior of 'House 4': Fig. 3.46). During our first season, we recorded the plan of our host's house in Yangjakot in detail (see Fig. 3.47). Beyond the core of the main building, a lean-to is attached to the north side and a small two-roomed structure along the southern side of the yard — one a guest room, the other a toilet/bathroom. (Though these are singularly 'modern' needs, they are rendered in the traditional vernacular style.) As shown on the plan, there is also a small byre on the north side, where a water buffalo is stalled. This lies on the far side of the approach path down to the house and is completely detached from it. This is important on two accounts. Firstly, in other villages where pastoralism is more widely practised, more elaborate adjoining barn structures were observed (see Warchok below: Fig. 3.44). The second point relates to the interpretation of Kohla itself. Particularly, whether a number of its small single-cell structures were also of ancillary status and not separate households as such. In the case of

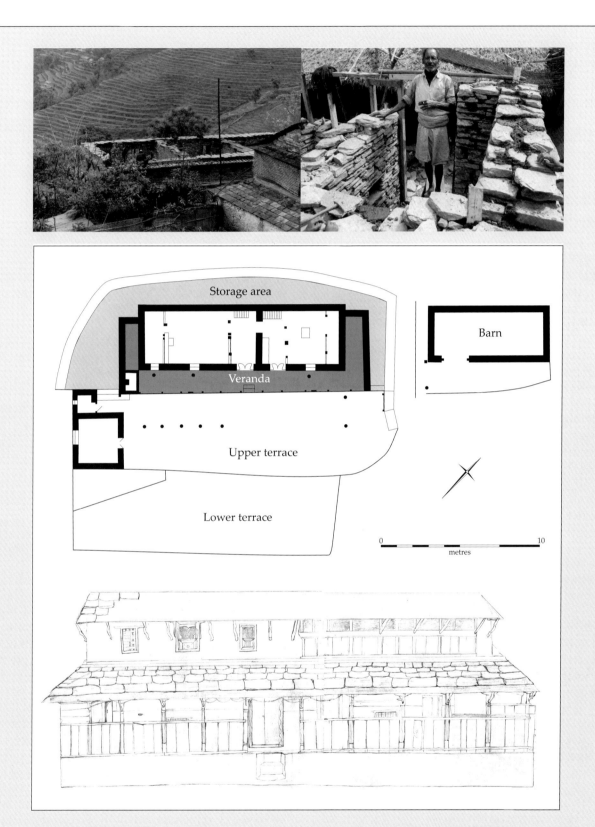

Figure 3.47. *Top, house construction in Yangjakot; middle, survey plan of Tara Devi Gurung and family house, Yangjakot (note their barn/byre on east side of access path/stairway), with Kaufmann's sketch-elevation of its frontage below.*

that site, it raises questions concerning the 'bounded-ness' of household space and also village sectoring.

As will become apparent in the ethno-archaeological study of contemporary Tamu-mai households in relationship to the plans of the upland sites, its relevance is severely limited by the occurrence of house platforms in the present-day villages. These are entirely absent in the highland settlement ruins, nor is there evidence of elaborate porches. This being said, while superficial similarities can be drawn between contemporary houses and those surveyed (e.g. robust stone construction, etc.), the Tamu-mai themselves admit that this is not a matter

of a direct linkage, and that prior to the last two centuries, their houses were of a lighter build. It has even been discussed whether earlier houses were of rounded form (Macfarlane 1976, 96, fig. 6.3; see also Tucci 1977, fig. 17). However, only one such vernacular building was observed of this type, and that belonged to a non-Tamu household in Pokhara itself. Rather, if in any way valid, this would seem to be a by-product of more organic, non-stone construction. Here, it is equally relevant that Pignède attributed the adoption of stone roofs to the cash input of Gurkha service and their subsequent emulation by others (1993, 72).

the complicated compounded ranges might even combine barns/byres within them and, hence, have not been so 'grand'.

It equally warrants mention that the settlement's only longitudinally cell-divided buildings are all located close together, in the west centre of the sub-Site I core (Structures 24 & 35: Fig. 3.43). Possibly relating to an elaboration of basic 'L'-plan buildings (perhaps by the addition of porches into the arms of the 'L'), then the immediate proximity of Structure 34 could also be relevant. If so, these three distinct buildings would be localized to an area of 1070 sq.m, with no other 'types' intervening between (otherwise, only Structure 3 in Kohla West might have a relationship to this building pattern).

The survey pottery
DAVID GIBSON

The pottery assemblage detailed here was collected over the 1994 and 1995 field seasons. The method of collection for the survey seasons was non-systematic fieldwalking, where vegetation permitted, principally through the examination of erosion scars and the sides of charcoal smokers' pits. The weather, especially on the first trip, was immediately 'pre-monsoon', with the occurrence of extremely heavy rainfall most days; this meant there was the continual possibility of the discovery of more pottery each day as erosion took place.

The total assemblage of sherds collected numbered 920, which are of varying condition, attributable to post-depositional factors. They were examined using a handlens (×10 magnification) and were classified by fabric, decoration and, where possible, form.

Eight main fabric types were recognized:

A - Light grey colour surface and margins, but with a slightly darker core. Having a smooth feel, inclusions of mica were small, less than 0.5 mm and infrequent; occasional organics burnt-out during firing were evident.

B - Uniform pale orange colour, with a slightly gritty feel. Inclusions

of mica were frequent, as were black, unidentified, angular ones, both were less than 0.5 mm in diameter.

C - Black surface (almost burnished) and margins with a dark grey/black core. Having a very smooth feel, inclusions of mica up to 0.5 mm are occasionally present; occasional organics have burnt-out during firing.

D - Uniform mid-orange oxidized ware with a smooth feel. Common inclusions of grog up to 2 mm and what appears to be quartzite; occasional organics have burnt-out during firing.

E - Uniform mid-orange/brown oxidized ware with a smooth feel. It contains frequent mica inclusions up to 1 mm, but mostly smaller.

F - Uniform mid-brown/purple reduced ware with a sandy feel. There are frequent inclusions of mica up to 0.5 mm and occasional larger ones.

G - Uniform pale/mid-buff with a smooth feel. There are frequent mica inclusions, with the majority less than 0.25 mm.

H - Buff surface with a light grey margins and core. Having a smooth feel, there are frequent large quartz, mica and black unidentified inclusions up to 1 mm.

No single fabric or fabrics stood out as markedly different, in terms of hardness or technological advance; though, Fabric D differed in using grog as a temper. The presence of mica in all fabrics suggests its presence within all the clay sources and, where clay was noted geologically during the expeditions, mica was present. The presence of burnt-out organics during firing in a number of fabrics is likely to be the result of poor sorting and preparation of the clay, rather than inclusion for temper, as they are not always present within one fabric type. Whether the pottery was clamp- or kiln-fired remains unclear, but clamp-fired techniques are still prevalent in the Kathmandu valley today (e.g. at Bhaktapur). The wide variation in finished product of the same fabrics suggests the quality control of the former. The same refinement of the pottery, with its often crude tempering indicated by the frequency of blow-outs by inappropriate inclusions, is found at all sites. There is no discernible variation of the quality between the sites in terms of fabrics.

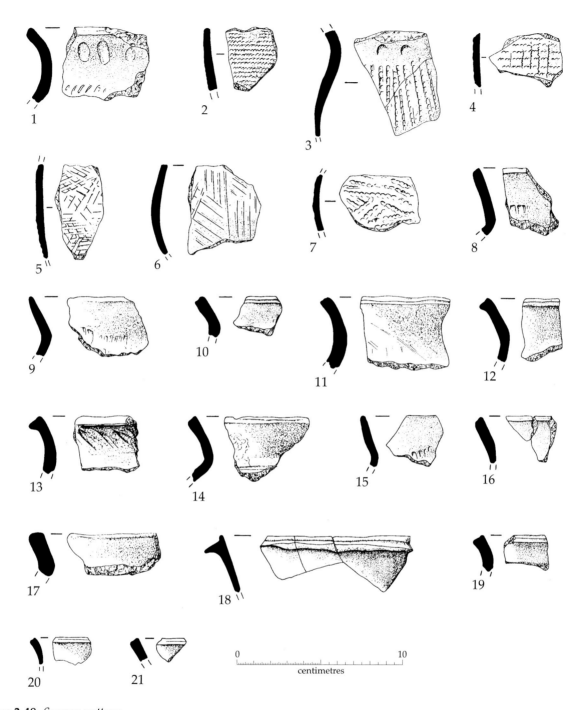

Figure 3.48. *Survey pottery.*

The survey pottery was variously hand-formed (the building or forming of the pot, without the use of centrifugal force), hand-formed with the addition of slowly thrown fitted-neck rims and wheel-thrown (occasional and difficult to determine from the abraded nature and sherd size). No complete vessel profile was recovered; the thickness of sherd walls was, in the main, 10 mm or less. The recovery of a possible waster at Kohla possibly provides evidence of on-site production.

Nine forms for decoration were distinguished:

1 - Grouped, sub-rectangular impressions, possibly by a wood or bamboo comb.

2 - Elongated, oval impressions, often distorted by the forming of the rim.

3 - Shallow, finger impression under rim, with diagonal, thick cord impressions below (Fig. 3.48:1).

4 - Wrapped, fine, horizontal twisted cord (Fig. 3.48:2).

5 - Shallow, finger impressions under the rim, with vertical, thick cord impressions below (Fig. 3.48:3).

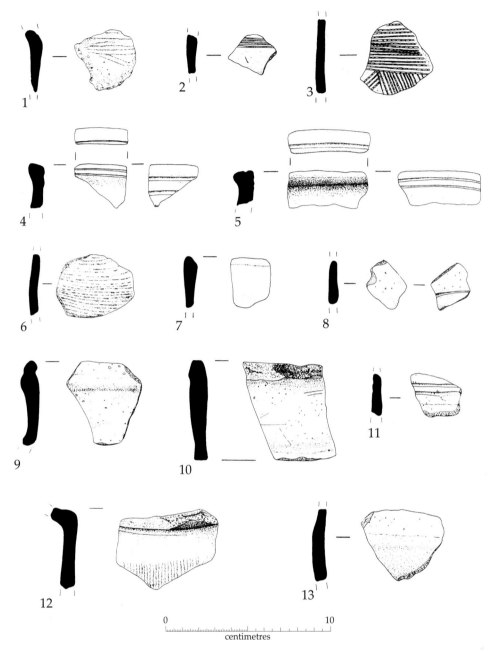

Figure 3.49. *Kohla survey pottery: 1) vitrified body sherd (A1); 2) body sherd (A2); 3) body sherd (A3); 4) rim (B1); 5) rim (B2); 6) body sherd (B3); 7) rim (B4); 8) body sherd (C1); 9) rim (D1); 10) rim (D2); 11) body sherd (D3); body sherd (E1); body sherd (G3).*

6 - Regular criss-crossing of thin twisted cord (Fig. 3.48:4).

7 - Criss-crossing with a wide-toothed comb (Fig. 3.48:5).

8 - Herringbone pattern with a wide-toothed comb (Fig. 3.48:6).

9 - Impressed thick cord (Fig. 3.48:7).

Decoration does not provide the same level of spatial patterning as fabric, with Fabric E being the most widely decorated medium (Table 3.3). On a number of sherds, there was evidence of decoration with black paint or slip, but no pattern of decoration could be distinguished due, perhaps, to the abraded nature of the sherds.

The pottery recovered from Kui Choh was of a much less abraded condition than the majority of the ceramics. The location of the pottery, immediately below the settlement, suggests that it may have survived in middens, which are now eroding. The remain-

Table 3.3. *Pottery: fabric/decoration type.*

Site/Fabric		1	2	3	4	5	6	7	8	9	Undec.
Yangjakot Palace Site											
Fabric B	Rim										3
	Body										4
Fabric E	Rim										
	Body							1	9		25
Kui Choh											
Fabric E	Rim	1	1	1							5
	Body			1	5	4	1	12	6	54	26
Fabric F	Rim										1
	Body	1			1			2	5		3
Fabric G	Rim	1									1
	Body				1			1	4		1
Nadr Pa Palace Site											
Fabric D	Rim										
	Body										1
Fabric E	Rim										2
	Body				1		2	3	29		22
Fabric F	Rim										
	Body				1				4		9
Nadr Pa Village Site											
Fabric E	Rim										4
	Body				1	1			9		19
Nadr Pa Ritual Cairn											
Fabric E	Rim								2		1
	Body										
Karapu											
Fabric A	Rim										
	Body										1
Fabric D	Rim										
	Body										4
Fabric E	Rim										
	Body										2

Site/Fabric		1	2	3	4	5	6	7	8	9	Undec.
Khuindo											
Fabric C	Rim										1
	Body										1
Fabric D	Rim										1
	Body										
Fabric E	Rim										2
	Body									6	45
Chikre											
Fabric A	Rim										10
	Body										95
Fabric E	Rim										
	Body										2
Kohla											
Fabric A	Rim			1							5
	Body										17
Fabric C	Rim										
	Body			1							1
Fabric D	Rim										3
	Body										96
Fabric E	Rim										
	Body				4	4			3	1	188

Table 3.4. *Pottery seriation of the environs sites (by altitude).*

Site	Total (no.)	Decorated (%)	Fabric:						
			A	C	D	E	F	G	B
Kohla	314	4.6	•	•	•	•			
Chikre	107	-		•		•			
Khuindo	56	10.7		•	•	•			
Karapu	7	-	•		•	•			
Kui Choh	139	74				•	•	•	
Nadr Pa	111	47.7			•	•	•		
Yangjakot	42	31				•			•
					shared fabrics				

Table 3.5. *Frequency of main worked stone types.*

Site	Chuni-holden	Querns	'Paddles'	Cupmark stones	Stele
Kui Choh	2	1	-	1	-
Nadr Pa	8	2	-	1	-
Karapu	1	-	-	-	-
Khuindo	-	-	-	1	2
Chromo	-	-	1	-	-
Chikre	-	-	-	-	-
Hachu	-	-	-	-	-
Michu	-	-	-	-	-
Kohla	2	2	1	-	1

ing pottery had suffered the extreme temperature and climatic conditions possible in the Himalayas, leaving it in a very abraded state. Many of their surfaces have been damaged by frost action.

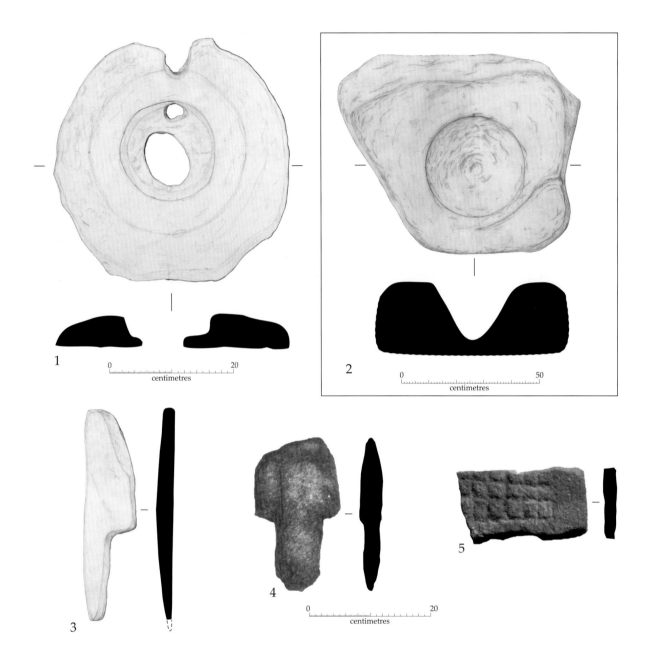

Figure 3.50. *Worked stone: 1) rotary quernstone, Nadr Pa; 2) ground-embedded chuni-holden, Kohla (see Fig. 3.13); 3) 'half-paddle', Kui Choh; 4) 'paddle', Kohla; 5) gaming board fragment, Kohla.*

Worked stone

The range and frequency of the main worked stone types that were recovered in the course of the site surveys is indicated in Table 3.5. As was discussed above, chuni-holden mortar stones do, indeed, seem to be a distinct 'type-artefact' of settlement *per se*. That none were observed on the pastoralist camp sites alone (i.e. without earlier remains), could provide confirmation that Yarjung's *Kuniholdo* was, in fact, a settlement site (see Chapter 2 above). Although, in all cases their numbers are too low to provide statistical validity, from the

table's listings an interrelationship could be postulated between recovery of chuni stones, and the querns (all seemingly of rotary-type; see Gajurel & Vaidya 1994, 306–9). Taken together, their distribution could be used to argue that crop production was a more central facet of the lower settlements — from Karapu and below — than those in the uplands. Kohla aside, their paucity on the other sites (those above Karapu) is marked, whereas, in contrast, their occurrence at Kohla could indicate the relative scale of its crop consumption.

Given the high number of chuni found at Nadr Pa, it is noteworthy that still another is said to hang in the branches of a tree nearby (i.e. was carried upwards through its growth). This stone could not, however, be found there by our team; a similarly elevated chuni apparently also occurs within Kohla's environs. (The rumoured situation of these mortars is vaguely evocative of the 'hanging pot' sites mentioned by Yarjung in Chapter 2; though whether this implies a distinct suspended-vessel form or just subsequently 'tree-raised' vessels is unknown.)

The potential associations of cupmark stones/ boulders and the standing stone uprights are discussed below (Chapter 4). Little, though, can be said of their distribution, given that they occur both above and below the Karapu upland/lowland interface (especially as a stele was present at the 'non-ruin' pastoralist camp at Khohgya, above Yangjakot).

Not surprisingly, the widest range of worked stone types was recovered at Kohla. Not only does this include the categories discussed above, but also a paddle-like object (23 × 7–13 × 2–3 cm), found in front of Structure 1 (Fig. 3.50:4). Our workmen thought that this could relate to food preparation (i.e. a stone version of a wooden rice 'paddle'), but it would seem inordinately heavy and unwieldy for such a purpose. Other suggestions were an architectural ornament or a funerary marker. Whatever the case, it was clearly a 'type', as a matching example was also found at Chromo (a single 'bladed', more club-like object was also found at Kui Choh: Fig. 3.50:3). Other objects from Kohla include a single, granite schist roof slate (38.5 × 28 × 3 cm), an ironstone 'wedge' (possibly for splitting timber) and a hole-pecked stone. The latter was flat (25 × 17 × 6 cm) with a single cup-hollow (60 mm dia.; 15 mm deep). While possibly footing a door pivot, this may just have been the start of a more ambitious cupmark 'motif', such as were found on other sites (see Chapter 4 below).

Perhaps the most remarkable stone item found at Kohla was a fragment of a gaming board, that has 6 × 3 squares 'etched' into its surface (24.2 × 12 × 3.8 cm: Fig. 3.50:5). With its squares left raised to a height of 4 mm, this clearly was more than just for immediate/one-off 'play' and much care had evidently gone into its execution. It may relate to either a parcheesi- or ludo-derivative game, perhaps *Tharki* as played in Manang (D. Gibson pers. comm.).

Discussion — diverse architectures

In an effort to provide further context for the upland ruins, in 1995 all 61 buildings within the Tamu-mai village of Warchok were surveyed (Fig. 3.44). Including ancillary barns and a shop, this involved 45 houses *per se*, of which 35 were said to be occupied (unfortunately,

time did not permit us to include the village's small southern Blacksmiths'/Tailors' 'quarter'). All were of rectangular plan and each had a veranda on at least one side, and most on three (including some 'veranda-ed' barns — 49 per cent; 40.4 per cent on two sides and 10.6 per cent on one side alone). While most of the houses with verandas on three sides fit the usual 'front-and-two-widths' pattern, five had them along two lengths and one width. These tend to be situated along the eastern edge of the village. There, the houses effectively have two 'fronts'; one overlooking the terraced valley slope below and, the other, on to the main trail.

The survey was undertaken to begin to provide statistical comparison for Kohla's ruins. To this end, when comparing the Warchok buildings, verandas are not included within the calculation of their dimensions (platforms being difficult to define *vs* walls). Nor are its houses 'compounded', inasmuch as barns and associated houses are treated separately; such direct knowledge of associative function is obviously unavailable for the upland ruins.

The Warchok buildings are markedly smaller than those at Kohla. Ranging from 13.8–72.3 sq.m, 65.6 per cent fall between 20 and 40 sq.m, whereas the Kohla ruins range from 24.3–189.7 sq.m, with 63.1 per cent falling between 40 and 80 sq.m (Fig. 3.51). More obvious is the difference in their respective breadth/ length ratios (B/L). The width of the Kohla buildings varies from 4.9–7.9 m, with most falling between 5.5 and 6.5 m and they have a B/L ratio of 1/1.3–1.6 (range 1/1–1.9), whereas most of the Warchok buildings are 3.9–4.5 m wide (3.2–5.2 m range) and have a B/L ratio of 1/1.6–1.8 (range 1.3–1/2.8). (With the addition of veranda space there is greater equivalence; Warchok range 15.7–82.1 sq.m — plus one at 131.2 sq.m — with 57.4 per cent falling between 40–80 sq.m.)

Apart from the fact that they share rectangular plans and high-quality drystone construction, this suggests that the Warchok/Tamu-mai and Kohla building styles vary significantly, with the absence of encircling verandas being only the most obvious differentiation (Fig. 3.52). This is not to deride contemporary building traditions. Their floor space may actually be greater than that at Kohla, if the upper, gable storey is included (there is little evidence of such at Kohla). Nevertheless, at ground level they have little in common, with the breadth/length ratio probably being their most telling constructional trait. The squarer plan of many of the Kohla buildings could suggest greater affinity with a tradition of flat-roofed construction and courtyard plans north of the Himal (see Chapter 4).

The basis of such comparisons has already been questioned, as they presuppose 'timeless' vernacular building traditions. Effectively denying history to the 'ethnographic', as mentioned, this is especially relevant among southern Himalayan communities, where outside capital has had a major impact for almost 200 years through foreign military service (i.e. the Gurkhas). We were informed that Tamu-mai houses were not always so solidly constructed, and apparently, instead, had thatch/wood (bamboo) super-structures upon low stub-wall footings (Macfarlane recorded similar observations at Thak; 1976, 96; see also Macfarlane & Gurung 1990, 8 & 9).

Apart from the fort at Karapu and the palace at Nadr Pa, no 'proper' house ruins (i.e. stone-built) have been surveyed south of Khuindo. Although village terracing has been apparent, there have been no upstanding buildings as such, and only denuded house platforms (without evidence of verandas). Less substantial construction techniques could also explain why early buildings at the Yangjakot 'South' site (otherwise only evidenced by pottery and scorched surfaces) cannot be identified. The house 'platforms' at Nadr Pa and Kui Choh are, in fact, directly comparable to the Warchok houses (Fig. 3.52). At the former site, they range in size from 3.5–5 × 7–10 m, with most falling between 4–5 × 6–8 m (B/L range 1/1.4–2.4; most 1/1.4–1.6). Those identified at Kui Choh seem somewhat larger and range in size from 4.5–5 × 7.5/9 m (Structure 2 being larger; 6.6 × 12 m). To compare the platforms with standing ruins/ buildings is not, of course, entirely valid, as we cannot be certain of the situation of the house to their platform-terraces. The two definite buildings at Nadr Pa have low surviving walls — one on three sides (0.3 m high) and, the other, on four (0.3–0.5 m high); they lie just inside the platform/terrace scarp (i.e. with little berm). Perhaps even more telling of their superstructure, relatively little rubble was found associated with the platforms. While, at that site, much of it could conceivably have been employed in later pastoralist building, this is not the case with Kui Choh and generally there seems to be no evidence for full stone-walling (*vs* only stub footings).

What becomes equally relevant in this context is that 'special' buildings in the lower upland sites — the palace at Nadr Pa or the fort at Karapu — are actually smaller in area than a number of the larger buildings at Kohla, even those not accredited with 'palace' status. Questioning a direct link between oral history and the upland ruins, this could suggest that *'folkloric' ascription is contextual*; it is obviously 'big/ complex' structures within the settlement ruins that have been singled-out for designated value (see Fig. 5.4). In other words, the distinction of what is 'special' is not based upon any kind of absolute measure, but what immediately surrounds it (seen in comparison with insubstantial house platforms, Kohla-size full-

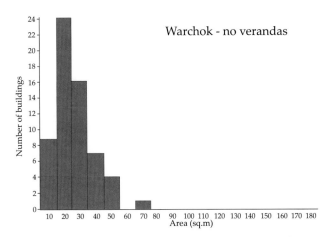

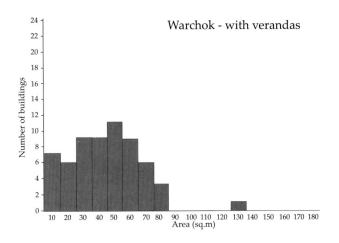

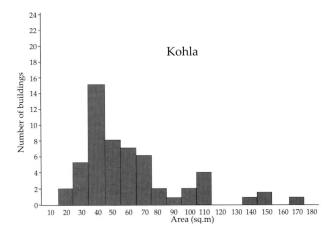

Figure 3.51. *Kohla/Warchok house-size frequencies.*

stone buildings would all seem unique within 'low-upland' sites).

What does this indicate, apart from the fact that building size (and 'robustness') seems to reduce with altitude? Numerous scenarios could be postulated to account for these changes in building styles. For example, that environmental adaptation prompted the

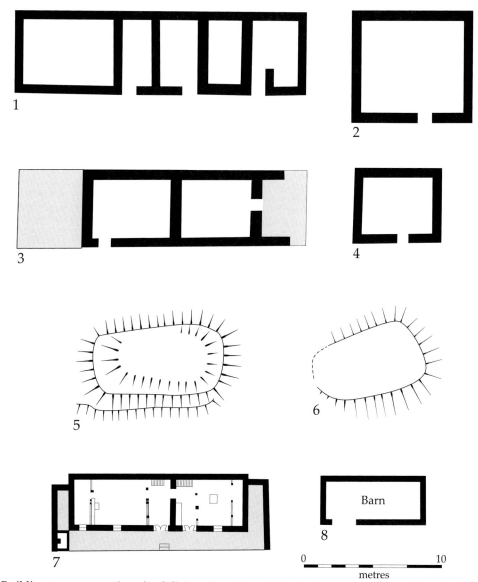

Figure 3.52. *Building-type connections (and disjunctions): 1 & 2) Kohla Structures 53 and 27; 3 & 4) Khuindo Structures 1 and 2; 5 & 6) Kui Choh Structures 1 and 4; 7 & 8) present-day Yangjakot Village, the Tara Devi Gurung and family house (and its adjacent barn; note porches grey-tone indicated).*

use of new materials (bamboo *vs* stone). Yet, that stone was predominately used in the distant 'highland' past and also in present-day villages in the 'low-uplands' implies that there is not a direct co-relationship, and that social factors must have played a significant role (i.e. there is no evidence that availability was the sole determining factor). The more recent adoption of stone clearly reflects greater wealth (capital) and, perhaps, a sense of home security, given that men have been/are absent for so long in foreign service.

Upland settlement systems

Of the sites visited in the course of our surveys, nothing has a comparable impact to Kohla itself. Although,

for our Tamu-mai colleagues the shrine at Nadar Pa was held to be very sacred, and other important locations were recognized *en route* (e.g. where the Ghale King lost his leg in battle), only Kohla gave rise to intense emotions, and it alone is held to be *the* place or home of the ancestors (despite the fact that there should logically be a more direct linkage to the settlements immediately above extant villages). However, the 'specialness' of Kohla also relates to the quality of its ruins themselves and their setting. Yes, the site has a unique status in the Tamu-mai cultural narrative, but its density and the height to which its buildings survive also make it a 'classic' ruin. There is a genuine and obvious sense of many people having lived there in the past and, conjuring up the ethos of other great 'lost cities', nothing else seen in the uplands comes close to having its qualities.

Based on their shared construction techniques and robust architectural style (and also common pottery types; see Gibson above), the sites recorded above Karapu would all appear to relate to a 'cultural horizon' and interrelated settlement system, whose extent and character will be further explored in Chapter 5. However, at this time what warrants emphasis is the evidence of control or regulation of the upland routes. This is suggested in the manner in which the small 'isolated' buildings flank either side of the lower trail at Chromo. Demonstrating a relationship to travel, the one had a porters' rest bench built into its side. Less obvious was why the other had three lintel-capped, window-like openings at ground level. Yet, the fact that the one trail-side building at Chikre (Structure 10, removed from the main settlement) also had comparable low recesses, could indicate that they somehow also related to through 'traffic'.

These evidently trail-related buildings range in size from 4–4.2 × 5.4–7.2 m, and are generally comparable to the two structures at Kohla East also thought to have a traverse-based function: Structures 50 (4.35 × 6 m) and 51 (4.45 × 5.45 m), the former also having an exterior rest bench (and a narrow vertical slot through one wall). Interestingly enough, Structure 13, fronting onto the main 'plaza' at Kohla, also has a series of low window-like openings in its eastern, square-side front. The purpose of these is unknown, but the argument could be proposed that they also had a trail-related function, and are comparable to similar structures at Chromo and Chikre (and possibly also Michu and Hachu).

The main sites below Karapu — Nadar Pa and Kui Choh — also appear related. This is primarily based on the evidence of their quite different domestic architecture, as their buildings are marked by low, house platforms and a relative paucity of building stone. The 'palace' at Nadar Pa is, of course, quite a different matter, being arguably two storeys high and well-built in stone. Its precise relationship to the nearby settlement site is unknown, as they may either have been directly contemporary or the 'palace' somewhat later (it being unlikely to have survived in such conditions had it been 'ancient'). Although difficult to quantify, and perhaps partially a product of the local stone, the quality of its construction seems rather more finished than the upland buildings (Kohla, etc.). It is conceivable that this 'palace' was actually some manner of tower 'fort-house'. Although it lacks any accompanying earthworks, as regards its (now missing) upper wall-'slots' it may be relevant that

Fri Desideri wrote in 1721 of the forts of Kathmandu Valley that they resemble 'our country dovecots' (i.e. implying high structures with firing loopholes: in Whelpton 2005, 33). In contrast, Kui Choh seems basically a ramparted, hillfort enclosure, with an associated settlement (see Howard 1995, 23–4, fig. 4 for comparable 'terrace-type' fortifications at Kaski and Lamjung). Unfortunately, the scale of its occupation — continuing down the site's steep and heavily wooded northern slope — was not detailed in its entirety. It is interesting, nevertheless, that the settlements (*per se*) at both Nadar Pa and Chui Koh seem substantially larger than the upland village sites, apart from Kohla (i.e. Khuindo and Chikre).

Lacking any definite structures as such, the Yangjakot 'site' (if that is what it is) would probably be equivalent to the lower level settlements (i.e. sub-Karapu), and/or may simply be an older component of the extant village itself.

Recognizing these two settlement types — respectively above and below Karapu — the status of that site is itself clearly pivotal, though this, in part, may well relate to the ambiguity of its results. Unlike the lower sites, Karapu does seem to have evidence of stone-built houses, even though it is difficult to differentiate these from more recent pastoralist shelters. This may well accord with its environmental situation, as it lies that amount higher and above the forest, and certainly it is a very exposed locale. Its defensive potential is unquestionable, and it commands a junction of major trails — southwest to Yangjakot, southeast to Warchok and north to Tapron and Lamjung Himal. Accordingly, there is little doubt that, like Chui Koh (and possibly the Nadar Pa tower 'palace'), this site was also fortified. With walls twice the thickness of the 'domestic' ruins (Fig. 5.4), the stone-built 'square' on its crown was arguably also a 'tower fort'. While its size and situation could generally compared be to the 'tower house' forts of Mustang (e.g. Jarakot and Lubla: Howard 1995, fig. 6; see also Seeber 1994; Harrison 2003), the Karapu enclosure differs in the paucity of its internal divisions and drystone construction technique (as opposed to shuttered-clay/-mud).

The transitional situation of Karapu, in effect bridging the upland and lower level settlement types — Yarjung's 'gateway' between the village zone and the wilderness (see Chapter 2) — may also be reflected in the pottery from the surveys. As demonstrated in Table 3.4, only there were all the fabric types found and, otherwise, certain wares were restricted to the sites above and below it (Karapu and the upland sites having a far lower frequency of decorated wares). In this capacity, it may well be relevant that, in his commentary, Yarjung mentions the occurrence of ancient pottery production at both *Sa Pu Cyo* below Karapu and *Sa Pu Neh*, adjacent to Kohla itself (Chapter 2).

The lower-level fort sites (probably including Karapu also) may well relate to the period of the 'Twenty-four Kings' and broadly date to the fifteenth/sixteenth centuries. A time of unrest, with petty 'kings' and 'princes' ruling small polities, it would be these circumstances that would have given rise to the need for fortification, however modest these may have been in some cases. In this regard, these ruins — especially those immediately above the extant villages — are probably comparable to those 'Ancient Fortresses' visited by Pignède in the west of Tamu-mai territory; namely that at Ghandrung and those on the ridge-tops overlooking the river valleys of the Modi and Barudi:

> I have visited the sites of two forts occupied by these kings. The foundations of stone and certain protective works are still visible (walls, ditches). These forts were situated on almost inaccessible promontories, controlling vast expanses (Pignède 1993, 198, fig. 3).

Pignède related that, after the reign of the Ghale, the valley of the Modi was ruled by two 'independent' families (i.e. non-southern Hindu). These 'little states' apparently lost their independence during the later eighteenth century and, thereafter, the local administration of the area devolved to the village headmen (*kroh/khhro*: Pignède 1993). Temple records that his guide, Damarsingh, reported that there are three groups of ruins above the village of Tangting (1993; Damarsingh also related the existence of stone-built sites in that area when he travelled with us in 1994). Messerschmidt similarly mentions the ruins of a fortress at Suilikot in Lamjung (1976a, 16). In all likelihood, this, like Pignede's fort sites and those we saw at and above Yangjakot (and probably also Karapu), were abandoned when the region was annexed by the Gorkha during the second half of the eighteenth century, if not before. Certainly they lack the more elaborate defensive architecture of later fort designs, such as internal firing steps and cannon embrasures (see Howard 1995, fig. 5b; H. Gurung 2002, fig. 23 respectively for the fortifications above Pokhara at Sarankot and Kahun). Ragsdale, alternatively, describes the establishment in 1791 of a fort by two brothers, at 'Lamnasa' in the District of Kaski (in 'real-life' the village of Mauja), at which time hill-top forests were apparently protected by royal decree for the cover they afforded to forts (1990, 3).

It is difficult to estimate the age of the region's extant villages. Messerschmidt attributed the establishment of 'Ghaisu' to the early nineteenth century (1976b, 173; Sikrung in 'real-life') and Pignède similarly calculated that Mohoriya was founded between 1815 and 20 (it having 12 houses 30 years later; Macfarlane 1976, 211). However, Mohoriya, like Thak, falls within the 5000–7000 ft (*c.* 1665–2335 m a.s.l.) lower zone of 'new settlements'. Founded since the late eighteenth century, their situation is attributable to access to irrigated rice agriculture. Based on historical accounts and information derived from the *pye* (outlined in Chapter 4 below), before that time most of the Tamu-mai are thought to have practised a more pastoral economy at higher altitudes and lived in villages at 8000 ft (*c.* 2665 m a.s.l.), such as Siklis or Ghandrung (Macfarlane 1976, 27–8).

Chapter 4

Approaching Kohla

Christopher Evans
with contributions by Eleni Asouti, Paul Craddock, Dorian Fuller,
David Gibson, Alan Macfarlane & Ezra Zubrow

When undertaking archaeological fieldwork in multi-disciplinary circumstances it is the act of excavation that usually divides researchers. Whereas, prior to that point, archaeologists and anthropologists (and, in this case, shamans, porters, pastoralists, etc.) can interpret landscape collectively and on a relatively equal footing, digging brings specific methodologies and the possibility of independence from immediate analogy. Arguably, it is this that allows archaeologists to 'go off' on their own. Although there was clearly potential for interpretative discrepancy, with Kohla's excavations cut short by political events, this never transpired within this project. While a benefit, in that it allows for greater coherence of approach, it in effect means that insufficient archaeology was undertaken to significantly challenge 'the present'. Yet enough was done to disturb and there is no easy fit between the past/present 'story'. Perhaps, in the end, this sense of interpretative tension or disquiet is itself an appropriate outcome.

The excavations

In April of 2000, two weeks' fieldwork was undertaken at Kohla. As the first excavation in this area of the Himalayas, our approach was necessarily cautious. With the depth and complexity of the strata unknown and, until our 'eye was in', we had no wish to open large areas and, instead, concentrated upon section-controlled sondage exposures. At the same time, it was obvious that the interior of at least one of the buildings had to be tested. It was, therefore, decided to focus the investigations in the north-central settlement (Fig. 4.1), thus avoiding the potentially 'public' buildings to the south while trying to achieve coherent results from one area. (This was as opposed to dispersed small-scale test pitting across the settlement's three sectors in a belief that — given the overall paucity of *context* — the basic principles of the site's layout first needed to be grasped, before formalized sampling procedures could be meaningfully adopted.)

Work centred upon Structure 27, a simple square-plan building, which was excavated in opposed quadrants. Beyond this, and in order to comprehend

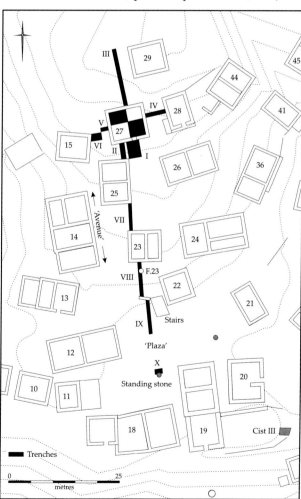

Figure 4.1. *Kohla 2000: trench plan (see Fig. 3.32 for location).*

Figure 4.2. *Kohla 2000 - photographic mosaics: top, looking north with Trench IX in foreground; below, looking south with Structure 27 in central foreground.*

the dynamics of what was evidently the settlement's terraced hill-side layout, trenches were extended along both the north–south and east–west slopes from the structure's central axes. Whereas the latter only interlinked that building with its two immediate 'neighbours' (Structures 15 & 28; Trenches IV–VI), the north–south trench-line was more extensive (Trenches I–III, VII–IX). Eventually continuing over more than 60 m and covering a *c.* 8 m drop in slope — from the crown of the northern hill down to the southern central courtyard 'plaza' — it also interconnected with Structures 23 and 25 (Figs. 4.1 & 4.4). (To avoid unnecessary disturbance to their floor strata, the interiors of the latter were not trenched, and only their exterior wall faces and foundations were exposed.) Finally, a small sondage was cut at the foot of the large standing stone within the southern central courtyard, in order to simply prove whether it was 'old' (i.e. deeply embedded), which indeed proved to be the case. In the course of the fieldwork, 121 contexts were excavated and 48 structural features were identified and recorded.

Somewhat surprisingly, the sub-soils consist of heavy tan/brown clays, and not bedrock (see e.g. Fig. 4.6). Although discrete stratigraphic horizons were recovered, the sequence proved to be quite shallow,

with no more than 0.75 m of strata encountered. The area's acidic topsoil has clearly impacted on bone survival. Aside from some animal teeth and burnt bone, the few faunal remains recovered were only very small and decayed.

From the outset, it warrants mention that the recovery of postholes in all trenches but IX and X was unexpected. A number of these proved very substantial. Based on the restricted exposure of our narrow trenches, it is difficult to ascertain any pattern among them. Some may well relate to the main stone buildings and, for example, may have supported porches or lean-to sheds. Generally, their density and situation would, however, suggest that they should be attributable to 'pre-stone' structures. To this extent, they are largely phased with 'early' surfaces present in Trenches I, II, V and VI (found cut by stone building footings). These were most obvious in the latter, western two. In Trench VI, two such early horizons were identified, including an upper burnt surface, which extended east across the base of Trench V and into the northwestern quadrant of Structure 27 (no early postholes were, however, found within the interior of that building). Samples of this burnt layer from Trench VI ([080]) were wet sieved and, aside from producing quantities of charcoal, numerous small clay crucible

Figure 4.3. *Kohla 2000: A) Structure 27 with Quadrant A right and 'D' left (with doorway threshold visible); B) Trench IV and east face of Structure 15; C) Structure 27, Quadrant A, with raised F.2 bench set along base of the northern wall right and hearth F.28 against western wall; D) Trenches V and VI (note burnt surface horizons).*

fragments were also recovered. It is clear that to come to terms with the nature of this early occupation and distinguish plans of its evidently timber buildings, larger excavation exposures will be necessary in the future.

Structure 27

Extending over *c.* 8 × 7.35 m (externally), the design and layout of the building proved to be straightforward. Seemingly packed with clay, its walls were 0.6–1 m high and generally 0.55–0.65 m wide. It is clear that its construction had occurred within a broad lateral cut (F.27), and the northern back wall was dug down into the natural clays to a depth of *c.* 0.9 m (Fig. 4.4). Thereby also supporting the terraced edge, that wall alone was 0.85 m wide. As it was not dismantled by us, no foundation as such was discerned, and it may well have been without a footing. Otherwise, the foundations of the east and western walls were set in construction trenches, 0.25–0.3 m deep; the trench-built footings of the southern front are 0.45–0.6 m deep (the base evidently stepping up with the slope midway along its east–west length). Although no trace of any walled internal division was found within the building, its roof may have been supported on free-standing posts. In this capacity, three possible stone slab, post-pad settings were tentatively identified along the building's central

north–south axis. Occurring on the section-line, the ambiguity of their definition is an outcome of an alternative quadrant(-only) excavation technique.

Among the other architectural features present was a raised stone 'bench', which apparently ran along the length of the back wall (F.2; *c.* 0.4 m high and 0.35–0.55 m wide: Figs. 4.3:C, 4.4 & 4.5). While possibly also for seating and/or raised storage, it must have primarily served to buttress the north wall against the pressure of the terraced deposits behind. (Buckling at the middle of its length, the eastern and western walls also evidenced inward collapse at their mid-points.) Obvious attention had gone into the construction of the doorway, which, 1.05 m across, lies off-centre in the western portion of the southern wall (F.1: Figs. 4.3:A, 4.5, 4.6 & 4.7). The threshold was raised by 0.2 m in relationship to both the interior and exterior surfaces. It had an internal porch flanked by stub-walls that project for 0.45 m into the building's interior. While a stone rubble surface survives in front of the building's threshold in Trenches I and II, its floor only consisted of trampled clay and no paving level was present. A succession of simple flat, clay-based hearths was found — extending over 1.6 × 1.25 m — built against the face of the west wall and within the innermost quadrant (A; F.28: Figs. 4.3:C & 4.5). Possibly deriving from these, dumped deposits of charcoal were found just inside the eastern interior of the doorway.

Quantities of stone rubble were present within the structure and adjacent exterior sondages. This was duly separated from the spoil and stacked in a 'drystone-like' manner; Quadrant A produced

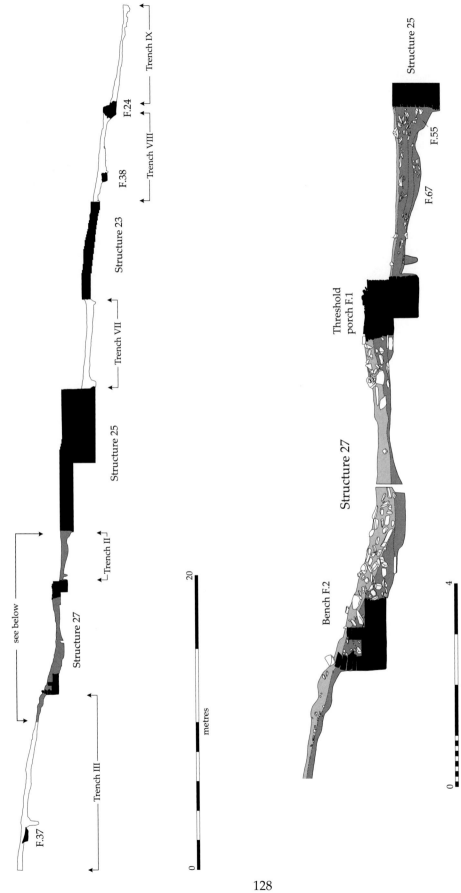

Figure 4.4. *Kohla 2000: composite north–south profile along length of trenches, with detailed section across Structure 27 below (and Trenches II & III).*

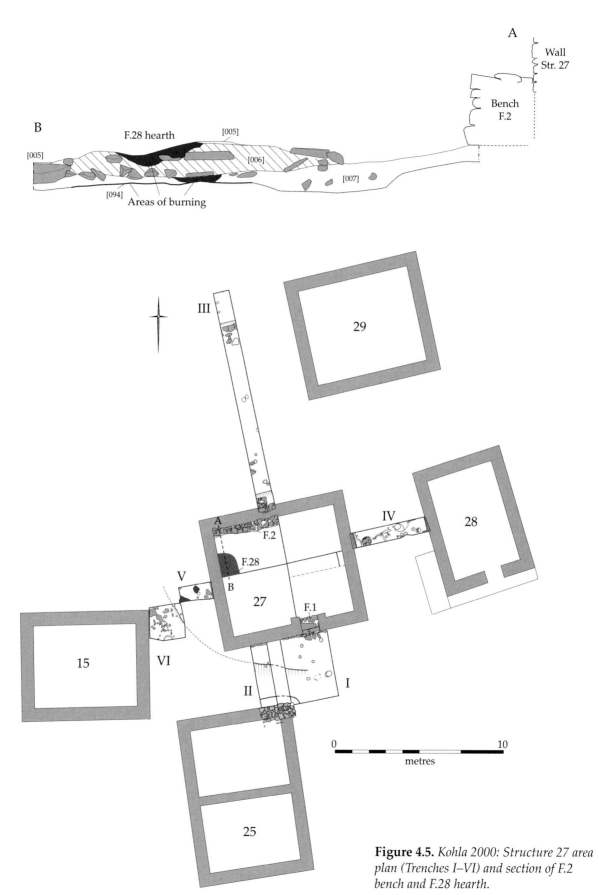

Figure 4.5. *Kohla 2000: Structure 27 area plan (Trenches I–VI) and section of F.2 bench and F.28 hearth.*

Figure 4.6. *Kohla 2000 - Structure 27: A) looking north to southern wall face with Trench I excavated in foreground (note postholes and profile of F.67 trough left); B) looking east with western wall visible in end of Trench V (foreground) and western wall of Structure 28 at foot of tree.*

A

B

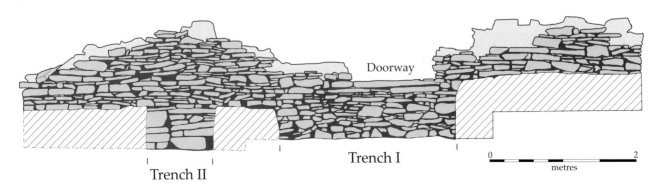

Figure 4.7. *Kohla 2000 - Structure 27: elevation of southern wall (note stepping of foundations; hachured line indicates masking of unexposed foundation courses).*

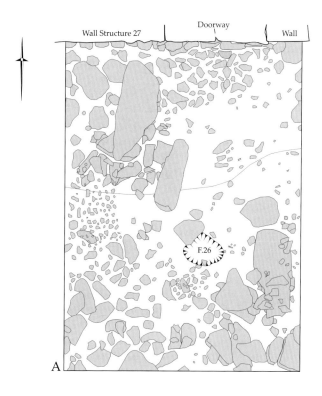

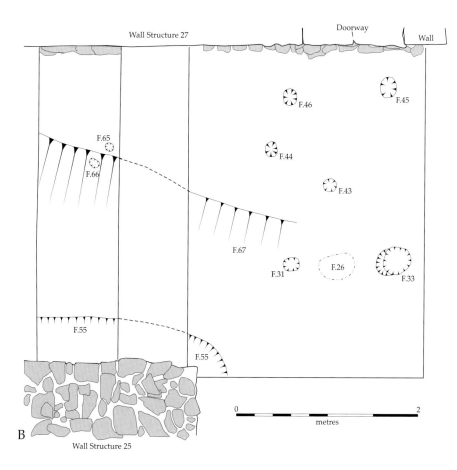

5.08 cu.m of stone and, D, 4.20 cu.m. If doubling this (in relationship to the structure's quadranted excavation), and including the rubble recovered from the exterior sondages, sufficient stone would be present to generate some eleven 0.15 m-high courses (*c.* 1.65 m). Adding to this the height of the building's extant walls suggests that it could only have ever stood 2–2.5 m high and be of a single storey. While very much only a rough rule-of-thumb measure, this would also correlate with the distance to which quasi-articulated rubble extended from the foot of its walls in Trenches V and VI (*c.* 1.5 m) and certainly indicates that the building could not have been two storeys.

Trenches I and II

Across the length of Trench II — the first of these two trenches to be cut — the level of the natural clay dropped, in the main, by *c.* 0.3 m over 2.6 m, down from the foot of Structure 27 to Structure 25 (Figs. 4.4 & 4.8). (Across the southernmost 0.5 m of the trench, the ground surface was truncated by the broad-profiled construction trench for Structure 27, which was 0.48 m deep; at the northern end, the 0.35 m-deep, vertically-sided cut for Structure 27 only extended for *c.* 5 cm beyond its wall face.) A broad, concave-profiled, east–west oriented trough (F.67; 1.5 × 0.1 m deep) interrupted the 'lie' or fall of the natural. Also distinguished at this level were three probable postholes (F.64–F.66); 0.1–0.18 m in diameter, these were 0.2–0.25 m deep and filled with mid-brown silty clay with charcoal. The one recorded in the eastern section (F.64) was found to be sealed by [011], a 2–5 cm-thick, primary 'occupation layer' which lay up to 0.15 m deep within the basal trough. This consisted of dark grey clay loam with extensive charcoal inclusions. It had a high density of pottery sherds and a few large stone slabs embedded within it. Otherwise, the overlying 0.2–0.35 m-thick topsoil and clay loam with rubble horizon was excavated as a single deposit ([004]). This, however, included within its central-southern length a distinct lower horizon (6 cm–0.12 m thick) of mid-dark grey silty loam, that must relate to occupation.

Figure 4.8. *Kohla 2000 - Trenches I and II: A) Trench I showing stone-strewn surfaces before threshold of Structure 27; B) showing postholes at basal level of Trenches I and II (note trough F.67 and F.55, the construction trench for Structure 25).*

Having rather summarily excavated Trench II, Trench I was laid-out to the east — with an intervening baulk — immediately in front of the threshold of Structure 27, for more detailed open-area excavation (2.6 × 3.5 m: Figs. 4.6 & 4.8). Whereas in Trench II there was doubt as to the interrelationship of the F.67 trough and Structure 25 (i.e. F.67 could have been a reduced 'behind-building' path), this was not the case in Trench I; the trough was clearly cut by the construction trench for that building. There, F.67 extended east into the sondage for 0.85 m, where, beginning to return southwards, it must terminate shortly thereafter.

In Trench II, the natural clays were sealed by [055]. Clearly cut by the construction trench for Structure 27, this was essentially a dark grey silty clay loam layer. It was flecked with charcoal and, having small, daub-like hardened clay fragments, it was obviously occupation-related (filling the F.67 hollow, there it inter-bedded with lenses of re-deposited natural clays). It sealed a series of postholes that must be associated with this usage:

F.43 - Sub-circular (0.15 m dia.) with a pointed base 0.55 m deep; fill, dark grey clay loam.

F.44 - Ovoid (0.14 × 0.16 m), 0.25 m deep; fill, as F.43.

F.45 - Ovoid (0.18 × 0.22 m), 0.55 m deep; fill, as F.43.

F.46 - Ovoid (0.15 × 0.18 m), 0.48 m deep, with a pointed base (leaning southwards); fill, as F.43.

(Note: cut F.33 was also only recognized at this depth, however, by the arrangement of stones in [055] at this point — that must relate to the post's packing — its attribution should clearly be later.)

This horizon was sealed by a make-up layer of quite clean, mid-brown clay (re-deposited natural), that carried a surface of mid-dark grey, slightly sandy silt loam with charcoal and hardened clay fragments ([012]/[054]). Embedded within this was a stone-paved 'way', including some very large slabs, which might relate to collapse from Structure 27 or else have been vertically set (i.e. standing stones). A series of postholes were found in association with it, and these may relate to a porch associated with Structure 27:

F.26 - Located immediately in front of the doorway of Structure 27, this was ovoid (0.40 × 0.46 m); its edges sloped down and, at c. 0.15–0.2 m depth, its form/plan was 0.25 × 0.4 m. From this level, it dropped vertically to a flat base, 0.65 m deep in total. It was filled with dark grey, charcoal-flecked clay loam, with the upper fill being stone-packed.

F.31 - Sub-circular (0.18 m dia.) and 0.38 m deep; fill, charcoal-flecked grey loam, with lenses of natural clay.

F.33 - Sub-circular (0.3 m dia.) with a flat base 0.5 m deep; fill, mid-brown clay, with large packing stones.

These and the [012]/[054] surface were here sealed by [008], the humic topsoil.

Trench III

This was extended across the northern hill-top, with the specific aim of investigating whether the recent construction of a large pastoralist shelter on its crown (obviously made of stone collected from the ruins) involved the complete dismantlement of early buildings (Figs. 4.4 & 4.9). This resulted in the discovery of an east–west oriented stone wall (F.37). Built in a cut, 0.8 m wide and 0.10–0.35 m deep (north side deeper than south), a 0.6 m-wide clay-packed wall was found to be carried on a foundation of large block-/boulder-like

stones. Lying c. 1.8 m south of the end of the trench, it is unfortunate that the cutting was not extended further to absolutely determine that it was not building-related (i.e. so that the trench could have potentially picked up a building's northern/back wall). While the quality of its construction led us to think that F.37 related to a terrace division, certainty in this manner is not possible.

A massive posthole was excavated on the southern side of this wall. F.36 was of ovoid plan (0.35 × 0.5 m), with a 0.25 m-diameter, sub-circular profile conjoining its southwestern side; 0.9 m deep, with depth it narrowed to a diameter of 0.28 m ([096]). It was filled with mid-brown clay with charcoal flecks ([095]).

Four postholes were excavated over the southern 2.4 m of this trench:

F.3 - Circular (0.3 m dia.), 0.2–0.3 m deep, filled with dark grey loam with charcoal.

F.4 - Sub-circular (0.26 × 0.3 m), 0.4 m deep, with a concave base and vertical sides; fill as F.3.

F.5 - Sub-circular (0.15 m dia.), 0.22 m deep, with vertical sides and a concave base; fill, mid-dark grey-brown clay loam.

F.6 - Sub-circular (0.15 m dia.), 0.36 m deep with rounded base; fill as F.5.

North of this grouping, three other definite postholes were exposed, but not excavated (F.56–F.58). At the north end of the trench, three further possible stake-/postholes were exposed, but these were thought no to probably relate to pastoralist shelters. It warrants mention that there is a suggestion that the main postholes were paired, and three such settings were apparent (F.3/6, F.4/5 and F.57/58).

Along the length of the trench, below the topsoil ([099] general number), the natural was found to show signs of weathering and evidence of occupation trample. Including charcoal flecking, quantities of pottery were recovered from this horizon ([018]; no pottery was recovered over the southernmost 1.5 m of the trench).

Trench IV

Extending the east–west section from across Structure 27, this trench ran east from that building to Structure 28 (Fig. 4.9). Exposed beneath the 0.25–0.6 m-thick layer of topsoil and grey-brown clay loam with rubble ([010] general no.), from approximately the mid point of the trench, the surface of the natural sloped down by c. 0.1 m over 2.4 m. In other words, it had not been truncated/terraced and carried no distinct sealing surface (cf. Trenches V & VI below).

The line of the trench fell just short of an exterior terrace porch that runs along the southwestern side of Structure 28. However, exposed in the southern face of the trench beside that building was a large, roughly dressed, stone upright (0.15–0.28 × 0.45 m × 0.8 m+) and which probably relates to that setting. This overlay the fill of F.63, the construction trench for that building's western wall, which sloped down broadly (0.15 m over 0.8 m), dropping to 0.25 m depth just before the wall itself. Its broad profile contrasts with the steep 'box-like' form of the construction trench for the eastern building (F.27); with a flat base 0.3 m deep, its vertical edge lay 0.35 m beyond that wall face. However, across the width of the trench, the distance which this construction cut extended beyond the wall narrowed markedly (to only 0.10–0.15 m width). The kink in its line could reflect a stepping of the depth of its footing, perhaps rising to the north in relationship to the level of up-slope terrace truncation.

Two major cut features were excavated in the surface of the natural:

F.7 - An ovoid posthole (0.60 × 0.93 m) with vertical sides coming

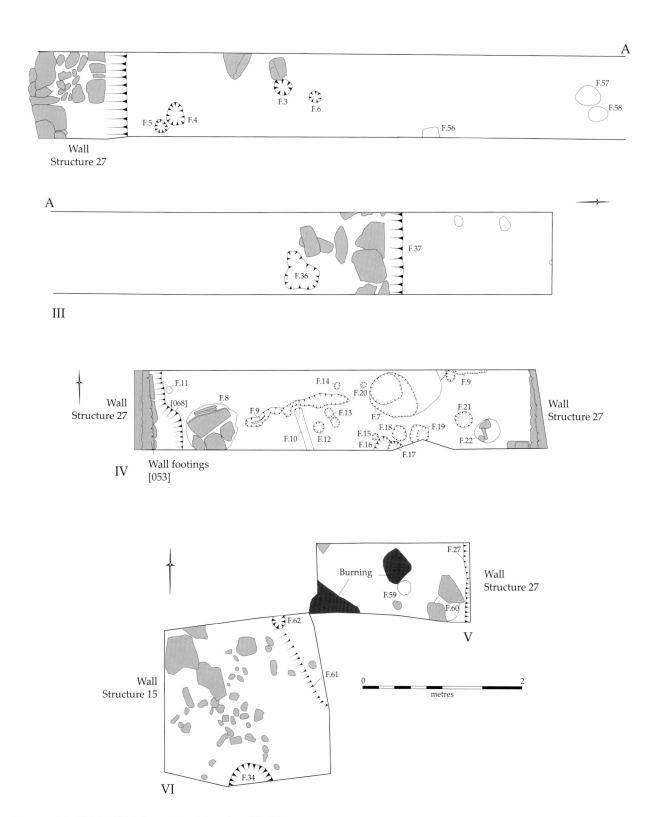

Figure 4.9. *Kohla 2000: base plans Trenches III–VI.*

down to a flat base 0.78 m deep. A discrete fill of re-deposited natural in its side indicates that it held a post 0.35 m in diameter; there was also evidence of stone-packing in its upper profile.

F.8 - This circular cut (*c.* 0.6 m dia.) had a flat base only 0.18 m deep. Large stone slabs had been carefully laid flat across its base (largest 0.04 × 0.28 × 0.5 m); a large slab had also been set vertically against its northern edge (0.02 × 0.27 × 0.38 m). Otherwise, this feature was filled with mid–dark brown silty clay, with lenses of re-deposited natural and flecks/small fragments of charcoal. While, in all likelihood, it also probably held a large, stone-packed flat-based post, the care given to its lining could suggest other functions (cold store?; cf. F.41 in Trench VIII).

Although still substantial (and seemingly 'real'), a number of somewhat smaller postholes were also excavated:

F.16–F.18 - This consisted of three inter-cut 'hollows' (*c.* 0.14–0.2 m dia.; 0.13–0.2 m deep). Though some, if not all three, probably represent postholes, they seem disturbed by rooting.

F.19 - An ovoid cut (0.18 × 0.2 m) tapering with depth to a circular form, 0.12 m in diameter; 0.35 m deep.

F.21 - Sub-circular (0.14 m dia.), becoming sub-rectangular with depth and tapering to a pointed base; 0.29 m deep.

F.22 - Sub-circular (0.3 m dia.) and 0.15 m deep. Although only distinguished at the level of the natural (and having an unclear relationship with the construction trench for Structure 28, F.63), its fill included large packing stones that projected above this height, implying that it must have cut through F.63.

Otherwise, a series of small 'holes' and channels were investigated (F.9–F.15 & F.20). Though possibly representing stakeholes, in all likelihood these were all products of tree-rooting.

Trenches V and VI

Metre-wide trenches were opened west of Structure 27, to extend the east–west transect to Structure 15; because of complications within the western of these (Trench VI), its width was doubled southward (Figs. 4.3:D, 4.6 & 4.9). The removal of the topsoil, grey-brown clay loam and rubble layers in each ([013] & [029] respectively) exposed a *c.* 1–3 cm-thick burnt occupation layer, with extensive charcoal inclusions and bright orange patches, indicative of *in situ* burning. In Trench V, this was clearly truncated by the construction trench for the wall of Structure 27 (F.27); cleaning of this horizon revealed two postholes (F.59 & F.60; respectively 0.15 & 0.3 m in dia. — unexcavated).

This horizon continued across the surface of the natural in the northeastern corner of Trench VI, west of which it bedded upon a layer of re-deposited natural clay ([080]); along the westernmost 0.5–0.6 m of the trench, these surfaces were definitely cut by the construction trench for Structure 15 (F.29: Figs. 4.3:B/D & 4.9). However, across much of this trench these layers were found to bed down into a 0.1–0.15 m-deep, flat-based cut (F.61), that continued west to and below Structure 15, definitely pre-dating that building. Extending throughout its base was what seemed to be another occupation layer of mid grey clay silt with charcoal, and which included a few large stone slabs within its base ([067]).

Two postholes were excavated within this trench. The one, F.62 (0.15–0.18 m dia.; 0.25 m deep) cut into the natural in the edge of the F.61 'terrace' cut. The other, F.34, was much larger and, located along the southern edge of the trench, seemed later. Probably cutting the [080] surface, it was itself truncated by the wall trench of Structure 15 (F.29). F.34 was 0.55 m in diameter and 0.9 m deep, its

sides tapering with depth to a rounded base. It was filled with mid-grey-brown clay loam with charcoal flecks, lenses of re-deposited natural and stone rubble.

The evidence of these two trenches is crucial for the understanding of the settlement as a whole, as they definitely attest to a phase of occupation prior to both the stone buildings, Structures 15 and 27. Although presumably relating to timber-built structures, with so limited exposure, little can be said of this occupation. What is, however, unequivocal is that it involved a degree of lateral terracing. Possibly demonstrated by cut F.61, this is more clearly seen in the fact that, east of this point, the natural ground surface was flat to where (sealed by the burnt occupation layer) it was truncated by the construction trench for Structure 27.

We cannot be certain whether there was an abandonment interval between this early usage and the construction of the stone buildings. Although the construction trenches for the latter were most apparent where they cut the 'obvious' layer of the lower burnt occupation, there were suggestions that they were cut from higher in the profile. This is clearest — though still with a considerable ambiguity — in the case of Structure 15, as hints of its construction trench could be distinguished higher in the upper clay loam/rubble layer. This could suggest, at least in this immediate instance, that the two phases of occupation may not have followed directly upon each other.

Trench VII

With its northern end marked by the southern wall of Structure 25 (and its 0.55 m+-wide and 0.3 m-deep flat-based construction trench: F.55), the trench continued south for 5.95 m to Structure 23 (the natural sloping down by 0.45 m over its length: Figs. 4.4, 4.10: D & 4.11). The northern wall of the latter was not itself trench-built (F.39). Rather, its base lay some 0.2 m above the 'truncated' level of natural behind it (i.e. worn or eroded away, see below). Sloping down from the level of the Structure 23 wall base, a 0.3 m-wide and 0.2 m-deep, concave-profiled gully (F.49) ran parallel with it. While possibly an earlier structural feature, in all likelihood this related to that stone building and was an eaves-drip trough.

Across the southernmost 2.75 m of the trench, the sloping surface of the natural clays dipped more markedly to form a broad, 0.1–0.2 m-deep hollow. Here was preserved a 0.1 m-thick occupation horizon, a mid–dark grey silty deposit with quantities of pottery ([063]), that was distinct from the light orange-brown silty clay which otherwise lay below the topsoil (with stones; [030] general number). Whilst possibly relating to a 'pre-stone' building occupation (here otherwise attested to by five unexcavated postholes, F.50–F.54), similar to the evidence of Trenches I and II as regards Structure 25, this material had probably been caught/dumped in a pathway behind Structure 23.

Trench VIII

Aside from exposing the lower face and construction trench for the southern wall of Structure 23 (F.39), a complex sequence of features was identified within Trench VIII (Figs. 4.4, 4.10PA/B & 4.11). F.38 was a 0.75 m-wide 'buried' wall (i.e. not visible at topsoil level), consisting of three courses of large stone slabs. Due to ground slope, only its northern up-hill side was trench-built (0.4 m deep); it had been laterally cut into the slope and there was no defining cut on its south side. On that aspect, the ground slope had been truncated and flattened over *c.* 1.9 m, and the southern face of F.38 had, therefore, been built free-standing. A few stone slabs lay embedded within the truncated surface of natural in front of the wall, and seemed associated with a thin burnt layer. In fact, under the topsoil, and held to a depth of 0.1–0.25 m before the wall (and otherwise extending as a 5–10 cm-thick layer over much of the base of the trench), the lower soil horizon had burnt clay/daub inclusions.

Figure 4.10. *Kohla 2000: A & B) Trench VIII F.23 capstone-sealed burnt deposit (A) with wall F.38 below (B; note southern wall of Structure 23 in end of trench); C) looking north along length of Trench IX with paved surface F.25 in foreground and terrace wall F.24 behind; D) Trench VIII showing full exposure of southern wall of Structure 25 (F.35) and construction trench (F.55).*

Abutting the north side of wall F.38 was a 0.5 m 'square' box-like cut, *c.* 0.2 m deep with a large slab laid across its base (F.41). Its excavator was able to identify the impression of subsequently removed vertical slabs in the sides of this feature and, therefore, this was probably either a stone-lined cist or hearth. Indeed, a concentration of charcoal was found upon the basal slab and a single burnt bone fragment was recovered. The interpretation of this feature group is further complicated by the fact that a cairn-like stone setting was found to seal it (F.23). Ringed by small stone rubble, a large concave slab capped a distinct heap of charcoal that was surrounded by sherds from a single broken pot (Fig. 4.12). What seemed to be horse teeth and small fragments of burnt bone were also recovered from these deposits. In short, this seems to relate to a ritual 'placement' and perhaps even a mortuary interment. If indeed the latter, by any measure, this would be a remarkable occurrence

within the core of a village.

While wall F.38 was clearly terrace-related, lying only 1.3 m south of Structure 23, it could also have footed a porch for that building (or, alternatively, have been the southern side of an earlier building). If so, the F.41 'box' hearth/cist may have been directly associated with it.

A series of postholes (distinct from areas of obvious tree-root disturbance) were excavated on either side of wall F.38:

F.40 - Sub-circular, *c.* 0.25 m in diameter with straight sides and a flat base; 0.39 m deep (fill, dark grey clay loam and charcoal flecks).

F.42 - Sub-circular, 0.35 m in diameter with vertical sides; 0.6 m+ deep; cuts F.41 and abuts wall F.38 (fill, upper profile void; below, grey loam).

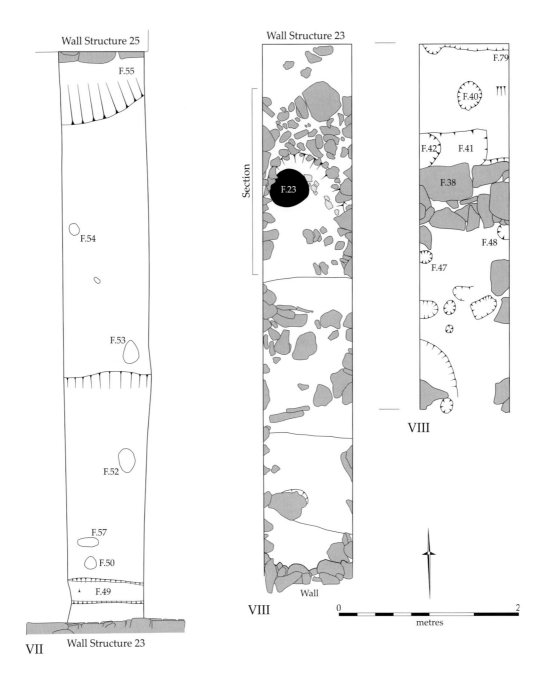

Figure 4.11. *Kohla 2000: base plans Trenches VII and VIII.*

F.47 - Sub-circular, 0.12 × 0.13 m+, 0.4 m deep, cutting into the top of natural along the southern foot of wall F.38 (fill, loose, dark grey clay loam, with remnants of decayed wood).

F.48 - A cut, *c.* 0.2 m in diameter, with a flat base (0.16 m deep), lying just south of wall F.38 (fill, loose and partially 'voided' dark grey clay loam).

Trenches IX and X

Trench IX extended south for 7.2 m from the line of F.24, a trench-built terrace wall (*c.* 0.85 m wide and 1 m high) that was visible as a surface feature (Figs. 4.4, 4.10:C & 4.12). From its foot the natural fell away by 0.6 m over 5 m down to the southern 'courtyard' before Structures 18 and 19. There, over approximately 200 sq.m, the ground surface is remarkably flat and the turf is spongy underfoot. Accordingly, within the trench the natural shelved at this point and it was found to be informally paved in flagstones, which extended around a large upstanding boulder. The surface of the natural appeared to have been truncated to accommodate this surface, and its northern edge is marked by a line of stone slabs (0.3–0.6 m wide) that seems to be some manner of recumbent wall, delineating the yard (all F.25). (In the 1994 survey, an exterior terrace-related staircase was identified immediately east of this trench.)

Trench X was opened at the northern foot of the large standing stone (set beside Structure 19), with the specific intention of determining whether this was 'old' or whether it had been recently set (Figs. 3.34:C/D, 4.1 & 4.12). Upon the removal of 0.3 m of humus, this stele was found to be embedded within the same paving recovered in Trench IX, thereby proving its antiquity (rising 1.65 m above the

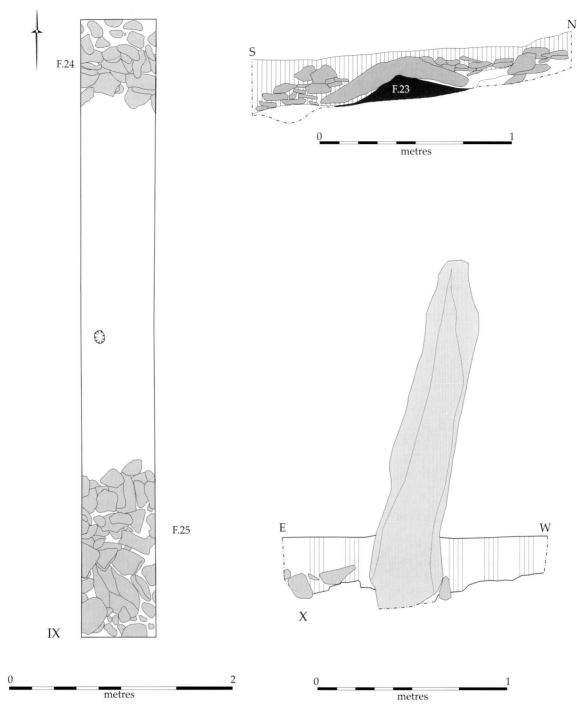

Figure 4.12. *Kohla 2000: base plan Trench IX with section of F.23 capstone deposit (Trench VIII; see Fig. 4.11) and stone upright, Trench X.*

contemporary ground surface). Aside from this determination, the importance of these two trenches is that they demonstrate the existence of formally defined 'public' space, within the core of the village settlement, which the standing stone itself is also clearly an expression thereof. Interestingly enough, no occupation surface was found sealing this paving. In fact, remarkably few artefacts were recovered in association, suggesting that deposition may not have been a major component of public activities.

Finds

The excavations proved surprisingly prolific. In total, more than 1200 sherds of pottery were recovered and their gross trench-densities are shown in Table 4.1.

Although such a limited excavation sample does not provide a sound basis for generalization,

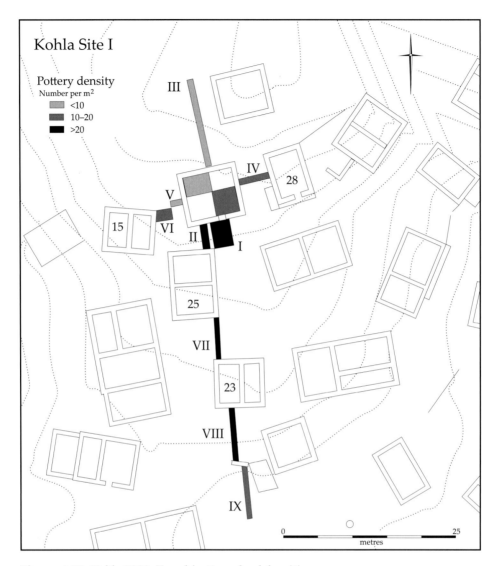

Figure 4.13. *Kohla 2000: Trench/pottery sherd densities.*

Table 4.1. *Pottery frequency (* indicates above mean densities — 15.8 sherds per sq.m).*

Trench	Sq.m	Pottery (no.)	Density (sherds per sq.m)
Str. 27	21.8	164	7.5
Quad A	10.25	31	3
Quad D	11.55	133	11.5
I	9.10	218	24*
II	3.30	93	28.2*
III	13.30	109	8.2
IV	5.00	64	12.8
V	1.90	8	4.2
VI	4.00	71	17.7*
VII	6.00	220	36.7*
VIII	5.60	165	29.5*
IX	7.20	90	12.5
X	1.40	2	1.4

trends may be suggested. Foremost is the relatively low densities within the interior of Structure 27 itself (Fig. 4.13). The terraced construction of that building probably resulted in the truncation of earlier occupation horizons and the re-deposition of their associated finds. Equally, these figures suggest — analogous to the maintenance of domestic space in villages today — that the building was swept out and, perhaps related, the densities in the doorway-related quadrant (D) were almost four times greater than the building's 'backspace' in Quadrant A. (Here, it is surely relevant that, as indicated in Table 4.1, aside from Trench VI, all the occurrences of above-mean densities occur in front of buildings. Abutting Structure 15, the location of the entrance into that building is unknown and the robust survival of the Phase 1 horizon in Trench VI also probably contributed to its densities.) The evidence that the houses were cleaned out could, by extension, imply the existence of midden dumps. Probably located at the fringes of the settlement's built-core, these were not located. Of course, this chain of argument presupposes that Structure 27 — with its low artefact densities — was a 'typical' house, as opposed to a meeting place, workshop, byre or shrine/temple. Only further excavation of a range of the site's structures will provide *comparative context* to permit such statements to be made with any confidence.

The densities across the surfaces in front of Structure 27 (Trenches I & II; 26.1 ave.) are roughly comparable to that before Structure 23 (VIII; 29.5), whereas, at 36.7 sherds per sq.m, the densities between Structures 23 and 25 are substantially greater. South of Structures 23 and the F.24 boundary wall, the density of Trench IX — running down to the 'plaza' — is relatively low (12.5), with the lowest density being in Trench X, at the foot of the main standing stone. While admittedly the paving was not removed across this area, this still suggests that the central 'public' space was kept relatively clean (with resultant dumping perhaps along the southern edge-of-settlement scarp) or that activities occurring there were not significantly artefact-related.

As outlined by Gibson below, the sheer quantity of the pottery recovered, and its range of decorative styles and fabrics (both wheel- and hand-made) suggests that the settlement had extensive trade/exchange links. A number of finds would, moreover, point to long-distance connections. Among these are turquoise and fossil coral beads probably deriving from Tibet (Fig. 4.14:4–8). Also found was a piece of a carved stone vessel and a rim/neck fragment from a fine bronze flagon (Fig. 4.14:1), both of which may well have been imported to the site.

Both stone and worked-down pottery gaming discs were recovered (and a drilled, round-worked, decorated sherd may have been utilized as a pendant; Fig. 4.14:10, 11 & 13). The ceramic small finds included what was probably a clay sling-shot and a 'top' or 'stopper-like' object of unknown purpose (Fig. 4.14:9). A large copper-alloy ring or bracelet and a miniature spatula-like piece (Fig. 4.14:2), as well as part of a silver earring or bracelet (Fig. 4.14:3), were also found.

Eight pieces of iron were recovered. Excluding a rod-like piece, five of these may be knives or other types of bladed implement (Fig. 4.15:1–4). Equally noteworthy were a number of small pieces of crucible from the lower burnt ground surface in Trench VI and, also, the presence of iron slag within three contexts (Trenches I & III; a piece of slag had also been found in the pre-excavation survey collections: see Gajurel & Vaidya 1994, 1–65 concerning Nepalese metalworking

traditions). Fortunately, fragments of the latter were present in environmental samples returned to Britain, and these we were able to have analysed.

Slag fragments
PAUL T. CRADDOCK

Only tiny fragments of slag from [080], weighing no more than a few grams were available for study and thus it is not possible to describe the metallurgical operations in any detail. However, examination by binocular microscopy showed that the fragments have a vesicular structure, typical of metalworking operations rather than metal-smelting, which usually generate a much denser slag largely free of gas porosity.

Qualitative analysis by energy dispersive, X-Ray fluorescence detected iron and silicon with some calcium, potassium and traces of zinc. The latter two elements are likely to come from the wood or charcoal fuel. The presence of crucibles suggests that some melting of non-ferrous metals was taking place, and this would create quantities of slag. The smithing of iron requires frequent reheating in a hearth, and this also generates slag.

Thus, the slag is likely to be a hearth slag, generated by high temperature metal-working, either in the melting of non-ferrous metals or the smithing of iron.

Illustrated small finds (Fig. 4.14)
Bronze
1) Bowl fragment (<14> [066], Tr. IX)
2) Object with flattened circular end with round shaft; ?miniature spatula (<6> [029], Tr. VI)

Silver
3) Ribbed earring or bracelet fragment (<37> [099], Tr. VII)

Beads
4) Hexagonal drilled stone (?coral; <17> [005]A, Str. 27)
5) Coral (<2> [004], Tr. II)
6) Turquoise (<4> [009], Tr. III)
7) Coral (<15> [002]A, Str. 27)
8) Turquoise (<13> [066], Tr. IX)

Clay/ceramic
9) Fired, either gaming piece or metalworking related (<25> [080], Tr. VI)
10) Perforated pottery disc (<16> [005]A, Str. 27)
11) Pottery counter/gaming token (<31> [095], Tr. III; F.36)

Stone
12) Whetstone (<34> [095], Tr. III; F.36)
13) Counter/gaming token (<32> [095], Tr. III; F.36)
14) Worked rock crystal blade (<29> [095], Tr. III; F.36)

Worked stone
Of the worked stone, a rock-crystal blade (Fig. 4.14:14) and a chert flake (?scraper) might attest to pre-medieval activity; a rectangular piece of blue quartz may have been somehow utilized (or curated). Otherwise, apart from a whetstone (Fig. 4.14:12), as shown in Figure 4.15 (5–8), the majority of these finds consist of various kinds of rubber/grinding stones, though one slab-like piece may have been from a quern. Two longer pieces appeared implement-like; the one being akin to a pick, and the rounded end of the other could

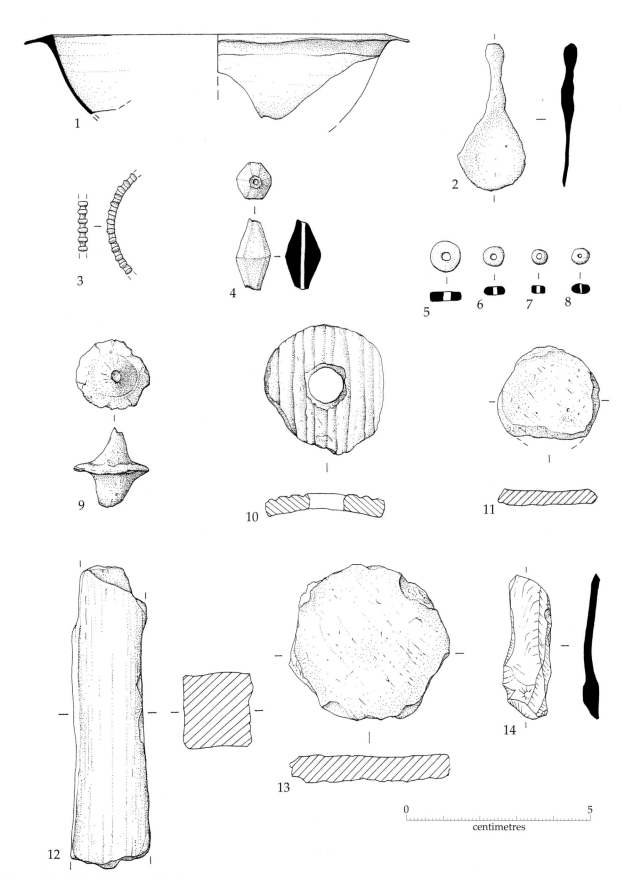

Figure 4.14. *Kohla 2000: small finds.*

Figure 4.15. *Kohla 2000: ironwork (1–4) and worked stone (5–7).*

suggest a mortar-pounding function. Two rather adze-suggestive pieces, smoothed on all sides, could also indicate mortar-related pounding or grinding. One of the other worked stones is particularly noteworthy (Fig. 4.15:7), though of entirely ambiguous attribution. Having a teardrop-like shape with an intentionally narrowed end, this has matching *c.* 4 cm diameter cupmark-like depressions on either of its faces, suggesting either its attachment (?for 'mass' hammering) or suspension (?a weight).

The category of 'architectural stones' was rather arbitrarily assigned to larger pieces. In two instances, this involved fragments that might have been either building sills or lintels; both were recovered in association with the fills of Structure 27. Similarly, a large slab was found lying on the buried ground surface in front of that building (Fig. 4.8:A). This might have served a comparable purpose or, alternatively, have been a recumbent standing stone, though of lesser dimension than that before Structure 19. Otherwise, the ridged form of two smaller fragments suggested a degree of working, though to what purpose is unknown.

Pottery
DAVID GIBSON
The total assemblage of sherds collected from the 2000 excavation season numbered 1275, which were of varying condition, attributable to post-depositional

factors. Although better preserved than the survey pottery, the material had still been subject to attrition with the leaching-out of organics due to acidic soil conditions and damage from frost action. Again, the sherds were classified by fabric, decoration and, where possible, form. The pottery from the excavation revealed five further fabric types in addition to those identified in the preceding survey seasons:

I - Pale buff/orange/brown with a smooth feel; slightly greyer core, with occasional mica inclusions up to 1 mm.

J - Pale buff/orange with a smooth feel; dark grey core and greyish margins, with grog tempering with frequent burnt- or leached-out inclusions.

K - Pale orange/buff with a rough feel; large mica inclusions up to 0.7 mm and occasional organics.

L - Mid grey with a hard feel; occasional small inclusions including mica and identified grey material.

M - Brick red with a hard smooth feel; well-fired with frequent grey inclusions (no mica) and occasional leached or burnt-out organics.

In terms of hardness or technological advancement/skill, none of the five new fabrics differentiated themselves from the remaining excavation or survey types. However, Fabrics J and M did not contain mica inclusions, tentatively suggesting differing clay sources. There is the possibility that Fabric J, as well as being tempered with grog, may have used organics as a temper; this may though just be the result of poor clay sorting.

141

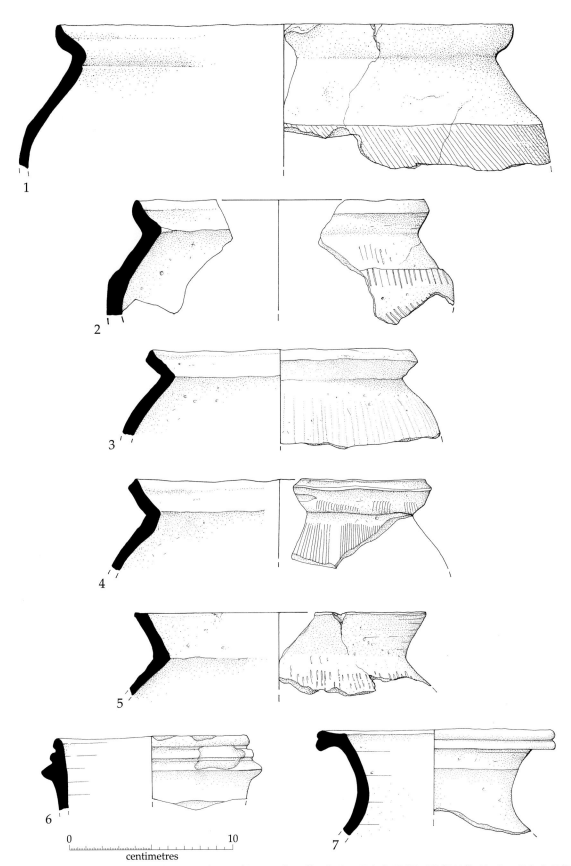

Figure 4.16. *Kohla 2000 - pottery: 1) rim, Fabric E (Str. 27, [005]); 2) rim, Fabric E (Tr. III [093]); 3) rim, Fabric J (Tr. VII, [064]); 4) rim, Fabric I (Tr. VII [063]); 5) rim, Fabric K (F.4 [016]); 6) rim (Tr. IX [066]); 7) rim, Fabric J (F.23 [06]).*

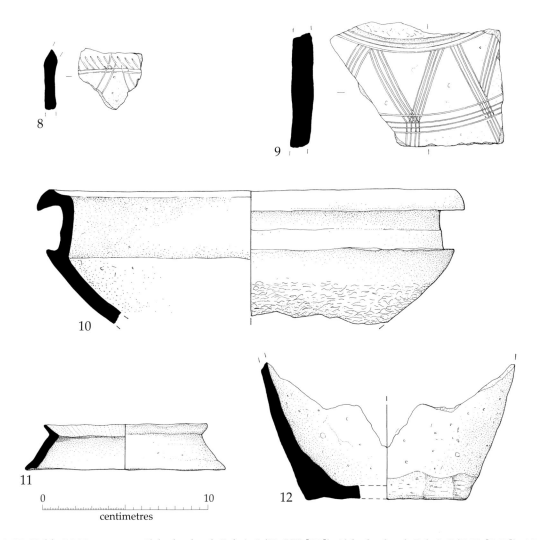

Figure 4.17. *Kohla 2000 - pottery: 8) body sherd, Fabric J (Tr. VII [03]); 9) body sherd, Fabric J (F.23 [065]); 10) rim, Fabric A (F.9 [031]); 11) pot stand, Fabric I (Tr. VII [063]); 12) base, Fabric J (Tr. VII [064]).*

The excavation pottery was both hand-formed (the building or forming of the pot without the use of centrifugal force), hand-formed with the addition of slowly thrown, fitted-neck rims and wheel-thrown pottery (occasional and difficult to determine from the abraded nature and sherd size). No complete vessel profile was recovered. The thickness of sherd walls was, in the main, 10 mm or less (Figs. 4.16 & 4.17). As with the survey pottery, whether the excavation pottery was clamp- or kiln-fired remains unclear.

The breakdown of sherds by fabric was as follows:

Table 4.2. *Fabric frequency.*

Fabric	A	B	C	D	E	F	G	H	I	J	K	L	M
Total	136	0	7	49	792	0	0	0	66	205	7	8	2

The percentage of each fabric (over 100 sherds) decorated by sherd number was as follows:

Fabric A   46% decorated
Fabric E   23% decorated
Fabric J   3% decorated.

This wide variance illustrates the differing treatment, in terms of decoration, of the varying fabrics. Because of the relatively poor condition of the sherds, it is difficult to know if this relationship is determined by the proportion of each pot being decorated, or whether individual pots in the same fabric were decorated or not.

The results of the excavation complemented the results of the survey. Fabrics B, F and G were not found at Kohla, being identified only at lower-altitude sites (with Fabrics I–M only found in the excavation phase and not during the survey). Based on the limited excavation areas, a number of contexts have been stratigraphically determined as 'early' in the site's sequence. In Trench VI, [080] ten sherds (five decorated) of Fabric A were found, with 11 sherds (five rims) of Fabric A, 49 sherds (four decorated) of Fabric E, seven sherds (a rim and a handle) of Fabric J and a sherd of Fabric L recovered in Trench I ([055]).

Other potentially early contexts include Trench II, [011] with seven rim sherds of Fabric C, 73 sherds (43 decorated and two rims) of Fabric E, two sherds of Fabric I and seven sherds of Fabric J. In Trench VI, [067] there were three sherds (two decorated) of Fabric A, five sherds (two decorated including a rim) of Fabric D, 34 sherds (seven decorated) of Fabric E and three rim sherds of Fabric L. Nine sherds (one decorated and a rim) of Fabric A, 60 sherds (two rims, four decorated) of Fabric E and ten sherds (eight rims, one decorated and a base) of Fabric L were recovered from Trench VII, [063].

Within the ceramic assemblage, five fabrics reached double figures in terms of sherd count: Fabric A, 136; Fabric D, 49; Fabric E, 792; Fabric I, 66; and Fabric J, 205. Fabric E was by far the most prevalent comprising 62 per cent of the total assemblage.

The excavation ceramic assemblage can be characterized as of relatively poor quality, in terms of technology and decorative appearance. The lack of attention to detail in the preparation and sorting of the clay is evident in the propensity for blow-outs and firing imperfections in the ceramics. These also suggest that the ceramics were clamp-fired, where temperature could not be maintained and regulated easily. The assemblage appears, in the main, to have comprised flat-bottomed jars and bowls with the occasional handle. More attention to detail has been taken with the rims, which appear to have been at least slow-turned; the bodies of the pots are often relatively crudely hand-formed.

The excavation sequence has demonstrated that Fabrics D and E, in particular, appear to be long-lived. They are also relatively widespread in the area, being recorded from the early excavation sequences at Kohla and at Nadr Pa.

Compared to the excavated assemblages of the Kathmandu Valley and northern India, or even the excavations of the last decade in Mustang at Khyinga (where 38,000 sherds have been recovered: Hüttel & Paap 1998), the total assemblage of 2195 sherds from the two seasons of field survey and one season of excavation is statistically small. However, a number of comparisons, in particular to Khyinga, can be made. There are a number of similarities, particularly in the use of thin- and thick-twisted cord decoration between the ceramics found at Kohla and those from its later phases. Obviously, without the direct comparison of sherds from both excavations, no comments on fabrics can be made, but the form and decoration of a number of ceramics seem stylistically similar. However, until more extensive excavation at Kohla is undertaken, these preliminary conclusions must remain tentative.

Archaeobotanical evidence

Eleni Asouti & Dorian Q. Fuller

The site is located in the transitional zone, between the upper montane forests of western Nepal (characterized by oak, spruce and fir) and those of eastern Nepal (characterized by rhododendrons, yew, fir and hemlock: see Allard above). As will be discussed below, the wood-charcoal data from the site is congruent with such an environment at the period of occupation. Five bulk samples from charcoal-rich contexts were collected during the 2000 excavations. A portion of these were used for radiocarbon dating, with the remainder given to the authors in London for archaeobotanical analysis.

The volumes and weights of the samples were recorded and they were sieved into standard size classes to aid analysis (>4 mm, 2–4 mm, 1–2 mm, 0.5–1 mm, <0.5 mm). All fractions of greater than 1 mm were sorted under an incident light microscope, with identification between 6× and 40× for the separation of seed, fruit and floral remains. All or half of 0.5–1 mm fraction was quickly scanned under the microscope from each sample, but little was noted in this size-range apart from wood fragments. Seeds and other non-wood remains were identified by morphological features in comparison to the Institute of Archaeology's reference collection. The finds of seeds are tabulated in Table 4.3, as is the overall weight and volume of samples, and also the weight of the >4 mm fraction and the counts of identified seed remains.

From the dry-sieved fractions of the archaeobotanical samples, the fraction >4 mm was targeted for microscopic analysis and identification of wood charcoal. Charcoal material was sub-sampled by counting from each >4 mm fraction to be examined, a total of 100 fragments. Although this number may not be considered as entirely satisfactory for tracing rare taxa in the assemblages, it still enables a sound preliminary assessment of sample composition, at least in what concerns the dominant taxa (cf. Asouti 2001). Furthermore, given the large size of the samples, and the lack of primary reference material from the region (see below), this sub-sampling strategy allows for the preservation of sufficient material for future analysis, under more optimal conditions.

Charcoal fragments were fractured by hand and/or pressure (with a carbon steel razor blade), in all three anatomical planes (Transverse, Radial Longitudinal, Tangential Longitudinal), and these were examined under a high-power Olympus BHMJ microscope at magnifications of ×50, ×100, ×200 and ×500. Since no primary comparative material (thin sections of fresh wood and/or modern charred specimens) was available in the first instance, the examined specimens were identified by comparison to published descriptions and microphotographs of Nepalese trees and shrubs (Suzuki & Noshiro 1988, Suzuki *et al.* 1991; 1999). Although the lack of original reference material is generally considered as a setback for the analysis of ancient specimens, these studies (particularly the very detailed anatomical descriptions accompanying each species) nevertheless provided a sound basis for attempting identification of the examined charcoal specimens to the genus and/or family level. Following this, selected specimens from each identified taxon were examined under the SEM (Scanning Electron Microscope), in order to verify the botanical identifications and produce high-quality microphotographs, suitable for publication and future reference. The original specimens used for this purpose are kept at the Laboratory of Archaeobotany and Palaeoecology at the Institute of Archaeology, University College London, together with the charcoal samples and the identified specimens from each sample; the remainder of the samples have been returned to Department of Archaeology, HMG, Nepal.

Fruits, seeds and flowers

Although the quantities of seeds and other non-wood finds were extremely few, they include a range of grain crops, and a couple of recognizable fruits (Table 4.3). Given the low number of samples and the small number of items in each, quantitative comparison between samples is unlikely to be meaningful. Calculations of relative frequency of species (from among all identified food plants in all samples) and ubiquity (the percentage of samples within which a species occurs) are provided at the right-hand side of Table 4.3. Most of these species were readily recognizable and are crops often found archaeobotanically (see Fig. 4.18).

Amongst the more surprising finds initially were the fragments of rice lemma and paleas, including some spikelet bases. While one fragment of rice husk is black, and perhaps charred, the other rice fragments are uncharred. This is in contrast to the rest of the assemblage which is charred. Apart from in exceptional environments, uncharred remains are regarded with suspicion as they are unlikely to survive, and are therefore more likely to be modern intrusions. The antiquity of the rice was tested by direct radiocarbon dating (Beta-173144, see 'Dating' section below), which

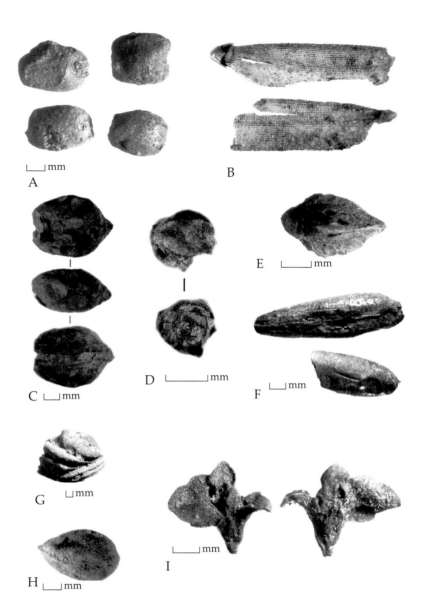

Figure 4.18. *Kohla 2000 - plant remains: A)* Triticum *grains from Trench VI ([080]), dorsal view; B) rice husk from Str. 27 ([003]); C)* Hordeum vulgare *from Str. 27 ([005]); D)* Setaria italica *from Str. 27 ([005]); E)* Fagopyrum *from Str. 27 ([003]); F)* Avena sativa *from Str. 27 ([003]); G)* Prunus persica *endcarp from Trench VI ([080]); H)* Cornus *type pit from Trench VI ([080]): I) two views of the flower from F.28 ([094]).*

proved that these remains are, indeed, modern. It seems probable that the small fragments of rice husk and spikelet bases represent contamination from the clothes or sacking of the excavators or other recent 'visitors' to the site. Further discussion of the plant remains concentrates only on those that were carbonized (charred) and can safely be inferred to be ancient.

The charred remains suggest that staple cereals were a major part of the diet during occupation of Kohla. This includes evidence for barley, a small-grained free-threshing wheat, and oats. A single grain of foxtail millet was recovered, which is characterized by its large embryo and the beaded surface texture on the preserved, adhering palea on its ventral surface (Fig. 4.18:D). Another identified crop which shows remarkable preservation is a single find of buckwheat. This triangular fruit retained the thin, veined, persistent

Table 4.3. *Archaeobotanical data: seeds, fruits, flowers (carbonized unless indicated).*

	F.23 [065]	Structure 27 F.28 [094]	Structure 27 [005]D	Structure 27 [003] C	Sondage VI [080]	Ubiquity	% total foods
Weight (g)	547.6	175.5	255.8	252.2	348.7		
Volume total (mL)	1150	395	375	414	751		
Volume >4 mm	856	125	180	180	350		
Cereals/ pseudo-cereals							
Wheat free-threshing (*Triticum* sp.) grains	1	1		2	4	80%	19%
Barley (*Hordeum vulgare*) grains	4		3	3		60%	24%
Oat (*Avena sativa*) grains				5		20%	12%
Oat (*Avena sativa*) grain fragments			2	21 (MNI 4)		40%	5%
Rice (*Oryza sativa*) spikelet bases - UNCHARRED (intrusive?)			1	3		40%	10%
Rice husk fragments - UNCHARRED (intrusive?)				2	2	40%	10%
Foxtail millet (*Setaria italica*) grain & husk			1			20%	2%
Buckwheat (*Fagapyrum* cf. *esculentum*)				1		20%	2%
Fruits							
Peach (*Prunus persica*) endocarp fragments			2		3	40%	12%
Cornus sp. stone					1	20%	2%
cf. *Cornus* sp. seed					1	20%	2%
Other							
Small Brassicaceae type				1			
Indet. fruit/nut fragments		5		1 (capsule)			
Indet. seed/tissue fragments	10	6	9	22	6		
Flower: Brassicaceae type		1					
Dung (sheep/goat?)	2				1		
Slag fragments					+		
Glass fragment (from bangle?)				1			
Felt(?) fragments				2			

calyx (sepals), in addition to the acuminate bracts that subtend these. Although the find is singular, it is clearly *Fagopyrum*. Reference material was not available to attempt to differentiate the common buckwheat (*F. esculentum*) from the tartary buckwheat (*F. tartaricum*), the latter of which can persist at higher elevations.

Finds of the characteristic endocarp of peach pits are likely to be from the well-known cultivated fruit, based on their rugose pattern and size (Fig. 4.18:G), although reference material was not available to rule out a range of indigenous wild *Prunus* spp. (cf. Polunin & Stainton 1984). A fruit stone generally similar to reference material of non-Himalayan *Cornus* spp., suggests the presence of a related species (Fig. 4.18:H).

The most remarkable find, in terms of archaeobotanical preservation, is a small, charred flower (Fig. 4.18:I). It appears to be a tetramerous flower, on which three of the four sepals are preserved, and also a single petal. It has a prominent pistil, which is congruent with an ovary of two fused carpels. The morphology of this specimen is congruent with a placement in the Brassicaceae (alt. Cruciferae), a family which includes some 54 species in 28 genera, many of which grow at high elevations and are characterized by minute tetramerous flowers (Polunin & Stainton 1984; Stainton 1988). No attempt has been made to further identify this specimen. Despite its remarkable preservation, it may not be of cultural significance and could merely represent a local wildflower incidentally included with fuel wood. The presence of a flower, however, does suggest that this fire burned, and, therefore, the site was occupied, during the flowering season, which is generally between mid-March and the end of May for Nepal (Polunin & Stainton 1984). This find does not, though, rule out occupation during other seasons.

In addition to the plant finds, fragments of slag were noted in one sample, and a fragment of a green glass object, perhaps a bangle,

in another. A few whole or fragmentary caprine dung pellets were encountered, although the main fuel for the fires appears to have been wood. Two small charred fragments of flat fibrous material were also encountered; these may be of animal hair and could represent carbonized felt.

The wheat grains recovered from Kohla are all abnormally small and stubby. The measurements of complete wheat grains are given in Table 4.4, and, as can be seen, their lengths are between 3.2 and 4 mm. This can be contrasted with the ranges and modal or average values from measured wheat assemblages from elsewhere in South Asia, such as charred wheat caches from Harappa, Mohenjodaro and Chanudaro, where lengths average between 4.5 and 5 mm, and widths between 2 and 3 mm (Vishnu-Mittre & Savithri 1982). Similarly, lengths above 4 mm and ranging to over 5 mm are reported for wheats from prehistoric/protohistoric sites of the middle Ganges Plain (e.g. Saraswat *et al*. 1994), Afghanistan (Willcox 1991), and Kashmir (Lone *et al*. 1993), although some short plump grains as short as 3 mm were reported in the latter study. The proportions of the Kohla grains, however, in terms of a length/breadth index and thickness/breadth index are comparable to these other assemblages (see especially Willcox 1991; Lone *et al*. 1993). The Kohla wheat is even small by comparison to the early free-threshing tetraploid(?) wheats of so-called 'parvicoccum' type known from the Neolithic Levant, reported to range from 3.6–4.9 mm in length (Kislev 1984, 66; Feldman & Kislev 2007). The significance of this distinctly small wheat-type is unclear, and it may represent the grains of a distinctive Himalayan strain. Given that modern botanical studies have not indicated the presence of tertaploid *Triticum durum* in the Himalayas, which is also largely absent from adjacent areas of the Indian plains, it is likely that the Kohla wheats were hexaploid bread wheats of some type. In the Kashmir Valley, the smaller grain

Table 4.4. *Wheat grain proportions, in mm.*

	Length	Breadth	Thickness	L:W(%)	T:W(%)
VI [080]	3.7	2.5	2.03	1.48	0.81
VI [080]	3.2	2.81	2.34	1.14	0.83
VI [080]	3.28	2.5	2.34	1.31	0.94
VI [080]	4	2.5	2.19	1.6	0.88
F.28 [094]	3.2	3.1	2.8	1.03	0.9
F.23 [065]	3.2	2.1	1.9	1.52	0.9
Str. 27 [003]	3.91	3.13	2.6	1.25	0.83

modality among archaeological wheats was referred to hexaploid *Triticum sphaerococcum* (Lone *et al.* 1993), although in general the widespread reporting of Indian shot wheat (*sphaeroccocum*) is problematic and remains poorly substantiated by detailed morphometric studies (see Fuller 2002; 2006, 22–4). Also, modern *T. sphaerococcum* is generally considered an adaptation to drought-prone arid regions, such as the Punjab and Baluchistan, and is, therefore, perhaps less likely to have been a crop above 1500 m a.s.l. in the Kashmir Valley. Thus, the possibility that some other small-grained wheat-type(s) evolved in the Himalayas deserves further research. However, there is also a possibility that small-grained free-threshing wheat diffused through the Himalayas from the northeast: the size range of the Kohla wheat is comparable to small round hexaploid free-threshing wheat reported archaeologically from East Asia, including Bronze Age central China and second-millennium AD Hokkaido, Japan (see Lee *et al.* 2007, 1088 and supplementary fig. 11).

Wood charcoal

Sixteen wood taxa were identified in addition to indeterminate woods of monocotyledons, dicotyledons and gymnosperms. The anatomical descriptions of the different wood taxa are provided in Table 4.5, with reference to accompanying plates, while quantified wood-charcoal results are found in Table 4.6.

The presence of apparent legume woods (family Fabaceae) requires further work. None of the published sources on Nepalese wood anatomy includes leguminous species, and reference material was not available to undertake such study. Based on Shrestha (1989), legume trees and shrubs mainly grow in the sub-alpine zone, in tropical and sub-tropical forests on much lower elevations, and do not, therefore, fit with the altitudinal zone of the site and the other high-elevation taxa identified in the charcoal record. Several species of leguminous shrubs are, however, reported up to and above 3000 m a.s.l. (see Polunin & Stainton 1984). Further comparative research on Nepalese wood anatomy is necessary before the presence of imported wood of low elevations, or one of the few high-elevation leguminous shrub species, can be confirmed.

Although the number of samples was limited and the frequency of seeds was low, a range of grain crops were identified which are likely to have contributed significantly to the diet of the inhabitants. All of these are species well-known in Nepalese agriculture today, but given the high altitude of the site and the tolerances of the crop species, it is unlikely that all of them would have been grown at or around Kohla. Oats and foxtail millet could not have been grown at this elevation, based on their modern distribution; both are cultivated in the sub-Himalayan tracts, with oats

reported below 1300 m a.s.l. and foxtail millet up to between 1800 and 2200 m a.s.l. (Manandhar 2002; Gaur 1999), although millets are also sometimes grown at higher elevations, where only summer cultivation is possible (Bishop 1990). For wheat, Kohla may have been close to, but still above, the altitudinal limits of cultivation, with reported upper limits of 2700–2800 and 3000 m a.s.l., respectively (Bishop 1990; Manandhar 2002; cf. Watt 1889–93). The two most tolerant of the crops recovered are buckwheat and barley, which are widely cited as cereals of the Himalayas, on the South Asian and Chinese sides, and barley, in particular, extends up to the limits of agriculture at *c.* 3500 m, while summer buckwheat may be grown at even higher elevations (Watt 1889–93; Anderson 1988, 181; Bishop 1990; Manandhar 2002).

In addition, a few species of gathered or cultivated fruits were recovered, including probable peach (see all wood charcoal of *Prunus* Type I), and dogwood (*Cornus* sp.). Of the latter, two species are reported as sources of edible fruits in Nepal up to elevations of 2600 m a.s.l. (Manandhar 2002). The peach is cultivated in Nepal (Manandhar 2002) and generally considered native to the mountains of central Asia or western China (Zohary & Hopf 2000). Evidence for the spread of peaches into South Asia begins in the Late Harappan period (from *c.* 1900 BC) and is focused upon Himalayan or foothill regions (Fuller & Madella 2001), including finds from the Neolithic of the Kashmir Valley at *c.* 1500–1600 m a.s.l. (Lone *et al.* 1993). While the bulk of peach cultivation is probably between 1000 and 2000 m a.s.l. (as reported by Manadhar 2002), peaches are known to be cultivated at high elevations above the 3000 m a.s.l. level in the Himalayas (Watt 1889–93; Bishop 1990, 239).

This evidence indicates that several species of grain crops must have been transported to the site from lower elevations, and, on the whole, it seems likely that agriculture was not a normal part of the economic activities carried out in the vicinity of Kohla. Generally, seed finds are extremely few, and of much lower densities than are normally encountered on agricultural sites in other regions of South Asia, where we expect that the regular processing of stored crops leads to the loss of grains and other plant parts that get incidentally charred (see Fuller 2002). While arguing from a lack of evidence is invariably weak, it is also notable that those species which could have been cultivated at this elevation (barley and buckwheat) are neither more frequent nor more ubiquitous than definitely transported species. This could suggest that all the grains are likely to have been transported to site from agricultural production, storage and exchange at lower elevations.

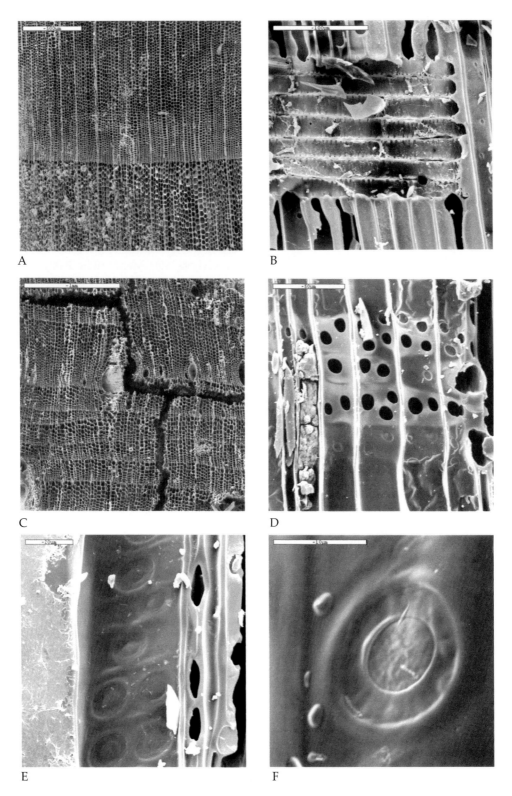

Figure 4.19. *Kohla 2000 - wood charcoal: A & B)* Abies spectabilis, *transverse section (A) and radial section showing characteristic nodular ray walls (B); C–F)* Tsuga dumosa *transverse section (C) and radial longitudinal section (D) showing crossfields with cypressoid pits; E is a radial longitudinal section with detail of axial tracheids showing single and double rows of bordered pits separated by crassulae and, F is a radial longitudinal section showing bands of thickening extending across the margo of a bordered pit.*

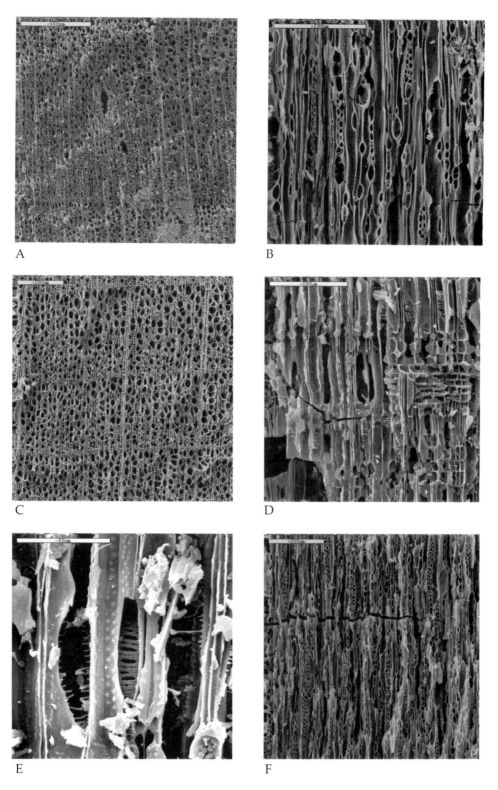

Figure 4.20. *Kohla 2000 - wood charcoal: A & B) Rhododendron type I, transverse section (A) and tangential longitudinal section (B) showing uni-, bi- and triseriate rays; C–F) Rhododendron type II, transverse section showing dense, solitary, angular pores (C) and radial longitudinal section showing rays and scalariform perforation plates (D; E is detail of the same); F is a tangential longitudinal section showing uni- to 4/5-seriated rays.*

149

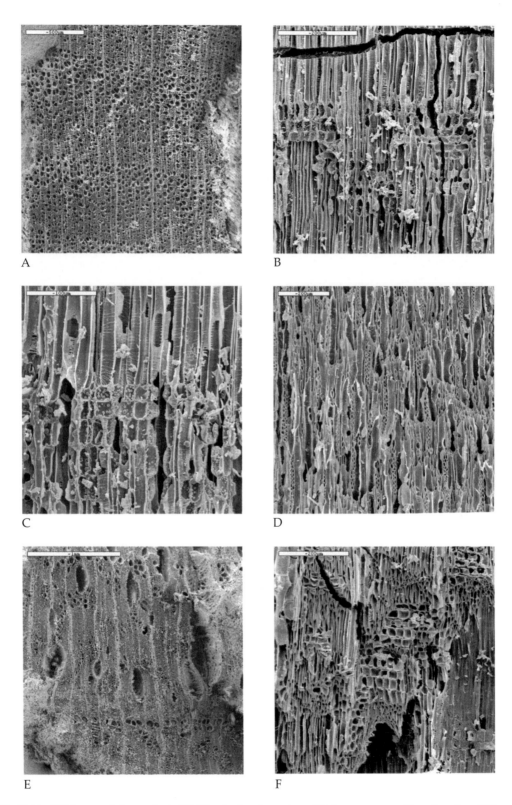

Figure 4.21. *Kohla 2000 - wood charcoal: A–D) Rhododendron type III, transverse section showing diffuse to semi-ring porous arrangement (A), radial longitudinal section showing rays and perforation plates (B), detail of radial longitudinal section showing distinct spiral thickenings (C) and tangential longitudinal section (D) showing uni-, bi- and triseriate rays; E & F) Fabaceae type II.*

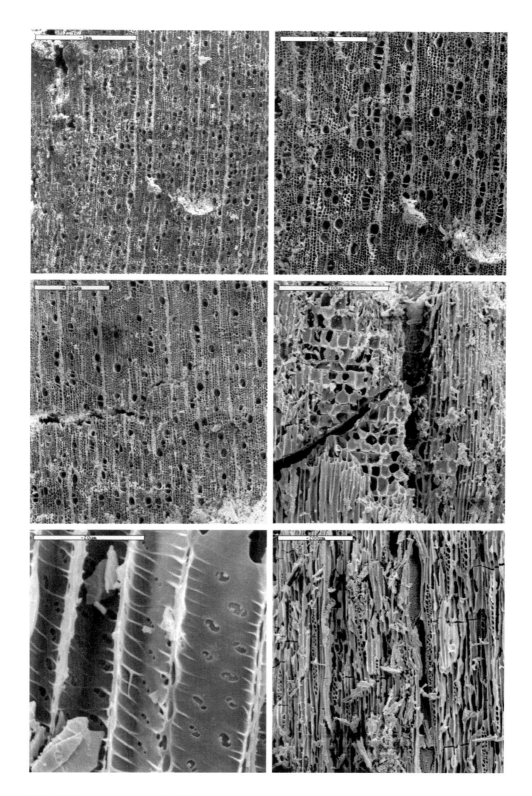

Figure 4.22. *Kohla 2000 - wood charcoal: Fabaceae type I.*

Table 4.5. *Wood taxa: anatomical descriptions.*

Taxa	Description
Gymnosperms	
Pinaceae	
Abies spectabilis (fir)	Earlywood–latewood transition gradual/abrupt. Resin canals absent. Average ray height 12–25 cells. Ray tracheids absent. Tangential ray walls nodular. Crossfield pits taxodioid, 1–3 per crossfield, piceoid in latewood (Fig. 4.19:A & B).
Tsuga dumosa (hemlock)	Earlywood–latewood transition gradual (in the examined specimens latewood width varies between 2/3 and 5 tracheids). Resin canals present. Axial tracheid walls with bordered pits, which are arranged in uniseriate or biseriate rows, occasionally separated by slight elevations (crassulae). Bordered pits usually with bands of thickenings extending across the margo. Average ray height 1–6 cells. Ray tracheids commonly present, with smooth walls. Crossfield pits cypressoid with wide elliptical apertures, 2–4 per crossfield, smaller in latewood (Fig. 4.19:C–F).
Taxaceae	
Taxus baccata (yew)	Earlywood–latewood transition gradual (growth rings indistinct). Resin canals absent. Average ray height 5–12 cells. Ray tracheids absent. Very distinct spiral thickenings in all the tracheids. Crossfield pits cypressoid or taxodioid (mostly cypressoid), 1–4 pits per crossfield.
Dicotelydons	
Aceraceae	
Acer sp.	Wood diffuse-porous. Pores relatively large, widely spaced, solitary and in radial multiples of 2–6 pores, rarely in clusters. Perforation plates simple. Spiral thickenings in all vessels. Rays slightly distended on ring boundary, of two distinct sizes: 1(2) and 3–4(5)seriate (the latter are more common), homogeneous, very rarely with square marginal cells. Vessel-ray pits simple and slightly enlarged. Libriform fibres present.
Araliaceae	
Brassaiopsis type	Wood ring to semi-ring porous. Pores sparse, solitary or in irregular clusters (forming a single row of pores at the beginning of the growth ring), occasionally in oblique to tangential arrangement. Perforation plates mostly scalariform (10 bars on average). Rays heterogeneous, uni- and multiseriate, the latter very broad, composed of procumbent cells with occasional sheath cells. Uniseriate rays consist of square to upright cells. Inter-vessel pits of two types: scalariform and opposite to alternate with elliptic to slit-like apertures. Fibre tracheids with bordered pits present. **Note**: Based on the published anatomical descriptions (Suzuki *et al.* 1999) the charcoal specimen examined resembles most closely *Brassaiopsis aculeata* and *B. alpina* (deciduous small trees found in the temperate and upper temperate zones of Nepal respectively). Most of the remaining species of this family (*Acanthopanax cissifolius*, *Brassaiopsis hainla*, *Hedera nepalensis*) are reported as having exclusively simple perforation plates. Another species of the genus *Brassaiopsis* (*B. mitis*) bears little similarity to the examined specimen concerning pore arrangement in the transverse section (pores in radial multiples) and lacking also the characteristic pattern of opposite/scalariform inter-vessel pits. The latter is also the case with *Pentapanax* spp. (also having simple perforation plates) and *Gamblea ciliata* (Suzuki *et al.* 1999).
Betulaceae	
Betula sp.	Wood diffuse-porous. Growth ring boundaries distinct. Pores relatively large, solitary and in radial multiples of 2–4, rarely in clusters. Rays slightly distended along growth-ring boundaries. Perforation plates scalariform (10–15 cells). Rays homogeneous to heterogeneous with one row of square marginal cells, bi- to 4-seriate. Ray vessel pits numerous, minute. Libriform fibres present.
Ericaceae	
Rhododendron sp.	Wood diffuse-porous. Pores solitary, small, numerous. Growth-ring boundaries distinct. Perforation plates scalariform (7/8–20/25 fine bars set at very small intervals). Rays heterogeneous, uniseriate and bi- to triseriate (the latter with uniseriate tails). Uniseriate rays are composed entirely of upright and square cells. Multiseriate rays consist of a central part of strongly procumbent cells and numerous rows of upright and square marginal cells. Spiral thickenings generally absent (occasionally present at vessel tail ends). Inter-vessel pits simple, circular to oval, mostly opposite. All transitions from perforation plates to inter-vessel pits present. Fibre tracheids with bordered pits present (Figs. 4.20:A–F & 4.21: A–D). **Note**: Three different morphotypes have been observed. Morphotype I (Fig. 4.20:A & B) was the most common and is described above. Morphotype II (Fig. 4.20:C–F) was very rare; its main characteristics different from above were the high density of seemingly more angular pores and the presence of 4–5 cell-wide multiseriate rays. Morphotype III (Fig. 4.21:A–D) was again very rare; diffuse to semi-ring porous, with distinct spiral thickenings on vessel elements and fibre tracheids alike. These features were not considered as sufficient for attempting to separate different species of *Rhododendron*. The main reason was that morphotypes II and III were present in very small numbers, hence not allowing a more secure evaluation of variation between different specimens. Features such as the presence of spiral thickenings and the arrangement of pores in transverse section are not necessarily related to species but may reflect growing habit. According to observations performed on modern material pore size, occurrence of spiral thickenings and the frequency of multiseriate rays are very variable: trees tend to present thickenings on both vessels and fibre tracheids, whereas shrubs tend to have narrower vessels with indistinct or missing thickenings (or restricted to tail ends: Suzuki & Ohba 1988).

Table 4.5. *(cont.)*

Taxa	Description
Fabaceae	Types I & II: identifications require further work.
Fagaceae	
Castanopsis type	Wood ring- to semi ring-porous. Pores relatively large, sparse, solitary, in radial to dendritic arrangement. Growth-ring boundaries distinct to indistinct. Perforation plates simple. Rays homogeneous, uni- to biseriate, consisting mostly of procumbent cells with square cells occasionally present at ray margins. Fibre tracheids present. Ray-vessel pits of various sizes, often kidney-shaped (Figs. 4.21:E/F & 4.22). **Note**: The other genera belonging to this family and native to the region are *Lithocarpus* and *Quercus* (evergreen oak). Their main difference from *Castanopsis* is the presence of compound and/or multiseriate rays. It did not become possible to locate this character in the examined specimens; however, the limited number of fragments present from this type and their small size do not allow the definite identification of *Castanopsis*.
Rosaceae (Maloideae)	
Indet. genus	Wood diffuse-porous. Pores medium-sized, dense, solitary. Growth-ring boundaries distinct. Perforation plates simple. Rays homogeneous to slightly heterogeneous with one row of square marginal cells, uni- to bi-seriate (mostly biseriate). Spiral thickenings generally absent (very faint spiral thickenings occasionally present in vessel tails and tracheids). Fibre tracheids present. Vessel-ray pits simple, rounded, slightly enlarged. **Note**: Due to the close anatomical similarities displayed between individual genera of Maloideae, it is not possible to separate them through observations on ancient material. Taxa indigenous in Nepal and abounding in the temperate zone include *Cotoneaster*, *Pyracantha*, *Pyrus* and *Sorbus* (Suzuki *et al.* 1991).
Rosaceae (Prunoideae)	
Prunus type I	Wood ring-porous. The beginning of the annual growth ring is marked by 1–2 rows of large earlywood pores (solitary or in clusters). Growth-ring boundaries distinct. Earlywood–latewood transition abrupt. Pores in latewood evenly distributed, sparse, solitary or more commonly in radial multiples of 2–3. Perforation plates simple. Very distinct spiral thickenings on vessel elements and vascular tracheids. Rays heterogeneous, uni- and multiseriate (5–10 cells wide on average; >10 cells also occur). Uniseriate rays consist of square and upright cells. Multiseriate rays comprise procumbent, square and upright cells. Fibre tracheids with bordered pits present. **Note**: The examined specimens closely resemble *Prunus persica* (deciduous tree cultivated or often wild in dry areas of Nepal: cf. Suzuki *et al.* 1991).
Prunus type II	Wood diffuse- to semi ring-porous. Pores relatively large, dense, arranged in short radial multiples of 2–3, occasionally in clusters too. Growth-ring boundaries distinct. Earlywood–latewood transition gradual. Perforation plates simple. Very distinct spiral thickenings on vessel elements and vascular tracheids. Rays heterogeneous, uni- and bi- to triseriate. Multiseriate rays consist of a central part of weakly procumbent cells and few marginal rows of square cells. Uniseriate rays are composed of square and upright cells. Fibre tracheids with bordered pits present. **Note**: No matching anatomical description was found in the literature in what concerns the width of the multiseriate rays and the arrangement of pores (semi ring-porous). It is possible that the examined specimens represent immature wood or they simply reflect differences in growing habit and environmental conditions from the material reported in the literature.

The seasonality of cultivation represented by these crops also shows variation. Wheat, barley and oats are winter crops sown between late September and mid-November, often rotated with summer/monsoon crops such as rice or millet, or fields are left fallow (Bishop 1990; cf. Watt 1889–93; Fuller 2002). Buckwheat grown in high-elevation regions is sown after the snows melt in May or early June and harvested after its short (*c.* three months long) growing season at the end of summer (Bishop 1990). Fruits of peach would normally have been available during summer, while *Cornus* spp. are reported to set fruits starting in November and into the winter. This could suggest occupation on the site to, at least, the beginning of winter.

Given the very limited number of samples examined from the site, and the lack of spatial and temporal depth, no comments can be made on issues such as vegetation change and (by inference) past climate conditions, based on the charcoal assemblage. Similarly, the sample population is not adequate for inferring differences in sample composition, introduced by context-related variation.

Based on the presence of taxa in the charcoal samples and the modern zonation of forest and woodland vegetation (described in detail by Shrestha 1989), it is possible to infer that the surroundings of Kohla had a tree- and shrub-cover characterized by mixed deciduous *Rhododendron* (the Nepali name for which is 'laligurans') forest and scrub. *Rhododendron* may be found at a variety of altitudes throughout Nepal (from *c.* 1000 m to 4500 m a.s.l.) and in association with almost all of the remaining taxa identified in the charcoal assemblages (including all temperate broadleaves

Table 4.6. *Wood charcoal quantified results*

	F.23 [065]	Str. 27 F.28 [094]	Str. 27 [005]	Str. 27 [003]C	Trench VI [080]
Abies spectabilis	1	1	1	3	
Tsuga dumosa					1
Taxus baccata	4				
Acer sp./spp.	6	11		5	8
Betula sp./spp.	10	2		1	
Brassaiopsis type				1	
Castanopsis type			1		
Rhododendron type I	40	46	37	40	54
Rhododendron type II	2	2	1	1	
Rhododendron type III	3	1	6	4	
Prunus type I	12				2
Prunus type II		1	7	1	3
Rosaceae-Maloideae	1	21	25	36	1
Rosaceae indet.	3		2	1	
Fabaceae type I	2		2		
Fabaceae type II		1			
Monocot. indet.	2	2			
Indet. Gymnosperms	2	4	6	3	8
Indet. dicot.	12	8	12	4	23
Total indet.	14	12	18	7	31
Total	100	100	100	100	100

and high-altitude conifers). Shrestha (1989) reports on the excellent burning qualities of *Rhododendron* as a fuel species (collected either by the lopping of branches or, at present illegally, the cutting of trees proper) and this may go some way to explaining the predominance of *Rhododendron* in the charcoal samples as a preferred fuel.

It is more difficult to evaluate the very low frequencies of conifers. Although sample size is too small to extrapolate a general pattern, these low frequencies may signify their low attraction as fuel species (particularly very resinous taxa such as *Tsuga* and *Pinus* — the latter completely absent from the examined assemblages — that can produce too many dangerous sparks) or, alternatively, their preservation as building materials. Shrestha (1989) mentions the local preference for *Tsuga dumosa* ('Tingray sallow') and *Abies spectabilis* ('Talis patra' or 'Thigay sallow') as timbers, presently bearing the brunt of over-exploitation due to both local use and exports abroad.

Temperate mixed forest formations include all the broadleaved taxa found in the charcoal assemblages. Members of the Fagaceae family in particular (including *Castanopsis*, *Lithocarpus* and *Quercus*; all furnishing good-quality firewood) are present throughout this zone. Modern vegetation records for the first two indicate their presence in the Mahabharat region of central

Nepal, just below the fir zone, where they grow inside pine ('Khotay sallow' *Pinus roxburghii*) forests up to an altitude of 2800 m a.s.l. (Shrestha 1989).

From the potentially cultivated species, it is interesting to note the presence of *Prunus* cf. *persica* (*Prunus* Type I), since it is matched in the fruit/seed record by peach endocarp fragments.

In conclusion, the preservation of charred plant remains was remarkable. This is evident in the retrieval of sizeable >4 mm fractions and the more than satisfactory preservation of the anatomical structure of individual wood fragments, as well as the remarkable flower and bract preservation in the seed assemblage. It is encouraging in terms of the potential of future studies. While the present assemblage was small, it represents the first evidence of this kind from this or adjacent regions at such an elevation.

This data set provides information of likely plant food that contributed a major part of the diet of Kohla's inhabitants, as well as wood resources that were utilized as fuel. The evidence for imported food grains contrasts with that of largely or entirely local wood fuel resources. While some of the food grains found could have been grown at this elevation, their scarcity suggests little or no agricultural production in the immediate vicinity of the site. As noted by Bishop in his study of subsistence in western Nepal (1990, 297), villages at this elevation that are agricultural normally produce a grain deficit and must rely on trade with lower elevations to fill it. Important trade products that are likely to have passed through or from Kohla, as part of this process, include timber, which was clearly available around Kohla, northwards and up to the treeless plains of Tibet, and Tibetan salt that has traditionally moved downward into Nepal, which lacks natural salt sources (Bishop 1990, 267, 297). Grains grown at lower elevations could have moved to higher zones, including Kohla, as part of the salt trade.

Dating

Based on the scale of subsequent tree-growth upon the ruins, it was thought that Kohla was generally of a medieval date and could be as much as *c.* 1000 years old. Having said this, by whatever affinities there are between its ceramics and those dated elsewhere in the country, a date range of anywhere between AD 500–1500 was possible. In order to bracket the sequence, two radiocarbon dates were initially submitted for analysis. The first was from the burnt, 'pre-stone' building phase in Trench VI; the second from charcoal dumped adjacent to the threshold of Structure 27 itself:

Interview: A hunter's perspective

Particpants:
Christopher Evans (CE)
Damarsing Tamu (DS)
Yarjung Tamu (YT)
Judith Pettigrew (video recording)
[translation, Tamu Kyui]

CE: It is the 13th of May [1994] at Kohla and we are here with Damarsing, extraordinary guide and former hunter [hunting now being banned in ACAP territory] to ask him a few questions about the landscape we are in. So, Yarjung, can you ask DS if he thinks that this would be a good place to live?

DS: [*via.* YT's interpretation] It is good place to stay for people, and difficult for growing food here; only six months is very nice, then afterwards covered by snow.

YT: So, that is the problem.

CE: So, there is snow here in the winter, all through?

YT: Yes, completely.

CE: What about in terms of food? Is there a lot to eat, animals, plants?

DS: I don't know what the ancestors ate. At the moment, we don't see any food growing here.

YT: Maybe barley, wheat?

DS: Maybe, but I can't say. Our ancestors lived here before, so maybe.

YT: Here, mostly millet, rice can't grow here. Only wheat, barley and mostly 'jungley' things, vegetables and that kind of things, that we have to eat now, which we know. Before, what our ancestors ate, we don't know.

CE: DS, if you could hunt here, could you live here off the land? Would there be enough game? Are there enough wild animals, enough deer, enough bear?

DS: Yes, there are plenty.

CE: When we go high up on the ridge and get above Kohla, are the type of animals you get there and the type of animals you get here any different? Is it all one zone going down to the river?

DS: Up to the hills?

YT: Yes.

DS: *Tui* deer, red deer?

YT: Yes.

DS: *Yeye* deer, *goral tosara*, it lives on the rocks, and another one is *kasturi*, musk deer. We have altogether four types of deer.

YT: Including musk deer, so that this is quite a rich place for animals.

CE: Would you get bears right the way through this area, would bears go down to the river?

YT: Yes.

CE: Does DS think they would have hunted at Kohla? Does he think that the people who lived in the village, would they have hunted bear?

DS: Yes, *they eat by hunting* [emphasis added].

YT: Yes, before, for our ancestors, it was mostly hunting.

CE: Mostly hunting?

YT: Yes, and also they didn't have guns at that time, they were using arrows and ...

CE: And maybe traps?

YT: Yes, traps and arrow, the traps are still used.

CE: Yes, like the one in the woods here.

YT: Yes [laughs].

DS: Before, there were no guns so they used bows and arrows.

YT: Yes, yes, they used a poison called *nhari*.

DS: If they went hunting with bows and poison arrows and spells [i.e. magic], and they didn't use them, then the poison, then the power of the poison will be lessened.

YT: Very strong poison they used in arrows.

CE: Does DS think they could have had horses here, do you think this is the kind of landscape you could have used horses?

DS: I don't know, maybe they came down riding horses. So that we saw the stable stone of the horse [before Structure 19], also we heard that the Ghale king's horse was tied there, so they must have been riding horses.

CE: In terms of other animals, is this land better for cows or sheep?

DS: Any animals can live here — buffaloes, sheep, cows. Buffaloes can't walk well on rocks, here it's quite flat so that it is good for buffaloes. In my opinion, this is a very nice place for sheep.

YT: For three kinds of animals, this is a very suitable place — buffalo, cow and sheep.

CE: Right, but could you keep them here all year or only for six months?

DS: Only during the summertime.

YT: Only when it is not covered by snow, at that time it is a good place, for six months it is not good [laughs].

DS: When winter begins, it is very frosty and very cold, from *Magh* (mid Jan. to mid Feb.). Sometimes there is snow in Tangting village. The bottom of the river will not be covered by snow. So it is not good to live here all the time.

CE: So what does DS think they would have done with the animals? Would they have taken them down to the valleys?

YT: Yes, before it snows they must go down.

CE: Right, we might, if we looked, find some very old shelters down by the lower river. Something contemporary with the villages?

YT: Yes.

CE: Good, well I think that's all for the moment.

YT: Yes.

CE: *Dhanyabad.*

A most knowledgeable and assured individual, in subsequent interviews Damarsing detailed the edible plants at Kohla, and also the specific uses and qualities of the 14 different kinds of bamboo growing in the area (distinguished by both their type and age: see Bhattarai et al. 2006 concerning traditional plant use in Manang).

---

1) [080] - 850±60 BP/cal. AD 1030–1280 (2 sigma/95% probability; Beta-149145)

2) [005]D - 750±50 BP/cal. AD 1200–1300 (2 sigma/95% probability; Beta-149144).

Subsequently, two further dates were achieved. The Beta-173144 assay is of charcoal from the F.23 capstone setting in Trench VIII, with the other being an AMS determination of one of the rice husks identified in the environmental samples (see above). The modern attribution of the latter clearly shows that the rice must have been intrusive and that the sample material was living within last 50 years. It must, therefore, have been introduced by recent 'visitors' to the site (e.g. pastoralists).

3) [065] - 1070±70 BP/cal. AD 790–1050 and cal. AD 1100–1140 (2 sigma/95% probability; Beta-173145)

4) [003]D - 111.0±0.5 pMC (108.7±0.5 pMC; i.e. post-0 BP; Beta-173144).

The three relevant dates would suggest that the settlement spans from *c.* cal. AD 1000–1300, though in this context two interrelated points warrant emphasis. Firstly, that coming from deposits much closer to the core of the main settlement, the [065]/F.23 date of 1070±70 BP was not from the primary occupation horizon within that trench. The earliest phases there must, therefore, date before that, and the wider range of their calibration spans could even suggest that the site's occupation started as early as the eighth century. Second, is to stress just how limited is the area of the overall site that was tested. Further work in other portions of sub-Site I and the settlement's other two sectors might well extend the range of this dating. Certainly, its various parts are unlikely to have been founded (and possibly not abandoned) at the same time; in other words, locally it might date earlier and, elsewhere, have continued later.

Discussion — layout and sequence

The recovery of the evidence of an early phase of timber buildings presents an intriguing dimension to the site's sequence. Certainly, one would now wish to know whether similar 'light' structures also preceded the stone buildings in the settlement's eastern and western sectors. In this regard it may, however, equally be the case that this early settlement was confined to, or at least focussed upon, the area of the central hilltop of sub-Site I and did not extend to its margins.

The evidence suggests that the character of the primary occupation differed from its 'developed' expression. Possibly relating to patterns of seasonal landscape usage (i.e. pastoral transhumance), 'prospection' (*viz.* the discovery of mineral ores) and/or trade, it suggests an immediacy of settlement. The use of timber would have been an obvious choice in a heavily wooded landscape, especially given the locale's clay sub-soils (i.e. stone would probably have had to be quarried from nearby slopes and outcrops).

In contrast to the robust stone buildings that came to dominate the site, a parallel could be drawn with the 'heavy' architecture of present-day Tamu-mai villages and the lighter-built structures that occur in the sites immediately above them (Khuh Chu and Nadar Pa). If so wishing, the timber structures both there and at Kohla could be interpreted as relating to 'arrivals' in the respective areas. While detailed comparison will not be possible without fuller exposure of the first-phase buildings at Kohla, and excavation of the lower sites, there do seem to be differences of kind. The Kohla remains suggest a 'heavier', more expedient timber-building (perhaps engendered by environmental/economic opportunism), whereas the house-plans at the village-environs sites rather suggest poverty. These observations may be biased by materials (hewn timber *vs* bamboo frame) and the immediate setting of the lower sites, as their settlements occur in

Pastoralist shelters and activity

Buchanan-Hamilton, writing of the Gurung/Tamu-mai in 1819, noted that they practised a predominantly pastoralist economy (see below), and both Macfarlane and Messerschmidt have commented upon the decline of their pastoral sector (respectively 1976 and 1976a). Certainly, the sheer frequency of pastoralist encampments in the uplands would bear this out, but, without very detailed survey, it is impossible to establish any statistical grasp on this. However, disused pastoralist sites seem to far out number active encampments, and they are found in almost all open clearings (and also in level forested locales; see Evans & Hodder 2006a, concerning the 'archaeology of woodland pastoralism' and the scale of clearings). Any sense of dating is, again, difficult (pottery does not seem to occur on non-ruin-related encampment sites). Nevertheless, by the degree of overgrowth upon them, many of the abandoned camps must, at least, be one or two centuries old. (Of the *phrohon* at Nadr Pa, the Ward President had no knowledge of the encampment — despite the obvious occur-

rence of 'shelter-type' settings — suggesting that they date before living memory; see Chapter 3 above.) Of course, this picture of more pastoral-based Tamu-mai communities would contrast with the key role of rice, which very much features within their rituals (effigy models, etc.), and this suggests a considerable 'lower-land' adoption, as it cannot be cultivated above the height of present-day villages.

In the main, two general types of pastoralist shelters (*phrohon*) can be identified within the area: small and generally 'lightly' built structures for sheep and goats; and much larger and more robust constructions for water buffaloes (though sheep/goats will also accompany the latter herds). Common to both are their timber frames, bamboo lathe-rafters and woven roof mats. The bamboo elements are easily removed and have been observed stored in caches — presumably at the end of the upland pasture season — both in the hollow trunks of lightning-struck trees and beneath the overhang of large boulders (Fig. 4.23:C). Although the smaller shepherd-type structures include areas of stone paving and slab-built hearths, stone is more extensively employed in the buffalo-type shelters. Not

Figure 4.23. *Pastoralist shelters at Kohla: A) the view looking south across the knoll of sub-Site I from the 'Saucer' Cist; B) detail of* phrohon *shelter; C) cache of pastoralist gear (roof lathes, bamboo rope, etc.) observed beneath a great boulder in valley below Kohla.*

only will this involve paving, but also surrounding walls on two to four sides. Covering upwards of 70 sq.m and more, the walls stand as much as 0.50–0.75 m high, and they often have a single, gabled end (recorded 1.20–1.85 m high: Figs. 4.23:A/B & 4.24). No evidence of the working of stone was observed (as opposed to selective collection) and, generally, the quality of the masonry does not compare to the 'ancient' upland building ruins. This, the fact that they are only 'half' masonry-built (the timber superstructure being carried above this level), and that relatively little rubble is associated with even abandoned shelters, means that they can usually be distinguished from buildings *per se*. However, this is not necessarily true on more low-lying campsites, and the slighter building traces on sites in the vicinity of inhabited villages can be difficult to distinguish from 'shelter' constructions.

Pastoralist camping has certainly impacted on the upland ruins and, as is clearly evident along the northern margin of the main Kohla settlement, their shelters have involved the robbing of building stone. (Charcoal-burning equally impacts on the sites immediately above inhabited villages, and the resultant pits have been seen cutting into ruins.)

Variations of *phrohon* construction observed include circular, corral-like bush surrounds at Khuindo and, perhaps more relevant, the incorporation of large stone slabs at Chikre. At the latter locale, there were a number of instances where slabs had been set vertically against the interior drystone wall-faces. However, in one instance large slabs alone appear to have been employed (the larger area of the shelter itself being defined by the extent of its floor paving: Fig. 4.24). Seemingly very old, it is conceivable that their associated walls had themselves been robbed. This, though, is unlikely, as it is not a matter of slabs being leant against the walls, but of having their bases buried (i.e. 'footed') to stand independently. What is crucial in this is the sense of a 'large stone' building technique, as the central gable-end slab of that structure almost approaches the scale of the central King's House standing stone at Kohla.

This building technique may relate to the occurrence of obviously recent standing stones on upland sites, perhaps demarcating and ritualizing rights to encampment. One had been erected (and is still venerated by offerings) on a pastoralist camp along the trail to Karapu, located approximately a half-day's march above Yangjakot. From this, one can only think that the standing stones at Khuindo also probably relate to seasonal pastoralist usage. (When camping at Tapron, asking about the significance of these stones, the local men were dismissive; they duly selected and erected a comparable stele within less than ten minutes.) Although much larger than any of these, this makes the village-context and the clearly 'ancient' attribution of the main Kohla upright all the more remarkable (see Bellezza 2002 concerning pre-Buddhist stele settings in Tibet; cf. Aldenderfer & Yinong 2004, 42–6).

Long interested in the ethnography and archaeology of pastoral transhumance (e.g. Evans 1983), we questioned our Tamu-mai colleagues — all of whom derived from either the arable-sector of nearby villages or resided in Pokhara itself — as to what this evidence of pastoralist activity in the landscape relates and whether the herders/shepherds might have a 'special' knowledge of the ruins. Their responses proved generally dismissive of the pastoralist sector and certainly did not privilege their potential familiarity with the sites in any manner. This becomes relevant given that the perceived northern roots/origins of the Tamu-mai clearly implies a greater emphasis on earlier (pre-)historical stock-raising and mobility. One interpretation of the suffix 'mai' in *Tamu-mai* is 'People of the Horse'. Horses are the common mode of transportation in Manang and Mustang, and some of the upland sites have distinct horse-related attributions — the 'tethering stone' for the King's horses at Kohla and the 'Racing Track' in a valley above the site. All this is despite the fact that the ranges above Tamu-mai villages today are considered far too steep to employ horses as pack animals (and the incredible capacity for human porterage is a key element of their identity and economy).

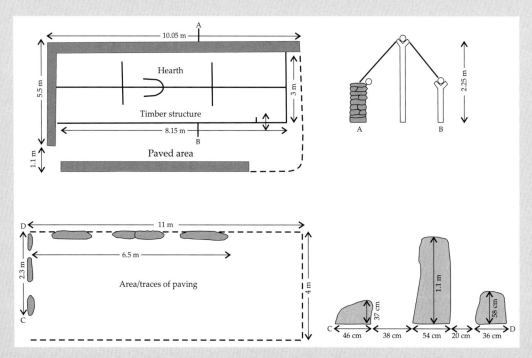

Figure 4.24. Phrohon *sketch plans, Chikre Toh (note upright 'stone slab-type' below: see Fig. 4.27:B).*

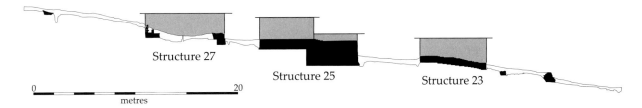

Figure 4.25. *Flat-roofed, stepped storey reconstruction of Kohla's buildings.*

the shadow of 'dominant' constructions — the stone 'palace' at Nadar Pa and the hillfort at Khuh Cho. Nevertheless, except for seeing a basic succession to timber-to-stone building techniques, the dynamics and character of the timber phases in these two landscape zones may well have been quite different.

Attributed to the main phase of the site's occupation, Structure 27 provides clear evidence of the terracing of the settlement and its buildings; it being cut back into the hill-side (Fig. 4.25). As a result, its foundations step up along their length, in compensation for the degree/axis of lateral truncation. Its northern back-wall was the most deeply downcut and, buckling due to down-slope pressures, the 'bench' was added along its length to provide buttress-support.

The evidence relating to Structure 25 is particularly informative of the arrangement of Kohla's buildings; 6.7 × 9.7 m in size, the length of this rectangular two-cell building runs down the hill slope. As exposed in Trench II, set on a 0.15 m-deep footing, its northern wall survives only 0.80 m high. However, on its southern downslope side, the wall is *c.* 2 m high (carried on a *c.* 0.3 m footing). Given that their top courses survive to approximately the same height, this indicates that, unless the floor level sloped markedly, the foundations and interior surfaces must step down along its length. It is logical to infer that this must occur at the point of its internal division, and the evidence suggests that the roof and storey level would have divided at this point. In other words, it was probably a split-level building, consisting of two interrelated, single-storey units. Although such arrangements are obviously possible in gabled structures, in a context of Himalayan vernacular architecture, it could even suggest a flat-roof construction; the roof of the lower unit being utilized as a raised 'yard' in front of, and accessed by, the higher back portion (Fig. 4.25).

Otherwise, no direct or unequivocal evidence of the buildings' roofing was forthcoming; the absence of stone slates need not necessarily imply a non-gabled construction, as timber shingles could have been employed. However, the quantity of small, and evidently much reduced, daub-like clay fragments recovered from the excavation of Structure 27 could attest to the collapse of a flat, packed-clay roof. Such a

roof design would obviously make little sense in the moist southern slopes of the Himalayas. Yet its design might have been *introduced* and, effectively, be an 'experiment' in the light of local environmental conditions.

Although also with an interior wall, the next building downslope, Structure 23, is of square-plan and more akin to Structure 27. In both of its exposures — Trench VII to the north and VIII to the south — its walls were only *c.* 0.6/0.65 m high. Situated at a point where the slope is only slight, it has not been significantly terraced into the hill; its internal, north–south wall need not relate to any kind of split-level arrangement, but only an interior *sub*-division.

Trenches IX and X clearly show that the settlement had well-maintained public space: the large paved plaza (with its standing stone) separating buildings along the central site's southern edge from those on the northern hill. Equally, the excavations demonstrated (particularly Trenches V & VI) that its apparent 'streets' or, better, 'alleys', were not formally laid-out but rather took the form of reduced hollow-way paths alongside the buildings.

The ascription of Structure 5 in Kohla West as being the 'palace' of the Ghale Kings may well be valid. Certainly, it is a very large and high building, and it undoubtedly includes the widest array of architectural details. (In comparison, the similar appellation of Structure 19 in the central settlement seems more 'folkloric' and perhaps less justified. Its central situation, size and proximity to the standing stone providing the sole basis of its entitlement.) In this context, the situation of Structure 5 — and also the potentially associated, two-storey Structure 6 'tower' beside it — immediately overlooking, and probably commanding the millhouses on the stream, evokes the story of the *pye* of the wealth of Lemko (the Ghale Raja's assistant) and the destruction of the watermills (Line 232; Chapter 2).

As there can be no disputing Kohla's extraordinary tri-partite layout, the issue here becomes how its sectoring is to be accounted for. In the *pye* translated in Chapter 2, it is clearly indicated that Kohla was founded by three clans, the Pamma, Kohlma and Lema (Line 146). Equally, while in his commentary Yarjung

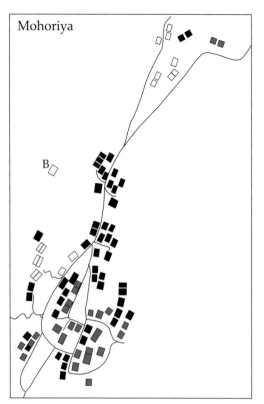
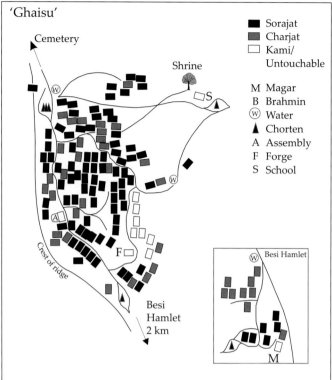

Figure 4.26. *'Present-day' Gurung/Tamu-mai village plans showing clan affiliation of households (after Pignède 1993, fig. 7 and Messerschmidt, 1976a, map 2; note that 'Ghaisu' is the real-life village of Sikrung/Siurung/Sere Nasa; Messerschmidt pers. comm.).*

stress that *Promo Haju*, opposite Kohla (though never visited by us), was also a 'mixed-clan settlement', by implication the other villages are thought to be single-clan villages. Indeed, Yarjung states that Chikre was solely inhabited by members of the Kromchain clan. Therefore, given this, in all likelihood Kohla's sectoring is best attributed to clan distinctions.

Based on information from his Lamjung companions, Messerschmidt's attribution of Kohla East as being the village's blacksmith quarter is of interest given the recovery during the survey of slag from that portion and also the workshop-suggestive arrangement of Structure 53. Yet here it is crucial to recognize that in a Nepalese context (and given the emphasis of Messerschmidt's study of Tamu-mai social structure and clan interrelationships: 1976a), that this entitlement now carries with it caste connotations. At least superficially, the inclusion of what are 'high-standard' buildings within that sector (Structures 48 & 52–4) could be enlisted to dispute such an interpretation, and in fact it has the highest ratio of 100 sq.m+ large structures on the site. More telling in this context is the evidence from the excavations themselves. The unambiguous occurrence of metalworking traces from within the hill-top core of the central settlement would

argue against such arbitrary 'clean/unclean' activity (and persons) distinctions. Admittedly only occurring in primary-phase contexts, this nevertheless suggests a greater sense of spatial dynamic and that the site's layout does not enshrine some manner of a pristine village 'model'.

As illustrated in Figure 4.26, the distribution of clan groups, as shown in the plans published of the villages of Thak, Mohoriya and 'Ghaisu', would offer the closest basis for settlement sub-divisions. Yet, while they reveal a propensity for lineage-based clustering, these do not result in comparably discrete or removed village sectors as at Kohla. Only the blacksmiths/former Untouchable houses stand off together from the main settlements in a similar manner, but their numbers seem relatively too small to constitute a comparable 'quarter' (see Pignède 1993, 199 concerning the seven 'quarters' of Ghandrung, and Macfarlane 1976, 14–19, appendix 3 for contemporary/historical village growth and development). In fact, in conversation, both the Tamu-mai and local *Dalit* former Untouchables are clear that the latter were not present with the Tamu-mai at the time of Kohla and the 'old' settlements (i.e. its blacksmiths must themselves have been Tamu).

Looking further afield northwards, employing a rammed clay (*pisé*) architecture, the dense warren-like quality of present-day villages in Mustang would offer no parallel with Kohla's plan (see *Goin' north* below and Harrison 1996; see Pohle 1988 for extant village plans in Manang). Nor, for that matter, do survey plans that are available for the 'early'/abandoned settlements in that area. The most ready example would be that at Phudzeling, which includes the upstanding ruins of some 34 buildings. Located in the lower Muktinath valley east of Kagbeni, this was partially excavated in the course of the Nepal-German High Mountain Project and, in the main, dated from the thirteenth–seventeenth centuries AD, though traces of a much earlier, Iron Age, settlement were also recovered (Simons *et al.* 1994a, 54–5). While the plan of some of its square and rectangular buildings would seem broadly comparable to those at Kohla and our other highland sites, aside from this and the settlement's south-facing locale, it has no obvious affinities to Kohla; in fact, foremost among their differences would be the Mustang settlements' direct association with the cave systems above them (see also Simons *et al.* 1994b, 109–17 concerning the much smaller, tenth- to sixteenth-century Mebrak settlement and *Goin' north* below for early sites in Manang).

The 'old' economy

Given the paucity of animal bone recovered at Kohla and the limitations it imposes on any attempt at economic reconstruction, we must turn to the observations of early travellers to Nepal for insights into the 'old' upland economy of the Gurung/Tamu-mai. Buchanan-Hamilton wrote of them in the beginning of the nineteenth century:

> Near the Magars was settled a numerous tribe named Gurung, whose wealth chiefly consisted in sheep … [and who] in the course of their pastoral life … frequent the Alpine regions in summer, and return to the vallies in winter. The men also employ themselves in weaving blankets; but they are a tribe addicted to arms … There are … several tribes of Gurungs, such as Nisi, Bhuji, Ghali and Thagsi. The latter live nearest the snow; but all the Gurungs require a cold climate, and live much intermixed with the Bhotiyas on both sides of the snow-covered peaks of the Emodus [the Himalaya], and in the narrow vallies interposed, which, in the language of the country, are called Langna. The Gurungs cultivate with the hoe, and are diligent traders and miners. They convey their goods on sheep, of which they have numerous flocks (1819, 27).

Hodgson's portrayal of their livelihood some 50 years later was very similar:

> They dwell mostly in small villages wherein each *Cot* [*kothi*, dwelling] is quite separate & they are adeal abroad in their goths or sheep sheds. They cultivate the ground to a considerable extent growing chiefly Makai [maize] & Kudo [eleusine, or raggee millet], making Dhero [gruel] from both & that is their favourite food. They also eat Makai dressed rice-wise & also such of their sheep as die, but they do not habitually eat their sheep. They milk them & make ghee [clarified butter] of the milk & shear & make Pankhi & Kamals [robes and blankets] of the wool; & using them also for carriage over the snow bringing back rock salt of Tibet. They are traders across the snows, taking hence cotton & rice & wheat & Dalls [lentils] & merchants' wares also either on the sheep or on their own backs. They dwell high in the lekhs [highlands] & their [agri-]culture is only Khuria [*khoriya*, swidden] & Bari [dry field], chiefly the former. They are also great Shikarees [hunters] & serve much as soldiers, having been renowned for hardihood since Prithi Narain's time [eighteenth century]. (As quoted in Messerschmidt 1976a, 33–4; 'makai dressed-rice-wise' would not seem to refer to rice but rather a way of preparing maize, presumably the boiling of kernels off the husk, A. Macfarlane pers. comm.)

Hodgson, thereafter, goes on to note that the Gurung/Tamu-mai are 'less agricultural than Magars' and that 'their herds are often very large [of] 1 or 2000 sheep & their dwellings [are] on the mountain tops'.

In this capacity, it is also worth recalling Macfarlane's resumé of the *pye's* information, concerning the early Gurung/Tamu-mai way of life:

> The Gurung consisted of small bands of wandering shepherds and hoe cultivators who circled the Himalayan foothills, moving from site to site every few generations. The 'pie' [*pye*] give glimpses of this existence. They recount, often in great detail, the various villages and regions through which the tribesmen wandered. Hunting was clearly an important part of the existence. Large-scale hunts, in which hunting dogs and beaters were employed in pursuit of deer, and a full-scale uniform (including special jackets, knives, kilts and blood-carrying flasks) was worn. Other 'pie' describe herding (including a man going off to live by himself in the forest to herd animals) — usually of sheep, goats, chickens, and long-haired animals (variety of Yak?) called 'Yo' and 'Pri' in Gurung (Macfarlane 1976, 25, see also 26–30; see also Pohle 1993 concerning the 'vertical dimension' of settlement and economy in Manang).

Although we must be wary of backdating nineteenth-century observations by half a millennium and more, in relationship to the archaeological data, the picture these accounts convey seems consistent with our findings and the economic possibilities of the area's highland zone. Admittedly, there are no direct correlates for the emphasis on hunting and the Gurung/

Tamu-mai's putative 'addiction to arms' (aside from the site's knives and perhaps the surveyed forts). The frequency of obviously very old camp sites throughout the uplands would, nevertheless, attest to the much greater importance of pastoralism in the past. That a number of Kohla's single-unit structures may actually have been animal byres could also be enlisted in support. Equally, that Buchanan-Hamilton notes that some of the Gurung/Tamu-mai were miners, recalls the evidence of Kohla's metalworking. That both he and Hodgson stress their role as traders provides a degree of context for the site's imported goods and, perhaps more importantly, this underlines that large-scale village subsistence would probably not have been possible at such altitudes within a 'closed system', but that they required sustained lowland connections. Here it is noteworthy, in the light of the changes which have occurred in village subsistence since the Second World War (see Macfarlane 1976; 2002), that the practices of their dwindling pastoral sector — with its emphasis on animals, 'movement' and diverse resource-zone exploitation (and which seemed so alien to many of our local village-/town-based colleagues) — is actually far closer to the 'old' Tamu-mai economy.

In his notes, Hodgson has the Gurung/Tamu-mai growing maize and millet and, practising a non-irrigation dry-field and/or swidden agriculture, trading in rice, wheat and lentils. Buchanan-Hamilton lists their arable produce, which includes barley, Uya (oats), Maniya or *Eleusine corocana*, Kangum (*Setaria italica*) and Phapar (buckwheat). It is when trying to evaluate these observations against the site's archaeobotanical evidence that the lack of pollen data from Kohla becomes critical (such sampling was to feature in the second excavation season — in hindsight, a misjudged decision). Out of Asouti and Fuller's identification of buckwheat, barley, millet and oats among its plant assemblages, it may only have been the first two of these that were actually grown on the site itself. (Although the one rice husk submitted for dating proved to be modern, that need not imply that all rice within the assemblage need be intrusive. Indeed, in the investigations within Mustang, rice was found to be imported into the area — as were also bamboo, lentils and hemp — from Period 2/400 cal. BC–cal. AD 100; otherwise barley and buckwheat were the main staples through the site sequences, starting at *c.* 1000 cal. BC: Knorzer 2000.)

The importation of crops would be consistent with the fact that only slightly upwards of an area of 1 ha within Kohla's immediate environs seems appropriate for arable production (i.e. level enough for fields). This was obviously insufficient to provide all of the arable needs of the site's population and clearly foodstuffs must have been brought in. It is always possible that other arable plots lay at a distance, either in cleared woodland at the same altitude or lower down by the riverside (at *c.* two hours' walking distance). Yet it should be stressed that no direct evidence whatsoever was found of fields at this height and that, at Kohla, it is just a matter of possibility given the lie of the land north of its eastern sector (though see Macfarlane below). This sets in context Asouti and Fuller's observations that, by the general paucity of its crop remains and that the obviously higher-elevation species occur at the same low frequencies as the rest, all the grain produce may have been imported. While the diet of the site's inhabitants evidently also included fruits (peach and dogwood/*Cornus* spp.), it can only be presumed that they primarily relied on meat and milk-based food stuffs.

In reconstructing the site's economic basis, the evidence of its charcoal assemblages must also be considered. Dominated by deciduous wood species, this contrasts with the site's immediate present-day woodland cover, which is largely fir, particularly juniper. One must be wary of drawing inferences from this and bear in mind factors of immediate environmental variability; *Rhododendron* does, after all, grow above this height (up to *c.* 4500 m a.s.l.) and, indeed, was seen above Kohla itself. Equally, an emphasis on resinous, deciduous woods could also have been a matter of selection and relate to their firing qualities in relationship to industrial processes. These caveats aside, the representation of woodland species within the assemblage could foster speculation that, in early medieval times, the area's environment was somewhat milder than today.

Attribution and abandonment

As discussed above, the site's series of radiocarbon dates would seem quite reasonable given the expectations of both its material culture and the scale of the tree-cover upon its walls. Admittedly, if the sampling had been broadened to include other sectors (and other portions of the central sub-site), its bracketing would probably be extended. Nevertheless, the dates generally seem acceptable. As discussed by Gibson above, some of the site's pottery is directly comparable to both Period II (late fourth–seventh centuries AD) and III (eighth–fifteenth centuries) types from the Khyinga site in Muktinath Valley, Mustang (Hüttel & Paap 1998). Equally, the unusual capstone ritual setting in our Trench VIII might have parallels with the wide array of 'foundation' and 'sacrifice-type' deposits found in first-millennium AD horizons at Khyinga (Hüttel 1997; Hüttel & Paap 1998).

If seeking a causality for 'arrival' in the area, a northern source would be logical. From the ninth century, the Tibetan empire was beginning to fragment and there were incursions into the Mustang area. From this time there was also the official spread of Buddhism, which may have encouraged migration by those groups still adhering to earlier shamanic-type practices.

Beyond a vague general correspondence between the 'life-style' of the pre-modern Tamu-mai in the reports of earlier travellers and the archaeological findings, the only definite basis by which to attribute the site seems to lie in its naming — 'Kohla, *The Three Villages*'. Certainly, its extraordinary plan directly complements and 'fulfils' this entitlement. Otherwise, the Tamu-mai have no unambiguous markers of group identity that could possibly have archaeological/past correlates. (They do wear coral and turquoise beads, such as were found on the site, but then so do many Himalayan peoples.)

Yet one 'finding', or rather the lack thereof, that warrants notice is the absence of any evidence of Buddhism. Of course, the basis of negative evidence can never be absolute, but, in this context, the most likely expectant 'type-artefact' would be *Tsa-Tsa*. These are variously small clay-moulded plaques and miniature stupas (often incorporating or holding the ashes of the dead) bearing Buddhists inscriptions. They are common findings on medieval sites of Buddhist affiliation. In the recent excavations at Sinja (whose ridge-top ruins were investigated over a smaller trench-area than Kohla), three were recovered (Evans & Gibson 2003). One was similarly found in the eleventh- to fifteenth-century occupation horizons (next to a 'mani-stone') in the Nepal-German excavations at Khyinga (Hüttel 1994, figs. 61 & 62; 1997, 63, fig. 63). Given the absence of these statuettes, and the site's date (and in the light of Kohla's 'ritual architecture' of cists and the standing stone), it can be said with some certainty that its populace would not appear to have been Buddhist. (Excavating the pre-Buddhist settlement at Dindun in western Tibet, dated to 400–100 BC, Aldenderfer actually found a standing stone within a chamber of one its houses; two others were also found on the eastern western approaches to the village: 2003b and Aldenderfer & Yinong 2004, 43–5.)

Finally, Kohla's abandonment needs to be accounted for. Social factors could well have participated and it can easily be envisaged that tensions might have developed between its sub-groups giving rise to communal fracturing, and certain sectors of the settlement might well have been abandoned before others. Yet this would not explain the 'loss' of the site as a whole. Positive choice may have been a motivation. Possibly involving the recognition that subsistence was too harsh at these altitudes, its inhabitants may simply have been lured downwards by the attraction of better climatic conditions and soil fertility. The problem with this line of argument is what seems to be the decline in the standard of village (and 'public') life in the possibly subsequent lower level sites (e.g. lighter-build structures, less formal village layout, etc.). If this is a valid inference, then we are left with 'negative' or reactive causes, and here, two suggest themselves: political and environmental factors. As to the latter, one would usually be wary of promoting an overt environmental determinism. Yet, here, we have to consider the special circumstances of these sites and especially Kohla. They occupied what can only be considered extraordinary 'niche' conditions and, in this context, the onset of the 'Little Ice Age' from the mid fourteenth century (e.g. Grove 1988; Vetaas & Chaudhary 2004) may have tipped the balance against permanent occupation at such heights (see Sinha *et al.* 2007 concerning changes in the Indian Summer Monsoon during the fourteenth–fifteenth centuries). Even slightly colder climatic conditions could have resulted in substantially greater snowfall extending the length of its ground cover to the point that arable cultivation became unfeasible, or meaning that the regeneration and availability of pasture was retarded to such a point that large herds could not be kept year-round at these levels. (The faunal remains from the Khyinga site in Muktinath Valley attest to a distinctly woodland environment and wetter climatic conditions, prior to the end of the first millennium AD: Hüttel 1997, 59.)

The other negative factor — relevant from the fifteenth century — is the incursion of Hindu(-ized) 'Kings' into the area. Direct conflict need not have been the cause of the 'Kohla system's' demise, but simply the disruption of trade connections with lowland communities, perhaps resulting in the loss of imported cereal food stuffs.

Operating together, these factors could have led to the abandonment of this upland zone for permanent settlement. If so, it should be recognized that both would only really have been influential from the fourteenth century, 50–100 years after the latest radiocarbon date from Kohla. Yet, as already outlined, this may simply reflect the limitations of the site's dating sequence (by number and the restricted distribution of samples) and all or part of the settlement could well have continued for upwards of a century thereafter. Equally, given the state of research in the region generally, we must be wary of leaping towards convenient, 'over-easy' explanations. Archaeology works on an inherently comparative basis to establish its operational logic and, put simply, there has as yet been too little excavation undertaken in this portion of the Himalayas to establish any real sense of broad patterning. This must await the future, thus ethno-historical data will for some time, if for no other reason than necessity, be heavily drawn upon to provide a sense of immediate 'framing' context (and this, *de facto*, will privilege past/present continuities). Moreover, this situation, in what can only be considered a highly marginal environment (i.e. a 'periphery'), is further compounded by the paucity of fieldwork within the immediate 'core'. Hüttel, for example, writing of the results of the Khingar/Khyinga site from 1991, remarked that of its some 6000 sherds, only 5 per cent (300) had any reliable diagnostic value and, lacking a regional sequence, that the role of imports from either India, the Tarai or Kathmandu Valley was paramount (1993, 4; see also Hüttel & Paap 1998); in this case, these distant 'core' sequences have still themselves to firmly established.

Here, one other potential caveat also looms. Given the resources that were brought to bear in the course of the Nepal-German High Mountain Project — especially the scale of its dating programme — from a normative chronological perspective (i.e. Western), one can only be surprised how little sense of 'solid' typological patterning seems to have been achieved. Yes, broad trends were distinguished (e.g. the date of the abandonment of the cave systems, etc.), but generally there seems little sense of under-lying material culture typology. This suggests, from a European perspective, that either the 'picture' is too complicated for ready appreciation or, alterna-tively, that the development of material culture in Nepal may have occurred according to a different sense of 'rules', whose rhythms (and seemingly long continuities) seem, at least for the moment, difficult to fathom.

Resourcing and leaving Kohla — some thoughts
ALAN MACFARLANE

Concerning the question why the Gurungs/Tamu-mai moved down from Kohla, I have faced the same problem in another Tamu village, Thak, across the valley from Kohla. Two hundred years ago, the vil-lage was located about 600 feet higher up the ridge. Before that, there are stories that it was even higher in the forest. Why did the villagers move down to the present village? Likewise, in another Tamu-mai village, Mohoriya, studied by Bernard Pignède, on a revisit some thirty years after Pignède's fieldwork in the 1960s, we found that many of the villagers had moved down near to the river, some thousand or more feet down the mountain.

The villagers in Thak gave several reasons to explain why their ancestors had moved. They said that at the higher location, the crops were more frequently destroyed by hail and gave this as a reason why the open land at that altitude was not used for crops nowadays. They said that marauding wild animals, and particularly monkeys and bears, which ate the crops, were more of a problem higher up. They also related that, as the population grew, the water supply ran out. They also suggested that, as the population expanded, more of their livelihood came from crops on terraces, particularly rice, which meant that it was better to live at an equal distance between the forest and the lower fields, so that there would be less carry-ing of heavy sacks of grain. They equally noted a shift from grazing and swiddening in the forest to arable agriculture, so that the forest became less important as a source of livelihood. Swiddening required a very large area of virgin forest. The latter was depleted as the population grew and swidden practices were banned early in the twentieth century.

Any of the above reasons, or a combination of them and those suggested elsewhere in this volume, could be behind the downward migration. What is obvious is that it is a movement which has occurred over a number of centuries and in almost all Tamu-mai villages.

Equally, we may wonder how the some 150–300 people thought to have lived at Kohla managed to obtain their basic grains, when there only appear to be one or two hectares or so of flat land to grow crops on near the village. There are various possible solu-tions. It seems very likely that some grain was brought up to the village, being exchanged for the forest and pastoral products or for the salt which the Tamu-mai had helped to bring down from Tibet. So it could be that, in effect, they only really needed gardens around their houses. The heavy meat and milk diet, plus forest produce (Tamu-mai used to gather many wild fruits and vegetables), would just need some supplements of grains, which could be traded.

Another possibility is that flat land was not really needed to grow crops. Much of the older production of grains in Thak was carried out by swiddening on quite steep slopes. There is no problem growing buckwheat, maize, millet and other crops on a slope, as long as there is rotation of the cultivated areas so that the land is not exhausted and hence eroded by the monsoon rains. So, quite large areas around the village may have produced a variety of plantains and grains, without the need for flat land.

Finally, as suggested, the Tamu-mai are very used to growing their grain an hour or more away from where they live. So, any flattish land within three to

Figure 4.27. *Stone upright settings: A) stele set by stream-head at pastoralist camp-site above Yangjakot; B)* phrohon *gable-end setting at Chikre Toh (see Fig. 4.24); C & D) Khunido showing standing stone ('C') and stele atop the great boulder ('D': see Figs. 3.26 & 3.27).*

five miles could be used. This is a pattern that can still be seen in lower Tamu-mai villages and I have also observed it in China.

Some combination of these was clearly also used in the old village above Thak, from which people migrated a couple of hundred years ago. Like Kohla, there is little flat land up there, yet people clearly managed for a few generations.

Fieldwork with shamans
Reflecting the manner in which great 'monumental' settings can attract diverse ideas and usages (see e.g. Bradley 2000), Kohla's cist settings could serve as a case study in the vagaries of interpretation (Figs. 3.37 & 3.38). If so wishing, an elaborate ritual framework could be identified as underlying the village's plan: the three cists marking a triangle, whose central axis

is delineated by the alignment of the 'King's' standing stone and the great 'saucer'. Pending excavation of any of the cists, all this seems far too fanciful. It is as if a kind of ritual interpretation, currently in vogue in British prehistory, is being too readily projected onto a site in a very different cultural context. Equally, as regards the consternation that the 'saucer's' interpretation caused during the 1994 shamans' visit (see *Travelling up*), the fact that the corpse of a cow then lay at its mouth evoked a sense of ritual slaughter, even though it probably had simply died huddled beneath the capstone's overhang. The pragmatic qualities of this setting as a shelter were amply demonstrated during the 2000 season. Feeling the night-time cold, a group of our men took to sleeping beneath its cover, making a fire at the mouth, whose heat reflected off the overhang. They even dug a slight drip-gully around the line of the capstone to catch run-off water. Altogether, an odd episode in the afterlife of this monument, this showed to what diverse purposes its cover could be put.

During discussions that followed the 1994 interpretative 'showdown', one shaman thought that the 'saucer's' shrine might mark where the king sat to address the people; another related the three cists to the various types of Tamu-mai shamans (Pachyu, Kyabri and 'Lama'), indicating that all three were then present in the village. Other discussions revolved around the idea that the cists were like 'Bhaya', places where bad and/or ill spirits (e.g. those killed in accidents or through suicide) are temporarily housed before being sent off in the *pye* ceremony. Yet it was noted that such box-like settings are destroyed in the course of the *pye* ritual. Alternatively, it was believed by some that these were places of 'long' rituals, probably relating to area gods. (Yarjung had apparently thought it was a *ta tay*, as described in the *pye* and which also occur in villages today. That is, the spot from where the village caller shouts out messages concerning what will happen in the village during the following day.) Finally, one other possible interpretation of the 'saucer' warrants mention — that the stone's usage pre-dates the village's occupation. This was raised by our HMG Nepal colleague, Uddhav Acharya. Much more familiar with the prehistory of the Indian sub-continent, he thought that it could well be a Neolithic megalith.

Whatever its origins, the sense of the 'presence' of this setting is unquestionable. It certainly commands the village below, and there can be no doubt that the stone setting had been *built* within its interior. Interestingly, albeit on a much smaller scale, two stone-slab, box-shrines were also seen at the site of Khuindo, both of which had bamboo-tube 'milk offerings' set within them. One of these was set at the foot of a large tree, within the interior of the main building on that site (Structure 3). The other lies at the base of a rock-face, atop which is poised another enormous, house-size boulder (Fig. 3.27:B & D). Giving a similar sense of 'commanding (geological) presence', when we scrambled upon it we found that a small stone slab had been set upright on its top (Fig. 4.27:D). (Another small stone stele had also been erected along the main axis into this site: Fig. 4.27:C.) No claim is being made that, in the case of this site, its uprights or box-shrines are particularly old. Indeed, they still seem to be actively used. Certainly, our visiting village-based shamans seem to have little immediate connection with any of these and this could suggest a degree of minor-scale 'megalithic' activity on the part of recent pastoralists. Here, it may be relevant that the head-suggestive boulder, set atop the

shrine within Kohla's 'saucer', is vaguely reminiscent of the 'footed', quasi-anthropomorphic stone uprights at the southern cairn/mound at Karapu (No. 7). (Pignède 1993, 316–18 describes village shrine buildings, with that at Mohoriya including three upright stones and a small statuette suggestive of a four-pawed animal. In this capacity, he speculated whether the Sildo festival and *koe* cult related to the Ghale kings and the 'ancient' political organization of the Tamu-mai.)

As regards the ambiguities of ritual, another anecdote deserves mention. Again, resonating in relationship to European archaeological practice, it also has implications for issues pertinent to local literacy and 'occupation' (see *Reading and scaling land* above). It was first at Khiondo in 1994, that we came across a stone pecked with cupmarks. A curious finding, but with little sense of any immediate context. This, however, changed in the following season. When surveying Nadar Pa, cupmarks were again seen across the top of a large boulder (Fig. 3.23). Located in the centre of the settlement, this had to be meaningful. Yet, on enquiring of our colleagues as to the significance of these stones, answers varied from 'providing water for fowl' to 'people just wasting time'. Knowingly, we dismissed such pragmatism, until one day in a village, we came across a man doing just that: clearly killing time, using the end of a large machete-like blade to aimlessly peck cupmark-size depressions in a slab. This does not, of course, necessarily imply that the cupmark stones we found on the sites were equally meaningless and, in this context, the obvious shifting of chuni-holdens — which after all appear like enormous single-cupmark stones — to trail-sides beside ruins may be related. (In 1994, we also saw cupmarks amid extensive rock-art panels, when touring Mustang: see Fig. 4.36 below.) This observation does, nevertheless, promote a degree of interpretative modesty.

In hindsight, it was difficult to envisage what one thought working with shamans would have been like (see e.g. Price 2001 concerning the archaeology of shamanism). Generally, there was surprisingly little sense of their direct connection with the work and it is probably safe to say that more was anticipated. Some episodes do, however, feature. In 1994, surveying Structure 6 at Kohla, we surreptitiously dug down in one of its corners to establish the foundation level. The hail, which fell immediately thereafter, seemed particularly intense and, continuing over the next two days, Yarjung and a number of our local colleagues felt certain that our activities had offended the local gods. We closed the small cutting, depositing coins both as dating evidence and as a public offering. That night, Yarjung was informed of this in a dream in which he was visited by his father, who directed that before any digging could occur on the site, we must make an offering of a sheep. This we duly did before commencing the excavations in 2000; a goat, however, having to serve instead (which the group then went on to eat) — such are the pragmatics of ritual in the real world.

Against this, only one part of the site was obviously held by Yarjung as being in anyway particularly 'special': the boulder-retained yard in front of Structure 30. His explanation for this was that perhaps it had been the house of a shaman. Otherwise, both he and the other shamans were greatly concerned with finding Kohla's cemetery. The three-day, commemorative burial rite — the *pai laba* — is the key ritual in Tamu-mai cultural life (see Pignède 1993, 369–82; Pettigrew 1995). They practice both

Figure 4.28. *Yangjakot Cemetery.*

inhumation and cremation, with the remains interred in small, cairn-like stone settings in cemeteries that lie outside of the core of their villages (Fig. 4.28; see Pignède 1993, 316 concerning Tamu-mai burial rites). It was clear that what our colleagues really wanted at Kohla was to be able to excavate the cemetery and 'hold the bones of the ancestors'.

Accordingly, during the 1994 season, Yarjung took to questing for the cemetery's location in the forest (running transformed as a 'panther'). Eventually, his father came to him in one of his dream-quests and told him to search for a lightning-struck, 'axe'-split juniper tree. There are apparently three types of lightning-hit trees: that which 'boils', so that it is completely dead; those that burn; and also the 'axe'-split. In the case of the latter, the 'axe' is not an implement, as such, but a kind of black stone that the lightning leaves embedded within the trunk — a notion which probably derives from the widespread idea of 'thunderbolts' (see Dart & Pradhan 1967, 654 concerning the notion of 'ax-thunder' elsewhere in Nepal). The search for the cemetery came to nought in the first year and, when back at Kohla in 2000, Yarjung continued in his pursuit. Eventually, he came to us on one of our last days, saying that he thought he might have found it, up on a narrow ridge a half kilometre or so to the northeast, some 150 m higher than the site. Visiting it with him, we found there are, indeed, a few small low, mounded cairns there, that could be denuded graves (possibly being Messerschmidt's *mo lhu* — the 'ruins of the underworld demons'). While not occurring in such numbers as to be conclusive, someday they should be tested to this end. What was, however, interesting

is that on pushing our way through the bush to the ridge's end, there stood a magnificent lightning-hit tree, Yarjung having to be reminded of his dream-quest of six years before. On the way down, limbs of it were hauled back to the camp and were eventually taken back to Kathmandu by one of our party, as apparently having lightning-struck wood in a house wards off lightning ever entering it.

One final aspect of Tamu-mai ritual life deserves attention: the key role played by rice, as indeed it does throughout Nepal generally. As variously discussed above, hunting seems to have featured in their former upland economy, and attributes of 'the wild' are a prominent part of shamanic regalia (see Messerschmidt *et al.* 2004, 55–6, 68 concerning hunting in Manang and also Reinhard 1974 and Oppitz 1983, 216–22 respectively among the Raute and northern Magar). Yet, employed in various forms of small moulded effigies relating to concepts of substitution (see e.g. Mumford 1990), rice also plays a major role in their rituals (and is certainly the staple of their diet). From this, if so wishing, a series of white-colour-based linkages could be postulated. This would interconnect rice with houses and men's traditional costume to the snow-capped peaks of the Annapurnas, and revolve around concepts of cleanliness and purity. Be this as it may, rice seems to have played no significant role in the traditional upland economy. This suggests one of two things: either, a remarkable ability for ritual adaptation to subsistence change or, if rice did feature in past rituals, it was a material rarefaction, whose status perhaps related to its importation into the high upland settlements.

Populating highlands — cultural demography
Ezra Zubrow

In effect testing oral sources with statistics, Zubrow's simulation studies below demonstrate that it would be quite feasible, over a period of some 700 years, for Kohla's c. 50 households (here presumed to have a population of 235) to have generated the current population of 120,000 Tamu-mai within its immediate districts. By extrapolation, in relationship to a larger Kohla settlement system (see Chapter 5 below), the potential total number of its multi-village households, as listed in the pye *(line 192; see Chapter 2 above), could theoretically come close to generating the total population of the Tamu-mai today (460,800 vs c. a half-million).*

Today, approximately 120,000 Gurung/Tamu-mai live in the Kaski and Syangja districts of mid-western Nepal (other sources have considerably different estimates: e.g. Eastern Gurung/Tamu-mai, 77,700; the Northern, 4090; and, the Western, 433,430). As outlined above, Kohla is said to be the last place they lived together as a people, and here, *c.* AD 1300 will be taken as the date of the site's abandonment. This contribution tries to determine whether this 'history' makes demographic sense. It briefly examines the demographic character of the Nepalese and Tamu-mai population, both historically and ethnographically. Then it uses archaeological data and simulation techniques to retrace the growth and the spread of the population.

According to UNICEF, contemporary Nepal's general demographic statistics (2003) are the following:

The total population is 25,164,000 (2003), of which 11,710,000 are under the age of 18 and 3,688,000 are under the age of five.

The life expectancy is 60 (2003), which is significantly better than the 1970 life expectance of 42.

The crude death rate is 10 (2003) per 1000, which is also significantly better than the 1970 crude death rate of 22 per 1000.

Under five mortality is 82 (2003), in comparison with 315 (1960).

The crude birth rate is 33 (2003) per 1000, down from 42 in 1970.

The annual number of births is 67,000 (2003).

Fifteen per cent of the population is urbanized, and their average annual growth rate from 1970–2003 is 6.3%.

The male median age is 19.7 and the female is 20 years, creating a total population median age at 19.9 years.

The population growth rate is 2.23%, estimated in 2004 (2003).

In 1976, Alan Macfarlane considered the population of the Gurung/Tamu-mai of Nepal. He examined a variety of anthropological and demographic characteristics and found that, in areas such as Thak, they coexist with other populations, making up 44.5 per cent of the ethnic grouping and 77 per cent of the households. Their demography focuses on the extended household, there being no local term for the nuclear family. It would appear that most villages are of the order of 100 households, and that the society is linked by kinship. Administrative wards are divided into smaller units (*tols* and *nasas*), which are recognized as hamlets.

Reviewing the literature, he found crude birth rates as high as 55 per 1000 (1969), but his fieldwork showed the crude birth rates could be as low as 17 and 18.1. However, when he adjusted it for all known missing people, he concluded that the crude birth rate is near 30/1000, substantially lower than Nepal as a whole. The average complete family size is 5.5, approximately 0.5 children fewer than Nepal as a whole. Age-specific fertility rates are difficult, but are estimated by cohorts as 90 (15–19), 297 (20–24), 278 (25–29), 260 (30–34), 215 (35–39), and 101 (40–44). Macfarlane finds the mean age of first childbirth is 23 at Thak, with a mode at 20, slightly more than the mode 18 found for Nepal in general. This relatively late begin-

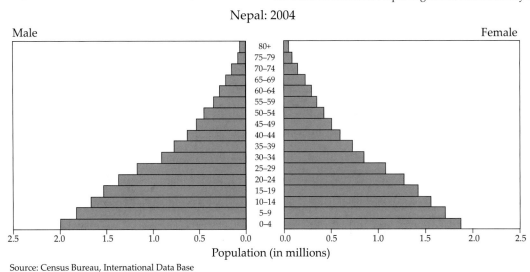

Figure 4.29. *The age structure of the population of Nepal (source: US Census Bureau, International Data Base).*

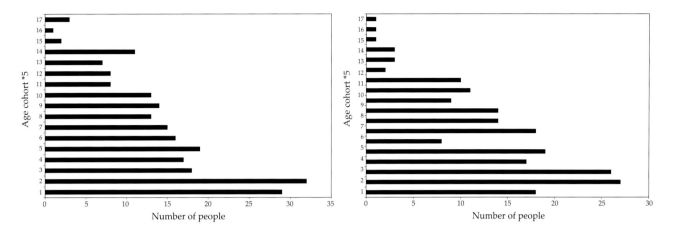

Figure 4.30. *Thak Village age structure: left, female; right, male.*

ning of childbirth is matched among the Tamu-mai with relatively early last childbirth. Their age of last childbirth is mean and mode around 36, in comparison with the Nepalese general population, with a mean age of 36.6 years and the mode of 39 years for the last pregnancy. Neither military service nor wealth seems to correlate with birth rates.

Reviewing the mortality literature as well, Macfarlane suggests that Tamu-mai's mortality is less than Nepalese general figures. He sees that they have a relatively low rate of mortality at childbirth, and an absence of particularly epidemic disease. The crude death rate for Nepal has fluctuatued from estimates as high as 30 to 32/1000, depending upon which census is used (1952–64). Macfarlane's estimates are much lower, at 15.5 over five years. Infant and child mortality ranges from 130–208/1000 for the country as a whole. Macfarlane found for the Tamu-mai that one in three of the children of women age 40 or more were dead and calculates a rate of 86/1000 on the ground. Mortality for men and women is low during the earlier years of marriage, and he found that, in the past, peak mortality was during the 40–49 cohort for women and 50–59 cohort for men; today it is in the 70–79 cohort.

The general age structure of the population of Nepal is somewhat between a third-world nation and a 'G7 Nation', as can be seen in Figure 4.29. Macfarlane's age pyramids for the Tamu-mai are much smaller and much less symmetrical, as can be seen in Figure 4.30. It seems to correspond also to the economy, in that it also fits midway between the developed and underdeveloped countries age-distributions.

The Tamu-mai's distribution, at least at Thak, clearly shows the evidence of World War I and World War II, in which many of their men went off to fight.

Village models and simulation

There are several village models that one may suggest. One is linear, in which a single village becomes a second village, and then becomes a third village, a fourth village, and so on down the line (Fig. 4.31). Another is the bifurcating or cascading pattern, in which the first village becomes two villages, which become four villages, which in turn become eight villages, etc. Of course, it does not have to be bifurcating, it could be trifurcating, or quadrifurcating, etc. Other patterns would be circular, essentially a linear pattern, in which the last village is attached to the first (Fig. 4.32), or an additive process in which one village continues and others enter the system at various times.

The simulation methodology is relatively straightforward. The fertility and mortality rates of modern Nepalese data were compared to Macfarlane's, as well as age-distribution data to the

various models developed by Coale Demeny, and it was decided that a 'South Model 2' fit the general mortality statistics. Using the South Model 2 mortality values, the age-specific fertility statistics were altered to increase the population to fit Macfarlane's estimates. The simulation is diagrammed in Figure 4.32 (right-side).

The initial parameters were set with the mortality rates and population as follows by age-cohort (for females; males are similar):

Age group (years)	M_x	l_x
0–1	0.00473606	20
1–4	0.0002365	14
5–9	0.00010783	10
10–14	0.00012651	9
15–19	0.00025751	8
20–24	0.000274	8
25–29	0.00031236	7
30–34	0.0004302	7
35–39	0.00066665	6
40–44	0.00109736	6
45–49	0.00177018	5
50–54	0.00281081	5
55–59	0.00481972	4
60–64	0.00769803	3
65–69	0.01205094	3
70–74	0.01998255	2
75–79	0.0334053	1
80–84	0.06015612	0
85–90	0.10403892	0
90+	0.20465792	0

The initial age-specific fertility rates were set to create a crude birth rate similar to the range of Macfarlane's above. The number of years was set conservatively at 700 years. The first set of simulations assume Macfarlane's values for fertility, age distribution and crude growth rates, and provides a good initial estimate. The second set

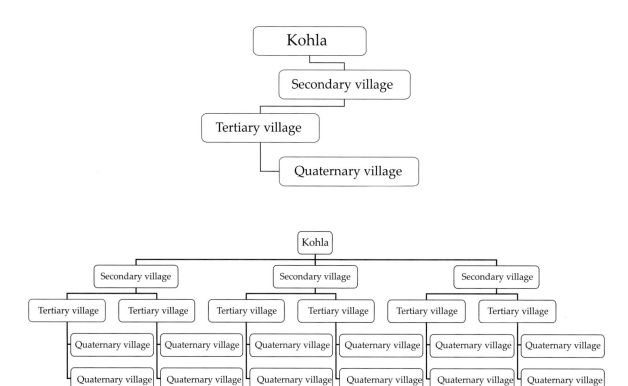

Figure 4.31. *Village-growth models: top, linear; below, bifurcating.*

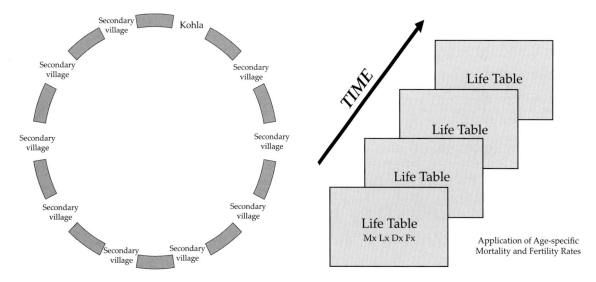

Figure 4.32. *Circular village process (left); right, visual representation of population simulation.*

of simulations vary the age-specified fertility rates, in order to make the population conform closer to the culturally informed history.

If one begins with the age-specific fertility rates to approximate Macfarlane's low crude birth rate of 15.5 per 1000, it would take 424 years, which corresponds generally with the cultural story of the Tamu-mai's arrival. The actual size of the present population would be 60,480 females and 59,898 males. This assumes that Kohla initially had 118 females and 117 males of all ages.

If one changes the age-specific fertility rates to correspond with the high crude rate (that Macfarlane believes to be 55 per 1000) with

same initial population, it would take 118 years to reach and surpass the local Gurung/Tamu-mai population today of 120,000. The actual numbers would be 62,069 females and 61,472 males. This is far shorter than what local history suggests and should be rejected.

Assuming that one wishes to have the population take close to 700 years for the growth, one may change the age-specific fertility rates to correspond with a crude rate of nine per 1000; in 698 years, the population would be 60,881 females and 60,296 males.

One may also change the size of the initial village. Assuming the initial village size of Kohla to be approximately half of the original assumptions, with 59 females and 58 males distributed similarly by age, fertility rates that create a crude birth rate of 10 per 1000 will bring the population up to the 120,000 number in 697 years. Doubling the initial village size requires a new rate of almost eight per 1000. This emphasizes that, under stable conditions, the growth is far more sensitive to the changing growth rates than it is to the size of the initial population.

Agricultural populations gamble with nature (see e.g. Zubrow & Robinson 2000). Do streaks of chance break the demographic bank? And if so, does it change one's interpretation of the cultural history?

> … in the seven years of plenty the earth brought forth in heaps … and the seven years of famine began to come according as Joseph had said and there was famine in all the lands… (*Genesis* ch. 41 verses 47 and 54).

One may change the stability of the conditions. To do so, random 'noise' may be added to the success of the growth rates. A large number of different noise regimes have been tried. For example, using a random number generator with a binomial distribution running 100 trials with a 90 per cent chance of success, it took 681 years to reach the total desired population. The age-specific fertility rates created a crude birth rate with a mean of 9.3 per 1000, the median 9.5 per 1000, and the standard deviation was two per 1000. This is, of course, a very favourable environment.

On the other hand, if one has sufficiently volatile conditions, either in fertility or in mortality, that the growth rate fluctuates significantly, then not only does the growth not take place, but the village becomes extinct. For example, in another set of simulations, where the mean growth rate could vascillate above and below stability by as much as 50 per cent, the population frequently became extinct. In this case, the age-specific fertility rates created a crude birth rate with a mean of 17.6 per 1000, the median of 31 per 1000, and the standard deviation was 288 per 1000. For example, using this unstable environment in several simulations, by the 167th year, the population had no females left in the child-bearing cohorts. In this case, the success of the Tamu-mai would have depended upon the existence of other 'founding' villages. In other simulations, the village goes extinct in the 28th year and the 110th. Survival under this regime for the Tamu-mai is very improbable, even with multiple villages. It takes more than 50 contemporaneous villages before one has a high probability of success. Clearly, a bifurcating, trifurcating, quadrifurcating or greater dividing strategy during those periods of sustained growth for Kohla would result in the best chance for creating the reality of the their cultural history. This would have been far more effective than either a linear temporal pattern of village creation or the circular process.

A more realistic volatile environment has fluctuation rates at 10 per cent. For a typical simulation, the age-specific fertility rates created a crude birth rate with a mean of 0.2 per 1000, the median of two per 1000, and the standard deviation was 57.2 per 1000. In this case, there is a majority of simulations in which the village continues. However, the size of the population comes nowhere near that needed for the cultural history. It reaches a maximum of 332 in the 46th year, but most of the time exists between 180 and 220. Under such conditions, any of the three strategies (linear, bifurcating and circular) would be sufficient to ensure the Tamu-mai historical phenomena. However, again the bifurcating structure more rapidly creates an earlier Tamu-mai settlement landscape that has the least risk of failure.

This contribution has four conclusions:
1. The Tamu-mai suggest that they arrived in central Nepal some 700 years ago and spread out from their 'home village' of Kohla. This paper shows it is not only demographically possible, but probable. In fact, if one uses Macfarlane's most probable demographic estimates for Tamu-mai fertility, mortality and growth,

the simulations show that their population would reach 120,000 without having to create unreal demographic conditions.

2. There are several different models of village budding and creation; five are briefly described.

3. Demographic cultural and environmental variability is modelled, by using random chance as a method. It shows that if the demographic system is sufficiently volatile, it would have been possible for founding villages of the Tamu-mai to go extinct without enough 'budded villages' to maintain their existence.

4. Finally, if the Tamu-mai relatively rapidly bifurcated, trifurcated, or quadrifurcated etc. from Kohla, relatively early during a short period of sustained growth, both the cultural history and the present demography would be expected.

In the case of the Tamu-mai, one may suggest that repetitive patterns of demographic feast and famine may cause hardship, but not extinction. Rather, *ethnic survival is the art of living in a village of such size as to know when to create the next one.*

Goin' north

Following the 1995 survey season, it was decided to take a short, reconnoitering trek north into Mustang and Manang (Fig. 4.34), to experience something of the land behind the Annapurnas and view sites that the Nepal-German project had brought to light. The trip was strictly for reference purposes. While observations were made of sites, the land and communities, it did not aspire to formal survey. Nevertheless, in contrast to the narrative section introducing Chapter 3, greater reference to 'prime' archaeological observations must here be made in order to provide a sense of 'framing context'.

Flying up to Jomson from Pokhara was chaotic, with days of delay, as the valley flight-route up was clouded in. Waiting in the airport, we — Evans, Pettigrew and Tamu, our three porters and Buwan Singh, a TPLS colleague — found that our mutual friend, Charles Ramble (now holding the Aris lectureship in Tibetan studies in Oxford), who was to join us, had forgotten his passport and so could not get permission to enter the region. One of his reasons for going was to accompany the playwright/director, David Lan, who was to scout-out locations for a documentary on local musical traditions. Trained as a social anthropologist (producing an important book, Guns and Rain: Guerillas and Spirit Mediums in Zimbabwe*), part of our way overlapped with Lan's and we, therefore, went together. We were a mixed party, as we also travelled with an old archaeological friend, Knut Helskog of Tromsø University Museum, from the northern tip of arctic Norway. As it happened, Knut, taking a break from fieldwork on his own 'Kohla Project' (studying the peninsula between Norway and Russia), is a renowned prehistoric rock-art specialist and, given our route, this proved fortuitous.*

A

B

Figure 4.33. *Manang Village: A) from east with temple right; B) house detail (foreground), note line-linked prayer flags running from temple up the hill-slope to the stuppa on its crown (see Pohle 1988 for local house and village plans).*

Up here, you're on a plateau behind the rain-shadow of the Himalayas. Demanding irrigation agriculture, it's very high and dry. This shows in the quality of light, which is almost crystalline, and it makes colours vivid — the sky incredibly blue, though much of the ground is a dusty grey/brown. The land is rugged and open, with far less tree cover than to the south. People ride horses, and it naturally makes you think of cowboy country. Yet these communities are largely of Tibetan/Buddhist affiliation (though with strong shamanic traditions), and you can see this in the land. Major landmarks, whether trees or prominent sites, are bedecked with prayer flags (Figs. 4.39 & 4.43:C). They are also set, strung with lines, up the slopes behind villages to corpse-exposure platforms on their crowns (Fig. 4.33:B). It comes as something of a shock that, walking the land as an archaeologist, you can recognize identifiable bits of human bone, dropped by vultures.

Buildings are different here. With substantially lower rainfall, roofs are flat (and can thereby be utilized) and most houses are built on courtyard patterns (Fig. 4.34). While Manang villages are compact and dense, most houses stand separately. They're in rough-hewn stone and, only having windows in their southern fronts, have a heavy 'block-like' appearance. In Mustang, houses are generally built in a pisé-style, with mud/clay and cobbles packed into shuttered lifts. There, buildings are often interconnected and the cores of villages have a 'warren-like' character (Fig. 4.36). Though neither of these vernacular styles have direct linkages to the architecture of Kohla (or for that matter present-day Tamu-mai villages), the Manang houses do have some general affinities (especially their 'L'-shaped arrangements, as opposed to 'U' or central courtyard plans).

Without roads, and maintaining vernacular traditions, these communities superficially have all the appearances of some manner of a 'remote kingdom'. Yet, they are far from isolated. Many houses have electricity, and satellite dishes perch on their roofs. This sense of 'connected-ness' and, at least for some, affluence, does not just derive from recent tourism. Both Manang Valley and the Kali Gandaki are great historical trade routes through the Himalayas, along which Tibetan salt and other goods have long travelled. The rights to this trade were held by family monopolies, many of whom have grown spectacularly wealthy. (A number of Kathmandu's Thamel District's more expensive hotels are said to be financed from such trade.) At a much more lowly level, we came upon evidence of this on the way; first, a small band of traders up from Gorkha selling wares in Manang, and then, a great sheep drive (its drovers on horseback), bringing down huge flocks from the north to Pokhara to sell for sacrifices during Dasain, the great Hindu festival. There is much entrepreneurism here and these are anything but isolated communities.

Walking out from Jomsom (passing the small, near-legendary guest house with its hand-painted sign announcing Jimi Hendrix's stay in the '60s), our way leads north, up to Kagbeni along the broad valley of the Kali Gandaki River. After some time, one of our party, hurriedly returning from relieving themselves, announced the 'discovery' of rock art. Deeply pecked in outcropping boulders and extending over at least some 60 × 70 m, the images ranged from cup-marks, simple geometric motifs and sun symbols, to human feet 'impressions', deer, axes and people (Fig. 4.35). In one instance, a figure appears to hold an axe, and, in another, there is a horse and rider, the latter possibly having a bow. With his background in Nordic rock art, Knut was ecstatic, and glorious hours were spent in their hasty documenta-

tion. Thereafter, going on, the questioning began: 'Was it indeed a discovery?'; 'Who could we turn to fund their formal recording?'; and 'How long would the work take?'. Of course, given their obvious quality and easy recognition, disappointment was inevitable. The next day, when talking with members of the German team, we learned that they knew of the rock-art panels and their publication was forthcoming. Although somewhat taken aback by the news, we had experienced with Knut a 'perfect day' and briefly enjoyed the true thrill of discovery, without the lingering burden of publication.

Lying just beyond and surrounded by its watered fields and orchards, Kagbeni is a large and densely-packed, almost urban-like space. It is commanded by a four-storey-high, pisé-built castle (Figs. 4.36 & 5.4). The town is situated at the southern border of the Kingdom of Lo, into which entrance is strictly regulated. Permits are expensive and, however much we wanted to visit it, entry was beyond our means. We consoled ourselves by viewing the larger-than-life mud-clay effigies built at either of the main gates of the walled precinct; a naked male at one, with a female opposite, whose genitals and breasts have been respectively snapped off and taken in the course of fertility rituals (their bodily parts being subsequently renewed annually: Fig. 4.38:A).

A series of close-set cave mouths can be seen high in the cliff face opposite the town. Such cave galleries are common in the region (some have already been passed getting here) and they have been surveyed by the Nepal-German project, with some also having open settlement sites at their bases below. Though cemeteries have been found within them (including grave-good accompanied mummies, in timber box settings dating to 300 BC), apparently most of the cave galleries themselves started as settlements. Originally being interconnected and accessed from the ground by timber scaffold gantries, many later became hermitage cells for lamas and nuns.

Based on Ramble's recommendation, at Kagbeni, we stayed in the Red House lodge. It's known for the hospitality of its hosts (two sisters) and also their private temple (awkwardly pressed into a small room is an enormous statue of the Buddha; plans of the building feature in Harrison's 1996 volume). Certainly, it's among the best accommodation in the region, though it is far from luxurious. During the afternoon, in the town's central quarter, we came upon a troop of young girls who had asked female elders to teach them traditional dance routines. Amid this strides Yarjung, with his video camera and his characteristic bravado. It resulted in one of the most endearing images of the project — a journeying, (post-) 'modern', Tamu shaman, tracing the migration routes of his ancestors, filming the dances of a Tibetan-Buddhist community (Fig. 4.38:B) — a picture that succinctly evokes cultural revitalization, travel and ethnic pluralism.

173

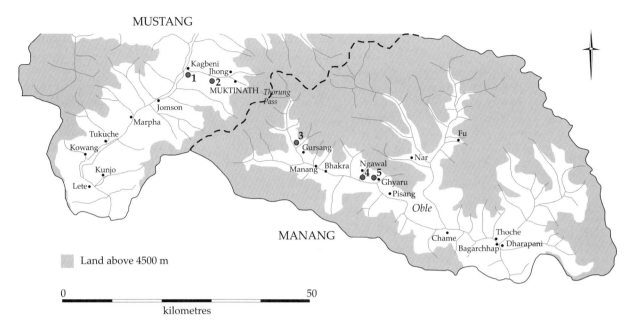

Figure 4.34. *The Mustang/Manang Trek: 1) Kak Nyingba petroglyphs; 2) the Khyinga site ; 3) the Kutsuan Site; 4) Palace of the Ghale Raja; 5) the Red Fort.*

From Kagbeni, our route runs east up the valley of Jhong Khola. The trail goes along the escarpment on the southern side, and more cave complexes can be seen in the cliff-face opposite. After a couple of hours walking, we reach the head of the valley. Here it strikes you just how different this landscape is as, reflecting restricted routes and 'pocketed' resources, four/five villages are there interlinked. With good soil and water sources, the area has an oasis-like quality. At Khyinga, we inspected the German-Nepalese excavations, which proved an important turning point for the project's researches. Almost tell-like, the sequence was some 5 m deep and, with occupation spanning from the second century BC to c. AD 1500, the archaeology was clearly very complex (Fig. 4.38:C & D). Although in many respects obvious, seeing it immediately struck one that any kind of simple, cultural-historical approach to the area's past would invariably fail — a Tamu-mai horizon could not be distinguished or attributed in such 'depth'.

Just above this point, we stop for lunch in the 'compressed', walled village of Jharkot. It's impressive in a dilapidated way. We visit its Buddhist temple, only to find that, like some eccentrically curated local museum, its backrooms are crammed with various 'artefacts', largely ancient arms and armour. It conjures up both the 'Wonder House' of Kim's Lahore Museum and Fisher's description of the contents of Thakali clan houses. Particularly, of the latter, the quixotic character claims that the wealth of the Khasa Malla was carried into the area (upon inspection by Fisher it proved but a sad array). Such mouldy storerooms of sanctified identity present an alternative model of 'collection', one other than western museums; they would someday warrant serious study in their own right.

Thereafter we go up to Muktinath, which is a renowned place of pilgrimage, and its shrine is duly visited. A very important local centre, Muktinath also hosts annual local horse races. The next morning, we had to leave when still dark and start climbing up to the Thorung Pass at about 4:00 am, as you've got to be certain of getting down to shelter on the other side before nightfall. Nearly 5500 m a.s.l. high at the top, it proved pretty gruelling, with two of our three porters dropping out due to altitude sickness. (Telling of the charged religious air of the locale, one of our men showed signs of possession the night before and had to be cured by Yarjung.) We also got ourselves spread out on the route: Yarjung having trouble with a leg and Evans feeling symptoms of altitude. Nevertheless, the way is startlingly beautiful; first, up steep scree and then, in the pass proper, where the route is flanked by high glaciers. There's no vegetation in these brilliantly barren lands, and certainly no obvious sites. At the summit, there are wayside cairns and little else, with the descent down leading through snow fields. Reaching the bottom and the lodge at Thorung Phedi, the start of the way up from the other side is marked by a series of cairns and quasi-anthropomorphic stone settings, with offerings for fortune on the trail ahead.

The next day, we descend south, down through the narrow, green valley of the upper Marsyangdi River. It's pleasant going; we stop at a large yak farm and pass an Austrian environmental research centre. On the way down to Manang, just above Kutsuan and some 2.5 km north of Gunsang, we come across a major settlement site (Fig. 4.39). While it, in part, includes the standing houses of a small hamlet, apparently only abandoned in the mid '80s, it otherwise seems entirely 'ancient'. Even though here

Figure 4.35. *The Kak Nyingba petroglyphs: top, portion of panel recorded by the Nepal-German team; below, our encounter, with Knut Helskog right. Recorded by Dr Predate Pohle, the Kak Nyingba petroglyphs is one of only three rock-art sites found in the course of the Nepal-German surveys in Mustang. It involves more than 770 individual motifs and includes 48 anthropomorphic figures (including riders on horse-/yak-back), weapons, cupmarks and various pre-Buddhist and Buddhist symbols (Pohle 2003, figs. 2 & 3). Its representation of forest animals — particularly deer — is thought to further support archaeological evidence that the region was formerly wooded and less arid. Although not absolutely dated, much of the imagery is clearly of pre-Buddhist affiliation and, based on affinities with Eurasian Animal Style sites in central Asia, might date back to the first millennium BC. The nearby abandoned settlement (after which the rock art is named) has subsequently been dated to the eleventh–fifteenth centuries (Pohle 2000; 2003) and this assignation would complement local oral traditions (Ramble 1983). A mortar-hole cut within the rock-art panels would indicate their connection with the village site, while engraved ramarildok gameboards are thought to relate to use by Tibetan-affiliated pastoralists.*

Figure 4.36. Kagbeni: Top, view of village from south (note the caves in the cliff-face left); below, detail of the pisé-built castle raising above the roof-tops of its houses.

Figure 4.37. *Manang Valley: Top, looking east down the valley-corridor with wall of the north side of the Annapurnas right, with the great basalt screen of Oble below.*

A

B

C

D

Figure 4.38. *In Mustang: A) male clay effigy figures at gates of Kagbeni Castle; B) Yarjung videotaping a women's dance group in Kagbeni, September 1995; C & D) the Nepal-German excavations at Khyinga (photographs C & D by K. Helskog).*

we're still well above the level of present-day cultivation, traces of terraced fields can be detected, extending for over half-a-kilometre around the site. It lies on either side of a small river, feeding into the Marsyangdi. On the north side is a 4–5 m-high mound that extends over c. 40 × 90 m. The remains of many stone buildings can just be made out within it (?15–20) and, along its southern riverside edge, their eroded walls are visible to a height of c. 1.2 m. Plain red wares are recovered, and this would definitely seem to be a major village site.

Approximately 150 m south of this is something quite different — an 8 m-high mound, 50 m across. It is not 'tell-like', as the rise proper seems geological (i.e. glacial). 0.8–1 m-high walls flank its sides and extend across its crown. At

least one very large building is evident (i.e. 'monumental'); over the remainder, small 'cells' are visible and quantities of pottery are present (including fine, wheelmade imports, and both scored and cord-impressed wares). This entire complex seems fortified and it probably represents a minor 'castle' or palace. Other small mounds and isolated building ruins are seen in its vicinity and this clearly is an important site; its location would probably have commanded movement along the main river valley.

Progressing downwards (and south), after a short while, the way turns east into Manang Valley proper (Fig. 4.37). The landscape suddenly opens up, it's less rocky and the entire valley bottom is cultivated. At this time of year, the crops are ripe, with buckwheat and apples grown (and

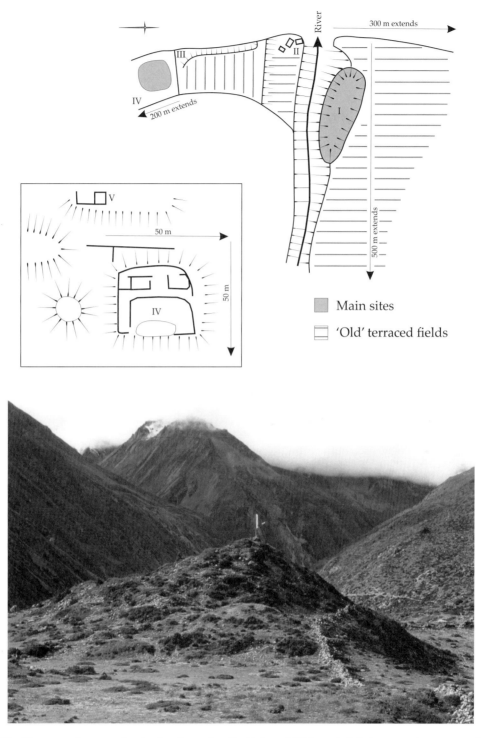

Figure 4.39. *The Kutsuan site: top, sketch plan (note detail of Mound IV inset left; below, southern mound (V) with prayer flag. (Photograph: K. Helskog.)*

we get to eat tough yak meat). Compared to Mustang, the land — at least along the valley corridor — seems more lush, and there's greater colour, including the milky blue of the lake at the foot of the Gangapurna glacier.

From here it's a short walk amid walled paths and terraced fields, down to Manang village, where we'll spend the night. Just west of it, on the southern side opposite, is another cave complex. Five to six storey-levels high, they lie just above the height of the scree and some 50 m above the valley floor (Fig. 4.40). The next day, a comparable

Figure 4.40. *Cave galleries opposite Manang Village; note their height above the valley floor (A), with detail below (B).*

cave gallery is seen opposite Bhakra/Braga (three storeys high, with ten openings 80 m above the plain). According to Yarjung, the western half of the village is itself 'caved' behind the houses, though none is visible. Yarjung explains that, while Bhakra was originally a Tamu-mai village, it is now of Manangbe/Tibetan-Buddhist affiliation.

Going down the valley, between the villages, the landscape is park-like and dotted with tall pine. A kilometre of so south of Bhakra is what seems to be a deserted village (with associated hamlets, south of the river). Like some sort of ghost town, only one house is currently inhabited, and we learn that this is an entirely transhumant settlement. It apparently exists in a clientage relationship with Bhakra, each of whose households have some 40 head of yak, cattle

and sheep/goats. Each year, these are taken into the uplands and that's where they are now, only coming down again in October, when the snows start falling higher up. The main ('empty') settlement consists of about 40 buildings, only two of which are of the local, 'formal', 'L'-shaped, two-storey plan, with the rest being low, single-storey and squarish.

Thereafter, it is a longish walk to the next village, Ngawal, which lies up on the escarpment, some 250 m above the valley floor. This interval seems something of a divide, as, south of Bhakra, no cave sites are seen. Located on a distinct promontory, some 0.5 km south of Ngawal, is the 'The Fortress of the Ghale Raja'. While in some respects comparable to the main Kustan mound, it is probably the most relevant site examined during this trek. In the main,

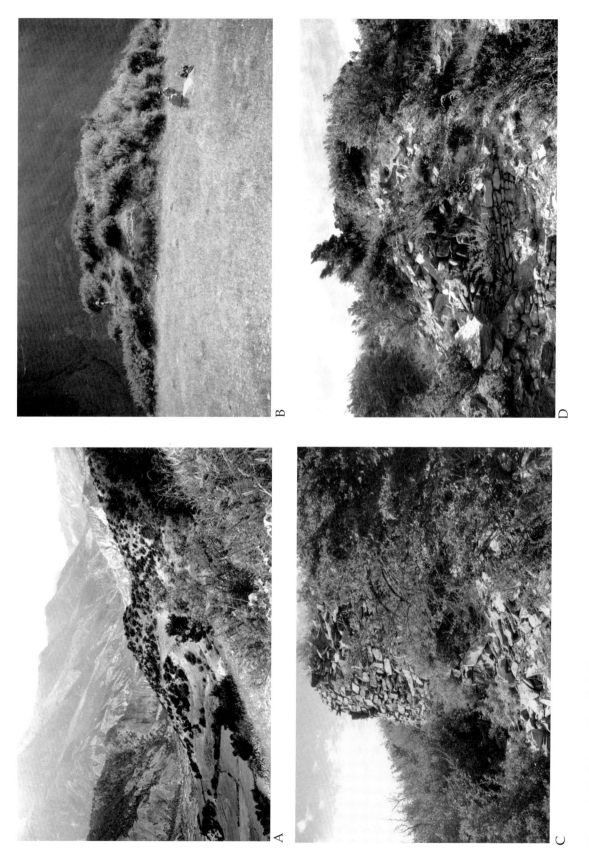

Figure 4.41. *Palace of the Ghale Raja: A) as seen from the west; B) the rise of its mound from the north; C & D) masonry visible along its southern flanks.*

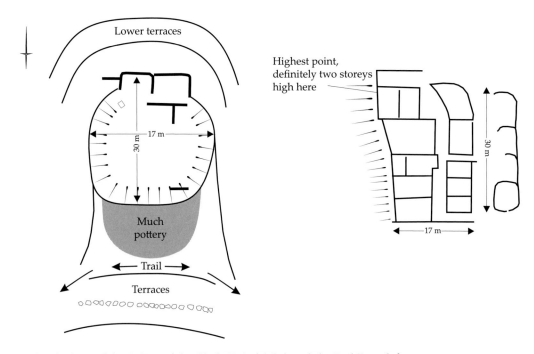

Figure 4.42. *Sketch plans of the Palace of the Ghale Raja (right) and the Red Fort, left.*

it consists of a distinct mound, c. 30 m in diameter and 4–5 m high (Figs. 4.41 & 4.42). A number of drystone structures are evident within this core (i.e. protruding from its flanks), with walls 0.5–0.8 m wide and standing up to 1.2 m high. At one point, a burnt layer could been seen extending beneath the stonework, and this suggests more than one phase of occupation. Evidence of two or three terraces is apparent along the southern riverside slope. Their walls are very high (c. 1.6 m) and these may also be components of the main complex.

The site would have dominated this length of the valley and, on the whole, it does seem 'fort-like'. As compared to the similarly situated Red Fort someway beyond (see below), it is considerably more eroded and, at least superficially, appears older. Much pottery is scattered around (all of it red wares), with cord-impressed pieces and five or six organic-tempered sherds present. As was the case throughout this trip, being outside of our 'zone', we have no formal permission to undertake any kind of fieldwork within this region. Moreover, some of the locals are clearly suspicious of our group and any recording has to be surreptitious. Therefore, pottery has to be left on-site, and surveying is only a matter of discrete sketching (given the conditions, it would be unwise to take tapes to these sites).

From here, we go onto the Red Fort, located on the escarpment level, west of the village of Ghyaru, at the boundary with Pisang. Although of more recent attribution (apparently being associated with the Nepal/Tibetan War of 1856), it's still very impressive. Its construction seems quite different from that of the Ghale Raja Fort, being built of slate slabs bonded in red clay (hence the source of its

place-name), and wooden stringer courses are also integral to its fabric (Fig. 4.43:A & B). Standing to a maximum height of 4 m, and at points clearly up to two storeys high, in the main this consists of a large, sub-rectangular 'block' structure (17 × 30 m), with some 13 rooms sub-divided by corridors. Well-built with tight corners, this was probably a single building and generally seems comparable to the castle at Kagbeni. Certainly, its core-structure contrasts to the ranges of rounded-corner 'domestic cells', that extend around its eastern, western and northern sides. Those on the north side appear newer/cleaner and may relate to the occupation of either hermits and/or pastoralists. From its degree of survival, this certainly appears of more recent date than the Ghale Raja's Fort. (Though interestingly, 'Tamu-mai/Gurung' informants from Ngawal related that the Raja's fortress belonged to their ancestors and that it was contemporary with the Red Fort, the latter being the 'House of the King's Lama' — in other words, the Ghale King's Lama! In this case, time/landscape have clearly been conflated into one unified narrative.)

From the Red Fort, we clearly see Oble. Looming up like a great basalt wall, it's different than anything else around and really is commanding (Fig. 4.37). Mumford in his book, **Himalayan Dialogue** of 1990, mentions that there are ruins around its foot. You really want to strike out to it, but it is at least 5 km distant and our time has run out, and to make our booked flights we must head back the same way we came. Returning over Thorung La and its loose downslope scree, Evans's knee gave out. After hours of agony, a man leading a horse eventually passed by and this was duly hired. Reaching Muktinath, Knut was also

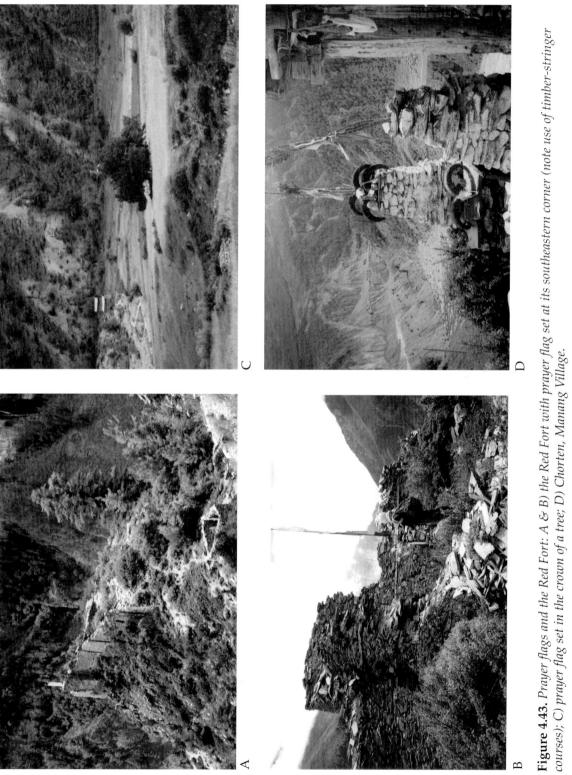

Figure 4.43. *Prayer flags and the Red Fort: A & B) the Red Fort with prayer flag set at its southeastern corner (note use of timber-stringer courses); C) prayer flag set in the crown of a tree; D) Chorten, Manang Village.*

convinced of the logic of this transportation. Both rode out the next day, on the small local mounts, to a guest house between Kagbeni and Jomson. Wakening at an ungodly hour, the next morning we catch the flight back to Pokhara aboard a worryingly-aged ex-Soviet helicopter.

This journey north should have been more. We should have got into the local highlands and met with its pastoralists, to discuss the high mountain routes. Equally, we should have gone on to Oble and recorded the sites at the mountain's base, and then continued down and gone out via Ghanpokhara. (Aside from the TPLS's 'round' trek in '92, all of the project's journeys went out the same route as we came in. Though arguably a waste of effort in terms of experiencing land, this always proved crucial in the provision of context. It was by first overviewing everything that a sense of relative value could be established, so that on the return route you knew what warranted re-appraisal or more detailed recording. Albeit a casual methodology, it allows you to mull over findings and eventually 'spiral' towards some degree of knowledge — first seeing things fresh and later in perspective as context builds up.) In the case of the '95 trek, however, needs pressed and, despite its brevity, a lot was learned. Primarily, this allowed a hands-on appreciation of the real environmental and cultural/ethnic differences on either side of the Annapurnas, and the degree to which they are a major geographical and cultural divide. Yet equally crucial was also the experience of landscape corridors *and the penetration of the area's great routeways, both Manang Valley (west–east, then southward) and the Kali Gandaki (north–south).*

Chapter 5

Landscape, Histories and Narrative Trails

Christopher Evans

Newly arrived and quite ignorant of the languages of the Levant, Marco Polo could express himself only by drawing objects from his baggage — drums, salt fish, necklaces of wart hogs' teeth — and pointing to them with gestures, leaps, cries of wonder or of horror, imitating the bay of the jackal, the hoot of the owl.

The connections between one element of the story and another were not always obvious to the emperor; the objects could have various meanings: a quiver filled with arrows could indicate the approach of war, or an abundance of game, or else an armorer's shop; an hourglass could mean time passing, or time past, or sand, or a place where hourglasses are made (Italo Calvino, *Invisible Cities* 1972; emphasis added).

There are no easy or grand conclusions to such a project, especially one whose researches were so obviously cut short by circumstance. Rather, appropriate to the dense histories of Geertz's 'thick description' (1973) or Calvino's 'un-obvious connections', it is essentially a matter of teasing-out what have been its key themes. Although avenues of future research have been highlighted, rooted in *the construction of the past in the present* — and its corollary, 'the past in the past' — the project of history must invariably remain open-ended.

From the outset, a sense of baseline should be declared. Given its extraordinary tripartite layout (and dating), the site of Kohla seems undoubtedly to be the Kohla of the *pye* — 'The Three Villages' settlement — and therefore, in the context of the region's ethno-history, there can be little doubt of its Tamu-mai attribution. This does not, though, imply that the question from where in the north, as a people, they originated has been resolved. However, funded by the European Science and Humanities Foundation, a major study of the genetic make-up of Himalayan peoples (including the Tamu-mai/Gurung) will shortly be published (Kraayenbrink *et al.* forthcoming; see also Gayden *et al.* 2007). In effect, there looms the possibility of *an* answer. This is an intriguing situation. Operating out

of Cambridge in the latter half of the 1990s, we had the opportunity to conduct DNA trials amongst the local populace had we so wished. Yet this always seemed, if not wrong, then at least an uncomfortable option. Perhaps it was simply too onerous a responsibility, but we didn't want to introduce hard genetics into the ethnic cauldron of Nepalese cultural politics.

With the prospect of hard science, therefore, left for the future, having 'established' Kohla's attribution (no more than what local communities have long known), there are a number of crucial issues to explore. Among these are: how the site was remembered and elements of its ruins identified; what is the nature of the interface between archaeology, cultural history and myth/oral texts; the role 'epics' play in the conceptualization of landscape; and, finally, how Kohla has recently been deployed in the construction of group identity. Before proceeding, it is, however, appropriate to begin with the project's finale, a great gathering of shamans in 2002.

The conditions of remembering (and forgetting)

It was to bring a degree of closure to the project that the meeting of shamans was held at the Pokhara *Kohibo*. The event proved extraordinary; 108 shamans and their apprentices attended, with many travelling more than two-day's journey by foot and/or bus to participate (Fig. 5.1). It began with suitable preliminaries and announcements of intent, with prestige and 'positioning', of course, playing a part. Yarjung started by presenting transcribed volumes of his *pye* to the TPLS. Despite the fact that he also donated a laptop computer to encourage other shamanic 'teams' to follow his example and record their knowledge, this naturally gave rise to some inter-village discontent. Thereafter, having framed a series of historically relevant interview questions, each of the village-shaman groups was duly interviewed by the project's anthropologists, and asked to outline their *pye* relating to Kohla and the downward migration.

Figure 5.1. *The Pokhara shamans' meeting: above, Pachyu shamans; below, the Kyabris.*

With most sleeping and dining in the lodge-*cum*-museum building, the meeting was both highly productive and appropriately chaotic, as the shaman groups discussed matters among themselves while awaiting their turn to be interviewed (with almost all lingering on till the gathering's close). It is impossible to convey the sense of lively creativity — the jostling for attention, the encounter with distant colleagues and undercurrents of village (and town) rivalry — in contrast to the dignified poise of senior delegates. Mass shamans' meetings are very rare (usually only two or three 'teams' at most ever work together) and, not surprisingly, it was punctuated by, and gave voice to, many things. Worried from the outset that sufficient numbers would attend, the shamans were offered the standard ritual day-rate payment for their participation. Remarkably, in the meeting's plenary session, they passed a motion to donate *en masse* their fees to further shamanic training and translation.

By the normative reckoning of modes of knowledge and group memory, the meeting should have been a defining milestone for Tamu-mai studies and

identity (Evans 2004). With Yarjung's formal presentation of his transliteration of the *pye*, an oral tradition was committed to the printed page, thereby marking the shift from *an embodied to a textual cultural record* (see Goody 1987 concerning 'the interaction of the written and oral'). Accordingly, a tale outlining the competition between a Tibetan lama and a 'Paju' (Pachyu) shaman is relevant:

> The Paju was angry that he had lost the contest. In despair the Paju took all of his written texts and threw them into a fire, where they burned to ashes. Then he heard the voice of a god above: 'Although you have destroyed your books you must do your rituals by remembering the knowledge that your books contained.' The Paju ate the ashes of the burned texts and thus swallowed the knowledge. To this day, the lama has to read his texts, but the Paju chants his learning from memory (in Mumford 1990, 53).

Unlike, for example, Luther's translation of the gospels or, in an Asian context, Mergen Geegen's translation of the tenets of Buddhism into Mongolian (see Humphrey 2001; Evans & Humphrey 2003), appropriate to

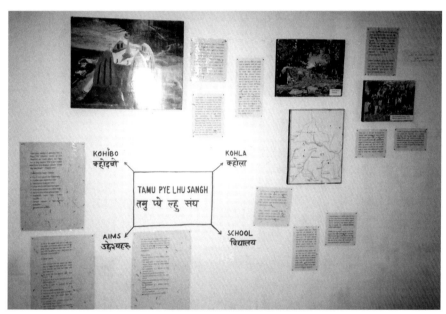

Figure 5.2. *The Pokhara shamans' meeting: above, shamans appraise the transcription of the* pye *at the Pokhara meeting (this photograph records the actual moment of 'the interface between the oral and the written': cf. Fig. 2.2); below, display within the Kohibo showing the linkages of the TPLS' long-term agenda (note that the Kohla display upper right balances the Kohibo/Kohibo left).*

our over-documented times, the actual moment of this 'world-turning' among the Tamu-mai was captured (Fig. 5.2). Yet, was it just that? While not at all equivalent to Tibetan-Buddhism's deep reliance on texts, some Tamu-mai shamans are known to have scrolls (Macfarlane, in Pignède 1993, 457, n. 120; see also Oppitz 2004 concerning Qiang shamans' divination books). Alternatively, a significant proportion of them are functionally illiterate and some even chant by rote, as they do not understand *Cho Kyui*, the Tamu ritual

language. Though occurring against a background of incipient orthodoxy amongst Pokhara's Tamu-mai community (e.g. in architecture and burial rite; see above and Evans 2004), perhaps even more telling is that Yarjung's texts are eccentric. They are in *Cho Kyui*, but written in a personally adapted Devanagai script (i.e. 'Nepali'), and it remains to be seen whether they will take root and have significant impact.

With the outcome of this 'moment', therefore, held in abeyance, what is crucial is the outcome of the meeting's interviews, and the remarkable degree of correspondence of what is chanted by the shamans. While for our surveys the constraints of time made absolute quantification impossible, the results would suggest that Strickland's estimation of the very high level of recital accuracy is, indeed, valid (1982); essentially they all chant the same thing. This extraordinary homogeneity of such a widespread oral tradition reflects on no less 'classic' themes than, for example, the works of Homer, and whether it is his poetry that has survived or only a version thereof (e.g. Kirk 1976; Sherratt 1990). Although collective correspondence lies at the heart of much scientific procedure (see e.g. Adkins 2003, 337–41 concerning the adjudication of cuneiform translation in the nineteenth century), in this instance the correspondence of memory need not itself necessarily ensure the historical accuracy of the *pye*'s content. Rather, it reflects the strength by which the Tamu-mai oral tradition has been maintained. Reinforced by the fact that the shamans' language is specialized and not in common usage (and therefore not prone to daily-life change or development), it is clearly *the exactitude of recital* and not *poetic embellishment* that has been fostered. Given the lack of variability in the *pye*'s recital, it is unlikely that its transcription will itself have a major impact on its content (i.e. *viz.* an 'enshrinement'; see Barth 1987, 78–80, 86–7). It is not a matter of a 'literal' orthodoxy in the face of multiple *versions*, but rather its impetus is the risk of wider cultural 'forgetting' or, at least, neglect. That is, the decline in the number of practising shamans and, with it, the worry that the tradition could thereby be lost. (There are also plans to establish a shamanic training school in Pokhara, with sponsored apprentices staying in the *Kohibo*.) In this context, transcribing the *pye* can be considered as an act of 'external storage' (Renfrew 1998), as opposed to a strictly embodied knowledge and cultural 'code'.

The loss of origin stories, and localized religions and oral histories generally, is a corollary of such prodigious feats of memory as the *pye*'s transmission attests to. In Plato's *Phaedrus*, Socrates relates the invention of writing to the Egyptian god, Theuth, who tries to sell it to King Thamus, on the grounds that it will make people wiser and their memories better. To this, Thamus duly replies:

> This discovery of yours will create forgetfulness in the learners' souls, because they will not use their memories; they will trust to external written characters and not remember themselves. The specific which you have discovered is an aid not to memory, but to reminiscence.

'Mass forgetting' need not just be the outcome of a lack of maintenance of oral traditions, but also religious conversion and one story eradicating or superseding another. The extra-regional spread of faiths, both those of historical times and presumably also religious 'movements' in prehistory, would have been accompanied by the loss — effectively an amnesia — of 'the local'. Of course, some origin narratives have proven resilient to conversion and, if not coexisting, then at least have still been remembered (abetted in historical times by subsequent written records); think of those of the Inuit and other American 'First Peoples' or, in Europe, Scandinavian sagas. Nevertheless, within the sweep of time, it is staggering to consider just how many clan histories and migration tales must, for example, have been forgotten in Europe's distant past.

Ricoeur has, in fact, argued that forgetting is a prerequisite for the *writing* of history (2004). Otherwise, the 'past as memory' would be like a life-size map and thereby useless, as its representation would not reduce, distill or symbolize the jumble of time and reality (see Margalit 2005). Yet great oral traditions like the *pye* are actually themselves more akin to texts than 'open memory'. It is not an unedited 'totality' of the past they convey, but structured narratives; they are, in effect, *living documents*.

Context and kingship

In the discussion of Kohla's radiocarbon dates in Chapter 4, while acknowledging that, due to its limited sampling, their span may well extend by one or two centuries beyond their actual assignation, the settlement is attributed to *c.* AD 1000–1300. This would broadly coincide with the impact of Tibetan culture and Lamaist Buddhism in Mustang from, at least, the later tenth century, and could, perhaps, provide an impetus for the migration of shamanic communities. The 'archaeology of religion' has, of course, its own pitfalls (e.g. Insoll 2004). Nevertheless, as discussed in that same chapter, it may be relevant that no material of Buddhist affiliation was recovered from any of the upland sites. Equally notable is the occurrence of standing stones in the 'public core' of both Kohla and Khuindo, given that, in a Tibetan context, Bellezza attributes such settings as pre-Buddhist (2002; cf. Aldenderfer & Yinong 2004, 42–6).

More in line with the AD 500 date postulated by Tamu & Tamu for the establishment of Kohla (1993), in Chapter 2 Yarjung relates that he still believes the settlement to be older and dates it to *c.* AD 300–600. Yet such an early attribution could be disputed by the evidence of the *pye* itself, as, in Line 120, it relates that the 'High country [Mustang] had a Tibetan king' prior to the foundation of Kohla. This is only a matter of detailing, and perhaps more telling are Yarjung's

Shamanic equipment — fighting sets

Having such a wide cross-section of the Tamu-mai shamanic community at hand during the 2002 Pokhara meeting, time was spent recording their apparel and equipment (Fig. 5.3). By reference to the migration epic, this allows for consideration of variability between oral records and material culture 'sets'. Of the latter, there is generally a close correspondence of their 'core' regalia, those items of costume and equipment that are *held to be necessary*. Yet, there are differences between what constitutes a specific object-type; the felt hats of the *Pachyus* were in a wide range of shapes, but all had cowry shells sewn on them and feather head-dress attachments. Equally, each practitioner would have a round flat-drum. Near universal in shamanic practice, these vary widely in size and decoration (note their almost emblematic prominence in the posed photographs: Figs. 1.4 & 5.3). Similar is the 'fighting hornbill', to combat evil. In the main, this involves a true hornbill's beak (imported from India), though for others a stork's skull and an iron bird-shaped implement were variously substituted. Their 'sounding' horns show comparable variety, ranging from conch shells to ram's horns and drilled-out human long bones. There are also items whose form is very similar, but whose usage differs. Iron-shoed quivers of porcupine quills are a case in point. Some employ

Figure 5.3. *The Pokhara shamans' meeting: top: left, a fully attired Kyabri, with a bedecked Pachyu to his right (note the latter's wildcat pelt belt and mountain pheasant-feather head-dress: cf. Fig. 2.2); below, a display table of shamanic equipment: 1) Pachyus' felt hats; 2) 'fighting' hornbill with stork's skull equivalent beside; 3) porcupine quill quivers; 4) various forms of horn; 5) set of miniature iron implements.*

these to 'fire' at witches (the quills metaphysically springing out *en masse*), while others have the quills bound together and, instead of being used as projectiles, they are rubbed against things to imbue strength.

As can be found through much of central Asia, the inventory of shamanic apparel showed a strong emphasis upon the 'wild', predominantly wildcat pelts, deer's feet and bird feathers. This is most clearly expressed amongst the *Pachyu* shamans, whose main task is to fight with witches (i.e. 'evil'). Despite almost two centuries of international interaction through Gurkha service, their 'weaponry' is inherently conservative, involving the bow, knives and other edged/pointed implements. The gun, or at least, representations thereof, for example, has no place (though it does feature in non-shamanic 'indigenous' art elsewhere in Nepal).

As illustrated in Figure 5.3, amongst the shamans' equipment are also sets of miniature 'edged' iron implements. Largely consisting of various forms of knives, axes and also bows (though the latter does not occur in the illustrated group; see, however, Herle 1994 and Macfarlane's note 39, in Pignède 1993), these also include blacksmithing tools. The latter are singularly interesting in the light of the oft-cited 'magical' status of metalworkers generally and, more specifically, caste proscriptions against blacksmiths amongst the Tamu-mai (especially given the recovery of slags and crucibles at Kohla). In this regard, issues of *transformation* — both of materials and change over time — seem apparent (see Evans 2004; forthcoming).

The use of these shamanic objects is essentially symbolic; their design does not entail functional refinement as, for example, the making of plough-ards. Based on the source of their parts, they can be more or less powerful, but as objects/weapons they cannot be made better. The necessary items fulfil named categories that have little potential for change; fully attired, the shamans may be wearing local versions of Adidas, but their shoe-style is not prescribed, so that this makes no significant difference to their costume (Fig. 5.3). What binds the material culture of the shamans together are *named* type-categories, rather than the specific form of 'the thing', with the shaman's power/strength largely relating to 'old' or embedded sources (though, obviously, at one time these things must have been 'new').

Similarly, it is categories and/or names that are the specific mnemonics of the shamans' recitation ('next we came to .. and .. did this'). The syntax and grammar of what binds them may vary, but the categories of memory show remarkable consistency — they are what is strictly memorized. The Tamu-mai oral record seemingly lacks the inherent ambiguity of material culture (i.e. 'artefacts'), it usually being held that the less precise meaning of 'things' is offset by their very materiality and long-term influence (e.g. Renfrew 1998). Yet, residing in the *embodied memory* of the shamans, in this case the oral record would assume a comparable, if not greater, longevity (see Mack 2003, 29–33 concerning great 'remembrancers' and the relationship of memory and cultural identity). In this context, *the drum* is arguably the most crucial element of the shamans' equipment. Providing performance rhythms, they effectively mediate 'text' and recital, and their pivotal role is succinctly expressed in a series of stories amongst the Qiang people of the Sino-Tibetan mountains of northwestern Sichuan:

> In the beginning, the *shüpi* or shaman *did* have written books. Every three years he would make a trip to a Buddhist lama to renew them. One day, on his way home after he had collected a new set of scriptures, he settled down under a tree for a nap. While he was asleep, a flock of sheep passed by and one of them ate his scriptures. When the *shüpi* woke up he realized the disaster that had befallen him. Having spent all the money he had taken for the trip, he did not want to go back to the lama to ask for another set of books, so he started to cry. A golden-haired monkey passed by and told the tearful man how to solve his problem. He instructed him to kill the guilty sheep and make a drum from its skin. When the shaman started to play his new instrument, he was able to recite a phrase from his lost books with each beat of the drum (Shaman Zhang Fuliang, in Oppitz 2003, 120).

The antithesis of such embodied shamanic oral texts would, of course, be the *Sir Guru Granth Sahib*, the great 'living book' of the Sikhs. Carried on a pillowed litter, it is literally put to bed each night in the Golden Temple at Amritsar.

remarks that the Tamu-mai's 'sacred texts' not only predate the invention of writing and letters, but 'our civilization and establishment as *a stable ethnic group*' (Chapter 2). The latter observation might admit correlation with the linguistic evidence (see Chapter 1), and suggest that the Tamu-mai emerged from a 'proto-grouping' — variously the *Tamu/Se* people as progenitors of the Tamu-mai, Thakali and Tamang — prior to the fourth century AD, and who probably arrived into Mustang from Tibet in the first millennium BC. This would generally correspond with the evidence of German-Nepalese researches in Mustang, and the observation that no single 'ethnic' identities/communities could ever be readily distinguished from its complex sequences (see Chapter 4).

Other facets of the archaeology that we found in the uplands fly in the face of the ready identification of the Tamu-mai with 'this past'. Yes, Kohla has a

superficial resemblance to present-day/historical villages, yet aspects of what was recovered do not easily fit with 'simple' village-type models. The occurrence of 'toll stations' and a dam, 'king's houses/palaces' and industrial quarters could suggest a more developed political economy than prevails today. Of course, in the same way that 'the ethnographic' is not pristine nor is it timeless, by focusing upon 'the people' as providing the thread of continuity, such discrepancies are not necessarily problematic.

Of Kohla's political economy, the status of its 'kings' deserves further exploration. Trying to gauge what level of hierarchy is expressed on the site, an anecdote arising from the Sinja Project investigations is relevant. In the autumn of 2000, after digging Kohla in the late spring, Evans and Acharya (joined by Gibson) excavated the ridge-top site of the summer palace of the Khasa Malla kings, in the west of the country (Fig. 1.7; Evans & Gibson 2003). Occurring along a royal 'road' linking northern India and western Tibet, the architectural and sculptural remains of this eleventh- to fourteenth-century dynasty — particularly their renowned lion figures — had first been brought to wider attention by Tucci (though he never visited Sinja itself; 1962, see also Bishop 1990).

The context of the fieldwork was fraught. Large numbers of Maoist insurgents were known to be active in the hills around the valley, the local police station had been attacked a number of times and the national army had just been called into the region. Moreover, the local villagers were suspicious. They suspected that the government had come to rob them of their past and, only after long and often unpleasant *en masse* meetings, were we able to proceed (and then under constant group supervision). Against this uncomfortable background, we embarked cautiously, as we did not want to open up anything that couldn't be finished given these tense circumstances. In the end, we spent most of our time regularizing and extending the trenches of Joshi, a Nepalese archaeologist who had cut sondages across the most obviously 'old' ruins on the ridge during the 1970s (his results being unpublished and their archives cannot be located). Of later medieval date (*c.* fourteenth/fifteenth–sixteenth century), the size and complexity of the standing remains were comparable to the largest buildings at Kohla, though the quality of the drystone work was inferior (Fig. 5.4). As assembled from relevant written sources, the description of Sinja's palace paints a grand picture: four storeys high, white-washed with fluttering banners along its walls. What we eventually unearthed was an extensive building range that was terraced downslope in four 'drops'. Indeed, at a distance, it would have appeared four storeys high. We had revealed, earlier, more robust, foundations in a deep sondage, and all this left us feeling confident that we had exposed a late vestige of the Malla's palace. Throughout, Kohla's 'kings' houses provided a sense of comparative scale.

On the second-last day, all this was soundly deflated. A local resident of a hamlet below called us over to view masonry exposed in the back of his property. We went eagerly, knowing that the fabric of his house included many finely worked stones and it lay adjacent to a spot where a number of the lion sculptures had earlier been set. Scrambling around his plot, there, in the approximately 3 m-high eroded edge behind, was a truly monumental architecture, consisting of robust stone footings and walls nearly twice the width of what we had investigated on the hill-top above. (The walls flanked a metalled roadway and seemed to relate to a gateway into the palace

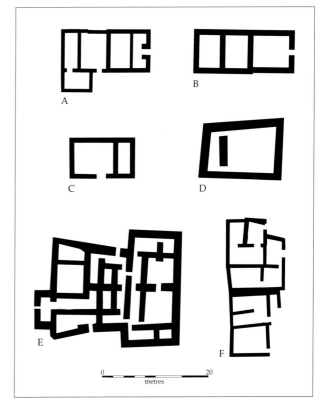

Figure 5.4. *'Great buildings': A & B) Kohla's 'King's Houses', Structures 5 (A) and 19 (B); C) Nadr Pa 'Palace'; D) Karapu, Structure I, 'Tower Fort'; E) Kagbeni Castle (after Harrison 1996, 28; see also 2003); F) Sinja 'Palace' (after Evans & Gibson 2003).*

precinct, with ancillary buildings extending off to one side.) This was an appropriately 'great' building. What we had been looking at on the ridge proper could only have been either a very poor 'last gasp' version of Sinja's palace or no more than an aspiring house.

Nothing we saw at Kohla would compare to this scale of architecture. This is not surprising as, in their time, the Khasa Malla controlled trans-Himalayan trade. This does no more than demonstrate that *the measure of social hierarchy/royalty is contextual.* Moreover, other qualities, such as sacred authority, may determine the basis of kingship from modes of leadership that otherwise might have amounted to no more than 'first amongst equals'. Indeed, while in the course of fieldwork Structures 5 and 19 at Kohla were always referred to as *King's Houses* ('king' being the termed used for the Ghale Raja in Tamu & Tamu's historical outline in Pignède 1993 and also in Yarjung's Chapter 2 commentary), in the translation of the *pye* above, the local hierarchy are termed 'chieftains', as opposed to the 'Tibetan King' of Mustang (Line 120, 121 & 125). It is in this regard that the 'latching-on' of the Ghale as *outsider* kings/chieftains to the Tamu-mai may resonate more widely, as the imposition of distant-source royalty is a widespread phenomenon in Asia (and Africa; see e.g. Helms 1988). However, in a particularly Nepalese context, this may equally tell of the nature of its hierarchies prior to the rise of the Gorkha Kingdom in the eighteenth century. Between the disputed poles of the Western Malla and Kathmandu's polities, Nepal's history is one of petty kingdoms riven by displaced (migrating) hierarchies (see Lecomte-Tilouine 2005 concerning Nepalese history more generally). This might well reflect on the limited carrying capacity of its mountainous regions. Unless controlling long-distance trade or else determined by other extraneous factors, its 'pocketed', small-valley-system geography is inherently decentralized, and would have discouraged the rise of major hierarchical systems. Against this, the importation and/or attachment of somehow enhanced 'others' — whether by religious or (invented) lineage affiliation — might have been a sufficient catalyst to foster strictly local royalties.

Admittedly, this is a speculative argument but, as has been emphasized in the work of Macfarlane (1976; 2002), the possibilities of Nepal's landscape in relationship to its demographic history is something that cannot be overlooked. Indeed, it is an issue that even frames the country's recent political troubles. From the perspective of visiting its highland villages (even better appreciated when flying cross-country), you cannot but be struck by the incredible human labour that has gone into the sinuous terracing of its fields. That backbreaking investment, which otherwise could have gone into so many other things (e.g. schools, roads and other infrastructure), is itself something truly *monumental*.

Ascription, serialization and landscape knowledge

The 'archaeology of the Ghale Raja' has itself effectively run as a secondary theme throughout this volume, with a palace/house and fort ascribed to them respectively in Kohla and Manang (Figs. 5.4 & 4.42). Yet these share no obvious attributes. Time and changing architectural styles may here be relevant, but equally this may tell of the *arbitrary* nature of oral-tradition associations. At Kohla, perceived social and architectural *difference* have been conflated in the attribution of Structure 5. That is, indeed, a different building and may have been a 'palace', but it could equally have always been of some other entirely different 'special' function.

It was difficult to fathom how aspects of the ruins were 'known' (i.e. named): Was something mentioned in the *pye*? Did it feature in local folklore or was it simply a matter of recent ascription? An obvious case in point was the standing stone in front of the main village's King's House (Structure 19). When we arrived in 1994, it was then said to be where the King had tethered his horses. Yet trying to tie down this appellation never resulted in a satisfactory answer. Regardless, the idea of the 'horse tethering stone' had significant interpretative implications, as it speaks of the difference of the 'King' and the public performance of office. It, moreover, indicates that horses were kept within Kohla's mountainous setting, where none are used today. The latter, of course, finds resonance in relationship to the suggested etymology however questionable, of *Tamu-mai* as 'people of the horse', and further evokes a northern 'Mongolian-type' identity (the *pye* does itself outline that horses were kept at *Tasa Khowa*; see Chapter 2, Line 193). Nevertheless, the interview with Damarsingh in Chapter 5 demonstrates the kind of persuasive (and circular) logic bound with such folk ascription. Asked whether Kohla's inhabitants had horses (the question itself being, of course, leading), he replied: 'I don't know, maybe they came down riding horses. So that we saw the stable stone of the horse, also we heard that the Ghale king's horse was tied there, so they must have been riding horses'.

With so little context, there was never really any basis to evaluate this information (though see also the rock column 'dog-hitching post' atop *Oble*: Mumford 1990, fig. 9). Yet when writing-up in 2004 some insight came from an unexpected source. Judith Pettigrew, travelling to the area in the course of other researches, visited the palace at Lamjung — attributed as still another seat of the Ghale Raja — and returned with the photographs that feature it in this volume (Fig. 5.5: A & B). There, standing proud in front of the restored palace, was an animal sacrifice stone with a drilled hole through its top. This provides a degree of support to Kohla's interpretation, inasmuch as palaces can have stele set before them. One of our party in 1994, who had also been a part of the TPLS trek of two years before, had worked as a government agricultural commissioner. This led him to travel widely throughout the district and he must surely have seen the Lamjung palace and could, in effect, have carried with him the implications of the palace's upright. Yet, this still does not account for Kohla's 'horse stone' interpretation and where the many sources of 'folk' appraisal may derive from (i.e. so many undocumented visits). Often of unknown provenance, clearly *the repetition of an entitlement* can itself promote 'enshrinement'.

Otherwise, given the remoteness of the ruins and the active Tamu-mai folklore relating to them, who has had access to these areas to keep the 'story' alive and fixed? Kohla lies well off trekking routes, and village-

192

Figure 5.5. *Palace architecture: A) Lamjung Palace, with detail of sacrifice stone (B; photograph J. Pettigrew); C) the 'old' palace at Gorkha (HMG Dept. of Tourism, Nepal).*

based collection for plants and firewood would not go above the level of Karapu. Local people traverse the uplands for special occasions, such as inter-village visits and the Rhodi-related tours of youngsters, but the site is off any of these trails. Therefore, one is left with transhumant pastoralism and, until of late, the activity of hunters. (Though hunting was banned from Annapurnas with the creation of ACAP in the 1970s, we encountered professional hunting parties whilst in the uplands and bear-traps that had recently fallen into disuse were observed around Kohla.) As discussed above, attributes of the 'the wild' — variously pelts, feathers and hooves — are a crucial component of the shamans' apparel. In this capacity, it is surely relevant that, in the *pye*, the original discovery of Kohla as a locale is accredited to hunters, as within the predominant village-based framework of Himalayan communities, it is only they and pastoralists who regularly reconnoitre and traverse land. Other long-distance trade and pilgrimage routes could be another mechanism of 'outlying' landscape familiarity, but none pass near Kohla.

Seasonal, extra-village land-use 'cycles' — hunting and pastoralism — are, therefore, probably crucial as to how Kohla is/was known. As we have attempted to illustrate in Figure 5.6, it is by these means that the location was first encountered and, having established the settlement there, how the landscape beyond/below became known (surely augmented by trade connections). Thereafter, upon Kohla's (*et al.*) abandonment and a shift to more low-lying locales, the activities of hunters and pastoralists were probably the principal means by which an active connection was maintained with the earlier settlement sites.

To physically move through land, by these various means, is also to travel through time and connect with the past. In other words, *landscape binds up the past and present*, and variously structures (pre-)history and holds knowledge. A salient factor is, of course, the degree to which these travels are/were 'informed'. Prior to the 1992 TPLS trek (when 'shamans and elders' first really travelled the uplands *en masse*, following Yarjung's earlier journey), and aside perhaps from Ghanpokhara's pastoralists (see Chapter 4 above and Messerschmidt 1976b), the main basis of any knowledge of the ruins would have been snippets of generic information gleaned from village shamans and, otherwise, 'folk-type' ascription projected upon what was seen. Furthered by the project's expeditions, since the early 1990s a story of the past in 'real' landscape is being forged and situated. This reflects a major transformation of the *pye* narrative. Essentially, having a linear structure downward/southward through time, only through its recital and the 'backward' soul journey of the dead (in part, accompanied by shamans) does it have cyclical qualities. Now that some shamans (in the company of 'seniors and others') have begun to traverse the uplands and view sites, this is becoming something other than just a metaphysical encounter. The narrative is increasingly rooted to specific places, with visits thereto akin to *pilgrimage*. Indeed, in Chapter 2 Yarjung relates that he would like to see Kohla become a place of pilgrimage for the Tamu-mai.

When involved in fieldwork, we also variously re-enact or, in contrast, disavow mythologies. As with pilgrimages, *expeditions* are themselves a structuring device or legacy, in which we anticipate roles and don reactions accordingly (e.g. the 'arduous journey'). Archaeology certainly has its own ethos of myth. It is predominantly driven by discovery and revelation, such as finding the lost kingdom and/or city. Read the clues, undergo the hardship of travel, and eventually, deep within jungles or high in mountains, the long-sought answer will be stumbled upon and/or unearthed. Although admittedly common to much detection or scientific enquiry in general, unique in the case of expedition-based archaeology is the physical re-enactment of this 'scenario-cum-structure' (see Helms 1988, 80–94 concerning 'the ritual of travel'). Crucial to this is the idea of *journeying towards knowledge*, with the on-the-ground searches otherwise

substituting for long hours of laboratory work. This, of course, is only true of 'visitation' to research areas, and see, for example, Evans & Hodder (2006a,b) concerning sustained working in land; the loneliness of the 'view from the tent' being more integral to the alienation and deeply embedded adoption-cycle of anthropological experience (see e.g. Clifford & Marcus 1986, and also Yarjung's comments concerning the two disciplines in Chapter 2 above.)

Apparently, British officers of the 1903 Expeditionary Mission to Tibet were staggered to learn that lamas there then still believed the world to be flat (Allen 2004, 56; see also Tucci, in Maraini 2000, 281). This epitomizes the contrast of diverse culture geographies. In this case, one revolved around the exact trigonometries of army engineers (precise mapping being an adjunct of imperialism: see e.g. Stone 1988; Harley 1988) and, the other, the elaborate sacred geographies of Tibetan-Buddhism, of which symbolic enumeration and landscape 'personification' are key facets (e.g. Michaels 2003, 16; Dujardin 2003, 24 & 28; Evans & Humphrey 2003). The latter has Lhasa and Mount Kailash as the centre of its world; the other, London, or at least the Greenwich meridian. Clashes of world-views and geographies have, of course, occurred in many colonial and other historical cross-cultural circumstances. Yet this sense of an encounter of geographies is, of course, something quite different from the simultaneous co-existence of multiple cultural landscapes within one topography. Take, for example, Manang Valley: for its Buddhist communities, it is primarily a locale of concentric 'centrings': ringed zones of inside/out in relationship to village boundaries (and the temple precincts at their cores) and up/down in relationship to local mountain deities (e.g. Ramble 1995; Gutschow & Ramble 2003; Michaels 2003, 16–18; see also e.g. Allen 1972 and Gaenszle 1999 on vertical 'tiering' and classification generally). Yet, at the same time, like a handprint over the land, running across the valley are various historical, long-distance routes. Distant, non-residential communities (and sub-sectors thereof) have crossed it for trade, pilgrimage and also in their migrations. All have articulated the land and have their places within it; clearly it is not a matter of one cultural landscape, but many.

Situated at the western foot of the Thorung La Pass in Mustang, Muktinath offers an even more obvious case in point (see e.g. Messerschmidt & Sharma 1982; Messerschmidt 1989; Ehrhard 2003; Sihlé 2003), and is also insightful for the manner in which natural features can foster cultural places. It is certainly a 'charged' and significant locale for the Tamu-mai, and the possession of one of our team members there has been outlined above (see *Goin'*

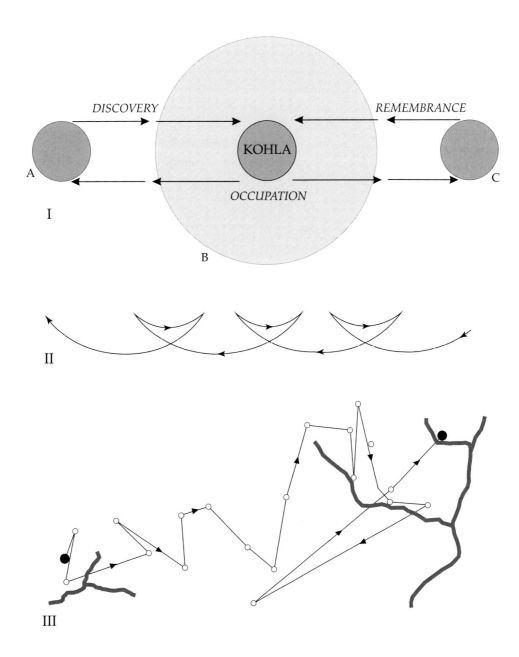

Figure 5.6. *Landscape 'cycling' and paths of knowledge: I) schematic illustration representing the movement/ reconnaissance of hunters and pastoralists, first from settlements north of the Annapurnas (A) leading to the discovery of Kohla's locale and later ensuring its remembrance from historical/present-day villages (C); 'B' indicates range of Kohla's larger contemporary settlement system and resource catchment. II) Magar shaman's forward/back dance routine (after Oppitz 1999, fig. 2; Oppitz sees this movement as an interaction between a clockwise life-direction and, its anti-clockwise opposite, the death-direction; its general right-to-left progression relates to the east–west 'sunwise' directionality of life). III) Tamang shamans' zig-zag recital traverses of ritual landscape 'stations' (circles, with grey tone indicating rivers; Höfer 1999, fig. 4); compare this to Figure 3.14's mapping.*

north, Chapter 4). Equally, for Tibetan-Buddhists, it is sacred for the shrine of the Serpent Deity, *Gawo Jogpa*, with Muktinath's Tibetan name, Chu-mig-brgya-rjsa — 'Hundred-odd Springs' — relating to the waters that rise there and which are channelled through

108 spouts. However, its greatest prominence is for Hindus, as a shrine of Vishnu, and 'Muktinath' itself accordingly translates as 'Lord of Salvation'. It also known by two other names, whose meanings are variants upon this and, too, as 'Salagrama' (by which

it has been identified in the *Mahabhaata*). The latter refers to its abundant fossils and, in fact, within its main temple Vishnu/Gawo Jogpa is represented as a black ammonite. There is, moreover, also a pool there, on whose surface methane naturally burns, and which is held to be sacred by both Hindus and Buddhists. That fire burns on water is understood to symbolize the world's harmony at the beginning of time, and Buddhists apparently collect rocks/fossil and soil from the location to respectively set into chortens and onto their fields to restore the qualities of the 'good age' (see Mumford 1990, 97).

As one of the eight most sacred shrines for Hindu Vashanavites, Muktinath has been a renowned place of pilgrimage for centuries and draws its faithful from both throughout Nepal and South Asia. Each year, it attracts thousands, mainly by one of two southern routes: along Manang Valley and over Thorung Pass; or up the Kali Gandaki River Valley from Pokhara. These are difficult ways that involve many days of travel, and during which there are proscriptions upon what sustenance Brahmins can partake of (and their social interactions generally). Conceptually, the landscape they traverse is not the same as for the Tamu-mai and other local communities; just as Muktinath itself is clearly a 'simultaneous locale', imbued with the different meanings of these diverse groups. (Today, it also has an existence as an 'electronic place' and there are numerous web-sites dedicated to it.)

Grappling with the complexities of such intensely multi-cultural/-dimensional landscapes, it may be useful to refer to Ingold's concepts/degrees of landed tenure (1986a,b). The immediate environs of Tamu-mai present 'home' villages are certainly envisaged as sedentary-type *territories*, with their transhumant pastures as outlying pockets thereof. Yet, linking them and extending through the historical/mythical landscape 'behind' (i.e. northward), relations are more akin to modes of hunter/gatherer *tenure*, with its investment localized to *paths and places*. The key point is that with historical migration, cultural landscapes are not a matter of territory *or* tenure as an either/or category, but of their multiple co-existence in relationship to past/present. By these means, within one area, the 'home territories' of its resident communities may be variously crossed by the paths and dotted with the places of other groups. Equally, these most basic ways of conceptualizing land — effectively, the 'circle' and 'line' — are, if not universal, then at least widespread, and landscapes will invariably have 'insiders and outsiders':

There is a sense in which an [English] open-field parish in the late eighteenth and early nineteenth centuries could be said to have a different geography according to who was looking at it: thus, for those of its inhabitants who rarely went beyond the parish boundary, the parish was so to speak at the centre of the landscape … For those inhabitants accustomed to moving outside it, however, and for those travellers who passed through it, the parish was … defined not by some circular system of geography but a linear one (Barrell 1972, 95).

Once accepting the premise that people moved in the past (as indeed they do today), variously carrying with them, 'dropping' and re-enacting their cultural geographies, then simplistic single-perspective phenomenological approaches to landscape (presuming cultural-topographic constants/uniformitarianism; e.g. Tilley 1994) are clearly woefully inadequate. Informing this is a concept of *serial culture geographies* (Evans 1998); for Tibetan-Buddhists there is Mount Kailash, *the* sacred mountain, but as the religion has spread, so have other versions of that landmark. These subsequent, more immediate points of centring are both integral unto themselves and resonate in relationship to their original 'model'. For the Tamu-mai, *Oble* seems to perform a comparable role (Fig. 4.38; see also Mumford 1990, 171–3, 186–90, figs. 8–11). It straddles a major conceptual divide, between a rooted, quasi-historical geography and a more mythic, or at least less precise, landscape north behind it. (It also marks a cultural divide between what are the predominantly Tibetan-Buddhist groups of Upper Mustang and the shamanistic/Hindu communities below it; Messerschmidt *et al.* 2004, 15.) In the distant past, it is also clear that there were other *Obles* — other Mountains of the Dead — that being something that inhabited landscapes need to have looming behind them (see Michaels 2003, 16 concerning 'flying mountains'). The act of migration, thereby, pre-supposes shifting cognitive centres and that places have *versions* in land. In other words, *with movement, landscape must be re-invested*. It is as if a cultural 'blueprint' has had to be re-enacted, with the things that a lived landscape must have being re-introduced.

In the case of prehistoric Europe, this would seem to have involved the interplay of distinct suites of monuments (e.g. Neolithic causewayed enclosures and long barrows), whereas for Buddhist communities in Mongolia, this entails *the* temple, *the* sacred spring, tree and/or cave and mountain gods and oboo cairns (Evans & Humphrey 2003). In the face of the repetition of such sacred grammars of monument- or landmark-types, it would be extraordinarily naive to think that these only arise from immediate circumstances. The mountain behind a village may well be sacred. Yet, equally, it was a good place to have a village sited in the plain before it, and cultural investment may require a sacred mountain behind settlement. Crucial here is that most archaeologists only study immediate, local-area settlement systems, and that 'culture' usually plays itself out across a much wider scale. (Concerning the place and role of mountains in sacred landscapes and cosmologies of Asia see, for example, Huber 1999; Hegewald forthcoming and papers in Macdonald 1997, e.g. Diemberger, Ehrhard and Ramble. See also Oppitz 1999, fig. 6, 196–200 concerning the geographic fixing of the cosmological universe of the Magar and its ritual/mythological journeys; many of the latter also correspond with active long-distance transhumant routes.)

Identity and settlement histories

Based on the similarity of construction technique and architectural style, there is every reason to think that all the settlements recorded above Karapu are broadly contemporary, and related to the same 'cultural horizon' (the use of this term being informed by Chapter 1's discussion of its implications). As related by Yarjung, during the fieldwork period these were thought to be 'dispersion' settlements post-dating Kohla's occupation. Yet this may well reflect a too-literal acceptance of Kohla as *the* last place the Tamu-mai lived as a people. Having the quality of myth, this is not something that we can necessarily take at face-value; individual villages are not 'islands' in which a culture/people thrive in pristine isolation. Given this, three alternative explanations suggest themselves:

1. Ethnic group membership is/was fluid, and involved more than just an original or historical 'homeland'-source identity. In other words, by inter-group marriage and various other means of association, people have subsequently 'become' Tamu (see Fisher 2001 on 'fluid identities').
2. There was not just one wave of southward migration, but also others and these may have involved alternative routes.
3. Kohla was but the main village within a larger settlement system; in which case, the other above-Karapu sites could have been associated villages (i.e. contemporary), thereby allowing for higher historical population estimates.

None of these are necessarily mutually exclusive and it may well be that all are applicable. However, at this point we will specifically explore the last: the idea of there being a broader settlement system.

In relationship to Kohla, the sites at Chikre and Khuindo seem 'outpost-like' and certainly they could not have been settlements of the same order. Here, perhaps the most relevant evidence is the trail-specific buildings at Chikre, Chromo and Kohla itself (and

possibly Michu and Hachu). Whether to facilitate and/or control upland travel, these 'stations' suggest regular movement through the highlands. While possibly only relating to long-distance trade, inter-village traffic would also be likely and, therefore, from this (and the shared style of these buildings and pottery), the contemporaneity of these settlements could be further inferred.

As outlined in Chapter 2, the evidence of the *pye* would itself indicate that Kohla was not isolated and that, at least subsequently, it was associated with settlements at Khuindo, Chromo, Chikre, Karapu, Hachu, Michu, Pamro, Naudi Rabro and Lelkhu (the latter three locales not visited by us); with Tasa Khowa and Thulhey named as places respectively for pasturing horses and goats/sheep. (Tapron[m] is mentioned as where a family arrived, but is not otherwise detailed.) Having raised doubts of the 'myth' of Kohla as fostering the Tamu-mai as a whole, it does actually seem feasible that it was their source/mother village. As demonstrated by Zubrow's demographic simulations (Chapter 4), it would be statistically possible for the 192 households enumerated within the *pye* to have generated their total present-day population of some half a million. Moreover, reiterating a point he raises, such population growth would, in fact, be far more sustainable when spreading the 'net of chance' between multiple/allied settlements, rather than by only concentrating population in one major village.

In an effort to further understand Kohla's settlement system, it is worth comparing the recovery of buildings on the sites we inspected with their listing in the *pye*:

Table 5.1. *Comparison between* pye-*enumerated and survey-distinguished households/buildings (the collective figure of 30 households at Michu, Hachu and Pamro cannot be evaluated, as the latter was not surveyed).*

Settlement	On-the-ground	*Pye* enumeration	Ratio
Kohla	55	80	1/1.5
Chikre	5/6	20	1/3.3–4
Khuindo	4	19	1/4.75
Chromo	2	8	1/4
Karapu	4	20	1/5

Given the degree of disturbance by pastoralists (especially north of its central sub-sector), that Kohla might, at its maximum, have seen 80 households seems quite reasonable from the 55 buildings recorded. Providing a ratio of 1/1.5 between the *pye's* enumeration and what was apparent on-the-ground, this is far higher than the 1/4–5 figures from the other sites. Even if we were to subtract Kohla's 21 single-cell buildings from its recovered total (on the basis that they may not all have been houses *per se*), this still only give a ratio of 1/2.35 and suggests that other factors must account for its greater 'representation' or survival. In other words, it is difficult to account for the degree of discrepancy between the *pye's* enumeration and how few buildings were evident at the other sites. Either it must be a matter of 'literary' exaggeration (for the extra-Kohla sites), or that Kohla's ruins have somehow been specially protected from pillaging/robbing. Alternatively, houses on the other sites might have been of a less robust building technique and hence are not as readily distinguished or have not survived as well.

Accepting that, for whatever reason, Kohla seems to be markedly 'different', it is worth interrogating the *pye* and the survey data for what they might tell of the character of its settlement system. In both, a tripartite ranking seems to be apparent. Below Kohla, there would be 19/20-household *villages* at Chikre, Khuindo and Karapu. Beneath this would be the eight households of Chromo and the 30 collectively enumerated for Michu, Hachu and Pamro. Assuming that the latter three were broadly equivalent settlements (though this might be at odds with Yarjung's remarks that Pamro was a mixed clan settlement, implying that it might have been larger), then it is perhaps reasonable to assign these to a lower level, 8/12-household tiering. These small settlements would essentially seem to correspond to the survey's trailside 'toll stations', and are best thought of as small *hamlets* (though their discrete trailside 'toll' function was also a part of the larger settlements — Chikre and possibly even Kohla). While the difference between a trailside 'hamlet' and 'village' would be in the magnitude of 100 per cent (i.e. 10 *vs* 20 households), the four-fold distinction between the three subsidiary village sites and Kohla itself would, again, emphasize the latter's unique status. In this capacity, while it would be logical to see Kohla's western and eastern sub-sectors as each being the equivalent of the subsequent 20-household villages settlements, this would not seem to be the case. With those sectors respectively having six and nine buildings *per se* recorded, if applying the site's 1.5 *pye*/survey ratio, this would amount to nine and 13.5 households, with both being more comparable to 'hamlet-scale' settlements (though subsequent population growth could be a factor given the settlement-dispersion/-off-shoot model).

Do we find any other expression of this apparent settlement ranking amongst the sites? Subtlety is, of course, impossible in this as no sites apart from Kohla were excavated as such. Nevertheless, these distinctions find expression in something so basic as the respective ranges of their building sizes. At none of the three recorded 'toll station' hamlets was

a building present with an area greater than 33.5 sq.m (Michu, Structure 1). In contrast, on the village sites (Kohla excluded), while also including a number of comparable small structures, a number were larger than 50 sq.m and in two instances were greater than 100 sq.m: Khuindo, Structure 1 and, if combined, Chikre Structures 2/3 would both cover *c.* 103 sq.m. However, at Kohla 12 buildings were larger than this, with five having areas greater than 150 sq.m. In this vein, there is also the manner in which the settlements were laid out. While the hamlets essentially straddle trails, the villages are arranged in a linear fashion (though no pattern as such could be distinguished for Karapu), whereas only at Kohla was there a sense of formal public space, with alleyways and 'plazas'/courts, etc.

Beyond this, though obviously contingent upon the relative size of their settlements (and, accordingly, the length of our stay at each locale), is that differences also seem reflected in the quantity of surface finds from these respective site categories. No ceramics whatsoever were recovered from the hamlets. Of the village sites, not surprisingly, most pottery was forthcoming from Kohla (and it had the greatest range of basic types represented; 4 *vs* 2/3); nevertheless, sherds were recovered from each. Unfortunately, the low density of the main worked stone-types recovered precludes any meaningful discussion of their distribution by site. It is, nevertheless, noteworthy that only at Kohla and Karapu were *chunis* found. As discussed in Chapters 3 and 4, the latter may reflect that site's interface with the 'lowland' settlements. Otherwise, the paucity of these mortars (and also querns) in the uplands could further attest to the reduced role of crop production in the highlands and, in contrast in this immediate context, the scale of Kohla's consumption.

Other potential distinctions of 'ranking' could also perhaps be anticipated, but, without further investigation, cannot be adequately addressed. Did, for example, industry (i.e. metalworking or large-scale milling) only occur at Kohla? Equally, did the smaller villages also include the residences of clan chieftains, or were these restricted to Kohla, where alone the 'houses of kings' occurred?

Finally, the *pye's* enumeration of the Kohla settlement's houses might indeed reflect upon one other aspect of its system. This relates to the land's carrying capacity. Its 20-household villages would suggest populations in each of perhaps 80–100 persons. While seemingly high in the light of the paucity of actual buildings apparent, nevertheless, it is conceivable that, by concentrating on pastoral activities, such communities would reflect the upper size limit of settlements, given the nature of the land and a 'reasonable' expectation of their resource catchments. By the same token, based on the *pye* data, Kohla would itself have had a population of some 300–400, which seems extraordinarily high considering its locale. Sustained perhaps by trade and taxation, Kohla may well have had to import food stuffs. It is this, and what seems to be the obvious presence of a public authority, that primarily distinguishes it from the other settlements.

Acknowledging that Kohla related to a broader settlement system, the issue then becomes the question of its overall size and configuration/orientation. Any interpretation in this regard can only be tentative based on the partial (and biased) nature of our surveys. Due to the project's 'host' connections, we repeatedly went up from Yangjakot and, therefore, it is natural to privilege this north–south axis into the uplands. Such an orientation would complement the general downwards shift of villages over time, with the settlements at Nadar Pa and Kui Choh (respectively above Warchok and Yangjakot) as the natural successors of, for example, Khuindo, Chikre and Kohla itself. Yet here we must be wary of too readily identifying our traverses with those in the past. There are other routeways through these lands, and it is unfortunate that — as we always intended to — we were unable to approach Kohla from different directions: going west from Ghanpokhara (as privileged by Messerschmidt 1976b); and east from Tangting. Not coming in along the latter route is particularly regrettable, given the report of ruins above that village (Damarsingh pers. comm. and in Temple 1993). Although involving a very steep climb, it is the most direct way to Kohla and can apparently be negotiated in a day. Given this, it is conceivable that the Kohla 'system' was actually riverine, along the Gnach Khola and, apart from Kohla, what we have recorded (and even then in part) are only its 'headwater sites'.

The issue of Kohla's orientation in landscape equally reflects upon the route by which it may have been first reconnoitred. Within the *pye,* there is a strong sense of north-to-south movement, and particularly relevant is the story of the hunters coming down through the Annapurnas and recognizing the qualities of Kohla as a place. Yet this need not necessarily define a direct route and there are many other lateral 'possibilities'. Yarjung has identified the pass over Ekrai Mountain as the most likely way by which Kohla's inhabitants originally reached the site through the mountains, but this is certainly not a major or easy route. (The 1992 TPLS trek going up from Kohla into Manang, crossed it and the going proved difficult. High and cold, though eventually 'do-able', it was not easy to work out a trail.) Here, of course we must

guard against too-normative readings of landscape (i.e. what is 'arduous'), but essentially there are two obvious ways into Kohla from the north. One, east through Manang Valley, along the Marsyandi River and then down to and west from the area of Ghanpokhara (which first implies traverse over the Thorung La pass into Manang). The other, more major, way would be down through the valley of the Kali Gandaki, then up the Madi River Valley to Tangting, and from there east into Kohla.

The possibility of these more indirect (though easier) routes to some extent could question the steady, southward impetus of the Tamu-mai narrative. Can we actually accept the idea that *a* people move *en masse* from village-to-village only to cross the Annapurnas, settle as a group at Kohla (and subsequently its related settlements) and then disperse to lower historical village locations? While seemingly born out in the consistency of the recital of the *pye*'s 'historical' data — and, as evoked by its refrain, 'Tamu people crossed many rivers and hills' — can this really be the case? Of the much more localized settlement dislocations described in the Northern Magar origin stories, the search for good hunting grounds and the spirit-vexed or unhealthy state of villages (e.g. scabies- and fever-infested) have variously been identified as motivating factors (and 'the whip of the querulous ancestors whims'; Oppitz 1983, 201–2). Yet, based on known evidence, as outlined in the *pye,* social/cultural groups simply do not move in such a unilineal manner over centuries, let alone millennia. Therefore, is this really a matter of a partial, historical myth/'truth' that has been regularized? Although a compelling story on which to focus identity, when pressed some people will admit to the possibility of a different historical reality and acknowledge that there might well have been another route down the Kali Gandaki into the Ghandrung area. What this simply attests to is that 'pasts' are complicated and can simultaneously entail contradictory ideas. This, moreover, is comparable to the fact that today the Tamu-mai seem so thoroughly settled and village-based (though, admittedly, having a large 'away' urban and overseas component), while in their past, pastoralism loomed so large and *historical movement* (i.e. sustained migration) is such a major facet of their identity.

Past/present — new orthodoxies

Memory does not, of course, equate with chronology as, unaided, it fragments and becomes disjointed. In Figure 5.6 patterns of landscape 'prospection/migration' and 'settlement' are shown as if unfolding in time. Following the path of writing, they are depicted as if progressing forward from left to right, whereas 'remembrance' is backward (right to left). This is logical, as memory invariably implies reversal and cannot work forward (though past-influenced presents are often projected into the future). It does not, however, mean that memory necessarily flows successively, like an uninterrupted stream, from the present backwards.

Yarjung has constructed his *pye* map from the more recent villages back through time (from left to right) and ultimately to the origins of the world (Figs. 2.4 & 2.5). In this manner, it is the opposite of the *pye* itself, that runs from the past to the 'more' present — from Line zero through to 509 (see Fig. 5.6 and Höfer 1999, 222 concerning how the northward 'verbal journeys' of Tamang shamans reverse the narrative chain of their cultural myths). Yarjung's approach is oddly reminiscent of how the archaeologist Christopher Hawkes advocated the study of the past should best be understood. In contrast to the other leading prehistorians of his day (e.g. Childe, Piggott or Grahame Clark), whose approaches were inherently evolutionary and 'origins-led', he was primarily concerned with the prehistoric/Roman interface of proto-historical studies and proposed that the past should be conceived of backwards: that is, from the known to the unknown, and present/recent to the distant past (see Evans 1998). Crucial to this is what is held to be the starting point of study, whether it lies in theory ('origins' inherently being an ideal/theoretical construct) or is empirically led. From the perspective of methodology, the latter 'Hawkesian' approach is how much landscape survey advances in the search for fixed points by which to hang sequences upon. Take, for instance, the upstanding remains of what are known to be medieval fields, that may overlie traces of an earlier boundary system. The absolute date of the latter may not be established, but, in reference to historical datums, it can then be attributed to pre-medieval times. Also often rooted in the most 'knowable', typological datums — be they pottery- or building-styles — can equally anchor *relative* sequences. The logic propelling such systems only really changes when either dated imports are recovered (e.g. Wheeler's use of Roman coins in India's sequences) or, since the second half of the twentieth century, when absolute-dating techniques such as radiocarbon are introduced.

Present-to-past tensions or, at least oscillations, are even reflected in the act of excavation itself. In stratified sites, we *dig down* going deeper into the past, but invariably sites are 'written up', dealing with the earliest expression/phases first and progressing to the most recent (see e.g. Thomas 2004 for further discussion). A comparable dualism can even be found in the paths or tracks that feature in so much European-tradition landscape painting. Such routes are essentially a contemplative device of space/time and, of course, we equally contemplate our pasts and futures. Think, for example, of Hobbema's *The Avenue at Middelharnis* of 1689 in the National Gallery, London (Fig. 5.7), though any number of similar compositions could be cited instead. With its lowland-scape split by a tree-flanked road that runs through its centre, does this way lead forward or back? The route narrows with depth and, by the conventions of perspective, it is thereby held to *carry* the viewer *back* into the picture plane. Its relationship to time is, therefore, ambiguous. The picture's path both carries us forward in time and space, and also back into itself. It can simultaneously be where 'we', the viewers, are going, but equally — by turning around and glancing over our shoulder — where we've been.

If understood to be the latter, then this further comments on the nature of paths linking the past/present. Behind, in time, things seem narrow, and forward/near the way widens. This foreground broadening suggests other possibilities. Had not historical contingency intervened, the later/'near' expression of something in the past — be it a pottery-style or building-type or even 'a people' — could well have been very different. If, for example, in a given year, a certain pass through the mountains had been blocked with snow and impeded migration or any number of small events, ranging from the travels of individual members of a community to the chance impact of distant visitors on 'the local', then the outcome of history (and the present) could have been re-directed.

What all this underlines is that the study/construction of the past is not just a matter of either/or — from the present back or from the past forward — as their interrelationship soon enfolds as a hermeneutic. This can variously be conceived of as a circle, hopefully spiralling towards some sense of 'best fit' resolution (Hodder 1999; Evans & Hodder 2006a), though in a Himalayan context, the forward/back progression of shamans' dances may be more appropriate (with the zig-zag recital 'paths' of Tamang shamans, perhaps, being an even more accurate image: Fig. 5.6:II & III). Whatever, with fieldwork moments of quasi-independent knowledge emerge and coalesce, such as with Kohla and its radiocarbon assays. Yet, despite that scientific support the site now has, Kohla still does not stand alone; it remains 'named' and part of a broader narrative binding up the past and present. The hermeneutic of this interaction, in fact, resonates with the cyclical structure of our fieldwork treks. It was only going there and back again, along the same route, that allowed any sense of context

200

Figure 5.7. *The Ambiguous Path - Forward/Back: cartoon rendering of Hobbema's* The Avenue at Middelharnis *of 1689 (V. Herring after The National Gallery, London original). The ambiguous time/space directionality of such 'way pictures' is, in this case (and typical of much Dutch landscape painting), clarified by a close reading of its moral intent. Arguably, a parable in landscape, the clue lies in the age and management of its trees. The saplings being pruned in the right foreground obviously represent the 'disciplined grooming of youth'. Otherwise, the trees mature with perspective depth along the 'proper route', and the avenue's straight upright trunks are the result of regular 'shred' pruning and demand near-constant care (R. Darrah pers. comm.). The central wood-lined path leads to the industrious trading port of Middelharnis, with its prominent church steeple. However, to achieve that end, the viewer/individual must first avoid the 'wrong way': the unkempt woodlot left and, also, the middle-ground right-fork, whereupon a gentlemen converses with a young lady (presumably of ill-repute).*

There is, of course, a vast Western canon of allegorical landscape imagery and it is an ethos that has even extended to garden design (e.g. Charlesworth 2003). This sense of the 'moral way' is perhaps most succinctly rendered in Victorian/ Edwardian versions of the game, 'Snakes and Ladders' (thought itself to originate from India); its players rising when landing on the squares of virtue (faith, thrift or generosity, etc.) and descended down its snakes through the encounter with sin/evil (vanity, greed or drunkenness, etc.).

to be assembled. 'Going up' into the highland from today's villages was, in effect, to progress back from the present, while on the downward-legs we worked back from the past to the present.

Ultimately, Kohla's narrative is one of *loss* and dispersion from the place of final collectivity (and the rule of 'kings'). Yet, with its very distinct tripartite layout, Kohla may simultaneously have been both a 'first' and 'last place' — somewhere of coalescence and the coming together of migrating groups (and their stories) and from where one identity and *the* single-past narrative was forged (see also Ramble 1997b concerning potential myths of 'northern'/Tibetan descent and

migration). The active construction of group identities, both in the past itself and the present, has drawn upon pasts as a basis of legitimacy, difference and authority. In this manner, the building of group identities is not dissimilar to the forging of narratives (or even individual personalities). Adopting a suitable style/stance and tone — just as in the narrative portions of this text itself, personas have been donned — facets are variously emphasized, backgrounded or even denied. The borders between narratives, histories and fictions become vague as the structures of cultural identity and stories interweave and play-out over time. The difference in the construction of group identities and cultural

Figure 5.8. *Electronic Communities and Overseas 'Fosterings': Tamu Pye Lhu Sangh, UK Branch (est. 2005) festival poster (above, note the central image of the Pokhara Kohibo) and below, their 'Tamu History' web-page.*

narratives, as opposed to those of individuals, lies in the importance of *shared* cultural understanding (i.e. language) and experience (i.e. history). Yet these identities and narratives, at least the latter, need not amount to a universal understanding. Here the role of cultural authority in fostering dominant stories and myths becomes significant, structuring how orthodoxies come into being. The oral and written past will always have been disciplined by predominant social actors; what is crucial is who sponsors(-ed) that past to 'act'.

Propelled by political, demographic and economic change (e.g. urban migration), Pokhara has now become a new centre of Tamu-mai collectivity (and there are even overseas 'fosterings'; see Fig. 5.8). Today, new orthodoxies are there being actively promoted, with the past being enlisted and sponsored in the cause of the present. For example, Macfarlane introduces his 1997(a) paper by quoting from a fax he received in 1992, outlining a series of resolutions that had then just been passed by a nation-wide Gurung (Tamu-mai) conference held in Pokhara:

1. Gurung history was written and distorted by Brahmins.
2. There are no inferior and superior clan groups in Gurung society.
3. The traditional Gurung priests are the Pachyu and the Klabri; Lamas are a more recent addition.

While the rationale behind the first two should be obvious in the context of this volume and the current understanding of Tamu-mai history (with the second relating to their egalitarian ethos *vis-à-vis* caste relations; see also Glover 2004), it is the third which need concern us. Over the last decades, the livelihood of shamans has come to be threatened by Lamaist practices. Relating to this, the resolution represents an attempt to produce an official version of the past. The Lamaist component of their rituals is thereby stamped as being later than 'indigenous' shamanism, implying that *the/a* past can be publicly endorsed. (Hay-Edie 2001 presents a comparable UNESCO-sponsored adjudication of the cultural landscape of Dolpo as a Bonpo World Heritage Site, which implies only one reading of land.)

To 'Western' sensibilities, there can be something disturbing about such a formal adjudication of history. Yet it is necessary to see this within the broader dynamics of group identity (re-)formation and, in effect, *becoming Tamu* (again). Once more, this finds resonance with the past, as it is only a sixth of the way through the *pye* (line 79) that 'the people' achieved the entitlement 'Tamu' (implying that they were something different before). Equally, over the last 15 years there has been a re-formulation of their identity, a new 'becoming Tamu', in contrast to the Nepali-defined 'Gurung' (see e.g. Macfarlane 1997a, 189–90; Pettigrew 1995; 2000).

An intentional linkage has certainly been made by the TPLS between the *Kohibo* and Kohla. The Kohla Project itself came to be bound up with these processes, with the University of Cambridge, in effect, serving as a basis of outside authority. This, of course, is the potential price of any *engaged archaeology*. Any research must ultimately be considered an *intervention* and, one way or another, fieldwork is implicated in the broader construction of the past itself. The moot point is whether this is an active or passive engagement. Invariably, there are pitfalls with such approaches, primarily the risk of misuse by fostering an historically informed ethnic chauvinism. Though, returning to Ingold's arguments of land/territory relations cited above (1986a), there can be some assurance in the tenured (-only) character of the Tamu-mai to the past. Theirs is not a matter of indigenous territorial land claims (see e.g. Rowlands 1994), but the recognition of their routes ('roots') and the axis of their arrival into Nepal. Nevertheless, finally completing this text during the summer of 2005, the celebration of multi-ethnicity which first propelled the project in the early 1990s now seems a much more fraught and complex undertaking.

The project did succeed in its most basic directive. Based on our interim reports and various presentations during the course of fieldwork, today Kohla features in both the historic consciousness of the local communities (now as a 'real place') and in recent 'official' histories (e.g. Whelpton 2005, 13). Beyond this, the degree to which the project realized its broader community-based aims is as yet unknown, and this must await the final reception of its publications and archives. Yet, as should be clear from this text (and our conduct throughout), in such involvement there is always the pressing need to act responsibly and not to compromise professional ethics to immediate agendas. The doubts and alternative interpretations that permeate this volume, are those common to any thorough archaeology; *situating practice* does not bring with it any greater absolutism.

Political events in Nepal cut the project short. Though amply demonstrating the quality of the upland sites and that archaeological fieldwork is feasible in these extreme conditions, the excavations were effectively stillborn and they (and this volume) should have been so much more. We should have gone on to sample a range of Kohla's public spaces (and its 'back' middens, etc.) and also its diverse structures. Thereafter, one of each of its main building types was to have been selected from its 'quarters' for full excavation (including one of the King's Houses), with the aim of also reconstructing at least one as a guest lodge-*cum*-display area for visitors. Full environmental sampling should have been undertaken (especially for pollen) and the site's environs thoroughly surveyed for its resource potential, particularly metal ores.

Equally, we wanted to proceed northwards, and further explore sites and routes out through the Annapurnas that way, just as we should have also gone down through Tangting to see if that was the main route to the site and record the settlement ruins said to lie in that direction. Moreover, it was always the intention of the project (and in our agreement with the government) to test-excavate and date the other sites found on the Yangjakot/Karapu route north. Ultimately, there was even the aim of having Kohla accredited as a World Heritage site, and also plans to extend the survey throughout the ACAP territory and train their rangers in the detection and protection of sites.

Yes, much was intended, but contemporary events intervened. While risking the cliché of a truism, what this demonstrates is the constant impact of history. There is/was never a timeless past, just as there is no pristine ethnography. Faced with the scale of what occurred in Nepal, one would have to be extraordinarily single-minded to think that the termination of the Kohla Project was itself a major loss, and such events certainly put archaeology into perspective. History is unfolding in the country; for some a source of hope, for many others a cause of personal tragedy. Whatever the outcome, it will not bring about a clean slate, free of social/ethnic rivalry and the vestiges of the past (both real and mythical). *The world is invariably mixed*, and naiveté can never be a valid response to the sweep of time and events, whether in the past or present.

References

Adkins, L., 2003. *Empires of the Plain: Henry Rawlinson and the Lost Languages of Babylon*. London: Harper Collins.

Aldenderfer, M., 2003a. Moving up in the world. *American Scientist* 91, 542–9.

Aldenderfer, M., 2003b. Domestic rDo ring? A new class of standing stones from the Tibetan plateau. *The Tibet Journal* 28, 3–20.

Aldenderfer, M., 2005. Caves as sacred places on the Tibetan Plateau. *Expedition* 47, 8–13.

Aldenderfer, M., forthcoming. Defining Zhang zhung ethnicity: an archaeological perspective from far western Tibet, in *Proceedings of the Tenth IATS Conference*. Leiden: Brill.

Aldenderfer, M. & Z. Yinong, 2004. The prehistory of the Tibetan plateau to the seventh century AD: perspectives and research from China and the West since 1950. *Journal of World Prehistory* 18, 1–55.

Allard, D.J., 2000. The Subalpine Fir Forest Zone of Lamjung Himal, Nepal: Vegetation Types, Forest Dynamics and Human Impacts. Unpublished PhD thesis, University of Cambridge, Department of Geography.

Allen, C., 2002. *The Buddha and the Sahibs*. London: John Murray.

Allen, C., 2004. *Duel in the Snows: the True Story of the Younghusband Mission to Lhasa*. London: John Murray.

Allen, N., 1972. The vertical dimension in Thulung classification. *Journal of the Anthropological Society of Oxford* 3, 81–94.

Alt, K.W., J. Burger, A. Simons, *et al.*, 2003. Climbing into the past — first Himalyan mummies discovered in Nepal. *Journal of Archaeological Science* 30, 1529–35.

Anderson, B., 1991. *Imagined Communities*. London: Verso Publishing.

Anderson, E.N., 1988. *The Food of China*. New Haven (CT): Yale University Press.

Arnold, D., 2004. Race, place and bodily difference in early nineteenth-century India. *Historical Research* 77, 254–73.

Asouti, E., 2001. Charcoal Analysis from Çatalhöyük and Pynarbay, Two Neolithic Sites in the Konya Plain, South-central Anatolia, Turkey. Unpublished PhD thesis, University College London.

Auster, P., 1987. *In the Country of Last Things*. London: Faber.

Barrell, J., 1972. *The Idea of Landscape and the Sense of Place, 1730–1840*. Cambridge: Cambridge University Press.

Barth, F., 1987. *Cosmologies in the Making*. Cambridge: Cambridge University Press.

Basso, K., 1984. 'Stalking with stories': names, places and moral narratives among the Western Apache, in *Text, Play and Story: the Construction and Reconstruction of Self and Society*, ed. E. Bruner. Washington (DC): American Ethnological Society, 19–55.

Bellezza, J.V., 2002. *Antiquities of Upper Tibet: Pre-Buddhist Archaeological Sites on the High Plateau*. Delhi: Adroit Publishers.

Bellezza, J.V., 2004. Ancient Tibet: bringing to light the forgotten. *Athena Review* 3, 1–11.

Bellwood, P. & C. Renfrew (ed.), 2002. *Examining the Farming/Language Dispersal Hypothesis*. (McDonald Institute Monographs.) Cambridge: McDonald Institute for Archaeological Research.

Bender, B., 1999. Subverting the Western gaze: mapping alternative worlds, in *The Archaeology and Anthropology of Landscape: Shaping your Landscape*, eds. P. Ucko & R. Layton. London: Routledge, 31–45.

Bhattarai, S., R.P. Chaudhary & R.S. Taylor, 2006. Ethnomedicinal plants used by the people of Manang District, central Nepal. *Journal of Ethnobiology and Ethnomedicine* 2, 41.

Bishop, B.C., 1990. *Karnali under Stress: Livelihood Strategies and Seasonal Rhythms in a Changing Nepal Himalaya*. (Geography Research Papers 228–9.) Chicago (IL): University of Chicago.

Bista, D.B., 1967. *People of Nepal*. Kathmandu: HMG Ministry of Information and Broadcasting.

Bista, D.B., 1977. Patterns of migration in Nepal, in *Himalaya: Ecologie-Ethnologie*. Paris: Centre National de la Recherche Scientifique, 397–9.

Boon, J.A., 1982. *Other Tribes, Other Scribes*. Cambridge: Cambridge University Press.

Bose, N.K., 1941. The Hindu methods of tribal absorption. *Science and Culture* 7, 188–94.

Boulnois, L., 1989. Chinese maps and prints on the Tibet-Gorkha War of 1788–92. *Kailash* 15, 85–112.

Bradley, R., 2000. *An Archaeology of Natural Places*. London: Routledge.

Buchanan-Hamilton, F., 1819. *An Account of the Kingdom of Nepal*. Edinburgh: Archibald Constable.

Buchli, V. & G. Lucas, 2001. *Archaeologies of the Contemporary Past*. London: Routledge.

Calvino, I., 1972. *Invisible Cities*. Turin: Giulio Einaudi Editore.

Caplan, L., 1990. 'Tribes' in the ethnography of Nepal: some comments on a debate. *Contributions to Nepalese Studies* 17, 129–45.

Caplan, L., 1995. *Warrior Gentlemen: 'Gurkhas' in the Western Imagination*. Oxford: Berghahn.

Chakrabarti, D., 1988. *A History of Indian Archaeology: From the Beginning to 1947*. New Delhi: Munshiram Manoharlal.

Chakrabarti, S., 2002. Giuseppe Tucci: his realm of archaeological adventure and discovery in Trans-Himalaya, in *Perspective of Buddhist Studies: Giuseppe Tucci Birth Centenary Volume*, ed. P. Jash. New Delhi: Kaveri, 98–104.

Charlesworth, M., 2003. Movement, intersubjectivity, and mercantile morality at Stourhead, in *Landscape Design and the Experience of Motion*, ed. M. Conan. Washington (DC): Dumbarton Oaks Research Library and Collection, 263–85.

Chatterjee, A., 2002. Tucci's scientific expeditions to Nepal and the Bon religion, in *Perspective of Buddhist Studies: Giuseppe Tucci Birth Centenary Volume*, ed. P. Jash. New Delhi: Kaveri, 86–97.

Chemjong, I.S., 1958. *Introduction to Limbu-Nepali Dictionary*. Kathmandu: Nepal Academy.

Chemjong, I.S., 1967. *History and Culture of the Kirat People*. Phidim: Tumeng Hang.

Des Chene, M., 1992. Traversing social space: Gurung journeys. *Himalayan Research Bulletin* 12, 1–10.

Des Chene, M., 1996. Ethnography in the *Janajati-yug*: lessons from reading *Rodhi* and other Tamu-mai writings. *Studies in Nepali History and Society* 1, 97–161.

Childe, V.G., 1947. *History*. London: Cobbett Press.

Clifford, J. & G.E. Marcus (eds.), 1986. *Writing Culture: the Poetics and Politics of Ethnography*. Berkeley (CA): University of California Press.

Coningham, R. & A. Schmidt, 1998. Ancient Buddhist sites in Nepal. *Minerva* 9, 40–42.

Coonerton, P., 1989. *How Societies Remember*. Cambridge: Cambridge University Press.

Darnal, P., 2002. Archaeological activities in Nepal since 1893 AD to 2002 AD. *Ancient Nepal* 150, 39–48.

Dart, F.E. & P.L. Pradhan, 1967. Cross-cultural teaching of science. *Science* 155, 649–65.

Dewey, C., 1972. Images of the village community. *Modern Asian Studies* 6, 291–328.

Diemberger, H., 1997. Beyul Khenbalung, the hidden valley of the Artemisia: on Himalayan communities and their sacred landscape, in *Mandala and Landscape*, ed. A.W. Macdonald. New Delhi: D.K. Printworld, 287–334.

van Driem, G., 2002. Tibeto-Burman phylogeny and prehistory: languages, material culture and genes, in *Examining the Farming/Language Dispersal Hypothesis*: eds. P. Bellwood & C. Renfrew. (McDonald Institute Monographs.) Cambridge: McDonald Institute for Archaeological Research, 233–49.

Dujardin, M., 2003. Demolition and re-erection in contemporary Rukubji, Bhutan: building as cyclical renewal and spatial mediation, in *Sacred Landscapes of the Himalayas*, eds. N. Gutschow, A. Michaels, C. Ramble & E. Steinkellner. Vienna: Austrian Academy of Sciences Press, 19–38.

Duncan, J.S., 1990. *The City as Text: the Politics of Landscape Interpretation in the Kandyan Kingdom*. Cambridge: Cambridge University Press.

Ehrhard, F.K., 1997. A 'hidden land' in the Tibetan–Nepalese borderlands, in *Mandala and Landscape*, ed. A.W. Mcdonald. New Delhi: D.K. Printworld, 335–64.

Ehrhard, F.K., 2003. Pilgrims in search of sacred lands, in *Sacred Landscapes of the Himalayas*, eds. N. Gutschow, A. Michaels, C. Ramble & E. Steinkellner. Vienna: Austrian Academy of Sciences Press, 95–110.

Evans, C., 1983. On the Jube line: campsite studies in Kurdistan. *Archaeological Review from Cambridge* 2, 67–77.

Evans, C., 1990. 'Power on silt': towards an archaeology of the East India Company. *Antiquity* 64, 643–61.

Evans, C., 1998. Historicism, chronology and straw men: situating Hawkes' ladder of inference. *Antiquity* 72, 398–404.

Evans, C., 1999. Cognitive maps and narrative trails: fieldwork with the Tamu-mai/Gurung of Nepal, in *Shaping Your Landscape: the Archaeology and Anthropology of Landscape*, eds. P. Ucko & R. Layton. London: Routledge, 439–57.

Evans, C., 2004. Material and oral records: a shamans' meeting in Pokhara, in *Material Engagements: Studies in Honour of Colin Renfrew*, eds. N. Brodie & C. Hills. (McDonald Institute Monographs.) Cambridge: McDonald Institute for Archaeological Research, 165–80.

Evans, C., forthcoming. Worlds in small: carrying and modelling knowledge.

Evans, C. & D. Gibson, 2003. The Sinja Valley excavation in 2000 AD. *Ancient Nepal* 153, 15–42.

Evans, C. & I. Hodder, 2006a. *A Woodland Archaeology: the Haddenham Project*, vol. I. (McDonald Institute Monographs.) Cambridge: McDonald Institute for Archaeological Research.

Evans, C. & I. Hodder, 2006b. *Marshland Communities and Cultural Landscape: the Haddenham Project*, vol. II. (McDonald Institute Monographs.) Cambridge: McDonald Institute for Archaeological Research.

Evans, C. & C. Humphrey, 2002. After-lives of the Mongolian Yurt: the archaeology of a Chinese tourist camp. *Journal of Material Culture* 7, 189–210.

Evans, C. & C. Humphrey, 2003. History, timelessness and the monumental: the oboos of the Mergen environs, Inner Mongolia. *Cambridge Archaeological Journal* 13(2), 195–211.

Evans, C., J. Pettigrew, U. Acharya & Y. Tamu, 2002. The Kohla Project 2000: the first season of excavation. *Ancient Nepal* 150, 1–19.

Feldman, M. & M. Kislev, 2007. Domestication of emmer wheat and evolution of free-threshing tetraploid wheat. *Israeli Journal of Plant Sciences* 55, 207–21.

Fisher, W.F., 2001. *Fluid Boundaries: Forming and Transforming Identity in Nepal*. New York (NY): Columbia University Press.

Fricke, T., 1986. *Himalayan Households: Tamang Demography and Domestic Processes*. Ann Arbor (MI): UMI Research Press.

Fuller, D.Q., 2002. Fifty years of archaeobotanical studies in India: laying a solid foundation, in *Indian Archaeology in Retrospect*, vol. III: *Archaeology and Interactive Disciplines*, eds. S. Settar & R. Korisettar. New Delhi: Manohar, 247–363.

Fuller, D.Q., 2006. Agricultural origins and frontiers in South Asia: a working synthesis. *Journal of World Prehistory* 20, 1–86.

Fuller, D.Q. & M. Madella, 2001. Issues in Harappan archaeobotany: retrospect and prospect, in *Indian Archaeology in Retrospect*, vol. II: *Protohistory*, eds. S. Settar & R. Korisettar. New Delhi: Manohar, 317–90.

Fürer-Haimendorf, C., 1975. *Himalayan Traders: Life in Highland Nepal*. London: John Murray.

Gaenszle, M., 1999. Travelling up — travelling down: the vertical dimension in Mewahang Rai journeys, in

Himalayan Space: Cultural Horizons and Practices, eds. B. Bickel & M. Gaenszle. Zurich: Völkerkundemuseum, 135–63.

Gaenszle, M., 2004. Brian Hodgson as ethnographer and ethnologist, in *The Origins of Himalayan Studies: Brian Houghton Hodgson in Nepal and Darjeeling 1820–1858,* ed. D.M. Waterhouse. London: RoutledgeCurzon, 206–26.

Gajurel, C.L. & K.K. Vaidya, 1994. *Traditional Arts and Crafts of Nepal.* New Delhi: S. Chand & Co.

Gaur, R.D., 1999. *Flora of the Distirct Garhwal, Northwest Himalaya (with ethnobotanical notes).* Srinagar, Garhwal: Transmedia.

Gayden, T., A.M. Cadenas, M. Reguerio, *et al.,* 2007. The Himalayas as a directional barrier to gene flow. *The American Journal of Genetics* 80, 884–94.

Geertz, C., 1973. Thick description: towards an interpretative theory of culture, in *The Interpretation of Cultures,* ed. C. Geertz. London: Basis Books, 3–30.

Glover, W., 1970. Cognate counts via the Swadesh list in some Tibeto-Burman languages of Nepal, in *Occasional Papers of the Wolfenden Society of Tibeto-Burman Linguistics,* vol. III: *Lexical Lists and Comparative Studies,* ed. F.K. Lehman. Urbana (IL): University of Illinois, 23–6.

Glover, W., 2004. Ouch! Don't Print That! Political Correctness in Gurung Lexicography. Paper presented at the Asia Lexicography Conference, Chiangmai, Thailand.

Gombrich, E., 1982. Mirror and map: theories of pictorial representation, in *Image and the Eye: Further Studies in the Psychology of Pictorial Representation.* London: Phaidon Press, 172–214.

Gomme, G.L., 1890. *The Village Community: With Special Reference to the Origin and Form of its Survivals in Britain.* London: Walter Scott.

Goody, J., 1987. *The Interface Between the Written and the Oral.* Cambridge: Cambridge University Press.

Gosden, C., 1999. *Anthropology and Archaeology: a Changing Relationship.* London: Routledge.

Gosden, C., 2004. *Archaeology and Colonialism: Cultural Contact from 5000 BC to the Present.* Cambridge: Cambridge University Press.

Graafen, R. & C. Seeber, 1992–93. Important trade routes in Nepal and their importance to the settlement process. *Ancient Nepal* 132–3, 34–48.

Grove, J.M., 1988. *The Little Ice Age.* London: Methuen.

Gurung, G.M., 1988. The process of identification and Sanskritization: the Duras of West Nepal. *Kailash* 14, 41–61.

Gurung, H.B., 1983. *Map of Nepal: Inventory and Evaluation.* Bangkok: White Orchid Press.

Gurung, H.B., 2002. *Pokhara Valley: a Geographical Survey.* Kathmandu: Nepal Geographical Society. (First published in 1965 by the Dept. of Geography, School of Oriental and African Studies, University of London.)

Gurung, S.B., 1957. *Gurungko Vamsavali.* Benares: Gurung Welfare Association.

Gutschow, N. & C. Ramble, 2003. Up and down, inside and outside: notions of space and territory in Tibetan villages of Mustang, in *Sacred Landscapes of the Himalayas,* eds. N. Gutschow, A. Michaels, C. Ramble & E. Steinkellner. Vienna: Austrian Academy of Sciences Press, 137–76.

Harley, J.B., 1988. Maps, knowledge, and power, in *The Iconography of Landscape,* eds. D. Cosgrove & S. Daniels. Cambridge: Cambridge University Press, 277–312.

Harrison, J., 1996. *Himalayan Buildings: Recording Vernacular Architecture in Mustang and the Kalash.* Kathmandu: British Council/Goethe Institut.

Harrison, J., 2003. Kings' castles and sacred squares: the founding of Lo Monthang, in *Sacred Landscapes of the Himalayas,* eds. N. Gutschow, A. Michaels, C. Ramble & E. Steinkellner. Vienna: Austrian Academy of Sciences Press, 55–66.

Hay-Edie, T., 2001. Protecting the treasures of the Earth: nominating Dolpo as a World Heritage Site. *European Bulletin of Himalayan Research* 20, 46–76.

Hegewald, J.A.B., forthcoming. Mandirs, maps and cosmologies: the role of landscape in Jain art and identity.

Helms, H.W., 1988. *Ulysses' Sail: an Ethnographic Odyssey of Power, Knowledge and Geographical Distance.* Princeton (NJ): Princeton University Press.

Herle, A., 1994. Museums and shamans: a cross-cultural collaboration. *Anthropology Today* 10, 2–5.

Hernon, I., 2003. *Britain's Forgotten Wars.* Stroud: Sutton.

Herzog, M., 1952. *Annapurna.* London: Jonathan Cape.

Hitchcock, J.T., 1966. *The Magars of Banyan Hill.* London: Holt, Rinehart and Winston.

Hodder, I., 1982. *Symbols in Action.* Cambridge: Cambridge University Press.

Hodder, I., 1999. *Archaeological Process: an Introduction.* Oxford: Blackwell.

Hodgson, B.H., 1838. Origin and classification of the military tribes of Nepal. *Journal of the Asiatic Society of Bengal* 2, 217–24.

Hodgson, B.H., 1847. On the Aborigines of the Sub-Himalayas. *Journal of the Asiatic Society of Bengal* 17, 73–8.

Höfer, A., 1999. *Nomen est numen:* notes on the verbal journey in some Western Tamang oral ritual texts, in *Himalayan Space: Cultural Horizons and Practices,* eds. B. Bickel & M. Gaenszle. Zurich: Völkerkundemuseum, 205–44.

Holmberg, D., 1989. *Order in Paradox: Myth, Ritual and Exchange among Nepal's Tamang.* Ithaca (NY): Cornell University Press.

Hopkirk, P., 1996. *Quest for Kim: In Search of Kipling's Great Game.* London: John Murray.

Howard, N., 1995. An introduction to the fortifications of central Nepal. *European Bulletin of Himalayan Research* 9, 20–31.

Huber, T., 1999. *The Cult of Pure Crystal Mountain: Popular Pilgrimage and Visionary Landscape in Southeast Tibet.* New York (NY): Oxford University Press.

Humphrey, C., 1978. Swords in ploughshares: the Gurung Gurkhas of Nepal. *New Society* 1.

Humphrey, C., 2001. Contested landscapes in Inner Mongolia: walls and cairns, in *Contested Landscapes: Movement, Exile and Place,* eds. B. Bender & M. Winder. Oxford: Berg, 55–68.

Hutt, M., 1994. *Nepal: a Guide to the Art and Architecture of the Kathmandu Valley*. Gartmore, Stirling: Kiscadale.

Hüttel, H.-G., 1993. Excavations at Khingar Mound 1991. *Ancient Nepal* 134, 1–17.

Hüttel, H.-G., 1994. Archäologische Siedlungsforschung in hohen Himalaya: Die Ausgrabungen der KAVA im Muktinath-Tal/Nepal 1991–1992. *Beiträge zur Allgemeinen und Vergleichenden Archäologie* 14, 47–163.

Hüttel, H.-G., 1997. Archäologische Siedlungsforschung in Hohen Himalaya: Die Ausgrabungen der KAVA im Muktinath-Tal/Nepal 1994–1995. *Beiträge zur Allgemeinen und Vergleichenden Archäologie* 17, 7–64.

Hüttel, H.-G. & I. Paap, 1998. On the chronology and periodization of Khyinga settlement mound. *Beiträge zur Allgemeinen und Vergleichenden Archäologie* 18, 5–26.

Ingold, T., 1986a. Territoriality and tenure: the appropriation of space in hunting and gathering societies, in *The Appropriation of Nature: Essays on Human Ecology and Social Relations*, ed. T. Ingold. Manchester: Manchester University Press, 130–64.

Ingold, T., 1986b. 'Changing places': movement and locality in hunter-gatherer and pastoral societies, in *The Appropriation of Nature: Essays on Human Ecology and Social Relations*, ed. T. Ingold. Manchester: Manchester University Press, 165–97.

Ingold, T., 2000. To journey along a way of life: maps, wayfinding and navigation, in *The Perception of the Environment: Essays in Livelihood, Dwelling and Skill*, ed. T. Ingold. London: Routledge, 218–42.

Ingold, T., 2004. Culture on the ground: the world perceived through the feet. *Journal of Material Culture* 9, 315–40.

Insoll, T., 2004. *Archaeology, Ritual, Religion*. London: Routledge.

Jackson, D.P., 1976. The early history of Lo (Mustang) and Ngari. *Contributions to Nepalese Studies* 4, 39–56.

Jackson, D.P., 1998. Notes on the early history of Se-rib and nearby places in the upper Kali Gandaki Valley. *Kailash* 6, 195–227.

Jasanoff, M., 2005. *Edge of Empire: Conquest and Collecting in the East, 1750–1850*. London: Fourth Estate.

Jones, S., 1997. *The Archaeology of Ethnicity: Constructing Identities in the Past and Present*. London: Routledge.

Karan, P.P., 1960. *Nepal: a Cultural and Physical Geography*. Lexington (KY): University of Kentucky Press.

Kaufmann, D., 2000. Housing Culture: an Ethnoarchaeological Approach to Tamu-mai Houses. Unpublished BA Dissertation, Cornell University.

Kawaguchi, E., 1909 [1995]. *Three Years in Tibet*. Delhi: Book Faith India.

Keay, J., 2000. *The Great Arc: the Dramatic Tale of how India was Mapped and Everest was Named*. London: Harper Collins.

Kirk, G., 1976. *Homer and the Oral Tradition*. Cambridge: Cambridge University Press.

Kirkpatrick, W., 1811. *An Account of the Kingdom of Nepal: Being the Substance of Observations made during a Mission to that Country in the year 1793*. London: Printed for W. Miller by W. Bulmer & Co.

Kislev, M., 1984. Emergence of wheat agriculture. *Paleorient* 10, 61–70.

Knorzer, K., 2000. 3000 years of agriculture in a valley of the High Himalayas. *Vegetation History and Archaeobotany* 9, 219–22.

Kraayenbrink, T., P. de Knijff, G.L. van Driem, *et al.*, forthcoming. *Language and Genes of the Greater Himalayan Region*.

Kraemer, K.-H., 1998. The *Janajati* and the Nepali State: Aspects of Identity and Integration. Paper presented at the First Annual Workshop of the Himalayan Studies Network, Meudon, CNRS.

Kwon, H., 1993. Maps and Actions: Nomadic and Sedentary Space in a Siberian Reindeer Farm. Unpublished PhD Thesis, University of Cambridge.

Lecomte-Tilouine, M., 1993. *Les dieux du pouvoir: les Magar et l'hinduouism Népal central*. Paris: CNRS.

Lecomte-Tilouine, M., 2002. La désanskritisation des Magar: ethno-historie d'une group sans historie. *Purusartha* 23, 297–327.

Lecomte-Tilouine, M., 2005. The transgressive nature of kingship in caste organization: monstrous royal double in Nepal, in *The Character of Kingship*, ed. D. Quigley. Oxford: Berg, 101–21.

Lee, G.-A., G.A. Crawford, L. Liu & X. Chan, 2007. Plants and people from the early Neolithic to Shang periods in North China. *Proceedings of the National Academy of Sciences of the USA* 104, 1087–92.

Lone, F., M. Khan & G. Buth, 1993. *Palaeoethnobotany: Plants and Ancient Man in Kashmir*. New Delhi: Oxford & IBH Pub. Co.

Losty, J.P., 2004. The architectural monuments of Buddhism: Hodgson and Buddhist architecture of the Kathmandu Valley, in *The Origins of Himalayan Studies: Brian Houghton Hodgson in Nepal and Darjeeling 1820–1858*, ed. D.M. Waterhouse. London: Routledge-Curzon, 77–133.

Macdonald, A.W., 1973. The Lama and the General. *Kailash* 1, 225–33.

Macdonald, A.W., 1989. Note on the language, literature and cultural identity of the Tamang. *Kailash* 15, 165–77.

Macdonald, A.W. (ed.), 1997. *Mandala and Landscape*. New Delhi: D.K. Printworld.

Macfarlane, A., 1976. *Resources and Population: a Study of the Gurungs of Nepal*. Cambridge: Cambridge University Press.

Macfarlane, A., 1989. Some background notes on Gurung identity in a period of rapid change. *Kailash* 15, 179–90.

Macfarlane, A., 1997a. Identity and change among the Gurungs (Tamu-mai) of central Nepal, in *Nationalism and Identity in a Hindu Kingdom*, eds. D. Gelleer, J. Pfaff-Czarnecka & J. Whelpton. Amsterdam: Harwood, 185–204.

Macfarlane, A., 1997b. Gurung buildings, in *Encyclopaedia of Vernacular Architecture of the World*, ed. P. Oliver. Cambridge: Cambridge University Press.

Macfarlane, A., 2002. Sliding downhill: some reflections on thirty years of change in a Himalayan village. *European Bulletin of Himalayan Research* 20, 105–24.

Macfarlane, A. & I. Gurung, 1990. *Gurungs of Nepal*. Kathmandu: Ratna Pustak Bhandar.

Macfarlane, R., 2003. *Mountains of the Mind: a History of a Fascination*. London: Granta.

Mack, J., 2003. *The Museum of the Mind: Art and Memory in World Cultures*. London: British Museum Press.

Maine, H., 1871. *Village Communities in the East and West.* London: J. Murray.

Manandhar, N.P., 2002. *Plants and People of Nepal.* Portland (OR): Timber Press.

Maraini, F., 2000. *Ancient Tibet* (1951). London: Harvill Press.

Margalit, A., 2005. Review: Ricoeur's *Memory, History, Forgetting. The Times Literary Supplement* 5348 (30 Sept), 9–11.

Mathur, S., 2003. *An Indian Encounter: Portraits for Queen Victoria.* London: National Gallery Company.

McHugh, E., 1989. Concepts of the person among the Gurungs of Nepal. *American Ethnologist* 16, 75–86.

McHugh, E., 2001. *Love and Honor in the Himalayas: Coming to Know Another Culture.* Philadelphia (PA): University of Pennsylvania Press.

Messerschmidt, D.A., 1976a. *The Gurungs of Nepal: Conflict and Change in a Village Society.* Warminster: Aris and Phillips.

Messerschmidt, D.A., 1976b. Ecological change and adaptation among the Gurungs of the Nepal Himalaya. *Human Ecology* 4, 167–85.

Messerschmidt, D.A., 1976c. Ethnographic observations of Gurung Shamanism in Lamjung District, in *Spirit Possession in the Nepal Himalaya,* eds. J. Hitchcock & R. Jones. Warminster: Aris and Phillips, 197–216.

Messerschmidt, D.A., 1989. The Hindu pilgrimage to Muktinath, Nepal, part 1: Natural and supernatural attributes of the sacred field. *Mountain Research and Development* 9, 89–104.

Messerschmidt, D.A. & J. Sharma, 1982. Social process on the Hindu pilgrimage to Muktinath. *Kailash* 9, 139–57.

Messerschmidt, L., T.D. Gurung & F. Klatzel, 2004. *Stories and Customs of Manang.* Kathmandu: Mera Publications.

Meyer, K. & S. Brysac, 2001. *Tournament of Shadows: the Great Game and the Race for Empire in Asia.* London: Little, Brown and Co.

Michaels, A., 2003. The sacredness of (Himalayan) landscapes, in *Sacred Landscapes of the Himalayas,* eds. N. Gutschow, A. Michaels, C. Ramble & E. Steinkellner. Vienna: Austrian Academy of Sciences Press, 13–18.

Miehe, G., 1982. *Vegetationsgeographishce Untersuchungen im Dhaulagiri und Annapurna Himalaya.* (Band 66, 1.) PhD thesis. University of Gottingen, Gottingen. Dissertationes Botanicae, Vaduz.

Montgomerie, T.G., 1875. Extracts from an explorer's narrative of his journey from Pítorágarh, in Kumaon, via Jumla to Tadum and back, along the Káli Gandak to British Territory. *The Royal Geographical Society Journal* 45, 350–63.

Morillon, F. & P. Thouveny, 1981. Settlements and houses in the Thak Khola, in *Man and his House in the Himalayas: Ecology of Nepal,* ed. G. Toffin. New Delhi: Sterling Publishers, 172–89.

Mumford, S.R., 1990. *Himalayan Dialogue: Tibetan Lamas and Gurung Shamans in Nepal.* Madison (WI): University of Wisconsin Press.

Myrone, M., 2002. *George Stubbs.* London: Tate Publishing.

Narharinath, Y. & K.B. Gurung, 1956. *Gurung Ghale Raja Hamko Vamsavali.* Kathmandu: History Association.

Northey, W.B., 1928. *The Gurkhas: Their Manners, Customs and Country.* London: John Lane.

Oestigarrd, T., 2000. *The Deceased's Life Cycle Rituals in Nepal: Present Cremation Burials for the Interpretations of the Past.* (BAR International Series 853.) Oxford: Archaeopress.

Opptiz, M., 1983. The wild boar and the plough: origin stories of the northern Magar. *Kailash* 10, 187–226.

Oppitz, M., 1999. Cardinal directions in Magar mythology, in *Himalayan Space: Cultural Horizons and Practices,* eds. B. Bickel & M. Gaenszle. Zurich: Völkerkundemuseum, 167–201.

Oppitz, M., 2003. A drum in the Min Shan Mountains. *Shaman* 11, 113–48.

Opptiz, M., 2004. Ritual objects of the Qiang shamans. *RES* 45 (Anthropology and Aesthetics), 10–46.

O'Toole, F., 2005. *White Savage: William Johnson and the Invention of America.* London: Faber and Faber.

Owen, R., 1859. Report on a series of skulls of various tribes of mankind inhabiting Nepal. *Report of the British Association for the Advancement of Science* 1859, 95–103.

Paddayya, K., 1995. Theoretical perspectives in Indian archaeology, in *Theory in Archaeology: a World Perspective,* ed. P. Ucko. London: Routledge, 110–49.

Pandey, R.N., 1987. Palaeo-environment and prehistory of Nepal. *Contributions to Nepalese Studies* 14, 111–24.

Pandey, R.N., 1997. *Making of Modern Nepal: a Study of History, Art and Culture of the Principalities of Western Nepal.* New Delhi: Nirala.

Peissel, M., 1992 [1967]. *Mustang, a Lost Tibetan Kingdom.* New Delhi: Book Faith India.

Pettigrew, J., 1995. Shamanic Dialogue: History, Representation and Landscape in Nepal. Unpublished PhD Thesis, University of Cambridge.

Pettigrew, J., 1999. Parallel landscapes: ritual and political values of a shamanic soul journey, in *Himalayan Space: Cultural Horizons and Practices,* eds. B. Bickel & M. Gaenszle. Zurich: Völkerkundemuseum, 247–70.

Pettigrew, J., 2000. 'Gurkhas' in town: migration, language and healing. *European Bulletin of Himalayan Research* 19, 7–39.

Pettigrew, J., 2001. Observations during the State-of-Emergency: Nepal, December 2001. *European Bulletin of Himalayan Research* 20, 125–31.

Pettigrew, J., 2003. Guns, kinship and fear: Maoists among the Tamu-mai (Gurungs), in *Resistance and the State: Nepalese Experiences,* ed. D. Gellener. London: Hurst and Co., 305–25.

Pettigrew, J., 2004. Living between the Maoists and the army in rural Nepal, in *Himalayan People's War: Nepal's Maoist Rebellion,* ed. M. Hutt. London: Hurst and Co, 261–83.

Pettigrew, J. & Y. Tamu, 1999. The Kohla Project: studying the past with the Tamu-mai. *Studies in Nepali History and Society* 4, 327–64.

Pignède, B., 1993 [1966]. *The Gurungs: a Himalayan Population of Nepal.* Kathmandu: Ratna Pustak Bhandar.

Pittman, R. & W. Glover, 1970. Proto-Tamang-Gurung-Thakali, in *Occasional Papers of the Wolfenden Society of Tibeto-Burman Linguistics,* vol. III: *Lexical Lists and*

Comparative Studies, ed. F.K. Lehman. Urbana (IL): University of Illinois, 1–8.

Pohle, P., 1988. The adaptation of house and settlement to high altitude environment: a study of the Manang District in the Nepal-Himalaya. *Journal of the Nepal Research Centre* 8, 67–103.

Pohle, P., 1993. The Managis of Nepal-Himalaya: environmental adaptation, migration and socio-economic changes, in *Nepal, Past and Present*, ed. G. Toffin. Paris: CNRS, 323–46.

Pohle, P., 2000. *Historisch-geographische Untersuchungen im Tibetischen Himalaya. Felsbilder und Wüstungen als Quelle zur Besiedlungs- und Kulturgeschichte von Mustang (Nepal)*. (Giessener Geographische Schriften, 76/1 and 72/2.) Giessen.

Pohle, P., 2003. Petroglyphs and abandoned sites in Mustang: a unique source for research in cultural history and historical geography. *Ancient Nepal* 153, 1–14.

Polunin, O. & A. Stainton, 1984. *Flowers of the Himalaya*. New Delhi: Oxford University Press.

Price, N. (ed.), 2001. *The Archaeology of Shamanism*. London: Routledge.

Ragsdale, T.A., 1989. *Once a Hermit Kingdom: Ethnicity, Education and National Integration in Nepal*. Kathmandu: Ratna Pustak Bhandar.

Ragsdale, T.A., 1990. Gurungs, Goorkhalis, Gurkhas: speculations on a Nepalese ethno-history. *Contributions to Nepalese Studies* 17, 1–24.

Ramble, C., 1983. The founding of a Tibetan village: the popular transformation of history. *Kailash* 10, 267–90.

Ramble, C., 1995. Gaining ground: representations of territory in Bon and Tibetan popular tradition. *Tibet Journal* 20, 83–124.

Ramble, C., 1997a. The creation of the Bon mountain of Kongpo, in *Mandala and Landscape*, ed. A.W. Mcdonald. New Delhi: D.K. Printworld, 133–232.

Ramble, C., 1997b. *Se*: preliminary notes on the distribution of an ethnonym in Tibet and Nepal, in *Les Habitants du Toit du Monde. Etudes recueillies en hommage à Alexander W. Macdonald par les soins de Samten Karmay et Philippe Sagant*, eds. S. Karmay & P. Sagant. Nanterre: Société d'ethnologie, 485–513.

Ranger, T. & E. Hobsbawm (eds.), 1983. *The Invention of Tradition*. Cambridge: Cambridge University Press.

Rappaport, J., 1990. *The Politics of Memory: Native Historical Interpretation in the Columbian Andes*. Cambridge: Cambridge University Press.

Reinhard, J., 1974. The Raute: notes on a nomadic hunting and gathering tribe of Nepal. *Kailash* 2, 233–71.

Renfrew, A.C., 1998. Mind and matter: cognitive archaeology and external symbolic storage, in *Cognition and Material Culture: the Archaeology of Symbolic Storage*, eds. C. Renfrew & C. Scarre. (McDonald Institute Monographs.) Cambridge: McDonald Institute for Archaeological Research, 1–6.

Ricoeur, P., 2004. *Memory, History, Forgetting*. Chicago (IL): University of Chicago Press.

Rowlands, M., 1988. Repetition and exteriorisation in narratives of historical origins. *Critique of Anthropology* 8, 43–62.

Rowlands, M., 1993. The role of memory in the transmission of culture. *World Archaeology* 25, 141–51.

Rowlands, M., 1994. The politics of identity in archaeology, in *The Social Construction of the Past: Representation as Power*, eds. G.C. Bond & A Gilliam. London: Routledge, 129–43.

Said, E., 1994. *Culture and Imperialism*. London: Vintage.

de Sales, A., 2000. The Kham Magar country, Nepal: between ethnic claims and Maoism. *European Bulletin of Himalayan Research* 19, 41–71.

Salter, J. & H. Gurung, 1996. *Faces of Nepal*. Lalitpur, Nepal: Himal Association.

Saraswat, K.S., N.K. Sharma & D.C. Saini, 1994. Plant economy at ancient Narhan (*c.* 1300 BC–AD 300/400), in *Excavations at Narhan (1984–1989)*, ed. P. Singh. Varanasi: Banaras Hindu University, 255–346.

Seeber, C.G., 1994. Reflections on the existence of castles and observation towers in the area under investigation, the South Mustang. *Ancient Nepal* 136, 80–87.

Sharma, P.R., 1973. Review article: Kirkpatrick's 'An Account of the Kingdom of Nepal'. *Contributions to Nepalese Studies* 1, 96–105.

Shennan, S., 1989. Introduction: archaeological approaches to cultural identity, in *Archaeological Approaches to Cultural Identity*, ed. S. Shennan. (One World Archaeology 10.) London: Routledge, 1–32.

Sherratt, E.S., 1990. 'Reading the texts': archaeology and the Homeric question. *Antiquity* 64, 807–24.

Shneiderman, S. & M. Turin, 2004. The path to Jan Sarkar in Dolakha district: towards an ethnography of the Maoist movement, in *Himalayan 'People's War': Nepal's Maoist Rebellion*, ed. M. Hutt. London: Hurst & Co., 79–111.

Shrestha, B.P., 1989. *Forest Plants of Nepal*. Kathmandu: Educational Enterprise Pvt. Ltd.

Shrestha, N.R., 1993. Nepal: the society and its environment, in *Nepal and Bhutan Country Studies*, ed. A.M. Savada. Washington (DC): Federal Research Division, Library of Congress.

Sihlé, N., 2003. Muktinath: dans le haut Himalaya, un lieu saint où se rencontrent les cultures, in *Himalaya-Tibet: le choc des continents*, ed. J.P. Avouac. Paris: CNRS, 152–6.

Sill, M. & J. Kirkby, 1991. *The Atlas of Nepal in the Modern World*. London: Earthscan Publications Ltd.

Simons, A., 1997. The cave systems of Mustang — settlement and burial sites since prehistoric times, in *Proceedings of the 13th Conference of the European Association of South Asian Archaeologists in Cambridge 1995*, eds. R. Allchin & B. Allchin. Cambridge: Ancient India and Iran Trust, 851–61.

Simons, A. & W. Schön, 1998. Cave systems and terrace settlements in Mustang, Nepal: settlement periods from prehistoric times up to the present day. *Beiträge zur Allgemeinen und Vergleichenden Archäologie* 18, 29–47.

Simons, A., W. Schön & S.S. Shrestha, 1994a. Preliminary report on the 1992 campaign of the team of the Institute of Prehistory, University of Cologne. *Ancient Nepal* 136, 51–75.

Simons, A., W. Schön & S.S. Shrestha, 1994b. The prehistoric settlement of Mustang. *Ancient Nepal* 137, 93–129.

Sinha, A., K.G. Cannariato, L.D. Stott, *et al.*, 2007. A 900-year (600 to 1500 AD) record of the Indian summer monsoon precipitation from the core monsoon zone of India, *Geophysical Research Letters* 34, L16707, doi:10.1029/2007GL030431.

Sinha, S., 1965. Tribe-caste and tribe-peasant continua in central India. *Man in India* 45, 57–83.

Sinha, S., 1973. Re-thinking about tribes and Indian civilization. *Journal of the Indian Anthropological Society* 8, 99–108.

Skar, H.O., 1995. Myths of origin: the Janajati Movement, local traditions, nationalism and identities in Nepal. *Contributions to Nepalese Studies* 22, 31–42.

Snellgrove, D.L., 1961. *Himalayan Pilgrimage: a Study of Tibetan Religion by a Traveller through Western Nepal.* Oxford: B. Cassirer.

Snellgrove, D. & H. Richardson, 1968. *A Cultural History of Tibet.* London: Weidenfeld and Nicolson.

Sørensen, M.L.S., 2002. *Gender Archaeology.* Cambridge: Polity.

van Spengen, W., 1987. The Nyishangba of Manang: geographical perspectives on the rise of a Nepalese trading community. *Kailash* 13, 131–282.

Stainton, J.D.A., 1972. *Forests of Nepal.* New York (NY): Hafner Publishing Co.

Stainton, A., 1988. *Flowers of the Himalaya: a Supplement.* New Delhi: Oxford University Press.

Stein, R.A., 1972. *Tibetan Civilization.* Stanford (CA): Stanford University Press.

Stiller, L.F., 1973. *The Rise of the House of Gorkha.* (Series 14, vol. 15.) New Delhi: Bibliotheca Himalayica.

Stocking, G.W., Jr, 1987. *Victorian Anthropology.* London: Collier Macmillan Pub.

Stone, J.C., 1988. Imperialism, colonialism and cartography. *Transactions of the Institute of British Geographers* 13 (new series), 57–64.

Strickland, S.S., 1982. Beliefs, Practices and Legends: a Study in the Narrative Poetry of the Gurungs of Nepal. Unpublished PhD Thesis, University of Cambridge.

Strickland, S.S., 1983. The Gurung priest as bard. *Kailash* 10, 227–65.

Strickland, S.S., 1987. Notes on the language of the Pe. *Journal of the Royal Asiatic Society* 1, 53–76.

Suzuki, M. & S. Noshiro, 1988. Wood structure of Himalayan plants, in *The Himalayan Plants,* vol. 1, eds. H. Ohba & S.B. Malla. Tokyo: University of Tokyo Press, 341–80.

Suzuki, M. & H. Ohba, 1988. Wood structural diversity among Himalayan *Rhododendron. IAWA Bulletin* (new series) 9, 317–26.

Suzuki, M., S. Noshiro, A. Takahashi, K. Yoda & L. Joshi, 1991. Wood structure of Himalayan plants (II), in *The Himalayan Plants,* vol. 2, eds. H. Ohba & S.B. Malla. Tokyo: University of Tokyo Press, 17–66.

Suzuki, M., S. Noshiro, A. Takahashi, K. Terada, K. Yoda & L. Joshi, 1999. Wood structure of Himalayan plants (III), in *The Himalayan Plants,* vol. 3, ed. H. Ohba. Tokyo: University of Tokyo Press, 119–72.

Tamblyn, B., 2002. Ancient dialogue amidst a modern cacophony: Gurung religious pluralism and the founding of Tibetan Buddhist monasteries in the Pokhara Valley. *European Bulletin of Himalayan Research* 22, 81–100.

Tamu, B.P. & Y.K. Tamu, 1993. Long road to Gandaki. *Himal* 6, 27–8.

Teltscher, K., 2006. *The High Road to China: George Bogle, the Panchen Lama and the First British Expedition to Tibet.* London: Bloomsbury.

Temple, M., 1993. The ruins of an early Gurung settlement. *European Bulletin of Himalayan Research* 7, 43–8.

Thomas, J., 2004. *Archaeology and Modernity.* London: Routledge.

Tilley, C., 1994. *A Phenomenology of Landscape.* Oxford: Berg.

Tucci, G., 1956. *Preliminary Report on Two Scientific Expeditions in Nepal.* (S.O.R. x. 1.) Rome. I.S.M.E.O.

Tucci, G., 1962. *Nepal: the Discovery of the Malla.* London: G. Allen & Unwin Ltd.

Tucci, G., 1977 [1953]. *Journey to Mustang, 1952.* Kathmandu: Ratna Pustak Bhandar.

Turin, M., 2006. Rethinking Tibeto-Burman: linguistic identities and classifications in the Himalayan periphery, in *Tibetan Borderlands,* ed. P. Christiaan Klieger. (Tibetan Studies Library, vol. 10, no. 2.) Leiden: Brill, 35–48.

Turner, V., 1974. *Dramas, Fields and Metaphors: Symbolic Action in Human Society.* Ithaca (NY): Cornell University Press.

UNICEF, 2003. *At a Glance: Nepal.* http://www.unicef.org/infobycountry/nepal_statistics.html

Vetaas, O.R. & R. Chaudhary, 2004. *The Effect of Glacier Meltwater on an Agro-Pastoral Society in Himalaya, Nepal.* http://www.unib.no/people/nboov/melt2k.htm.

Vinding, M., 1998. *The Thakali: a Himalayan Ethnography.* London: Serindia Publications.

Vishnu-Mittre & R. Savithri, 1982. Food economy of the Harappans, in *Harappan Civilization: a Contemporary Perspective,* ed. G.L. Possehl. Warminster: Aris and Phillips Ltd, 205–22.

Waterhouse, D.M. (ed.), 2004. *The Origins of Himalayan Studies: Brian Houghton Hodgson in Nepal and Darjeeling 1820–1858.* London: RoutledgeCurzon.

Watt, G., 1889–93. *A Dictionary of the Economic Products of India* (8 vols.). London: W.H. Allen and Co.

Whelpton, J., 2005. *A History of Nepal.* Cambridge: Cambridge University Press.

Willcox, G., 1991. Carbonised plant remains from Shortugai, Afghanistan, in *New Light on Early Farming: Recent Developments in Palaeoethnobotany,* ed. J. Renfrew. Edinburgh: Edinburgh University Press, 139–54.

Wolf, E.R., 1982. *Europe and the People without History.* London: University of California Press.

Zohary, D. & M. Hopf, 2000. *Domestication of Plants in the Old World.* 3rd edition. Cambridge: Cambridge University Press.

Zubrow, E.B.W. & J. Robinson, 2000. Chance and the human population: population growth in the Mediterranean, in *Reconstructing Past Demographic Trends in Mediterranean Europe,* eds. J. Bintliff & K. Sbonias. Oxford: Oxbow Press, 133–44.